Additional Praise for *The Great Reformer*

"A biography that delves deep into the Argentine pope's personal history and ideological roots . . . Ivereigh argues with passion and rigor."
— *The Economist*

"[An] invaluable new biography."   — *The Telegraph*

"A richly researched, artfully constructed, and consistently compelling account of a remarkably complex and controversial life . . . [A] masterly account."   — Peter Marshall, *The Times Literary Supplement*

"Ivereigh simply tells us about Jorge Mario Bergoglio—and he does this very well—and his book ought to be read by everyone who wishes to know more about this very singular pope."   — *Irish Independent*

"Austen Ivereigh's *The Great Reformer* is no insta-book, but a gracefully written and meticulously researched account of Francis's life. . . . It is the best English-language biography of the pope to date, and— more important— raises provocative questions about the future of the Church and the relationship between religion and secular modernity."
— Molly Worthen, *The New York Times Book Review*

"A fine new biography . . . A comprehensive book . . . Fair, judicious, and compelling."   — Father James Martin, *The New York Times*

"In print just twenty months after Francis's election, *The Great Reformer* gathers a vast amount of oral and written testimony to explain his origins and career and to suggest where he might be headed. . . . Ivereigh deepens our understanding of a man whose personality and prophecy may change the Catholic Church forever."   — *National Catholic Reporter*

"Austen Ivereigh's *The Great Reformer* benefits from the privileged insights of some of those instrumental in securing Bergoglio's election, and from Ivereigh's own intimate knowledge of his Latin American background."
— Eamon Duffy, *The New York Review of Books*

"The most expansive and important biography of Bergoglio yet published . . . Beautifully written, well crafted from beginning to end."
— *The Christian Century*

"A meticulous and lovingly written biography that will please both knowledgeable and amateur readers."
— *Library Journal*

"An admiring defense of the new pope . . . A quick, efficient job of fairly sketching this extraordinary life."
— *Kirkus Reviews*

"Consider this book the cornerstone of any collection on Pope Francis and twenty- first- century Christianity."
— Ray Olson, *Booklist* (starred review)

"[Ivereigh] is the ideal papal biographer. . . . With its wealth of biographical information that offers an in-depth look at formative influences, this is the best examination of the current pope to date."
— *Publishers Weekly*

"An in-depth picture of Jorge Bergoglio . . . already being spoken of as the definitive biography of this pope."
— *Christian Today*

"By telling his personal story more richly than heretofore, the book helps to illuminate why and how [Francis has] had such a dramatic impact in a relatively short time as pontiff . Here is a full portrait of a man shaped by many 'crucibles' of leadership."
— Jeff Kehoe, *Harvard Business Review*

"The author's deep familiarity with Argentine language, culture, and history sets this work apart from other English-language papal biographies. As an English-language account of the pope's Argentine heritage, this book will be hard to beat."
— *Catholic Herald*

"*The Great Reformer* is a rooted, lively, insightful read."
— *National Review*

"[*The Great Reformer*'s] depth is unparalleled in the quickly growing Francis biography genre, and the reader can't help but come away with a deeper understanding of Jorge Bergoglio."
— *Our Sunday Visitor*

"Terrific ... Among other things, [Ivereigh is] masterful in explaining how navigating the ideologically charged period of Argentina's 'Dirty War' prepared the pontiff to try to hold a divided Church together."
— John Allen, *Crux*

"In a graceful style, Ivereigh illuminates Bergoglio's path from tango-loving teen to Vatican heavyweight with copious anecdotes and historical and theological insight. His rigorous research unveils fascinating details and does not skip the controversies that intervened along the way."
— Kenneth A. Briggs, *The Philadelphia Inquirer*

"*The Great Reformer* is a magnificent book that should gain a wide readership. It is a tour de force of biographical research and good judgment."
— John Cavadini, *Commonweal*

"Austen Ivereigh's new biography, *The Great Reformer* ... is a highly significant— and successful— achievement."   — *CathNews New Zealand*

"Austen Ivereigh has done a great service in writing *The Great Reformer* . . . The book brings to light several major themes in the life of Jorge Bergoglio that are crucial to understanding this pope and his papacy."
— *The Catholic World Report*

"The best available chronicle of the formative events in the life and thinking of Jorge Mario Bergoglio"
— George Weigel, author of *Evangelical Catholicism*

"Well written, full of information; this is the best biography of Pope Francis to date."
— Thomas Reese, author of *Inside the Vatican: The Politics and Organization of the Catholic Church*

"*The Great Reformer* helped me to realize anew the sheer magnitude, power, and influence of Benedict's humble and courageous decision and Francis's bold and daring revolution of tenderness inaugurated on March 13, 2013. If you wish to understand Pope Francis, read this book."
— Father Thomas Rosica, CSB; CEO, Salt + Light Catholic Media Foundation

"Probing, comprehensive, eminently readable, and absorbing . . . In a growing list of books on the first Latin American pope, Ivereigh's is uniquely well informed and persuasive."
— Charles J. Chaput, O.F.M. Cap., Archbishop of Philadelphia

"Austen Ivereigh has produced about the best one-volume biography of Pope Francis that you'll find. . . . Ivereigh is able to give us a realistic and insightful account of what Bergoglio is up to as pope, and where he is taking the Catholic Church."
— David Gibson, author of *The Rule of Benedict: Pope Benedict XVI and His Battle with the Modern World*

"No recent pope has gotten a biography as sensible, as culturally adept, and as attuned to the ongoing moment as this one."
— Paul Elie, author of *The Life You Save May Be Your Own* and *Reinventing Bach*

"In Austen Ivereigh's engaging work, we come to more fully learn and appreciate the circumstances and influences that shaped Jorge Bergoglio's journey: first as a young Jesuit leader, then as Archbishop of Buenos Aires, and now as shepherd of over one billion Catholics. The many fascinating events and challenges recounted in *The Great Reformer* demonstrate that the key to understanding Pope Francis and his vision for the Church begins above all by recognizing his unfailing faith in the love and mercy of Jesus Christ."
— Cardinal Timothy M. Dolan, Archbishop of New York and author of *Praying in Rome: Reflections on the Conclave and Electing Pope Francis*

The GREAT REFORMER

Francis and the making of a radical Pope

AUSTEN IVEREIGH

ALLEN&UNWIN

First published in the United States in 2014 by Henry Holt and company, LLC.

First published in Great Britain in 2014 by Allen & Unwin
This paperback edition published in Great Britain in 2015 by Allen & Unwin

Allen & Unwin
c/o Atlantic Books
Ormond House
26–27 Boswell Street
London WC1N 3JZ
Phone: 020 7269 1610
Fax: 020 7430 0916
Email: UK@allenandunwin.com
Web: www.allenandunwin.co.uk

A CIP catalogue record for this book is available from the British Library.

Paperback ISBN 978 1 76011 348 3
Ebook ISBN 978 1 74343 950 0

Internal text design by Meryl Sussman Levavi
Printed and bound by CPI Group (UK) Ltd, Croydon, CR0 4YY

10 9 8 7 6 5 4 3 2 1

For Linda

CONTENTS

PROLOGUE

THIS BOOK CAME out of a minute's meeting with Pope Francis in St. Peter's Square in June 2013. My colleague and I had been given sought-after front-row tickets at the Wednesday audience, when there is the chance to speak to the pope as he moves along the row chatting briefly to delegates and guests. He took over two hours to reach us, because after his address—the usual mix of homespun humor and startling metaphors—he disappeared for what seemed like an eternity among the ones he calls God's holy faithful people. They, the *anawim*, the poor of God, not we, the front-row ticket holders, were his priority.

It was a sun-struck day and the exertion had taken its toll: by the time he got to us, Francis, at that point seventy-six years old, was sweating, hot, and breathless. But what most struck me was the energy he gave off: a biblical blend of serenity and playful joy. The archbishop of Canterbury, Justin Welby, put it well after he met Francis some days later. The Argentine pope, he said, is "an extraordinary humanity, on fire with Christ." If joy were a flame, you'd need to be made of asbestos not to get burned.

Francis had fascinated me more and more since the rainy night of his election on March 13, 2013. I was up on a TV platform overlooking St. Peter's Square conducting minute-by-minute commentary for a British news channel. It had been an hour since the white smoke, and we were waiting, with the globe's media, for the twitch on the balcony curtains.

Some minutes before Cardinal Jean-Louis Tauran came out to announce the new pope, I had a tip-off from my old boss, the retired archbishop of Westminster, Cardinal Cormac Murphy-O'Connor, who had taken part in the pre-conclave discussions but was too old to take part in the conclave itself. He told my emissary that, as it had been a short conclave, the new pope could well be Jorge Mario Bergoglio.

Bergoglio? It was a name from the past. I knew his country: it began with parakeets in hot humid rainforests, continued in vast herds of cattle and horses in great prairies between the mountains and the ocean, and ended with penguins on ice floes floating past spouting whales. It had once been a wealthy nation, one that saw itself as an outpost of Europe stranded in Latin America; later it was a textbook study in failed promise, a warning of how deep-rooted political polarities can paralyze society. I recalled a trip to Argentina in 2002 to write an article about the country's economic collapse, when people spoke highly of their aloof and austere cardinal; but also further back, to the early 1990s, when I had lived in Buenos Aires while researching a doctoral thesis on the Church and politics in Argentine history. Over a number of visits, in the midst of attempted coups and currency crises, I had come to love that beguiling city; and living there for many months at a time, my Spanish had sprouted the inflections and idioms of *porteño* Spanish. It was all—as W. H. Hudson titled his memoir of Argentina—*Far Away and Long Ago*. Now Bergoglio had brought it back.

I had another memory, of the April 2005 conclave that had elected Benedict XVI, when I had been in Rome with Cardinal Murphy-O'Connor. Some cardinals had been making a bid to find a pastoral alternative to Joseph Ratzinger and were looking to Latin America, the Church's new hope. A few months later, an anonymous cardinal's secret diary revealed that Bergoglio of Buenos Aires had been the other main contender in that election. But after that, he had seemed to fade, to the point where almost nobody in 2013 thought he was *papabile*. That's why I was so glad for that tip-off: the Argentine cardinal hadn't been on my list, or almost anybody's. At least when the balcony curtains finally opened and the new pope was announced, I could say who it was and something about him. It didn't go so well for some commentators on other channels.

Afterward, the consensus seemed to be that Bergoglio had just emerged, that there had been no group of cardinals working for his election. But if that was so, why did my old boss seem so sure, before the conclave, that it would be him? I sensed there was more, that Bergoglio had not faded at all but had simply been invisible to our Eurocentric radar, and that there had been a group organizing his election.

But that wasn't my main curiosity. What I really wanted to know was who he was, how he thought, how being a Jesuit shaped him, where he stood among all those controversies I had studied so long ago. In those first hundred days of the electrifying Francis pontificate, he had taken the Vatican, and the world, by storm—flipping the omelet, as he liked to say. People were trying to fit him into straitjackets that just didn't apply in Latin America, and even less in Argentina, where Peronism exploded the categories of left and right. The misreadings had given rise to contradictory claims: A slum bishop who was cozy with the military dictatorship? A retrograde Jesuit who became a progressive bishop? Some tried to claim he was both, and had "converted" during his Córdoba exile in the early 1990s. Those in Argentina who knew him well said this just wasn't true. But what alternative account existed?

The first Argentine biographies, hastily assembled by journalists who had spent years reporting on him, were full of fascinating stories and insights, and this book owes much to them. But their focus, understandably, was on Bergoglio's latter years as cardinal, for which there was an abundant paper and Internet trail, leaving virtually untouched his thirty years as a Jesuit—the time of the controversies, as well as the period when his spirituality and vision of the world had taken shape. What exactly had gone wrong between Bergoglio and the Jesuits? If I could understand that, I felt, it would all be much clearer.

When I met Francis for that brief minute in the hot square, I took comfort from the hand he had placed firmly on my arm. I don't mean that he wanted this biography—he hates the idea of books about him; he wants to deflect attention to where it belongs—but the firm grip gave me encouragement: as a foreigner who had long grappled with Argentina's complexities, and knew the Jesuits, perhaps I was well placed to help outsiders understand the Francis enigma.

In October 2013, I left for Buenos Aires for an intense five weeks of interviews and research, scooping up copies of most of what he had written, much of which was long out of print. I retraced Bergoglio's steps beyond Buenos Aires to San Miguel, Santa Fe, Córdoba, and Entre Ríos, as well as over the Andes to Santiago de Chile. There have been other trips in the course of this book: to Rio de Janeiro, Brazil, for World Youth Day in July 2013; and twice to Rome, for the consistory of cardinals in February 2014 and the canonizations the following April of John XXIII and John Paul II. In dozens of interviews with Jesuits, ex-Jesuits, and others close to him from his twenty years as a bishop, archbishop, and cardinal, the missing narrative began to take shape. I realized that many of the important stories about Francis had not yet been told and that only by grasping the deep past—Argentina's, the Church's, the Jesuits'—could Francis's thinking and vision be understood. *The Great Reformer* is, necessarily, not just Bergoglio's story but those other stories too.

Many biographies are written after their subject retires or dies. During the seven months this was written, December 2013 to June 2014, its subject became a global phenomenon. It was impossible not to see the links between Bergoglio and Francis, or to pretend that the reader would not be thinking of Francis while reading about Bergoglio. I knew the canvas had to be broader than the Bergoglio backstory, that the fast-unfurling Francis pontificate needed to be seen through his biography. Yet to constantly refer the reader forward to Francis would not only disrupt the narrative but commit the crime of hagiography, reading the past through the eyes of the present, as if his life had been a warm-up act for the papacy. My solution is to begin each chapter with an important episode (a trip or a document) from Francis's papacy that the reader can keep in mind: that way, some interesting—and sometimes provocative—connections can be made with his past without disturbing the flow or the integrity of the narrative. In the epilogue, I draw together both streams, analyze his first year, and suggest where this remarkable papacy is taking the Church.

The Great Reformer is, then, chronological but not rigorously so: it zooms in on stories that bring our subject into focus and then pans back to take in the land and history that shaped him. In the early chapters, where I have called him "Jorge" until he was ordained, there are excursions into the divisions and tensions in Argentine political and church history that are essential to understanding his vision. The Jesuit story, worldwide and in Argentina, past and present, figures strongly: both Saint Ignatius's *Spiritual Exercises,* which have so deeply formed Bergoglio's thinking, spirituality, and leadership, and the struggles within the Society of Jesus (the Jesuits) over its renewal after the Second Vatican Council, play a major role in the first half of the book. Throughout, *The Great Reformer* takes seriously Bergoglio's Jesuit spirituality of discernment as the key to his decision making. He made and makes judgments not just on the basis of information and interests, but where he saw God's will, and its opponent: the temptation of the "bad spirit."

During the writing of this book, I have read thousands of Bergoglio's words: from his first published article in 1969 through to his retreats and homilies as cardinal. (He is a natural writer: vivid and precise.) Most of his early writings and almost all of his homilies exist only in Spanish, and the translation is almost always my own, even when another translation exists, unless otherwise specified. The same is true of the interviews, almost all of which were conducted in Spanish, heroically transcribed in Argentina by Inés San Martín (now Rome correspondent for the *Boston Globe*), and translated by me. In order to avoid excessive notes, quotes should be assumed to come from those interviewees (listed at the back) unless otherwise specified. In the Note on Sources is a detailed list of writings, interviews, and other resources on which this book has drawn.

THERE are many stories in *The Great Reformer* that have drawn attention for the new light they cast on areas of controversy or important episodes in Francis's life. But there is a narrative thread, captured in the title, that runs through them all: of a church leader who from an early age felt called to be a reformer, and was given the authority to do so. This is a story not just of the man but his three reforms: of the Argentine Jesuit province, of the Argentine Church, and now of the universal Church. His lodestars have been two French theologians, Yves Congar and Henri de Lubac, who taught him how to unite God's People by a radical reform that will lead them to holiness. If the reader comes to see that thread and understand this papacy better as a result, the book's purpose will have been accomplished.

Some of the best stories and insights in these pages came out of fascinating meetings of great warmth and intensity, in Argentina, Rome, and elsewhere. There are many listed in the Note on Sources; but I wanted generally to thank here those—they include Jesuits, cardinals, and confidants of Jorge Bergoglio's, some of whom did not want to be mentioned—who went into tense or complex territory at my probing, and others who entrusted me with confidences that could easily be misused. I hope that, even when it comes to conclusions they might not agree with, *The Great Reformer* repays the confidence they placed in me.

When the original edition came out in November 2014, a few mistakes were pointed out to me that have been corrected in reprints. They were generally small matters of detail that did not affect the reader's understanding of Francis or the accuracy of the account. But one slip deserves comment. In my account in Chapter Nine of the conclave that elected Francis, I inadvertently gave the impression that Bergoglio in some way consented to the efforts by a group of cardinals who were seeking his election. That is not what I intended, and it was not true; but the phrasing was seized upon and given that meaning, and subsequently exploited by traditionalist bloggers who were claiming that Benedict XVI's resignation and therefore Francis's election were invalid. As Vatican spokespeople and serious commentators have made clear, these claims have no foundation; in addition, press statements from the Vatican and from the cardinals concerned, as well as my own, have all made clear that no such approach to Bergoglio was ever made, as the wording now makes clear. Bergoglio may have been aware of the efforts being made to elect him, but he had no part in them.

In every other respect, the insights and revelations of *The Great Reformer* have stood up well—even in Argentina, to where I returned in April 2015 to write the new epilogue and to present the Spanish edition at the Buenos Aires book fair. I was a little nervous at how it would be received; I am, after all, a gringo writing the story of their pope. Fortunately, many of those close to Francis—friends of his, and now friends of mine—who helped with the original research were on hand to praise the book. Those friends' further insights and comments have enriched the new epilogue, and therefore the world's understanding of the holy whirlwind that is Pope Francis.

Buenos Aires, Feast of St. Joseph the Worker, May 1, 2015

THE GREAT REFORMER

ONE

FAR AWAY AND LONG AGO

(1936–1957)

THE FIRST POPE born of immigrants in the New World chose for his debut journey outside Rome a small Italian island on whose stunning beaches thousands of bloated bodies had over the years turned up with the tide. Francis had learned from newspaper reports soon after his March 13, 2013, election that more than twenty-five thousand North Africans had lost their lives this way—far more than the six thousand who have died in the US desert crossing from Mexico. Who knew? Appalled that few seemed aware or to care, he opted to make Lampedusa, 180 miles off the coast of Africa, his first papal visit—to the peripheries of Europe. There, on July 8, he wept for the dead and made migration a pro-life issue.

The Mass he celebrated on the island's sports field was a penitential Eucharist, one that begged forgiveness. During the homily he took God's famous question to Cain in Genesis—*Where is your brother?*—and asked: "Who is responsible for this blood?" Speaking from an altar made of the wood of one of the capsized rafts, clinging to his white skullcap in the wind, he said he was reminded of a character called L'Innominato in Alessandro Manzoni's novel *The Betrothed*: a tyrant who is nameless and faceless. Then he switched to Jesus's parable of the Good Samaritan, likening "us"—he always included himself—to the Levite and the priest who pass by on the other side: "We see our brother half dead on the side of the road, and perhaps we say to ourselves: 'poor soul . . . !', and then go on our way," he ventured. But the real sting was in his denunciation of what he called a "culture of comfort, which makes us think only of ourselves, makes us insensitive to the cries of other people." It caused people to live now in "soap bubbles." Thus, he said, we have "globalized indifference."

The new pope had come to afflict the comfortable. He had linked those who lived well to the penniless migrants who died at sea. But he knew guilt alone was no good.

Francis was a member of the Society of Jesus, and while he had long been a bishop and dispensed from his Jesuit vows, he continued to put "SJ" after his name. He was deeply imbued with the spirituality of the Society's founder, Saint Ignatius of Loyola, creator of the famous *Spiritual Exercises*, who had urged people in prayer to beg the Holy Spirit (or, as he put it, "to ask for the grace") to feel what was needed—delight at seeing Jesus, say; or awe at the sight of the crowds; or sadness at the foot of the Cross. Now, in Lampedusa, the first Jesuit pope led the world on a spiritual exercise, urging anyone listening to "ask for the grace to cry for our indifference, to cry for the cruelty in the world, that is in us, that is in those who anonymously make decisions that produce dramas like these." He was inviting the world to *feel*, because unless the heart was in play, nothing would change.

Suddenly Lampedusa, and the tragedy that it symbolized, appeared on the lips of news readers, who explained how unstable boats overpacked by human traffickers often capsized in the crossings, and how vehicles of hope turned into floating death traps. A result of sorts came three months after the pope's visit, when 366 Somalis and Eritreans died after a fire broke out on their boat close to Lampedusa. The world for once sat up and took note. A year later, it was still news when divers found the ship, with the bodies still in the wreckage, huddled together at the bottom of the sea.

Francis, arriving in Assisi the day after the boat fire, declared a "day of tears" for the victims. Politicians and newspaper editors, sensing a new unease, began to say that maybe immigration policy wasn't just about how to keep people out; maybe it should also be about how to bring people in. A year later, the European Union created a new agency, Frontex, whose ships and helicopters would rescue migrants in peril. Francis had broken a soap bubble.

Later that year he went to another island on the peripheries of Europe, celebrating Mass at the shrine of Our Lady of Bonaria in Sardinia, which had given its name to the Argentine capital. There he spoke to jobless miners, telling them that he knew what it was like to suffer from financial crisis because his parents lived through the world depression and had often spoken of it. He had learned that "where there is no work, there is no dignity," he told them, adding that it was an "economic system that brings about this tragedy, an economic system that has at its center an idol which is called money."

Migration and jobs: these were the issues with which he began his papacy, the issues the poor cared about.

He knew what it took to leave one land for another, "that fortitude, as well as the great pain that comes from being uprooted," as he once put it, speaking of his grandmother Rosa. Francis was born to an American nation forged from millions of similar deracinations. Nostalgia—from the Greek words *nostos* and *alga*, a yearning to return to the place—ran in his veins. When we lose it, he said in 2010, we abandon our elderly: caring for our old people means honoring our past, the place we come from.

On Lampedusa he had gone out in a boat and laid a floral wreath in the sea. There was a reason why the fate of the migrants struck him, as he said in his homily on the island, "like a painful thorn in my heart." Maybe they reminded him of the time many years before he was born when five hundred passengers, almost all in steerage class, drowned off the northeast coast of Brazil.

It was October 1927 when the Italian passenger ship en route to Buenos Aires went down after a cracked propeller shaft damaged the hull. The *Principessa Mafalda* was among the fastest and most luxurious ships of her day, the transport of choice for celebrities such as the Argentine tango singer Carlos Gardel. It was Italy's *Titanic*, a disaster of human arrogance and incompetence.

Jorge Mario's grandparents, Giovanni Angelo Bergoglio and Rosa Margarita Vasallo di Bergoglio, together with their six children—including Francis's father, Mario—had bought steerage-class tickets on that ship. But because the proceeds of the sale of their Turin coffee shop had taken longer than expected to arrive, at the last minute they had swapped the tickets for passage on the *Giulio Cesare* a month later.

Their lucky escape was part of Bergoglio family lore.

IN emigrating to Argentina, the Bergoglios were following a path taken by hundreds of thousands of Italians before them.

According to the old Latin-American joke, while Mexicans are descended from Aztecs and Peruvians from Incas, Argentines are descended from boats. In the period of mass emigration to Argentina, between 1880 and 1930, so many boats came from Italy that the writer Jorge Luis Borges used to declare playfully that he couldn't be a pure Argentine because he had no Italian blood. A glance at the Buenos Aires telephone directory tells the same story—as does a list of its cardinal archbishops in the twentieth century. Only one (Aramburu) was of Spanish extraction; the others—Copello, Caggiano, Quarracino, Bergoglio—were all *tanos*, as they are known in Argentine slang. The Italians gave Argentine cities not just trattorias, pizzas, exquisite gelato, and the custom of *ñoquis* (gnocchi) on the last Friday of each month, but bequeathed to Argentines an instantly recognizable musicality of speech along with those famously emphatic arm gestures.

As immigrants usually do, the newcomers were joining relatives. Giovanni Angelo Bergoglio's three brothers had done well in Paraná since arriving seven years earlier in that thriving river port upstream from Buenos Aires. From the profits of their paving company, the future pope's great-uncles had raised an impressive four-story residence with a pretty turret, the only one in town with an elevator. The family nicknamed it the Palazzo Bergoglio.

For Giovanni Angelo and Rosa, it was the second major move in a few years. They had married and raised their six children in the town of Portacamaro—where Bergoglio is quite a common surname—in Asti, in the Piedmont region of northwestern Italy. They were of peasant stock but, like many at the time, were moving into the middle class by educating their offspring. In 1920, they had moved thirty-four miles west to Turin, where the coffee shop they ran just about covered the children's schooling. The future pope's father, Mario, their only son, born in 1908, was a *raggionere*, an accountant who worked in the Banca di Italia.

When, after a five-week crossing, the Bergoglios disembarked in Buenos Aires in January 1928, the country's model of export-led growth, which had made it the world's eighth-largest economy, more akin to that of Canada and Australia than Latin America, was about to come to an end. The Wall Street Crash the following year, which triggered the Great

Depression, would eventually leave them penniless, forcing yet another fresh start. That recession, and the world war that followed a decade later, would change Argentina's place in the world, triggering a new turbulence in its economy and politics.

But as they stepped from the *Giulio Cesare* into the torrid heat of midsummer Buenos Aires, that new horizon was still invisible to Mario's parents and siblings. Rosa clung to her fox-fur coat as if it were winter, for sewed into its lining were the proceeds from the Turin coffee shop. The Bergoglios barely had time to take in the great avenues and stately buildings of belle époque Buenos Aires, the "Paris of South America," before making haste upriver to a new life in Entre Ríos.

✿

ALTHOUGH Argentina had become independent from Spain back in 1816, for many decades afterward it was a nation-state only on paper. In the absence of a central authority, the idea of a united nation governed from Buenos Aires by lawyers and merchants—the ambition of the so-called unitarians—provoked only chaos. From the 1830s to the 1860s the country was a confederation of self-governing provinces ruled by caudillos, cattle ranchers with armies of cowherds or gauchos. The greatest of these caudillos were Juan Manuel de Rosas in the province of Buenos Aires, Estanislao López in Santa Fe, and Facundo Quiroga in La Rioja. Their immense cattle and sheep estancias, some of which were as large as European nations, contained at the time most of the nation's power and wealth. Of these three the most successful, most enduring, and wealthiest was Rosas, the "restorer of the laws," who sat astride the period 1835 to 1852 like a creole Napoleon. Despite a fearsome reputation as a disciplinarian, he was a well-read, accomplished manager and a pragmatic leader, whose political strength lay in his close rapport with the gauchos. He understood their needs and their culture, and the importance of discerning the right moment to act. Later, Bergoglio would deduce from a letter Rosas wrote to Quiroga his own principles of good government, not least that "reality is superior to the idea."

Only with the defeat of Rosas in 1852—improbably, the Tiger of the Pampas retired with his wife to a cottage in Southampton, England— were the architects of the liberal project free to reverse that principle. What followed was the attempt to graft a new idea of a nation, one that was modern, liberal, enlightened, and cosmopolitan, onto the rootstock of a Spanish Catholic colony.

The emerging export economy was shifting the power and wealth to the cities, where the unitarian lawyers and merchants reigned. Yet, despite agreeing to a national constitution, what followed were more years of cau-dillo uprisings against the central government, until, in the 1870s, the War of the Triple Alliance against Argentina's neighbor Paraguay helped to settle the question. The national army, which returned victorious from that conflict, could now begin to impose the will of the state.

Schools and railways were built, and immigrants began to arrive. It was President Domingo F. Sarmiento's ambition to Europeanize Argen-tina. He dreamed of north European Protestants filling Argentina's empty spaces, consigning the so-called barbarism of the caudillos and the gau-chos to the past, and inaugurating a civilization of modernity and prog-ress, with Argentina increasingly absorbed into the international economy. The lodestars in this project—economically, politically, and culturally— were Britain and France; travel in their direction, signposted progress, would lead liberal Argentina out of its backward Hispanic, colonial, mixed-race past.

It is in this clash between modernity and the past, between the for-eign and the national, the old and the new, that the Argentine culture wars of the twentieth century have their genesis.

Argentina's mostly creole—that is, Spaniards born in Latin America— ruling class had a mentality not so different from the Jeffersons and Washingtons in the United States. But the religion of the Argentine lib-eral elite was not Deism or Unitarianism but Freemasonry, which gave its adherents an institutional base to rival the Catholic Church. Theirs was a mentality shaped by Social Darwinist ideas about science and the superi-ority of white (preferably Protestant) culture. Sarmiento and other late-nineteenth-century presidents were disappointed that the migrants who came were mostly Italians and Spaniards, rather than Swiss or Germans; and they saw the defeat of the savages of the plains as an inevitable tri-umph of racial progress.

In this enlightened, liberal view, the Catholic Church—and all religion—was a thing of the past, an affront to reason, the creed of the mixed-race, rural world that modern Argentina sought to leave behind. But they didn't want to eradicate the Church, only to control it. The population was not ready for too much scientific progress, said the main thinker behind the 1853 Constitution, Juan Alberdi, and in the meantime the divine sanction of religious morality "is the most powerful mechanism available for moralizing and civilizing our people."

Just as, in the United States, the world of the frontier cowboy was romanticized just at the moment it was disappearing, in 1870s Argentina stories of gaucho life in the pampas began to be popular. José Hernández's epic poem *El Gaucho Martín Fierro*, a favorite of Bergoglio's and considered the defining Argentine classic, is both a protest at the mistreatment of the rural poor at the hands of landowners and army officials, and a celebration of a way of life vanishing under the onslaught of barbed wire and foreigners. As Fierro complains of the Italian immigrants, "I'd like to know why the Government / enlists that gringo crew / And what they think they're good for here? / They can't mount a horse or rope a steer, / And somebody's got to help them out / In everything they do." Priests in Buenos Aires say Bergoglio could recite long passages of *Martín Fierro* from memory. As cardinal in 2002 he used it, in the middle of a devastating crisis, to help reimagine the nation Argentina was called to be.

By 1880, federalism was spent as a force, and the liberal project—centralizing, modernizing, capitalist—was unchallenged. Buenos Aires was made the federal capital, and the city of La Plata the capital of Buenos Aires province. National elections were held: presidents completed six-year terms and handed over to elected successors. As a democracy, it was far from perfect: until 1912 only naturalized citizens who were also male property owners could vote, and a single party, a coalition of provincial forces known as the National Autonomist Party (PAN), ensured its self-perpetuation by means both fair and foul. But it was stable, and what followed were five decades of rapid growth: finance and industrial goods poured in, along with millions of immigrants from southern Europe, while exports, mostly wheat, beef, and wool, flowed out. In this first era of globalization, triggered by massive cost reductions—the steam engine and the ship propeller had the same effect on that age as the microchip has on ours today—Argentina was the tiger economy of its day, proof, said its advocates, of the virtues of free-market capitalism.

Economists call it comparative advantage: what Argentina produced well and cheaply was what European countries needed, and vice versa. As demand for Argentine exports accelerated, the frontier was pushed back;

in 1879, the so-called Conquest of the Desert wrested eight million hect-
ares of land from the Tehuelche and Araucanian natives and handed
them over to just four hundred landowners. As huge swathes of territory
opened up, Argentina sent increasing quantities of food and raw materials to Europe's expanding industries and urban populations, while using
the currency it earned from its exports to buy in the industrial goods
and technology it needed to develop. Britain, then the world's leading
industrial power and provider of capital, was Argentina's main market,
its leading investor, and its major source of industrial goods. British capital-
ists invested in or ran the railway, the telegraph, the gaslights on the streets,
the postal service, and the Buenos Aires trams, as well as Latin America's
first ever underground train, Line A of the Buenos Aires *subte*, which,
decades later, would have one of its most loyal passengers in Cardinal
Bergoglio.

Together with New York—and in some years even more than New
York—Buenos Aires was the main destination of a vast transatlantic migration. In the 1880s, 1.5 million people entered Argentina, rising to a stagger-
ing 4.3 million between 1890 and 1914. Over a million Italians and some
800,000 Spanish made new lives there, alongside large communities of
Polish Jews and Syrian Muslims, as well as Welsh sheep farmers (who went
south, to Patagonia) and Swiss Protestants (who settled in Santa Fe). Buenos Aires alone went from a population of 180,000 in 1869 to 1.5 million in
1914. Immigrants were usually educated and socially mobile; they were
especially adept at creating small businesses, and soon came to outnumber
the native-born as owners of local industries. This was especially true after
1930, when Argentine exports and imports dropped sharply, and people
began to make locally what had previously been imported.

The main beneficiaries of Argentina's golden age were the families of
lawyers, landowners, and merchants with land and capital whom Argentines shorthand as "the oligarchy." Many were fabulously wealthy, the
Texas millionaires of their day, notorious for their elegance and extrava-
gance (the French for a time used the expression "as rich as an Argentine"). They moved out of the humid, mosquito-prone historic center of
Buenos Aires to build sumptuous mansions in the latest French styles in
the north part of the city cooled by the River Plate, known as the Barrio
Norte. In contrast, the southern part of the city, by the fetid river Riachuelo, was where the poor from the interior would start out, crowded into

cheap housing known as *conventillos*—nurseries of crime, disease, and the sultry music known as *el tango*. In the late twentieth century, this is where most of the shantytowns, the so-called *villas miseria*, could be found.

The European immigrants were better off than those who came from the interior. They arrived, like the Bergoglios, with access to capital and learning and, on the whole, settled in the middle part of the city, in areas that ranged from working-class to petit bourgeois. In this respect, Jorge, born to Italian immigrants in the then lower-middle-class Buenos Aires barrio of Flores, the bull's-eye center of the city, was amazingly unexceptional. Because of this great European immigration of skilled workers Argentina, like the United States, became a nation with a large middle class, placing great store in hard work and progress; and in this, too, the Bergoglios were a migrant family straight out of Argentine central casting.

JORGE's grandparents and their children had been in Paraná for just two years when the world recession struck. The death from leukemia of the eldest brother, Giovanni Lorenzo, who headed the family's paving company, together with the economic crisis, which was at its worst in 1932, put the business under. The Bergoglio Palace was sold for a song, as was the family's marble tomb. The youngest brother made his way to Brazil, while Giovanni Angelo, with his remaining brother, headed with their families to Buenos Aires.

There they sought the help of a priest whom Giovanni's son Mario— the future pope's father—had come to know on his visits to Buenos Aires. Father Enrico Pozzoli belonged to the Salesians of Don Bosco, an Italian teaching order that was prominent among the urban working class both in Italy and in the Americas. Mario had known the Salesians back in Turin and had looked them up within months of arriving in Argentina, lodging with them in their guesthouse whenever he went to Buenos Aires. It was at the guesthouse that he met Don Enrico, who became, from 1929, Mario's confessor—a mentor, adviser, and spiritual director.

After the Bergoglios arrived, penniless, in Buenos Aires in 1932, Don Enrico arranged for them to be lent 2,000 pesos, with which the family bought a *confitería*, selling coffee and cakes. Mario helped out by making deliveries of cakes on a bicycle, until, as the economy began to recover, he got work as a part-time bookkeeper in various small firms. The Church in

Buenos Aires was a lifeline at this time for Mario, as for so many other families, mobilizing solidarity, weaving webs of support, just as it did seventy years later under Cardinal Bergoglio, during the brutal crisis of 2002–2003.

Mario had become part of a circle of young men around Don Enrico who used to meet with him at the Salesian church of St. Anthony of Padua in the working-class barrio of Almagro. In the group were the two Sívori Sturla brothers, who introduced Mario to their sister Regina in the church one Sunday in 1934. She was the daughter of an Argentine-born descendant of Genoese immigrants and a Piedmontese woman, Francisco and María Sívori Sturla, who lived just a few blocks from the church. One of Regina's uncles was a close friend of Don Enrico, with whom he shared a passion for photography; other uncles were active in the Catholic Worker Circles. This was the vibrant, thoroughly Italian and Catholic working-class world that shaped Jorge's childhood. It revolved around the Salesian fathers, who were famous teachers and confessors. Children were taught to ask for the blessing of Our Lady, Help of Christians, every time they said good-bye to a Salesian.

Mario Bergoglio married Regina Sívori on December 12, 1935. They had five children, of whom Jorge was the eldest. Until his death in 1961, Don Enrico was the family priest of both the Bergoglios and the Sívoris. "If in my family we live as serious Christians, it's thanks to him," Jorge later wrote. Don Enrico baptized Jorge on Christmas Day 1936, in the Almagro basilica of Our Lady, Help of Christians, eight days after he was born on December 17, with Jorge's paternal grandmother, Rosa, and his maternal grandfather, Francisco, acting as godparents. Although the Salesian was away for the birth and baptism of the next Bergoglio child, Don Enrico would baptize the three that followed.

Mario was by now doing the books for various small businesses in Flores. At first he and Regina rented, but soon after bought, a humble two-floor house, a *casa chorizo*, with kitchen and living room downstairs and bedrooms upstairs. It was there, at 531 calle Membrillar, that Jorge Mario lived shortly after being born a few streets away, and where his two brothers and sisters were born: Oscar, Marta, Alberto, and the last, in 1948, María Elena. His paternal grandparents, Giovanni and Rosa Angelo Bergoglio, lived close by in Flores. His maternal grandparents, Giovanni and María Sívori, remained in Almagro, four blocks from the church where Jorge's parents had met.

When Jorge was a child you could still see the remains of the fertile plots that gave Flores its name. Older residents recalled that the dictator Juan Manuel de Rosas had had a quinta there, and how Flores had been the first and only stop on the very first Argentine train journey in 1857. The station improvised for the occasion was then on the outskirts of Buenos Aires, and even in the 1940s, when Jorge was growing up there, it was a long way from the center. Since the city now has over ten million people, it feels far more central and middle-class than it would have done then: nowadays its streets are lined with pretty *casonas* adorned with curlicues and ironwork balconies, concealing patios or little gardens. But back then the houses were simple, just one or two floors, and the dusty streets turned to mud when it rained.

Jorge spent his first twenty years in that little house on calle Membrillar, his life revolving mainly around Flores and Almagro. Even after he left home, he seldom went far. During his thirty-three years as a Jesuit, he was mostly in San Miguel, in the province of Buenos Aires, a little more than an hour away; and in his fifties he returned to Flores as an auxiliary bishop. As archbishop in his sixties he lived in the Plaza de Mayo, half an hour directly east of Flores by bus or subway. Before he was made Christ's vicar on earth, he planned to live out his remaining years in Flores— specifically in Room 13 on the ground floor of the clergy retirement home on calle Condarco 581, which was being kept for him.

Seven blocks south of the Bergoglio house was their parish church, the impressive Basilica of St. Joseph of Flores, which hosted the funeral of the Buenos Aires governor, Manuel Dorrego. It was here, at seventeen, that Jorge had an experience in confession that unlocked his vocation, and whenever he returned as archbishop he would kiss the ornate wooden confessional where God had surprised him.

The basilica sits on Rivadavia Avenue, which was in colonial times the "royal road," the *camino real*, linking Buenos Aires to Upper Peru. Later it became the main east-west artery, marking the boundary between the wealthy north of Buenos Aires and its poorer southern half. Along the Rivadavia, underground, runs the subway to the Plaza de Mayo.

A few blocks north of Membrillar Street is the Mercy Sisters' convent, in whose little chapel the Bergoglios often heard Mass. The convent occupies the whole side of the square later named after it, the Plaza de la Misericordia, or Mercy Square. At kindergarten here, Jorge hated to be inside the classroom, wanting always to be outside. The nuns nowadays laugh that this was the first indication of what is now the pope's plan for the Church.

A Mercy nun here was one of the three key women in his childhood. Sister Dolores Tortolo prepared him for his First Communion ("from her I received a catechetical formation that was balanced, optimistic, joyful and responsible," he later recalled) at the age of eight. She would be a source of strength when, as a young seminarian, he lay close to death, and she was present at his first Mass in 1969. Whenever he came back to Flores, as Jesuit and later archbishop, he visited her in the convent. He was there in 2000 when she received an award for a lifetime's teaching, and spoke on that occasion of how she taught with her words and life the value of the interior life and fraternal love.

In the twilight of her life, when she was still mentally alert but physically paralyzed, the then cardinal would carry her to her room.

"So what was I like as a child?" he would tease her as he lifted her. "Tell the sisters!"

"You were terrible, terrible, as naughty as anything!" Dolores would cry, and the sisters would fall about laughing. (After he had gone she would tell them, giggling, that that was not true, that Jorgito, "little George," was always a good boy, happy and affectionate.) When Sister Dolores died in 2006, he spent the night in prayer next to her body in the convent chapel.

The sisters showed Jorge the meaning of God's mercy, and he would always speak of it, taking as his bishop's motto the Venerable Bede's account of Jesus recruiting the tax collector Matthew, *miserando atque eligendo*, which translates clumsily as "He saw him through the eyes of mercy and chose him." Bergoglio liked the way Latin had "mercy" as a verb, *miserando*, and so created the Spanish *misericordiando*—an activity of the divine, something God does to you. "*Dejáte misericordiar*," he would tell the guilt-ridden and the scrupulous, "let yourself be 'mercy'd.'" It was typical of the way he idiosyncratically appropriated a word, creating a *bergoglismo*.[1]

Speaking to journalists on the flight back from Rio de Janeiro in July 2013, Francis would proclaim a new age, a *kairos*, of mercy, recalling how, in the Gospel, rather than call him to account for the money he had squandered, the Prodigal Son's father instead threw a party. "He didn't just wait for him; he went out to meet him. That's mercy, that's *kairos*."

All his life, Bergoglio has insisted on this quality of God who takes the initiative, who comes out to find us, and surprises us with his forgiveness. "That is the religious experience: the astonishment of meeting someone who has been waiting for you all along," the cardinal said in 2010. "*Dios te primerea*," he added. "God beats you to it." *Primerear* is Buenos Aires slang meaning literally "to first" somebody. Used of God it is a *bergoglismo* that makes you smile, for you have a picture of someone dashing ahead, cheekily snatching the place you thought was yours.

※

THE single greatest childhood influence on Jorge Bergoglio was his grandmother Rosa, a formidable woman of deep faith and political skill, with whom he spent most of his first five years.

Back in Turin, Rosa had been heavily involved in Catholic Action, a national movement created by the Italian bishops that in the 1920s sought to defend the Church's independence from the all-absorbing state of the fascist dictator Benito Mussolini. Rosa was a regular speaker who worked closely with the Catholic Action national women's leaders of her day. The topics of her talks may not have been incendiary—Jorge kept one of her pamphlets, entitled "Saint Joseph in the Life of the Single Woman, the Widow and the Wife"—but because the fascists saw Catholic Action as a rival to the state, its speakers were constantly harassed and repressed, eventually provoking Pius XI's powerful 1931 antitotalitarian letter, *Non Abbiamo Bisogno*. When the fascists closed the venue where she was due to speak, Rosa would stand on a soapbox in the street, defying the henchmen; and one time she took to the pulpit of her church to publicly deplore Mussolini. The dictatorship was one of the factors behind her decision to emigrate.

"My strongest childhood memory is that life shared between my parents' house and my grandparents' house," Bergoglio recalled. "The first part of my childhood, from the age of one, I spent with my grandmother." Rosa began taking in Jorge after his brother Oscar was born, collecting him each morning and dropping him back in the afternoon. Rosa and Giovanni spoke with each other in Piedmontese, which Jorge learned from them—"I had the privilege of partaking in the language of their memories"—to the extent that today he can recite much of the romantic verse of the great Piedmontese poet, Nino Costa. Because his parents were anxious to integrate and therefore to downplay their origins, Jorge's grandparents were key to the boy's sense of identity as an Argentine of

Italian heritage. His father, Mario, in contrast, spoke only in Spanish; he was the immigrant moving on, seeking acceptance, never looking back to Piedmont with nostalgia, "which meant he must have felt it," Bergoglio later recalled, "since he denied it for some reason."

Bergoglio has always been convinced of the vital importance of grandparents—and especially the grandmother—as guardians of a precious reserve parents often ignore or reject. "I was lucky to know my four grandparents," he recalled in 2011. "The wisdom of the elderly has helped me greatly; that is why I venerate them." In 2012 he told Father Isasmendi on the community radio of the Villa 21 shantytown:

> The grandmother is in the hearth, the grandfather, too, but above all the grandmother; she's like the reserve. She's the moral, religious, and cultural reserve. She's the one who passes on the whole story. Mom and Dad are over there, working, engaged in this and that, they've got a thousand things to do. The grandmother is in the house more; the grandfather, too. They tell you things from before. My grandfather used to tell me stories about the 1914 war, stories they lived through. They tell you about life as they lived it, not stories from books, but their own stories, of their own lives. That's what I'd like to say to the grandparents listening. Tell them things about life, so the kids know what life is.

Rosa was a wonderful faith transmitter. She introduced Jorge to the saints and taught him the Rosary; and on Good Friday she took her grandchildren to see the crucified Christ and told them how he was dead but would rise on Sunday. Her faith recognized human goodness beyond the boundaries of religion. If at home with his parents the Catholicism was rather puritanical—"If someone close to the family divorced or separated, they could not enter your house," he recalled, "and they believed all Protestants were going to hell"—he learned a different message from Rosa. When he was about five or six, two women from the Salvation Army passed on the street. "I asked her if they were nuns, because they had those little hats they used to wear. She answered, 'No. But they are good people.'" Looking back he realized that this was "the wisdom of true religion. These were good women who did good things."

He recalled Rosa taking him to Mass at the Salesian oratory of St.

Francis de Sales on Hipólito Yrigoyen Street, explaining that the church had been visited by Cardinal Eugenio Pacelli when he presided at the 1934 International Eucharistic Congress in Buenos Aires. She would often tell stories about that mind-blowing event, pulling out old newspaper cuttings and explaining how that October 12 more than a million people had received Communion, almost half of them men (amazingly for the time, when many more women than men attended church); and how hundreds of thousands of people prayed in the streets of the city and queued to confess down the Avenida de Mayo. The Bergoglios were thrilled when Pacelli was elected Pius XII in 1939. Shortly after, Germany invaded Poland, World War II broke out, and émigrés in Buenos Aires spent years deprived of news of their families. Jorge would remember how, when he was nine, Italians celebrated the end of the war, rushing to give each other news of their relatives after Mass at the Basilica of Flores.

His grandmother also taught him to love Italian literature, reading to him above all the great novel by Alessandro Manzoni, *I Promessi Sposi* (*The Betrothed*), whose famous opening ("That branch of Lake Como that turns off to the south between two unbroken chains of mountains . . .") Jorge learned by heart. *The Betrothed*, which was first published in 1827, would always have a special place in his affections. It is the Italian equivalent of *War and Peace* or *Les Misérables*, an epic of love and forgiveness amid war and famine, with an unforgettable cast of pious lovers, cruel nobles, virtuous peasants, and a great range of ecclesiastical figures: a worldly country priest, a saintly friar, and an austere cardinal.

At the heart of the story are two lovers, Renzo and Lucia, whose desire to marry is thwarted by their parish priest, Don Abbondio, who is cowed by the local nobleman, Don Rodrigo, who lusts for Lucia. The lovers appeal to a saintly Capuchin Franciscan, Father Cristoforo, who confronts Don Rodrigo, who is enraged and vows to kill Renzo and abduct Lucia. The plot escalates as Father Cristoforo hides the lovers, who are separated, while Rodrigo secures the help of the murderous baron L'Innominato ("The Unnamed") in kidnapping Lucia. Enter, at this point, the austere and holy cardinal, Federigo Borromeo, in whose presence L'Innominato breaks down and confesses his sins. The novel's dénouement takes place in a lazaretto, a field hospital for victims of the plague outside Milan, where there are heartrending scenes of forgiveness and reconciliation, as victims and perpetrators come face-to-face at the instigation of the friar.

The Betrothed is a complex, multilayered novel with many themes that would be dear to Bergoglio as a Jesuit, bishop, and later pope: the mercy of God, offered even to the worst sinners; the contrast between the cowardly worldliness of some priests and the fearless austerity of others; the corruption of wealth and power in contrast to the virtuousness of ordinary people; the power of prayer and of forgiveness; the Church as a battlefield hospital. Cardinal Borromeo's pages-long rebuke of the cowardly Don Abbondio—"You should have loved, my son; loved and prayed. Then you would have seen that the forces of iniquity have power to threaten and to wound, but no power to command"—could almost be a manifesto for Francis's reforms.

His grandmother remained Bergoglio's great love. In the 1970s, by then widowed and frail, when she was looked after by Italian nuns in San Miguel, he visited often. "He adored her, she was his weakness," recalls one of them, Sister Catalina. "She only ever paid attention to what he said." As Rosa lay dying, Jorge kept vigil by her bed, holding her body until life left it. "He told us: 'At this moment my grandmother is at the most important point of her existence. She is being judged by God. This is the mystery of death.' A few minutes later," said Sister Catalina, "he got up and left, as serene as ever."

With Rosa and the maternal grandparents in the background, his parents in love with each other, and siblings at home, Jorge was a happy, well-adjusted child in a contented, stable Italian home. Mario was an essentially joyful man who seldom got angry, and in this, says María Elena, father and eldest son were alike. The Salesian family priest, Don Enrico, was a supportive presence, a regular visitor especially at the Sívori house where the whole clan would gather to eat ravioli with him.

Jorge's barrio had many playmates, who used to come together in the local square. Primary school (No. 8 Coronel Pedro Cerviño, at no. 358 Varela Street) was close by: there he was a diligent student who passed all his subjects. With his first-grade teacher, Estela Quiroga, he maintained a lifelong correspondence, relating to her each stage in his journey of faith, and she was present at his ordination to the priesthood in 1969.

María Elena—known in the family as Malena—was twelve years younger than Jorge. "I was the little doll and he was *el viejo*, the old man," she laughs. She remembers Sundays best, when they all went to the parish for Mass and came back to lunches that stretched far into the afternoon.

Materially, it was a simple existence: "We were poor, with dignity." There was no car, and they didn't go on vacation, as better-off middle-class families did. But there was food on the table—Regina's capelletti with ragú and Piedmontese risotto were high on the family wish list—and clothes to wear, even if they were recycled. "Mama succeeded in salvaging some article of clothing for us, even from our father's things: a ripped shirt or fraying pants got repaired and sewn up, and became ours. Maybe my brother's and my extreme frugality comes from this."

Faith was strong, and conventional. Mario led the family in praying the Rosary when he got back from work, and they were all at Mass on Sunday. But Jorge's father, whose qualification as an accountant was not recognized in Argentina, had to take on many jobs to make ends meet, and he often sat at home on weekends with huge ledgers, while playing operas and Italian crooners on his Victrola phonograph. To relax, the family played *brisca*, an Italian whist. Listening to opera with his mother and siblings on Saturday afternoons is among Jorge's fondest memories. To keep the children's attention, he recalled, Regina would offer a running commentary, whispering, for example, during *Otello*, "Listen carefully: he's about to kill her." Between the ages of ten and twelve his parents took Jorge to every Italian movie being screened in Buenos Aires that starred Anna Magnani and Aldo Fabrizi. *La Strada* and *Rome, Open City* were his favorites.

Then there was soccer. Jorge, a lanky kid, liked to kick around with friends but wasn't much good: he had flat feet. But Ernesto Lach, who used to play with him behind the parish church of the Miraculous Medal, says he was good on tactics, an opportunistic striker. Most of his playmates agree, however, that he was more at home with books. Everyone remembers him as studious, always with his nose in a text. But that didn't stop Jorge obsessively following soccer. From his dad he inherited a passion for San Lorenzo, the smallest and pluckiest of Buenos Aires's three major teams, founded by the Salesian missionary Father Lorenzo Massa back in 1907. Massa had been parish priest of St. Anthony of Padua where Mario and Regina met, and the club is under the protection of the Virgin Mary. After the team entered the major league in 1915, Father Massa secured a stadium where they could play known as the Old Gas Meter in neighboring Boedo, where Mario and his sons never missed a match. The team's big year was Jorge's tenth, when legendary striker René "the Egg" Pontoni lifted San Lorenzo to hitherto undreamed-of heights. "I didn't miss a single match of the champion team of '46, with the great Pontoni," Bergoglio later told the team.

Not long after Jorge began his Jesuit formation, in December 1961, Mario died of a heart attack while watching a match in the stadium. He was just fifty-one. Jorge's youngest brother, Alberto, who was with Mario at the time, never went back there. When he left for Rome in February 2013, Cardinal Bergoglio took a treasured relic that is with him now in the Vatican. That piece of wood from the Old Gas Meter contains a whirlwind of memories: of Don Enrico, of "the Egg" Pontoni, of his dad and brother, as well as that feeling when a roaring crowd leaps as one from the benches, punching the air. He has remained a lifelong devoted fan of San Lorenzo and, as Pope Francis, he continues to pay his annual membership fee. If you happen to be in St. Peter's Square during a Wednesday audience, and there's just been a match, and you have a San Lorenzo shirt on, you're sure to see Francis with a great grin on his face, finger-signing the score to you as he swings past on the popemobile.

THE Church that Jorge Bergoglio knew as a child in 1940s Argentina was vigorous, nationalistic, and closely identified with that part of Argentine society that transported General Juan Domingo Perón to power in 1946.

It had been very different in the mid-nineteenth century, before the immigrant flood started. The River Plate region had been on the peripheries of the Spanish colony, and the Church emerged from the internal battles following independence a feeble institution, heavily controlled by the state. The Church had just five bishops in 1869. They had been appointed by the state, had almost no contact with Rome, and showed little initiative. The great Catholics of that time were not bishops but missionaries like the man known as the "gaucho priest," Father José Gabriel Brochero (1840–1914), whom Francis, shortly after his election, placed on the road to sainthood. Father Brochero rode a mule, wore a poncho, smoked cheroots, drank mate tea from a gourd, and went about building churches, chapels, and schools, opening up paths and passages in the sierras of Córdoba, tending to the poorest in a model life of heroic self-abnegation.

As the immigrants poured into the cities, however, the Argentine Church began to grow both in capacity and in independence from the state. Two dates stand out. The first was 1865, when Buenos Aires was made the primatial see, the mother diocese, which by 1880 had eighty-four priests; the other was 1899, when Latin-American bishops met in Rome to agree to a sweeping range of reforms. The Church in Argentina became Romanized at about the moment when the state achieved dominance over the nation.

Over the next decades, state and Church developed vigorously alongside each other. As the state set about institution-building—spreading the railroad and the telegraph, creating a standing army—so the Church built seminaries and parishes, while new religious orders, especially of nuns, sprang up to manage hospitals and schools. Most of this activity was concentrated in the cities, especially in Buenos Aires and Córdoba, in contrast to the interior, where the dioceses remained vast, poor, and remote—and where the rural poor continued, until well into the twentieth century, to have little contact with the Church. Popular religion—which Bergoglio would always respect as an evangelized culture—has its origin here: country people ignorant of doctrine but with deep faith who, in the absence of clergy and churches, looked to devotions more than sacraments.

By the late nineteenth century the Church had grown in size and influence to the point where the liberals began to see it as a rival. In the 1880s, the Argentine government, in a display of secularist zeal, copied France by bringing marriage and education under the control of the state. The civil marriage law made the state the only legal witness to a wedding, while the education law banned Catholic teaching from public schools in favor of a compulsory secular morality that would create enlightened citizens. During the furious debates in Congress—in which the education minister declared the triumph of science over "thousands of years of mystical hysteria"—the government easily crushed the clutch of Catholic deputies and moved to quell the Church's objections by expelling the Holy See's apostolic delegate, temporarily suspending the bishops (who were state employees), and sacking the Catholic university teachers who had challenged the new laws. As the historian John Lynch puts it: "Argentina was living disproof that Latin-American liberalism was a tolerant creed."[2]

Yet the government had little appetite for disorder of the sort that had broken out during the conflict, when Freemasons torched churches and anticlerical mobs attacked the Jesuit-run Salvador College. French-style secularism was abandoned in favor of a conservative, almost English model of Church-state relations, in which agnostic rulers supported a tame Church as a bulwark of social order. Unlike in neighboring Chile, where state and Church amicably separated in the 1920s, Catholicism remained the official religion of the Argentine state, while guaranteeing freedom to other faiths. Argentine bishops received their salaries from the government, and the president was until recently required to be a baptized Catholic, with the power to veto the appointment of bishops. Church and nation have remained strongly entwined. Every day, after the 9:00 a.m. weekday Mass at the cathedral, sword-carrying soldiers in ceremonial uniforms march down past the side altars to stand guard at the flag-draped tomb of the liberator, General San Martín. And once a year, the Church reconsecrates the nation at the traditional May 25 Te Deum service, attended by the president and leading politicians, which, until Cardinal Bergoglio turned it into a prophetic challenge, was a tame, reassuring event.

The first of many papal letters deploring the iniquities of modern capitalism, Pope Leo XIII's *Rerum Novarum* of 1891 found a clear echo in Argentina, as did his objections to the free-market idolatry of the wealthy classes. The poverty of the laboring classes and what to do about it—the so-called social question—came to dominate Argentine politics, and lay behind growing social violence: in 1919 the Buenos Aires police chief was killed by an anarchist bomb and hundreds died in the subsequent crackdown. Yet while governments enacted public-order laws, they refused to intervene in the market; Congress blocked attempts by Catholic and socialist deputies to introduce even moderate social reforms.

The Church ran the only organized labor movement not led by communists or anarchists, and in its social teaching it had a clear alternative to both left- and right-wing ideologies. But attempts to translate these into a clear political alternative to the dominant liberal government foundered: the Christian Democratic Union's advocacy of the women's vote, a minimum wage, and labor laws made the bishops uneasy.

In the early 1920s, however, the accommodation of the bishops to the liberal state received a blow from Rome. When the government tried to name the new archbishop of Buenos Aires, the Christian Democrats and the Jesuits appealed to the pope, who refused the nomination: the post would be vacant for two years before a new candidate was finally agreed on. In the midst of this standoff between the Vatican and the Casa Rosada, the Argentine Church would increasingly find its prophetic voice, one that was sharply critical of liberalism in both economics and politics, and, in Church terms, ultramontane, looking to Rome rather than the state. Catholicism, in short, became antiestablishment. The Church was the major source of protests against the liberal economy and politics of the day, drawing on the social teaching of the popes and new nationalist thinking in Argentina, both of which would influence the Peronist government in the 1940s and 1950s.

The Church of the 1930s also acquired an impressive capacity for mobilization. The symbolic moment was the 1934 International Eucharistic Congress in Buenos Aires, two years before Jorge Bergoglio was born, but about which he had heard endless stories from his grandmother Rosa. In the history of the Argentine Church, it marks a before and after. The following years witnessed a dramatic expansion, a "Catholic spring": ten new dioceses were created; Mass attendance rose sharply, along with baptisms and marriages; the seminaries swelled; and vocations finally kept pace with population expansion. Schools multiplied, to the point where three out of four private pupils were educated by the Church.

It was also an intellectually confident Church, running a network of newspapers, magazines, and radio stations, along with the leading Church publisher of its day, Editorial Difusión, which in the 1930s sold six million books from a catalog of hundreds of titles. In the 1940s to 1950s, hundreds of thousands of Catholics—among them the young Jorge Bergoglio—joined Catholic Action's study circles. There were marches, leaflets, and speeches that laid the blame for social ills squarely at the feet of liberal capitalism, while urging workers to resist the blandishments of socialism and embrace Catholic social teaching. Yet Catholics and socialists still cooperated in Congress, finally persuading it to pass laws introducing Sunday rest and eight-hour workdays.

This was the Church—vigorous, confident, a little triumphalist—in which Jorge Bergoglio grew up. It was antiliberal in the particular Argentine sense of that word. Liberal was associated with the free-market, cosmopolitan, rationalist, authoritarian outlook of the Argentine belle époque; in the 1930s, it was a worldview that increasingly came to be seen as antithetical to the national interest.

The alternative to liberalism was a series of inchoate protests under the umbrella of nationalism. The movement had begun in academia, in studies of history and literature, but it became, in the 1930s, a social and political critique of the prevailing order. In shutting export markets to Argentine goods, the world economic crisis had exposed the country's dependence on foreigners, and comparative advantage began to look like a slavish subservience—one that the so-called oligarchy defended in its own interest rather than that of the nation as a whole.

This crisis of the liberal order caused nationalist intellectuals to challenge the liberal myth that Argentina had progressed by spurning its Spanish, colonial heritage; they began to look to an older, more authentic nation that had been suppressed by the liberals' cult of foreigners. In rejecting political and economic liberalism, the nationalists embraced what liberalism had scorned: the Spanish and Catholic tradition was now vindicated as the more "authentic" heritage, and the dictator Rosas came to be seen as a hero, one close to the land and its people.

Catholics were sympathetic to these new ideas because they rescued Catholic culture as a key actor in Argentine history—one that had been suffocated by what nationalists called foreignizing (*extranjerizante*) liberalism. Some of the more aristocratic Catholic nationalists looked, ironically, to right-wing movements abroad (this was the age of Franco and Mussolini), but the Argentine Church mainstream steered a course between both liberalism and totalitarianism. What Catholics sought was a government that would give a voice to the new urban masses disenfranchised by the liberal elite. They wanted government to be nationalist in the sense of being faithful to Argentina's traditions rather than a copy of France or Britain. And they wanted the government to take its economic and social policies from the social teaching of the Church, which meant a state that intervened to curb the excesses of the market and the growing gap between rich and poor.

By the time of the 1930 military coup, liberal republican democracy in Argentina had few friends. The introduction of universal male suffrage in 1912 had led to the electoral monopoly of a middle-class party, the Radical Civic Union (UCR), known as the Radicals. Despite their name, Radicals did not question the basic tenets of the economic model, but expanded state spending in order to secure electoral support through patronage, earning the enmity of the conservatives, now gathered in the modern successor to the PAN, the National Democratic Party (PDN). In 1930 the army moved to topple the Radicals in the name of rescuing the constitution, eventually handing power to the PDN, who reverted throughout the 1930s to their old practices of stuffing the ballot box, while excluding the Radicals from taking part in elections.

For this, among other reasons—there were monopoly concessions to the British, and widespread evidence of corruption linking the ruling classes to foreign business interests—the 1930s would be remembered as the infamous decade, the liberal era's last gasp, sandwiched between two military coups. The second coup came in 1943, in the midst of World War II, when Argentina—maintaining its traditional neutrality, in defiance of the United States' call for Latin America to back the Allies—was plunged into crisis by a US embargo on arms and industrial goods. The army took power in the midst of rising social protest and anger at electoral fraud, waiting on the outcome of the war. As the Allied victory began to look certain, a group of young army officers, headed by Colonel Juan Domingo Perón, took control.

Perón grasped that Argentina was on the cusp of revolution, that the old order had passed away and the task was to manage the transition to a new mass politics without falling into communism. While his fellow officers thought only of restoring the status quo after the war's end, Perón used his formidable political skills to construct a powerful new alliance of interests and values. Deploying the resources of the state at his disposal, he began dispensing favors to the labor unions and reaching out in various ways to the disenfranchised working-class majority. In less than two years he constructed a formidable movement, one that voiced the nationalist and Catholic values of the immigrant classes and offered concrete benefits to the poor.

When the war ended and elections were called, Perón was arrested; but on October 17, 1945—a date hallowed by Peronists ever since—tens of thousands of workers filled the Plaza de Mayo to demand his release. The army set the colonel free, and he coasted to a decisive electoral victory in February 1946, when Jorge was nine. Perón defeated a rainbow alliance of all the existing "liberal" political parties, ranging from left to right, assembled by the US ambassador in Buenos Aires, Spruille Braden, who misread Perón as a fascist. Perón won a second term in 1952, which ended three years later. Peronism transformed the Argentine political landscape and dominated the adolescence of the future pope.

THE first real crisis in the Bergoglio home happened in February 1948, when Jorge was twelve, and Perón had been in power for two years. As a result of complications with the birth of María Elena, Regina was bedridden for some time, suffering from a form of paralysis. While Rosa helped with the two youngest children, Alberto and María Elena, the family priest, Don Enrico Pozzoli, hastily found places for the three eldest at Salesian boarding schools. While Marta was sent to the María Auxiliadora school in Almagro, Jorge and Oscar were sent in 1949 to the splendidly named Wilfrid Barón de los Santos Ángeles school in the western district of Ramos Mejía.

Jorge, who boarded as a sixth grader, loved the school, which was named after a French immigrant millionaire whose widow funded its construction in 1925. "The day shot by like an arrow; there was never time to get bored," Bergoglio recalled in 1990 in a letter to the Salesian provincial, Father Cayetano Bruno. The school was permeated by a natural Catholic culture, in which going to Mass was as normal as studying or playing. The hours of studying in silence developed his concentration and focus, and he learned a wide variety of hobbies and skills: Father Lambruschini taught him to sing, Father Avilés how to make copies using gelatine, and a Ukrainian priest taught him how to serve Mass in the eastern rite—an unusual choice of pastime for an adolescent, but not at the Wilfrid Barón de los Santos Ángeles school.

In both study and sport, they were taught to compete "as Christians"—to strive for success, but never despising those who came second. They learned about sin, but also forgiveness: the Salesians "weren't afraid to confront us with the language of the Cross of Jesus," he recalled in the letter. Jorge learned to pray before going to sleep, to ask favors of the Virgin, and to respect the figure of the pope, then Pius XII. The Salesians also taught him a love of chastity, which Jorge—who arrived in the school just as he was coming into adolescence—came to see as healthy. "There was no sexual obsession in the college," Bergoglio wrote to Don Bruno. "I found much more sexual obsession later on among educators and psychologists who claimed to let it all hang out, but who looked at everything through a Freudian lens which saw sex everywhere."

Jorge's conscience developed fast that year: "I learned, almost unconsciously, to seek the meaning of things." He became aware of the existence of truth as something outside himself, of the need of values and virtues, and of his own responsibility for the world. The Salesians spoke often of the needs of the poor and encouraged students to go without in order to give to those in need.

He also learned about death. One night in October 1949 Monsignor Miguel Raspanti, one of the Salesian school inspectors, told the boys about the passing of his mother a few weeks earlier. "That night, without being afraid, I felt that one day I would die, too, and that it was the most natural thing," he told Don Bruno. He began to hear stories of how the old Salesians left this earth, and what made for what they called a good death.

At the end of the school year the Bergoglio boys returned home to find their mother, still unable to stand, peeling potatoes from a chair, with all the ingredients for their meal laid out. "Then she'd tell us how to mix and cook them, because we didn't have a clue," Bergoglio remembered. " 'Now put this in the pot and that in the pan,' she'd explain. That's how we all learned to cook."

Jorge first felt the stirrings of a vocation around age twelve or thirteen, although at that stage he was thinking about being a priest "in the way that you think about being an engineer, a doctor, or a musician," he recalled to Father Isasmendi. He clearly had it in mind when he fell in love with a girl next door of the same age, Amalia Damonte, to whom, in a burst of pubescent passion, he made a less than romantic offer. "If I don't become a priest, I'll marry you," he told her in a letter in which he also drew a pretty house with a red-tile roof where he said they would live. (The girl's father was furious: he beat her and forbade her to see him.) At school, he prayed intensely to discover his vocation following a talk by a Father Cantarutti, and discussed the possibility of priesthood with another of the priests, Father Martínez, who was famous as a "fisher of vocations." But the following year, 1950, he began secondary school, and the idea was pushed to the back of his mind until, four years later, the candle was lit again, and this time the flame did not go out.

AT the time Jorge began secondary school, Perón had been president for nearly four years and Argentina had been turned on its head. It was the high noon of the first Peronist term, remembered with awe even today as a time of massive state spending, a distribution of wealth in favor of the working class, and rapid industrialization—a nationalist project that in almost every respect reversed the previous liberal model. These were new times: Britain, impoverished by war, was no longer a key trading partner, and while the United States supplied manufactured goods, it already produced at home what Argentina offered to export. A more self-sufficient economy was needed. Perón's idea was to increase wages to create more consumption and encourage industries to meet that demand, while nationalizing everything that he could, such as oil, railways, and trams. Like the thinking behind Roosevelt's New Deal, the assumption of Peronism was that the economy could solve social problems and that the state could steer the economy.

The arguments about what Peronism was and is—authoritarian populism? left-wing nationalism?—miss the deeper point that it was a vehicle for Perón, not for any particular ideology. And Perón, far from being an ideologue, was an intuitive political genius with an uncanny ability to articulate the interests and hopes of the new classes—the immigrants and their children, the folk arriving in the cities in search of a better life. He understood their hopes and dreams, for he was one of them. The story of the handsome colonel and his pretty radio actress wife, Evita—both were born out of wedlock in small-town provincial Buenos Aires, conquering social stigma and disadvantage to make it to the top—and how they built a political movement that resonated with poorer Argentines, has been told often, in books and musicals and films. But outside the theater and myth, the reason that Peronism has endured beyond the deaths of its creators is that, in articulating the values and interests of this new Argentina, Perón created something far bigger than himself: a movement rather than a party, a culture rather than an interest group, a political hybrid so popular and absorbent that for decades it has dominated modern Argentina, overshadowing even those elections from which it was banned.

Among the many barriers smashed by Perón's 1946 electoral victory was the wall erected by Argentine liberalism against the Church. His was the first government in Argentina's modern history to gain its legitimacy from identifying with Catholic values and priorities—above all with the Church's social teaching, made popular in the Catholic and nationalist revival of the previous decade. The early years of the Peronist government looked like a high noon for the Church. Here, finally, was a government that would uphold Argentina's Catholic heritage, implement Catholic social teaching, and support the Church's work of evangelization.

Later, after the Second Vatican Council, the Church would no longer—at least officially—look to the state to be an instrument of its evangelization. But at the time, this was the default position taken by bishops in Catholic countries: the Church was the guardian of moral and spiritual values that the government should uphold and implement, while respecting the Church's freedom to Christianize society. Perón, eager for legitimacy—he gave no indication in his early life of being a believing Catholic, and little in his life story suggests much contact with the Church—embraced that idea, seeing his movement as the political incarnation of the "Catholic nation." It was an idea that lingered long after the furious conflict between Perón and the Church from 1954 to 1955 that led to his being ousted in another coup.

Just as Perón dispensed concrete benefits and real gains to the workers and their unions, and expected loyalty in return, he did the same for the Church: bishops and clergy received sudden increases in their salaries, seminaries were built, grants were offered to seminarians to study abroad, imported religious goods were tax-exempted, and Church organizations were offered state subsidies. But even more significant was the new openness to Catholic ideas. Perón explicitly identified his government's doctrine with the social teaching of the Church—he spoke of humanizing capital and dignifying labor—and recruited Catholic Action leaders to put forward proposals on issues they had long campaigned for, such as the family wage and regulation of child labor, that quickly became law. The Peróns even had a Jesuit priest as an adviser, Father Hernán Benítez, who expressly linked Peronism to the Gospel and Catholic social teaching.

But the relationship broke down because the Church refused to be bought. In the negotiations over a new constitution, Perón rejected the Holy See's call to remove the *patronato*, the colonial-era right of the state to control the Church in a variety of ways, which the 1853 Constitution had continued to uphold. The Vatican, recently emerged from the fascist era in Europe, was sensitive to the dangers of supposedly Catholic states seeking to use the Church as an instrument of social control. And it knew that long after the Peronist government had gone, another, more hostile government could use that power seriously to inhibit the Church's mission.

For his part, Perón was not about to renounce his constitutional power to appoint politically loyal bishops; it was the logical corollary of Peronism as the political embodiment of the Catholic nation.

Each side dug in. The Holy See, increasingly concerned by the attempted "Peronization" of the Church, refused to ratify new bishops, while for his part Perón, angered at what he saw as the Church's ingratitude, began to attempt to detach Christianity from the Church. A new state doctrine, *justicialismo*, made an appeal to Christian values that were identified with Perón rather than Jesus Christ ("Perón is the face of God in the darkness," declared Evita in her autobiography. "Here the case of Bethlehem, 2,000 years ago, was repeated; the first to believe were the humble.") The state began to create parallel institutions to compete with the Church, depriving Catholic organizations of legal recognition. Peronism no longer claimed to be practicing what the Church preached but to preach what the Church failed to practice.

In 1951, as the country prepared for elections, Evita became ill from cancer, dying the following July. Her appearances at the balcony of the Casa Rosada, giving impassioned speeches as the cancer wracked her body, would become iconic moments in Peronist mythology. Riding on a wave of sympathy for Evita, and backed by women to whom he had granted the vote in 1947, Perón swept the board in the 1952 elections.

Then came the decline. As the economy experienced a downturn, Perón became defensive and paranoid, descending into the authoritarian madness that commonly afflicts populist-nationalist governments in Latin America, whether of the right or left. Nation, state, and government merged: state officials were required to be party members, disagreement was framed as dissent, and opponents (whether Radicals, socialists, or Catholics) defined as enemies of the people. Official art featuring the chiseled features of the Peronist "New Man" began to appear, and *justicialismo* descended into a vortex of philosophical banalities and bizarre dualities. The funeral of Evita, which has its modern parallel in that of Diana, Princess of Wales, was an extraordinary moment of mass grief, but the government's attempt to create a cult of her—she appeared as a secular Virgin Mary on the school edition of her autobiography sporting a halo—marked a low point in relations with the Church.

In 1951 and 1952, Catholic activists moved from critical collaboration to disillusionment, and then into outright opposition. Having lost many of their leaders to Peronism, Catholic Action was rejuvenated by their return. Church newspapers and Catholic Action meetings reported on the new Christian Democratic parties in Europe, comparing them unfavorably with the government. Perón detected the birth of a Church-backed political rival in his backyard and ordered a clampdown.

In a speech in November 1954, Perón fulminated against priests meddling in politics and had a number arrested. Catholic Action was legally dissolved, and Church publications and radios were ransacked and closed down. In an echo of the Mexican Revolution, public religious acts were forbidden. A series of laws followed, aimed at restricting the Church and flouting its moral concerns, legalizing divorce and prostitution, banning religious education from schools, and derogating tax exemptions to religious institutions. The government began bestowing favors on Protestants and Spiritists, plastering churches with denials of Jesus's divinity.

As pastoral letters from the bishops were read out in parishes, lamenting these measures and accusing the state of attempting to create a parallel cult, Catholic Action, which at that time had seventy thousand active members, took to the streets. Networks of cells published and circulated pamphlets to counter the news blackout. Tactical commandos were formed to defend churches and prevent government stooges from interrupting Mass. But the main method of resistance was to organize public religious acts large enough to make the government's prohibition of them unenforceable.

On May 25, 1955, Perón boycotted the Te Deum at Buenos Aires cathedral, the annual ceremony of prayers for the nation attended by political and church leaders. Catholic Action began bringing people out on the streets in protest, culminating in Corpus Christi on June 11, a eucharistic procession of deep significance to Catholics. In spite of desperate government efforts to prevent it, more than a quarter of a million people processed silently behind papal and national flags in a definitive show of defiance.

Perón panicked and ordered the arrest of dozens of priests and the ransacking of Catholic Action's headquarters. The naval air force bombed the Plaza de Mayo, its planes bearing the slogan *Cristo Vence* ("Christ Conquers"), killing hundreds of counterdemonstrators organized by the unions. Recalling that moment in 2011, Cardinal Bergoglio told his friend Rabbi Abraham Skorka that the slogan "disgusts me, it makes me very angry. I am outraged because it uses the name of Christ for a purely political act. It mixed religion, politics, and pure nationalism. Innocent people were killed in cold blood."

In retaliation, twelve churches in the city center were gutted and burned. What followed were two months of further anticlerical campaigns and growing evidence of a series of military plots to unseat Perón. One of them, in September 1955, succeeded. It was known as the "Liberating" Revolution. The army had taken the reins again, called out from the barracks to restore order and the constitution.

The conflict between Perón and the Church did not lead, as might be supposed, to all Catholics becoming anti-Peronist. It was a family conflict, one that took place within the walls of the hallowed ideal of the Catholic nation. Perón, exiled in Spain, would in time make his peace with the Church, which was also keen to repair the breach. Seeing how ordinary people remained devotedly Peronist, in the late 1950s and especially in the 1960s, when Jorge was training as a Jesuit, many Catholics, fired by social justice, turned to Peronism, calling for the exiled leader's return. Bergoglio was never active in a political party and, after 1958, the year he joined the Jesuits, he never voted. But he always had a natural affinity with the cultural and political tradition represented by Peronism.

By persecuting Peronism, the army turned it into a martyr and increased the loyalty of ordinary people to the exiled leader. For the next three decades, from 1955 to 1983, the Peronist party was banned from every election except that of 1973, eighteen presidents served terms of an average of 1.5 years each, and the armed forces ruled for nineteen years. By the end of the 1960s, Argentina had the largest guerrilla force in the region, which would be defeated in the 1970s by one of the continent's most brutal military dictatorships. To explain why Argentina became the most unstable country in the Western Hemisphere, the account must always begin in the 1950s, when Catholicism and Peronism faced each other down, and the army tried to take the country back to the days before Perón ever appeared. From the 1950s to the 1970s Argentina was paralyzed by a political paradox that is hard for foreigners to grasp: the antiliberals (the nationalists, the Peronists) were popular and came to power by winning elections, while the liberals—the democrats, the pluralists—used dictatorship to keep the Peronists out of power.

BEGINNING in 1952, for five years, while he was at secondary school training as a chemist, Jorge was a member of the local Catholic Action in his
parish of Flores. Catholic Action was still a vibrant part of the Church—
more than one hundred aspirants, as the adolescent section was known,
met at the basilica at that time—and the nursery of many vocations to the
priesthood. It received a particular boost in numbers at the time of the
Church conflict with Perón, but at the end of the 1950s membership began
to decline.

Among the aspirants Jorge stood out as quiet, polite, and well read
(he helped to set up and run the bookshop in the parish narthex), but he
kept his vocation to himself. During the Church-state tensions of 1954–
1955 the aspirants concentrated on private charitable acts; but in 1956–1957,
Jorge with thousands of others took part in rallies in favor of allowing the
Church to run universities. There was also charitable work, visiting the
very poor in Flores, offering material help and comfort.

At weekly Catholic Action talks by priests, known as "Tribunes for a
Better World," Jorge drank in the core tenets of the Church's social teaching, still largely defined by the most recent papal letter on the subject
(known as a "social encyclical"), Pope Pius XI's 1931 *Quadragesimo Anno*.
Read through the eyes of contemporary political events, the encyclical
offered ammunition for both supporters and opponents of Peronism: on
the one hand it deplored liberal economics and called for unions and
state intervention in the economy; on the other, it sought to demarcate
the limits of the state's pretensions to control and shape society. For the
adolescent Jorge, who was eighteen when the Church-state conflict broke
out, it was a fertile environment for his awakening consciousness of faith
and political ideas.

The son of the head of his secondary school recalls his father repri-
manding Jorge for arriving at class with a Peronist insignia; college kids
were banned from wearing symbols of any sort. Yet Hugo Morelli, one of
Jorge's classmates who knew him well, claims that Jorge was anti-Peronist.
"I was Peronist and he wasn't, and we argued about it all the time." What
divides those two recollections was the growing Church-state tensions of
the 1950s, when many Catholics who had been pro-Perón turned against
him; by the mid-1950s, Jorge was one of them: he was attracted to socialism at the time. Later—in the 1960s and 1970s—he would come to respect
Peronism as the expression of the values of ordinary people.

The parrot next door to the school, on the other hand, had no doubt about its allegiances. Jorge's classmates vividly recall that during classes it would screech *¡Viva Perón, carajo!* ("Long live Perón, dammit!"), causing fits of giggles. In addition to Morelli, Jorge's classmates between 1950 and 1955 were Alberto D'Arezzo, Abel Sala, Oscar Crespo, and Francisco Spinoza; they became close friends with him and with one another and would have regular reunions later in life, when Bergoglio was cardinal.

The Escuela Industrial No. 12, which had started the year before in a private house in the barrio of Floresta, was an avant-garde initiative, part of the drive by the Peronist government to boost Argentina's industrial capacity. Jorge's father, Mario, was president of a civic association that raised funds for the school, and he secured his son's place there. There were just a dozen pupils at this time. Although the school followed the nationally agreed-upon curriculum of obligatory subjects, it gave extra time and resources to food chemistry, qualifying its students to work in laboratories.

His classmates paint Jorge as an ordinary young guy of his time, a warmhearted, book-addicted, but engaging companion. He teased them when their teams were thrashed by San Lorenzo, played basketball with them during breaks, and on weekends hooked up with them to go dancing with girls.

But their descriptions reveal two respects in which Jorge stood out. The first was his fierce intelligence: he grasped new ideas and information with a speed that ensured he always, and apparently without effort, came out head of the class (his "truly enviable intelligence was honestly far above ours," says Morelli. "He was always many steps ahead of us"). His classmates, who went on to have careers, as expected, in chemical industries, were clearly a bright group, which makes their awe of Jorge's brainpower significant. They admired his performance, too, outside chemistry class, especially in his top subjects of literature, psychology, and religion. But his brilliance didn't inspire resentment because he placed it at their disposal. "He supported us all the time if we had problems with any of the subjects; he always offered to assist," recalls Crespo. There are glimpses, in these remarks, of the future priest: he had a particular ability for solving problems, adds D'Arezzo, "whether in our studies or in our personal lives."

The second distinctive trait was his intense faith. "At that time, when we were fourteen or fifteen, he was already militantly religious," recalls Néstor Carabajo, who was part of a large group of fifteen to twenty guys, including Jorge, who often went on picnics in the Tigre Delta, an area of forest and grasslands just outside the city. Jorge, "with his baby face, always had staunch Catholic religious tendencies," agrees Morelli.

He and Crespo vividly recall a religious education class, a compulsory subject since being introduced by the military government in 1944, and subsequently ratified by Perón in his pro-Church phase. The teacher asked if anyone hadn't received their First Communion, which was a requirement of the course. Two of them raised their hands. "It was obvious he had spoken beforehand to Jorge," says Crespo, "because he told us: 'compañero Bergoglio has offered to be your sponsor in the Basilica of St. Joseph of Flores.'" After Jorge instructed his two classmates in the Church's understanding of the Sacrament of the Eucharist, he took them to receive their First Communion at St. Joseph's, and afterward to lunch at his house. He was fifteen at the time.

Jorge was by now working to earn money. His father had found him a job in his accountancy firm, initially just doing the cleaning, but later helping out with administrative tasks. He went on to do clerical work at a hosiery factory that was also one of his father's clients. Combined with his studies, these were long days, when he would often not return home until 8:00 p.m. But he loved to work, and his extraordinary capacity for it has impressed others throughout his life. As cardinal, he was evangelical about the vital importance of work for a person's self-worth and dignity, and he was a determined opponent of the scourge of long-term unemployment.

He did not take vacations but relaxed, above all in the summer, in the house of his maternal grandparents, where his great-uncles would teach him risqué Genoese ditties. There was a lot of adolescent hanging-out. Crespo recalls, "We always met in a bar on Avellaneda and Segurola, where we played pool. On weekends we met up in each other's houses and went to dance in a club in Chacarita because there were lots of girls there." Both he and Morelli remember Jorge going out with one of them. "Sure, he had a girlfriend," says Morelli. "He was kind of cautious, but he danced with the rest of us. But yes, he was cautious. We encouraged him."

Once he overcame his shyness Jorge loved to dance, especially the *milonga*. Among his favorites was Ada Falcón's version of "La Puñalada."

Anna Colonna, a friend in his parish circle, remembers him dressed in a suit, gallantly asking girls to take a turn with him. She was one of Jorge's group of friends who regularly organized *asaltos*, parties which lasted through Saturday nights in people's houses. The boys wore ties (white jackets if it was someone's birthday) and brought the drink, the girls the food. At dawn, the boys accompanied the girls to their houses, hoping for a kiss if they got lucky. But these were Catholic Action teenagers in the 1950s. "At eight o'clock the next morning," recalls Colonna, "we were all at Mass."

Colonna, who describes Jorge when she knew him as "very considerate, very sociable," says his great love musically was tango. "Jorge was a great tango dancer," she said. "He liked tangos a lot."

Tango, Bergoglio said in 2010, "comes from deep within me."

The emblematic sound of Buenos Aires was born as accordion music accompanying ritualized fights between tough men in turn-of-the-century tenements, especially down in the port area of La Boca. But over time it became respectable, morphing in the 1920s into music for couples to dance to—flirtatious, competitive, haughty. Then words were added: in the 1930s and 1940s, when the silky-voiced and astonishingly handsome Carlos Gardel crooned "El Día Que Me Quieras" ("The Day That You Will Love Me") on the big screen, tango became a craze, both in Argentina and abroad—and Gardel's tragic early death (which in Argentina has a national resonance as deep as the assassination of John F. Kennedy in the United States) only heightened his fame.

By the 1950s tango had been domesticated as dance music—Jorge particularly liked Juan D'Arienzo's orchestra—but it was also a poetic song form, to be listened to rather than danced to. Tangos used *lunfardo*, the dialect of Buenos Aires that creatively mixed Italian with old Spanish, creating memorable words and images that as cardinal Bergoglio often drew on. He followed the work of composers such as Enrique Santos Discépolo and singers such as Julio Sosa and Ada Falcón—the two contemporaries he admired most—for whom tango was also a form of social commentary, a lament for the erosion of values. Discépolo's "Cambalache," for example, sung furiously by a pin-striped Sosa in 1955 with cigarette in hand, propping up a bar, uses the clever image of a pawnshop window, in which a Bible is seen sobbing next to an old radiator. In the 2010 book *El Jesuita*, Cardinal Bergoglio quoted "Cambalache"'s famous line—"what the heck, everything's the same, and there in hell we'll all see each other anyway"—to deplore contemporary relativism.

Bergoglio always listened to tangos, including in the period of their revival, led by Ástor Piazzolla, in the 1970s. As a Jesuit he got to know Azucena Maizani, the first major woman tango singer, who dressed as a man to be taken seriously. When he gave her the last rites in 1970, he met around her deathbed the great tango artist Hugo del Carril, who was also from Flores.

When he was elected pope, Bergoglio's love of tango was cited by Argentina's media as proof—along with his devotion to San Lorenzo, and his attachment to the ubiquitous smoky green Argentine tea called mate—of his guy-next-door qualities. But in the 1950s tango was still edgy; it still, if dimly, suggested lipstick-smudged hookers fleeing pin-striped hoodlums down dark alleys. For a teenager thinking of priesthood, the attraction to it was unusual, and a sign that even then, in the confusion of adolescence, the margins beckoned.

GOD "got in there first" with Jorge on September 21, 1953, when he was six weeks shy of his seventeenth birthday. It was the start of spring, when across Buenos Aires the jacarandas detonate in purple sprays. He was on his way to meet his girlfriend together with his Catholic Action and school friends to celebrate National Students' Day. As he was walking down the Avenida Rivadavia past the Basilica of St. Joseph he knew so well, he felt an urge to go inside. "I went in, I felt I had to go in—those things you feel inside and you don't know what they are," he explained to Father Isasmendi.

> I looked, it was dark, it was a morning in September, maybe 9:00 a.m., and I saw a priest walking, I didn't know him, he wasn't one of the parish clergy. And he sits down in one of the confessionals, the last confessional as you're looking down the left side at the altar. I don't quite know what happened next, I felt like someone grabbed me from inside and took me to the confessional. Obviously I told him my things, I confessed . . . but I don't know what happened.
>
> When I had finished my confession I asked the priest where he was from because I didn't know him and he told me: "I'm from Corrientes

and I'm living here close by, in the priests' home. I come to celebrate Mass here now and then." He had cancer—leukemia—and died the following year.

Right there I knew I had to be a priest; I was totally certain. Instead of going out with the others I went back home because I was overwhelmed. Afterward I carried on at school and with everything, but knowing now where I was headed.

The religious vocation is "a call from God to a heart which is expecting that call either consciously or unconsciously," Bergoglio once explained. He accepted it not so much as God's will for him, but as his own deepest desire, even if God—in getting there before him, *primereando*—knew it before he did. In Saint Ignatius's three ways of choosing, this was clearly an example of the first: when you *just know*. In a 1990 letter, he described the experience as like being thrown from a horse.

For over a year he told no one at home, while undertaking what he describes as "serious spiritual direction" with the confessor he had stumbled on in the basilica, Father Duarte Ibarra, until the priest's death the following year in the Military Hospital.

At this time he was working, along with Oscar Crespo, in the Hickethier-Bachmann chemical laboratory at the corner of Santa Fe and Azcuénaga, and also earning money on occasional evenings as a doorman at tango bars. Crespo remembers how one day Jorge told him: "I'm going to finish secondary school with you guys, but I'm not going to be a chemist, I'm going to be a priest. But I'm not going to be a priest in a basilica. I'm going to be a Jesuit, because I'm going to want to go out to the neighborhoods, to the *villas*, to be with people."

This account suggests more certainty than in Bergoglio's own remembrance. Although he was clear about wanting to be a priest, "in truth, I wasn't very clear which direction to go in," he recalled in 2010. Crespo's memory suggests Bergoglio's direction was mapped out in his mind but was some way short of being a concrete plan. He knew no Jesuits until he reached the seminary, only Salesians and Dominicans. For a lower-middle-class kid from Flores, it wasn't easy to knock on the door of what was at that time a large, formidable order with a reputation for taking only the best educated—mostly the products of their own private schools.

"Some years passed before that invitation and decision were definitive," Pope Francis told young people in Sardinia in September 2013. "They were years of successes and joys, but also of failures, of fragility and sin. . . . But even in the darkest moments of sin and failure I looked at Jesus and he never left me alone."

They were also years of political experimentation. His friends remember his concern for social questions and his visits to deprived neighborhoods. He regularly digested a communist periodical and devoured every article he could find by Leónidas Barletta, a left-wing essayist and playwright. Jorge was never persuaded by Marxism, but contact with its rigorous theories helped sharpen his ideas. After he made a searing critique of trickle-down economics in his first major document as pope, he would be accused of being a Marxist by some conservatives in the United States. "Marxist ideology is wrong," he told a journalist, but "I have met many Marxists in my life who are good people, so I don't feel offended."

The good Marxist Jorge met at this time was Esther Ballestrino de Careaga, the third woman—after his grandmother Rosa and Sister Dolores—he has spoken about as a major influence on his early life. Ballestrino was a Paraguayan communist who in 1949, at the age of twenty-nine, had fled her country's dictatorship and moved to Buenos Aires with her daughters. For three years Esther was his "remarkable boss" at the Hickethier-Bachmann laboratory. She showed Jorge not only the importance of proper scientific work, repeating tests to eliminate possibilities—he was performing chemical evaluations of nutrients—but also taught him the rudiments of her native language, Guaraní, and many valuable lessons in politics. "I owe a lot to that woman," he said in 2010. "I loved her a lot."

They met again more than a decade later, when he was Jesuit provincial and her family was under surveillance during the military dictatorship. He agreed to hide her collection of Marxist books and to help her locate her daughter Ana María, a communist worker delegate, after she was captured and disappeared (she was eventually released). As result of looking for her daughter, Esther became one of the founders of the Mothers of the Plaza de Mayo, the human-rights movement that protested the mass disappearances under the Argentine military dictatorship in the 1970s. She was abducted along with French nuns by the military in June 1977 from the Passionist church of Santa Cruz where they were meeting.

When her remains were discovered and identified many years later, in 2005, Esther's other daughter, Mabel, successfully petitioned Bergoglio, then the cardinal archbishop of Buenos Aires, for her to be buried in the garden of the Santa Cruz church, because, Mabel said, "that was the last place they had been as free people." Naturally, he agreed. And that is how a communist atheist Paraguayan woman the cardinal had loved as a teenager came to be buried in the garden of the Buenos Aires church from which she had been taken to be murdered.

HAVING been accepted by the Buenos Aires diocesan seminary, Jorge was due to begin his studies at the start of the academic year in March 1956. He broke the news to his parents in November 1955, just after graduating as a technical chemist, two years after his experience in the confessional. The shock was particularly great for Regina, who had banked on his studying to become a doctor. That is what he had told her, and when she accused him of lying, he defended himself with proto-Jesuit deftness: "I didn't lie to you, Mom," María Elena recalls him telling her. "I'm going to study medicine of the soul."

Regina would not be the first mother to try to block her firstborn's bid to leave the nest. "I think she would have had the same reaction if he had announced he was getting married or moving abroad," María Elena believes. Although their father, Mario, was supportive, he backed Regina's bid to persuade Jorge to wait and get a degree. When Jorge refused, the atmosphere in the house turned thick with tension.

Guessing that sooner or later Don Enrico would be called in to adjudicate, Jorge arranged to see him. Father Pozzoli asked him about his vocation, gave him his blessing, and told him to pray and leave it in God's hands. Sure enough, someone at home soon suggested: why don't we talk to Father Pozzoli? With a straight face, Jorge agreed. The opportunity arose on December 12, 1955, two months after the army coup that deposed Perón, on the occasion of Mario and Regina's twentieth wedding anniversary, when Don Enrico celebrated a Mass for the family at the Basilica of St. Joseph. At breakfast afterward in a Flores café, the question of Jorge's vocation arose. "Father Pozzoli said the idea of going to university was a good one, but that one had to take things as God wants them," Bergoglio recalled.

And he began telling different vocation stories, without taking sides, and finally he tells his own story: how a priest put the idea to him of being a priest, how pretty soon afterward they made him a subdeacon, then a deacon, then a priest, how unexpected it all was. . . . By this point my parents' hearts had been softened. Naturally, Father Pozzoli didn't end by saying they should let me go to seminary, nor did he ask them to decide; he realized he had to just soften them up. That was typical of him. . . . You didn't know where he was going, but *he* did, and he generally didn't want to reach a point where it looked like he was "winning." When he sensed that he was getting what he wanted, he pulled back before anyone else realized. That way the decision was made freely, by the people involved; they didn't feel pressured. But he had prepared their hearts. He sowed the seeds, then let others have the satisfaction of reaping.

His parents acquiesced, but it took some years for Regina to accept. She didn't visit him until he was a Jesuit novice in Córdoba. In 1969, at his ordination, by then long widowed, and proud of his decision at last, she would kneel for his blessing.

Rosa, his grandmother, had long guessed this was where Jorge was headed, but she feigned surprise. "Well, if God is calling you, blessed be," she told him, adding that the doors were open if he decided to come back, and no one would hold it against him if he did. Her response was a lesson to him in how to walk with people making a major life decision.

When he broke the news to his friends, they were happy for him but sad to lose a dear companion. There were hugs, and promises of prayers. He was ribbed about the loss to San Lorenzo's future. A couple of girls—perhaps disappointed for themselves, as well as sad to lose him—sobbed.

When he knocked on the door of the seminary, in March 1956, Jorge was twenty, almost the age his father, Mario, had been when he boarded the *Giulio Cesare*.

THE MISSION

(1958–1966)

O N COPACABANA BEACH in the last week of July 2013 you could still find a fresh coconut to suck or a caipirinha sugarcane cocktail to sip, but the bronzed, bikinied beauties of Rio de Janeiro were nowhere to be seen—and not just because of the unseasonal rain and wind. Francis was in town, and Copacabana was now a beach of piety, every inch of its three-mile seafront occupied by young Catholics drawn from every nation. As pilgrim-in-chief of World Youth Day, Francis was there to lead the great crowds of the young. But he had a bigger mission in mind: the launch of his pontificate. "My papacy begins after Rio," he had earlier confided to a friend in Buenos Aires.

Francis had inherited the event, which had been in Benedict XVI's diary before he resigned. World Youth Day (WYD) is the Church's largest assembly, when hundreds of thousands of exuberant young pilgrims from across the world gather for days of teaching and prayer before a weekend of massive liturgies led by the pope, the final Sunday being the Day itself. Since it was begun by John Paul II in 1984, World Youth Days have injected vigor into the Catholic Church worldwide. A generation of Catholics can trace to their WYD experience their first emotional engagement with the faith: it's not just the music, and the silence, and the uplifting teachings, but the comfort and pride in the numbers involved. The record was set in Manila, Philippines, in 1995, when five million turned out for the final Mass, said to be the largest gathering in human history. The sociological theory of secularization, according to which humanity, and the young in particular, becomes less religious over time, has always been dubious as a generalization, and looks especially so during WYDs.

WYD can only hit Manila levels of attendance when the host country is both populous and churchgoing: Brazil is the world's largest Catholic country in the world's most Catholic continent. Rio is one of the world's great modern cities, famous equally for its glamour and its social divisions; what better platform for a pope setting out to heal those divides? Rio was not so far from Aparecida, Brazil's national shrine, where in 2007 the Latin-American bishops had gathered in a continent-wide meeting that produced a remarkable document steered by the then cardinal Bergoglio, and heavily influenced by his vision. The document had been ignored by Catholics outside Latin America, but now the River Plate and the Amazon were pouring into the Tiber. As Francis soon made clear, Aparecida was now the program for the whole Church.

Inevitably, Aparecida's gargantuan shrine basilica, second in size only to St. Peter's in Rome, was the first stop in what turned out to be a whirlwind five-day visit. After that the pope remained in Rio, where his schedule included a slum, a soccer field, a hospital, a cathedral, as well as many meetings: with drug addicts, civic leaders, bishops, presidents, young offenders, slum dwellers, and, of course, the people of Brazil, thousands of whom he met in hour upon hour of hugging and handshaking from his open-top popemobile. All of this was the lead-up to the main event, a weekend of massive liturgies on the Copacabana seafront, which as the week went on gradually disappeared under wave after wave of exuberant pilgrims, reckoned at close to four million on the last day. Rio, no stranger to exuberant crowds, had never seen anything like it. Despite the bizarrely inclement weather—the city seldom endures such cold and rain—Copacabana became *a praia da fé*, "the beach of faith," its fabulous natural setting permanently hugged by the open-armed Christ statue on the Corcovado mountain behind.

As Pope Francis touched down in Rio, it seemed as if a new wind of Pentecost now blew from the south. "This week," said Francis on Copacabana Beach, "Rio de Janeiro has become the center of the Church." The figures told their own story. In 1910, 70 percent of the world's Catholics lived in the north (mainly in Europe) and only 30 percent in the south, whereas in 2010 only 30 percent lived in the north and nearly 70 percent in the south. Some 40 percent of the world's Catholics were in Latin America, and if the Latin Americans living in North America were included, it was 50 percent. Spanish—or *castellano* ("Castilian"), as they prefer to say in Hispanic America—was now the most widely spoken language in the Catholic world. But what was most striking about the Latin-American Church was its demographic. Over 70 percent of Catholics are under twenty-five—precisely the reverse of Europe and North America. For energy, passion, and missionary resourcefulness, the Church of this continent leads the world.

The only question, in fact, was whether God was Argentine or Brazilian. Francis, in an interview with *TV Globo*, settled the matter. Because the pope was an Argentine, he conceded, God must be Brazilian.

The Cariocas—Rio dwellers—were soon smitten. A hurricane of affection blew toward Francis. The taxi drivers and the juice bar waiters, the TV pundits and the businessmen, the poor of the shantytowns, the favelas, took to him much as had the Romans in March. They loved his simplicity, his directness, his humility, his passion for social justice, his tireless capacity for vigorous hugging of the elderly and the disabled. They praised his well-aimed three-point speeches, his cozy references, and his vivid metaphors; his cheeky, almost conspiratorial manner with the young; his humor and his candor. But above all they loved him for being Latin-American, for putting people first, for unveiling the humanity inside the humblest hovel—and they loved him even more when, in continental fashion, things didn't always go as planned.

On paper, the visit looked familiar enough: the Alitalia Airbus A330 touching down on the airport tarmac, its cockpit flying the Vatican and local flags; the welcoming committee of politicians and bishops; the car drive to the city center, where he would board the popemobile to greet the multitudes. Yet in practice, almost everything was different. The first story of the trip was Francis carrying his own briefcase (it contained, he later told journalists, his prayer book or Breviary, a book in Italian on Saint Thérèse of Lisieux, and his diary), which was another nail in the coffin of papal monarchy: when had a pope ever carried anything himself? On the thirteen-hour flight, Francis seemed to be permanently active as he held meetings, revised texts, and spent what seemed like an eternity chatting with the pilots in the cockpit. "This pope has an extra-ordinary energy," an exhausted Father Federico Lombardi, the Vatican's spokesman, told journalists the evening of their arrival.

The real innovation of the flight was his handling of the *vaticanisti*, the Holy See–accredited journalists who accompany the pope on the papal plane. Rather than give scripted answers to pre-submitted reporters' questions, as happened on Benedict XVI's trips, Francis came back to greet them, ribbing them that journalists were not the saints to whom he had the strongest devotion. Meeting them one by one, he asked about their families and posed for selfies. The *vaticanisti*, who usually feel herded and neglected on such trips, were captivated. But they still needed a story, and he was careful to leave them with one—a five-minute reframing of WYD as inclusive of the elderly. "Many times, I think we do an injustice to the elderly by setting them aside," Francis said, "as if they don't have anything to give us. But they can give us the wisdom of life, the wisdom of the past, the wisdom of our country and our family. We need this."

On the return journey he would reward the press with a gift they were not expecting: a spontaneous, unfiltered, on-the-record question-and-answer session that lasted an astonishing hour and twenty minutes, during which Francis stood the whole time, thanking journalists for asking the kinds of questions—about gay people in the Curia, corruption at the Vatican's bank—which it is assumed popes go to great effort to avoid answering. His responses were so frank that the journalists had a choice of lead stories. In the end, it was his response to a question about gay people— "Who am I to judge them if they're seeking the Lord in good faith?"—that created the headlines and became the defining phrase of his early papacy.

Arriving at Galeão airport, Francis asked permission of Brazilians to pass through "your great heart" to "come in and spend this week with you." Quoting Saint Paul, he said, "I have neither silver nor gold, but I bring with me the most precious thing given to me: Jesus Christ." After the greeting rituals with Brazil's premier, Dilma Rousseff, she got into a helicopter, while he sat in the back of a Fiat hatchback with its window wound down, the papal arm hanging out. One of Ignatius of Loyola's early companions, Jerónimo Nadal, once said that Jesuits have different kinds of houses or dwellings, but their most peaceful and pleasant house was the journey, "and by this last the whole world becomes our house."

It wasn't long before Francis was stuck in a Rio traffic jam—his driver managed to turn off the road the police had cleared—and found himself mobbed by well-wishers. Many of the *vaticanisti*, who had been bussed in to the press center in time to witness the scenes on television, were horrified: surely anyone could attack him? But while the pope's secretary had his heart in his throat, Francis was delighted. He was there, after all, to meet people. "When I'm going down the street I wind the window down, so I can put out my hand and greet people," he later explained to Brazilian TV. "It's all or nothing. Either you make the journey as you have to make it, with human communication, or you shouldn't make it at all." He apologized to the Vatican and Brazilian security teams, who he knew didn't like it, but "they both know it's not because I wish to be an enfant terrible, but because I am coming to visit people and I want to treat them as people—touch them." But didn't it make him vulnerable? asked *TV Globo*. "I'm not aware," smiled Francis, "of being afraid."

After a rest day and the visit to Aparecida, Francis began wowing Rio. At the favela of Varginha—which used to be known locally as the Gaza Strip on account of its shoot-outs between rival drug gangs—Francis blessed the altar of the tiny breeze-block chapel of São Jerónimo Emiliani, which, with its eighteen simple wooden benches and brightly painted walls, its street dogs padding in and out, might have been Nuestra Señora de Caacupé in Buenos Aires, or indeed any chapel in any slum in any city of Latin America. Normally, a pope in such a place would have seemed a visitor from another planet, but with Francis it was the other way around. He was at home here, and if anything was out of place, it was the posse of journalists and the hundreds of flashing smartphones.

After some time spent hugging, handshaking, kissing, teasing, hair ruffling, laughing, blessing, and playing with those waiting to touch him—including an elderly lady so excited she needed a defibrillator—he entered a one-room, newly bricked house festooned in yellow and white balloons whose occupants had been chosen to represent all the other families in Varginha. The cameras couldn't follow, and inside Francis was able, for the first time since his election, to do what he spent much of his life doing, first as a Jesuit, and then as a bishop and archbishop—sitting with a family, listening to their stories, playing with their children, and leaving behind a little hope in warmed-up hearts.

Then he made his way to the favela's soccer field and called for the world to learn from the poor and change. "The culture of selfishness and individualism that often prevails in our society is not what builds up and leads to a more habitable world," he said. "It is the culture of solidarity that does so, seeing others not as rivals or statistics, but brothers and sisters."

The pope as missionary was something new.

Paul VI had traveled, a little, mostly for bridge-building meetings with political and religious leaders. John Paul II, until his infirmity, traveled constantly, like a great emperor organizing his populace, addressing great crowds in every place he visited. Benedict XVI, a regular but reluctant traveler, was shy and quiet-voiced, and liked to meet people in small groups. Francis was different again. He had neither the swagger of John Paul II nor the erudition of Benedict XVI. But what was fascinating was how, in meeting the crowds, he shifted the focus. With Paul VI, the attention was on the dignitaries he met; with John Paul II, it was inevitably on himself; with Benedict XVI, it was on the text he read. But with Francis the attention went to those he called God's holy faithful people. Here was a pope who, when he was among them, made ordinary people the protagonists.

At a meeting with Argentine pilgrims at Rio's cathedral, which he at the last minute added to the schedule, he was among his own again and visibly relaxed. He could lapse into the sonorous Spanish of Buenos Aires after days of effortful attempts at Portuguese and be intimate with his countrymen, to whom he confessed that in the Vatican he felt, at times, caged. "I want to tell you something," he told them, his voice slowing. "Do you want to know what I want to happen as a result of World Youth Day? *Quiero lío.* I want havoc."

> Sure, here inside there's going to be havoc, and here in Rio, too, but I want havoc in the dioceses, I want us out there, I want the Church to get out into the street, I want us to avoid everything that speaks of worldliness, of comfort, of clericalism, of being closed in on ourselves. The parishes, the schools, the institutions—these are all places to go out from, and if we don't get out from them we become an NGO, and the Church cannot be an NGO!

Hacer lío has a particular meaning in Argentina, where going out into the streets to bang saucepans and shout at the top of your voice indicates exuberant passion for a cause. But what did "create havoc" mean in Los Angeles or London? The confusion was even greater when a church news agency mistranslated the expression as "I want to create a mess," leaving Catholics in English-speaking countries perplexed as to what their pope was asking them to do.

But the address to Argentines showed, in close-up, the extraordinary bond Francis created with people. He demonstrated it even at the massive events on Copacabana Beach, when he was evangelizer-in-chief, rousing the young pilgrims with challenging questions and stark choices, inviting them to become missionary disciples "poised toward the peripheries . . . in the encounter with Jesus Christ." But even there, his quiet, firm voice created a different dynamic; he roused, not by matching the energy of the crowd but by achieving a strange kind of intimacy, as if dialoging with each person present.

This was never clearer than at the Stations of the Cross on Copacabana Beach on July 26. This traditional devotion imaginatively follows Jesus on the journey of humiliation and pain that ends with his death on the Cross; Catholic churches have the fourteen stations—stages—on their walls, traditionally in the form of white plaster images. Playing with this idea, the Brazilians hired an actor to play Jesus as a white plaster statue who came to life in scenes of modern suffering along the seafront. At the Tenth Station, Jesus, bruised and beaten, struggled up a bloodred ramp against a backdrop of neon signs of some of Rio's leading beachside hotels—a powerful symbol of poverty and suffering amid wealth. When he gave a meditation at the conclusion, Francis addressed the millions of pilgrims as if he were leading a small group on a Jesuit retreat, inviting them to identify with a character in the Passion story—Pontius Pilate, Simon of Cyrene, Mary, or the women of Jerusalem—and asking a series of searching questions, followed by long pauses.

At the following night's prayer vigil, Francis invited young people to become missionary disciples at the service of the Church—"athletes of Christ" who are training for something "much bigger than the World Cup." The training, he said, involved daily prayer, sacraments, and loving others ("learning to listen, to understand, to forgive, to be accepting and to help others, everybody, with no one excluded or ostracized") in order to build a more just and fraternal society, starting with each person. He asked them, in the manner of evangelical preachers, to respond, to give their "yes." But as the evening wore on, Francis calmed them, inviting them to kneel before what the Brazilian Church claimed to be history's biggest eucharistic host. There he took three million pilgrims into a place of depth and stillness, framed by the crashing Atlantic waves.

At the first service with the pilgrims, he watched a series of musical performances put on to welcome him. He shifted often in his chair; Francis is not a sedentary type and suffers from sciatica, which makes sitting down for long periods a chore. But there was one performance he appeared to enjoy the most: a choir of Guaraní people from the rain forests of Paraguay singing "Ave María" from Ennio Morricone's score of *The Mission*.

The 1986 film, directed by Roland Joffé, is a firm Jesuit favorite, not least for the Robert Bolt script, the Morricone theme music, and its actors—Robert De Niro, Jeremy Irons, and Liam Neeson playing priests and brothers in the Jesuit missions, known as "Reductions," of eighteenth-century Paraguay. *The Mission* tells the inspiring, ultimately tragic story of the century-long civilization that emerged from the encounter between Jesuits and the Guaraní natives, and its destruction on the orders of far-off rulers in collusion with greedy colonists.

The story of the Reductions taught Jorge Bergoglio important lessons, giving him a model for the evangelization he would promote as a Jesuit and bishop. They stood for a radical immersion in the life of the people, on the basis of an exchange of gifts—the Jesuits opening to the culture of the Guaraní, the culture of the Guaraní opening to receive the seed of the Gospel—while showing him how to inculturate the Gospel and to advocate for the poor. In pondering the Reductions' tragic end, he also took valuable lessons that would shape his political and historical consciousness.

❧

JORGE applied to the Society of Jesus while in his second year at the seminary in the barrio of Villa Devoto, where priests for Buenos Aires diocese are trained. Because the Jesuits before 1960 ran the seminary, he was in constant contact with them: the rector, his spiritual director, and many of the teachers were Jesuits.

The archdiocesean seminary, with its thick walls and iron grilles, was the formidable occupant of an entire block on José Cubas Street. It took boys as young as twelve into the minor seminary, some of whom stayed on to train as priests. The older ones, like Jorge, were known informally as *los viudos*, the widowers, because they were between minor and major seminaries. Formally he was a Latinist, one of those who had finished secondary school but needed a solid basis of Latin and Greek to advance to philosophy and theology studies at a major seminary.

His nickname at the seminary was El Gringo, perhaps because of his European features and tall frame. He is remembered as studious, low-profile, but approachable, well-mannered, and well-respected, a good conversationalist and (like everyone else at the seminary) a soccer player. Jorge González Manent ("Goma"), a friend from Flores Catholic Action circles, visited him on Sundays and found him "a normal guy, happy in life." The seminarians went out on weekends to help in parishes; Jorge's was San Francisco Solano in Villa Luro. The timetable was divided between communal prayer (Matins, Vespers, and Compline), Mass, study, meals in silence, and free time spent in organized sports, mainly soccer. Among those who taught there, and excelled on the pitch, was the handsome, upper-class Father Carlos Mugica, the reference point for a whole generation of activist slum priests who in the late 1960s would commit themselves to social revolution.

Part of the reason Jorge had taken time to enter the seminary was his difficulty in giving up marriage. People "want their cake and to eat it, too," he said in 2011; "they want what is good in the consecrated life and what is good in the life of a layperson, too. Before entering the seminary, I was on that path." Now, in his first year at the seminary, he was forced to make that choice again, after meeting at an uncle's wedding a young woman whose beauty and intellect sent him spinning. For days, whenever he tried to pray she would appear in his head. He was beset by doubts: was this a sign that he wasn't suited to celibacy? Could he live without sexual love, the companionship of a woman, the joy of children? He had taken no vows and was free to leave; should he?

Eventually he made his decision to stay, and found he could pray again. But he had been open to the alternative. When such moments occur, he would later say as cardinal, it may be a sign that a seminarian is unable to commit to celibacy and priesthood, in which case, "I help him to leave in peace, so he can be a good Christian and not a bad priest."

In his second year at Villa Devoto, Jorge began to discern in earnest the possibility of giving up training for diocesan priesthood to join the Jesuits. He admired their missionary spirit and discipline, their commitment to poverty, and, above all, their spirituality. As a Jesuit he would be a priest, but not one based in a parish; he would live in a community of other Jesuits and would be answerable to a Jesuit superior rather than to a bishop. It would also mean the longest period of training anywhere in the Catholic Church: at least a decade before he was ordained, and thirteen or fourteen years before he was a fully professed Jesuit.

As he was discerning that decision, he was brought down by an illness that took him to the edge of death. It began in August of 1957 with a devastating pleurisy that resisted antibiotics. Barely able to breathe, his life in danger, he was rushed to the Syrian-Lebanese hospital close to the seminary, where surgeons removed three pulmonary cysts and a small part of his upper right lung. He spent five days in an oxygen tent followed by an extremely painful post-op month during which he was pumped with saline with a catheter in his chest to remove the dead pleura and scar tissue.

For Jorge, then twenty-one, it was his first experience of intense physical suffering. At times delirious with pain, he begged his visitors to explain what was happening. His mother, among others, tried to comfort him by attempting to displace his thoughts: it will soon pass, she told him, it will all be okay, you'll be home before you know it. But Jorge wasn't reassured: the pain and danger of the moment were far more real than any future he was asked to imagine.

As Viktor Frankl, the Austrian psychiatrist and Holocaust survivor, would later show in his memories of the Nazi death camps, the secret to enduring great suffering is not to try to imagine its end but to find meaning in its present.[1] That is what Sister Dolores, the nun who had prepared him for First Communion, helped him to do when she visited. Her simple words—"with your pain, you are imitating Christ"—revolved in his head and brought peace. What had been pointless was now redemptive; the pain was no less, but bearing it became possible.

The meaning of pain, he would reflect years later, "can only be understood fully through the pain of God who became Christ." Christ's suffering on the Cross was intensely lonely. In any deep suffering, physical or spiritual, what a person needs is people who love them, who respect their silence, and who "pray that God may enter into this space which is pure solitude." Two seminarians, José Bonet Alcón and José Barbich, took on that role, taking turns at his bedside, sometimes spending all night at the hospital. When Jorge needed it, they donated their blood—a liter and a half in a person-to-person transfusion.

Among the other angels at that time was a ward sister who tripled his dose of penicillin and streptomycin because "she was daringly astute. She knew what to do because she was with ill people all day." He believes he is alive today because of her. The doctor, a good man called Deal, "lived in a laboratory," Francis told Father Spadaro, whereas the ward sister "lived on the frontier and was in dialogue with it every day."

Laboratory versus frontier: the choice was taking shape in his mind. As pope, Francis would challenge the Jesuits: "Are we consumed with zeal? Or are we mediocre, satisfied with our apostolic plans that come from a laboratory?" Where the laboratory for Jorge signified cerebral artifice, the frontier stood for immersion in human reality, alive with God's surprises.

While convalescing in September and October of that year, Jorge confided his thoughts about being a Jesuit to the family priest, Don Enrico Pozzoli. After again testing his call with some wise questions, the Salesian gave him the green light. In November 1957, he formally applied to the Society of Jesus and was accepted to start the following March.

Because of Jorge's tensions with his mother, Don Enrico was concerned about him returning home for the long intervening period, and arranged for him to spend the summer months in the retreat house his Salesian order ran in the mountains of Tandil, in the south of Buenos Aires province. There, in the Villa Don Bosco, in the company of vacationing priests and missionaries, Jorge recovered his strength. Some of those he met there would become lifelong friends.

Bergoglio's debt to Father Pozzoli is suggested by the warm tribute he paid to him in the title pages of his first book, *Meditaciones para Religiosos* (Meditations for Religious). Because Don Enrico was an outstanding watchmaker and a gifted photographer, Jorge describes him there as having "a very fine ear for the tick-tock of consciences and a very sharp eye for the imprint of God's love on people's hearts," one who "knew how to embrace in God's time the intricate passage of a soul, and to reveal the Lord's designs in each person's life." What he most admired the Salesian for was his rootedness: he was the "king of common sense," Bergoglio wrote in his 1990 letter to Father Bruno.

The legacy of Jorge's operation—to this day his voice is soft, and he gets breathless—has not prevented him from leading a normal life. But in removing part of his lung, the surgeons clipped his wings: while he kept his passion for soccer, he would no longer play it; and he would be exempted from the physically demanding activities during Jesuit training. His lungs were the reason why the Jesuit general rejected his application to go to Japan. Until his final mission in Rome, Bergoglio's frontier would always be close to home.

❧

JORGE'S decision to join the Society of Jesus while recovering from a brutal operation is striking, for the Jesuit story began, nearly five hundred years ago, with another man in similar suffering. Iñigo—later he Latinized it to Ignatius—was a thirty-year-old nobleman soldier from the Basque country in northern Spain whose leg was shattered by a cannonball while fighting the French. Carried in agony over the mountains from Pamplona to his home town of Loyola, he endured three leg operations without anesthetics, the details of which are best passed over, for they involved breaking his bones to reset them and sawing off a stump. He survived, just; and eventually, during nine months of convalescence in the top floor of the family castle in 1521, agonizing pain gave way to boredom and frustration.

Ignatius was the dueling, womanizing, outdoor type who sported a fashionable two-colored slashed doublet with a cuirass and coat of mail, and hair under a bright cap that flowed down to his shoulder. Confinement was crucifixion. Worse, there were no copies at hand of the gallant-knight-rescues-distressed-damsel tales he read so avidly, only his sister-in-law's pious tomes, specifically Ludolph of Saxony's four-volume *Life of Christ* and Jacopo de Voragine's *Lives of the Saints*.

He was in for a surprise. As he turned from one saint to another, repelled by their piety and penances, some of the stories began to appeal to him—especially that of Saint Francis of Assisi, who before his conversion was, like Ignatius, a minor nobleman who spent his time in vanities. Ignatius found that these stories lifted his spirits and brought out good and noble thoughts in him—"What if I should do this?" he wondered—whereas when he thought of the knights' tales, he felt dry and dissatisfied. Ruminating alone silently, hour after hour, intensely concentrated, he would lose himself in dreams and reveries; and as he came out of them, he began to detect feelings, motions of the spirit, which he learned to identify—by how they made him feel—as coming from either his own thoughts, or, if from outside him, from either God or what he called "the bad spirit" or sometimes "the enemy of human nature." He began to contemplate, and had a vision of Mary that for hours flooded him with happiness, together with a revulsion at his former dissolute life. Finally one night, alone in his fourth-floor bed under a brocaded canopy, God gained a follower: unobserved by history, the knight unconditionally surrendered.

As he developed in the spiritual life—the next fifteen years were spent as a pauper, in and out of religious houses, on the road and on ships, reading and reflecting, fasting and begging—Ignatius delved deeper into the motions of the spirit, coming to understand some of the subtle ways in which the bad spirit appears *sub angelo lucis*, in the guise of good, tempting with feelings that initially seem to be of God; and how sometimes you can only spot what he called the serpent's tail by tracing back the succession of feelings to the moment when the bad spirit took a person off course. Ignatius also came to understand that the spirits act differently with people, depending on their disposition. Thus in his famous seventh rule for discernment of spirits, the good angel touches a spiritually inclined soul gently, "like a drop of water which enters into a sponge," whereas a bad spirit will feel harsh, like water falling on stone. Conversely, a person who is not advancing in the spiritual life will experience the good spirit as something that clatters and interrupts, whereas bad spirits enter quietly, "as into their own home, through an open door."

The Spiritual Exercises, which Ignatius eventually published, after much fiddling, in 1548, is a slim volume of tips and techniques, an instruction manual more than a book to be read, that enables a monthlong retreat to be given as easily in the middle of a noisy city—as he did in Paris and Rome—as in a rural retreat. Its flexibility made it the perfect adjunct to the age of travel and discovery: Ignatius was born in 1491, the year before Christopher Columbus stumbled on the Americas. From the *Exercises* flows Jesuit spirituality: finding God in all things, not needing to retreat from the world; being contemplatives in action, leading active lives but rooted in prayer; and freedom and detachment, learning how to be free of idols such as status, money, and power in order to be more available for serving God and others. In bringing people into direct emotional encounters with Jesus Christ through graphic imaginative contemplations of scripture scenes, the *Exercises* offered a new way of evangelizing that spread like seeds in a storm.[2]

The construction of the *Exercises* is significant: they follow a forward-moving structure modeled on the spiritual path that Ignatius discovered in himself and others. Bergoglio once described that structure:

> The Principle and Foundation lays the groundwork by affirming the wisdom of indifference and explaining how "we ought to desire and choose only that which is more conducive to the end for which we are created" (SpEx 23). The First Week impresses with us two fundamental realities: we recognize and abhor our sins and their roots in the spirit of the world, and we converse about all this with Jesus "suspended on the Cross." There is only one sure way to enter into the labyrinth of our sins: by holding on to the wounded hand of Jesus. In the Second Week, we hear the summons to work for the Kingdom; we come to understand the meaning of the struggle and how much is at stake; we begin to comprehend that the only weapon by which we can win the battle is humility; and we make our election. In the Third and Fourth Weeks, we meditate on the paschal mystery and how we are integrated by means of it into the community and the Church. In the light of this mystery, we confirm the election we have made.[3]

This is the pattern of Christian conversion. It begins in a First Week experience, such as Jorge had at age seventeen, of God's merciful love—the dawning knowledge that we are in relationship with God, who created us and is faithful to us, despite our turning away from Him. The rest flows from this grateful realization.

As a Jesuit priest and provincial, and later as cardinal, bishop, and now pope, Bergoglio always insisted that the Church should offer people what he called this "primary proclamation"—the experience of God's merciful love—prior to (in the sense both of precedence and importance) the rest of Christian teaching. Hence Francis's controversial insistence, in his interview with Father Spadaro in September 2013, that the Church should not be obsessed with moral doctrines but should be like a battlefield hospital tending to the wounded. This, he explained, was "proclamation in a missionary key": only an experience of God's love can prepare the mind and heart for everything else the Church offers and teaches. It is an insight that comes from the First Week of the *Exercises*, just as Francis's major teaching document, *Evangelii Gaudium* (*The Joy of the Gospel*) flows out of the Fourth Week.

Ignatius shared his portable desert with women as well as men, married as well as single people. Among the last was a group of students he studied with in Paris, who became the first Companions of Jesus (the word *Jesuit* came much later—an unfriendly epithet that stuck). They, in turn, directed others, who in turn offered themselves, and the Society expanded in a viral, capillary fashion familiar to us in the Internet age. From the first ten companions in Rome—Bergoglio's favorite was the least educated of them, a brilliant French peasant named Pierre Favre whom within a year of his election Francis declared a saint—the Society's growth was little short of meteoric: by Ignatius's death in 1556, there were already more than 1,000 Jesuits in twelve provinces. In 1615 there were 13,112 members in thirty-two provinces, which by the mid-eighteenth century had nearly doubled. There were 36,000 Jesuits worldwide in 1965, although for most of the twentieth century the number was far lower— 23,000 in both 1945 and 1995. Yet even after shrinking, the Society of Jesus remains the Church's largest male religious order, active in 112 nations on six continents.

Ignatius and his first companions placed themselves at the service of the pope, promising to go wherever he saw fit to send them. This is the origin of the famous Fourth Vow Jesuits take of special obedience to the pope "in regard to the missions," which produced a moment of hilarity at a Vatican press conference after Francis's election. Was the pope, as a Jesuit, still bound by it? a journalist wanted to know. The Vatican spokesman, Father Lombardi, also a Jesuit, and still reeling from the news, could barely contain his laughter. "I imagine," he eventually managed, wiping his eyes, "that being pope now himself, this vow no longer applies."

Ignatius wasn't just a spiritual master. He was skilled in attracting bright young men, forming them, and fanning them out to the far corners of the earth while keeping them linked to him and to one another. "The flamboyant gentleman-at-arms," writes his biographer, Philip Caraman, SJ, "became a pivotal administrator, a level-headed patriarch of an ever-increasing family." He did it all from a small desk in Rome. Between 1540, when Pope Paul III authorized the Society, to Ignatius's death sixteen years later, the founder of the Jesuits wrote an astonishing seven thousand letters, full of encouragement, advice, news, and heartfelt promises of support and love.[4] Ignatius saw letter-writing both as an art and a ministry, a way of walking with others. In this respect Jorge Bergoglio is Ignatius's son: even as pope, he continues to handwrite huge numbers of letters, penning "F. Casa Santa Marta. 00120 Vatican City" on the reverse, should it need returning to sender.

Ignatius and Francis are alike, too, in that they fuse two qualities that are seldom found combined in a person. On the one hand, Ignatius (as does Francis) had raw political ability, which some might call charm: a capacity for reading people, earning their trust, inspiring them, organizing them to work for high ideals, together with enormous skills as a natural leader, teacher, and negotiator. On the other hand Ignatius (like Francis) was a mystic, who lived and led by discerning spirits, choosing whatever served the greater good, God's greater glory, which Jesuits describe with the Latin word *magis*. Spiritual guides are seldom good governors, and those in power are almost never saints. Ignatius and Francis are among the few who break the mold.

They share, too, a constant attention to spiritual discernment—where is God calling us? what are the temptations and distractions from this call?—in hours of dawn prayer as well as in reflecting on the most mundane of activities. It is a focus that brings a remarkable freedom from the habits and norms of the day, whether in the Church or society; and yet, paradoxically for the modern world (but not for a Catholic), it produces a radicalism rooted in obedience to the Church as God's instrument on earth. For both Ignatius and Francis, radical reform is ultimately about the courage to strip away the accrued layers of distraction to recover what has been lost. It is a going back in order to go forward. It is what makes them both great reformers.

THERE is a popular image of the Jesuits as an obedient, disciplined, well-trained Counter-Reformation army blindly obedient to the pope. There is some truth to it: the Jesuits would be for many centuries the defenders of papal universalism against the growing tendency of states to take control of the Church. But a more helpful analogy is to see the Society as a kind of dynamic global corporation, one that combines a clear common purpose and loyalty on the one hand with a reliance on individual initiative on the other. Its purpose, of course, is not shareholder profit but the building of God's Kingdom. But just as successful corporations invest heavily in developing and training their leaders, so the Jesuits stood out in early-modern Europe by the astonishing effort and resources they put into their formation, which remains to this day longer and more thorough than any religious order's.

A Jesuit spends two years as a novice—time to decide, with the help of the monthlong *Exercises*, if God is calling him to the Society of Jesus—before taking his first, "simple" vows of poverty, chastity, and obedience. He then begins anywhere between ten and thirteen years (depending on his preexisting qualifications) of "formation," toward the end of which he is normally ordained a priest. This might include initial university studies, but will always include some years of philosophy and theology study, broken by a two-year period of teaching (known in English as the regency). He will end with a kind of second novitiate, called a tertianship, during which again he repeats the monthlong *Exercises*. After this, the Jesuit will be invited to make his solemn profession, which includes the Fourth Vow.

Ignatius regarded this process not as hoops to pass through to "qualify," but as an opportunity for God to shape a mature human being: one who emerges, hopefully, as a self-reliant, mature, and wise spiritual leader, competent and broadly educated, able to be "sent" to where he is needed, whether to a university lecture hall or a hut in a far-off forest. Rather than tightly controlling his members, Ignatius governed loosely, relying on the Jesuits' developed capacity for discernment, and on an internal compass he called *nuestro modo de proceder*, "our way of proceeding." Jesuits are organized into provinces—a flexible unit that might include one or more countries, or (where there are many Jesuits) a region or region within countries—led by a provincial appointed for six years by the superior general in Rome. Apart from general congregations—once-a-decade meetings of all provincials, which set the general direction—provinces are largely self-governing.

Jesuits are famous for their individualism. It is said that when you've met one Jesuit, you've met one Jesuit. The long formation produces, by definition, leaders; and leaders, by definition, lock horns. The Society of Jesus, a Jesuit once ruefully observed, is essentially an "orchestra of first violinists." Because consensus can be difficult—*three Jesuits, four opinions*, say the Italians—the Society of Jesus sets great store by obedience.

Jorge's formation involved two years' novitiate, a year's juniorate (university-level humanities), three years' philosophy, three years' school teaching, three years' theology, and a year's tertianship. It lasted thirteen years, from 1958 to 1971. All but two of those years—the juniorate in Chile, and the tertianship in Spain—were spent in Argentina: the novitiate was in Córdoba, the regency in Santa Fe and Buenos Aires, and for six years (broken by teaching) he studied philosophy and theology at the Colegio Máximo, in the Buenos Aires province town of San Miguel. At the end of theology, in 1969, he was ordained a priest. In 1970, he took his final vows.

His formation coincided with a period of epochal change in the Church. Months after he began his novitiate, Pope John XXIII announced his intention to call a meeting of the world's bishops, the first in almost one hundred years, in Rome. The Second Vatican Council (1962–1965)—overseen first by Pope John; then, from 1963, by Pope Paul VI—unleashed reforms that transformed the way the Church related to the world and led to far-reaching internal changes. The Council would be Bergoglio's greatest teacher, and the single greatest source, later, of his pontificate. Among the changes the Council called for was for religious orders to return to the original charisms and activities of their founders. Leading this renewal-by-return would be one of his main tasks as provincial of the Argentine Jesuits in the 1970s.

Jorge's formation led him to draw deep from the wells of Ignatian spirituality and Jesuit history, developing a vision of formation that he would implement as novice master and provincial. At a time of crisis in the Society, on the eve of the Council, when many Jesuit students were leaving, Jorge discovered both internal spiritual clarity and a distinctive vision of the future of the Society and himself in it. His ideas were the product of different sources: the spirituality and ideas of the early Jesuits, as well as Catholic theology, especially of the Vatican Council, but also of the history of Argentina and the extraordinary role of the Jesuits in its formative period.

✥

THE Jesuits in the colonial era laid the foundations of modern Argentina. They were explorers and founders of settlements that later became cities.

They ran the largest and best-managed estancias (huge ranches) that lay at the heart of the colonial economy. They were protectors of the natives, opposing their abuse by the settlers. And they were the great educators of the time, founders of the colony's universities and colleges.[5]

They arrived in the River Plate within a generation of Ignatius's death, going among both conquered and unassimilated native peoples. There were no great sedentary civilizations in the region, only scattered clusters of seminomads, the largest of which were the Guaraní, who lived in the rain forests between the rivers on the border of today's Argentina, Paraguay, and Brazil.

When the Jesuits arrived in Tucumán from Peru in 1585, the heart of the River Plate province was not the Atlantic coast as it later became, but the mountains in what is today northwest Argentina, then part of Upper Peru, centered on the great silver mine at Potosí in today's Bolivia. Buenos Aires had just then come into existence as an entrepôt for contraband, through which silver was smuggled out and foreign goods smuggled in, bypassing the royal monopoly.

Spanish colonial policy prohibited the enslavement of natives; they were to be subjugated, gathered into a "Reduction" (from the Latin *reducere*, "to group together"), offered baptism, and assigned to a settler who could demand work from them. But the system quickly broke down. The settler, anxious to get rich, exploited his charges in brutal conditions, leading the natives to flee to the rain forest, where they were captured and sold as slaves; and the church mission, unfunded, quickly collapsed.

Shocked at the greed of the colonists, the wretchedness of the Indians, and the corruption of the Church, the Jesuits arriving in the 1580s sought to create a new kind of Reduction that would protect the baptized natives from the colonial population. Having won the trust of the Guaraní—who had escaped the worst of the settlers by living in the thick vast forests above the Iguazú Falls—they created in 1604 a new Jesuit province of Paraguay, separate from Peru, which would "take the missions to the Indians who were found on the periphery of the cities and at the edge of the conquered districts," wrote its first provincial, Father Diego de Torres.[6]

The Jesuits arrived in Guayrá, the land of the Guaraní, just as the Portuguese settlers in Brazil were making incursions into the area in search of slaves to work on their plantations. The Treaty of Tordesillas of

1594 demarcating Spanish and Portuguese boundaries was, at best, an arbitrary line that ran through today's southern Brazil and northern Argentina. Anxious about Portuguese incursions, the Spanish Crown saw the advantages of a buffer zone and agreed to the Jesuits' request for natives to be exempt from labor and taxes—and to be able to carry firearms to keep out intruders, whether Portuguese slavers or Spanish colonists. For their part the Indian chiefs, aware that they were surrounded by enemies, and impressed by the intelligence and understanding shown by the Jesuits, agreed to be "reduced" and to accept the authority and protection of the Spanish Crown. On the basis of this fragile balance of alliances and interests, expanding from the first one, at San Ignacio Guazú, a remarkable enterprise was born.

At their peak between 1640 and 1720, there were around 150,000 Guaraní in more than forty Reductions, served by around two hundred Jesuits. Most were in what is today northern Argentina. Each Reduction had just a handful of Jesuits, one of whom was the parish priest, who oversaw, in collaboration with the cacique, villages that varied from two thousand to ten thousand inhabitants. William Bangert describes a typical village in its heyday:

> From a central plaza, pointing north, south, east and west and built of the material of the area, even stone and adobe, spread the homes of the people, who sometimes numbered up to 10,000. Close by stood the assembly of workshops with tools for carpentry, masonry, metal work. Behind the homes stretched the fruit orchards, the pasture land for cattle, and the farms which provided wheat, rice, sugar cane and cotton. In the church, the noblest edifice of all and the center of community life, the Indians, instructed in the dignity of the liturgy and inspired by the beauty of the altar, sang their hymns and played musical instruments. . . . To establish such centers of faith . . . the Jesuits brought, in addition to the sacraments and the rewards of God, their skills as metallurgists, cattle raisers, architects, farmers and masons.[7]

The Jesuits didn't only evangelize the Guaraní, but formed them into a modern nation. The missionaries' respect for their language and culture was real: the Guaraní grammar books, catechisms, and other records they compiled show it. Where the native peoples' habits contradicted the Gospel, the Jesuits sought to change them, but they did so by first grasping the rationale for their behavior: the Guaraní custom of killing disabled children at birth, for example, was an imperative of the nomadic way of life, which the stable existence of the Reductions made unnecessary. In order to combat the destructiveness of alcoholism—the Guaraní were attached to a lethal fermented brew called *chicha*—the Jesuits encouraged the habit of drinking the smoky green tea called mate from a gourd through a straw, as Pope Francis does each morning.

Jesuits and natives shared an indifference to what obsessed the settlers—gold and silver—but they were not afraid of technology. The Jesuits introduced iron tools that led to a revolution in productivity that over time produced surpluses and wealth that were used for the benefit of the Reductions. As the taste for mate spread throughout the colony, the tea leaves, known as yerba, became their principal export.

Life was disciplined, a balance of work and prayer, punctuated by festivals combining Jesuit theatrical religiosity and local natural and tribal customs. The Guaraní were great musicians and craftspeople; from their schools and workshops came famous carved wood instruments and in time the most stunning churches in the region, incorporating native motifs and styles. The Reductions had large choirs and composers of a distinctive genre of sacred music, such as the Guaraní-composed "Ave María" that had entranced Pope Francis on Copacabana Beach.

In a talk Bergoglio gave in 1985 in Mendoza to celebrate the four hundredth anniversary of the Jesuits arriving in Argentina, he praised this "inculturation" as a model for missionaries and pastors, who need to recognize the inherent dignity of every culture and to become enmeshed with it, renouncing their own culture as far as possible and taking on the other. This degree of inculturation, he added, was costly, especially when a Jesuit is called to another mission and must go through the process again. "When he is moved, he feels pain," said Bergoglio. "If it doesn't hurt he's not a Jesuit."[8]

The Paraguay Reductions were the most famous and emblematic, but by no means the only, Jesuit missions in the River Plate. Across the colony the Jesuits became the advocates of subjugated natives, demanding they be remunerated for their labor, a stance that won the Jesuits few friends. In a 1977 talk in Santa Fe, Bergoglio recalled how the Abipone and Mocobi would gather in the Jesuit college in that city to discuss with its rector the advantages of being "reduced" with the help and protection of the Jesuits. Because of their bad experience with the colonists, the older natives preferred to remain nomads, but their chief or cacique, who trusted the rector, was persuaded that it was in their interests. The Jesuits acted, in this way, as seventeenth-century community organizers among the poor.[9]

Yet they also ran highly successful chains of ranches and plantations that became trade and manufacturing hubs, linked by a kind of parallel trade network, not unlike the monasteries of medieval Europe. Fewer than five hundred Jesuits in the eighteenth century ran these estancias as managers, deploying African slaves in common with other estancias of the time—a practice that the Jesuits seem not to have questioned.

The Jesuits benefited from centralized administration, command of large capital, and the ability to avoid taxation. The wealth accrued from the efficient management of this parallel economy paid for the Jesuits' formidable education network: by the mid-1750s there were Jesuit colleges in all the cities, of which those of Córdoba and Santa Fe were the oldest and most important. The point of Jesuit colleges in the colonial period was to form leaders for service to king and Church, with one of them—the *collegium maximum*, or Colegio Máximo—designated as the formation house for the Jesuits themselves. The Jesuit college was not just a set of classrooms: it was a community of scholars, a place of humanist research, and the heart of the cultural life of the creole elite. The Jesuits presided over the colleges as guardians of the colony's know-how: they were astronomers, botanists, pharmacists, printers, zoologists, cartographers, and architects, as well as theologians and jurists, admired not just for their knowledge and accomplishments but also for their discipline and personal austerity.

THE Jesuits were deeply unpopular with mid-eighteenth-century European monarchs looking to extend their control over society. This was an era when the Catholic Church had become increasingly yoked to the national state; the Jesuits, with their wealth and their loyalty to the pope, were out of step, and their independence now looked like insolence. What was especially offensive to the new generation of enlightened absolutists in the courts of Madrid, Lisbon, and Paris were the writings of the Jesuit theologian Francisco Suárez, whose theory of the democratic origin of authority was a standard text in Jesuit colleges of the time.

Suárez's theory can be summarized in four principles: no ruler has civil authority directly from God; those who rule receive their authority through the intermediation of the people; the people grant authority, and this is the source of a governor's legitimacy; the power, being transferred, can be withdrawn, and therefore power is circumscribed. Although these principles were little more than a restatement of the classic Catholic understanding of power, they appeared dangerously subversive in the era of absolutist rulers such as Carlos III of Spain, who claimed to govern by divine right and accepted no limits on his sovereignty.

The Reductions had been created in an era underpinned by those Suarezian ideas. The Guaraní had been melded into a nation; they were a people, a culture, with dignity and autonomy that the Crown should by rights protect and defend. But the new political ideology of absolutism had no time for such medieval niceties. The Reductions would be crushed by the stroke of distant royal pens on a 1750 treaty drawing new Spanish and Portuguese boundaries in South America.

In exchange for the port of Sacramento, Spain handed over to the Portuguese seven of the Reductions east of the new frontier, together with their inhabitants. It took eighteen years for the Spanish and Portuguese royal forces to dismember the Guaraní missions. The natives fought hard to protect their villages. More than ten thousand were killed in appalling massacres; thousands of others were captured as slaves or fled back to the forests. The Jesuit general in Rome ordered the missionaries to abide by the treaty and leave, but some refused and even took up arms in their defense—stances dramatized by Father Gabriel (Jeremy Irons) and Rodrigo (Robert De Niro) in *The Mission*'s tragic finale.

The next step was not long in coming. The Crowns of Portugal, France, and Spain expelled the Jesuits from their territories and seized their assets. A few years later, in 1773, harassed and threatened by those same monarchs, and politically captive to Madrid, Pope Clement XIV ordered the suppression and abolition of the Society of Jesus.

The departure of the Jesuits from the Spanish colonies was traumatic. On April 2, 1767, some 5,350 Jesuits across the world were surrounded, arrested, and put on boats bound for the papal states following a decree of Spain's Carlos III "for reasons he reserves to himself." From the River Plate sailed 457 Jesuits, of whom 162 were Spanish, 81 local, and the rest Europeans of different nations. Soon after, a royal decree ordered the suppression of all the teaching chairs associated with the Jesuits, as well as books by Jesuit authors. Carlos III was trying to eliminate not only a religious order but its seditious ideas.[10]

The Jesuit expulsion was Latin America's Boston Tea Party, a blow to the economy and well-being of colonial society from which it never recovered, and the cause of deep resentment in the creole population. It was followed by Carlos III's Bourbon Reforms, which sought to bring the American territories more tightly under Madrid's control, and which only heightened the resentment, severing the bonds of affection and loyalty between Spain and its territories. Within decades the territories had become independent nations. The architects of the new Argentine nation had been trained in Jesuit colleges—specifically, that of Córdoba—and when they declared self-rule in 1810 they did so appealing to those same ideas of Suárez that the colonial authorities had tried so hard to suppress.

In his 1988 speech on the Jesuit martyrs of Paraguay, Bergoglio saw in the Reductions an embodiment of the Suárez ideal—the Gospel, brought by the Jesuits, uniting the people, forming a Guaraní nation—and the 1750 treaty that ended them as the consequence of a brutal, detached, rationalist ideology. In Carlos III he saw a prince forgetting and betraying his people, and imposing an enlightened ideology that was divorced from the people themselves. Where the Jesuit Reductions were a project of the heart, paternalistic in the best sense of the word—caring, tender, seeking the freedom and well-being of their charges, incarnate in the cultural reality of the natives—their annihilation was the product of an ideology imposed from above: a project of the mind, coercing reality to fit an idea, which turns people into its instruments.

"The fruitful universality which integrates and respects differences was replaced by an absorbent metropolitan hegemony, of the most domineering kind," Bergoglio said of the Bourbon Reforms. "These lands, which were 'provinces' of the Kingdom [of Spain], were turned into colonies. There was no longer room here for projects of the heart: now was the era of the enlightenment of the mind." In the 1960s he would develop this dichotomy into something close to a doctrine, in which the poor, the *pueblo fiel*, are a kind of vaccine against the destructive effect of ideology, of left or right—whether the Bourbon Reforms, nineteenth-century economic liberalism, or twentieth-century Marxism.[11]

It is hard to think of a more thorough rejection of the Enlightenment project than in a retreat Bergoglio gave in the 1970s. "The worst that can happen to a human being," he said, "is to allow oneself to be swept along by the 'lights' of reason. . . . Our mission is instead to discover the seeds of the Word within humanity, the *logo spermatakoi*."[12] It is a theme Pope Francis returned to in his meeting in Rio with the bishops of Latin America, when he warned against making the Gospel an ideology—whether free-market liberalism, Marxism, or certain forms of "psychologizing." Noting that Gnosticism—an early Christian heresy—was the "first deviation" in the Church that has reappeared throughout its history, he told the bishops: "Generally its adherents are known as 'enlightened Catholics,' since they are in fact rooted in the culture of the Enlightenment."[13]

In the "Declaration of Principles" Bergoglio wrote as Jesuit provincial for the Universidad del Salvador in 1974, he portrayed the Society of Jesus's clash with the Bourbon state in Catholic nationalist terms, as defending an incarnate culture from a disembodied ideology. From the beginning, he said, the Society of Jesus has respected the diversity of cultures ("The truth of Christ is one, but many and unique are its human and historical manifestations"). Therefore

it is unsurprising that the Society should find itself confronting the growing liberal-bourgeois claim to homogenize the historical and human reality of the world, by means of a centralizing statism and an enlightenment rationalism, to the detriment of the multifaceted richness of the created world. . . . In China as well as in the River Plate, the Society refused to act as the religious justification of European expansion, in endowing the people of their missions with the social and organizing elements that allowed them freely to develop their unique culture, integrating them into the universality of a Faith which they assimilated as their own. The Society is, from its foundation, universalist; and for that reason opposed to the homogenizing internationalisms which, either by "reason" or by force, deny peoples their right to be themselves.[14]

Fifteen years after Pope Pius VII reestablished the Society in 1814, the Jesuits returned to the River Plate—now independent from Spain—at the invitation of the dictator Juan Manuel de Rosas. It didn't go well. When the Jesuits refused to put his portrait on their altars and preach against his political enemies, they were again expelled, and would not return until after the dictator was deposed. In the 1850s some churches were returned to them, and by the 1870s the Jesuits had reestablished themselves as educators in different cities, founding or refounding prestigious schools such as the Colegio de la Inmaculada Concepción in Santa Fe and the Colegio del Salvador in the capital. They were also entrusted with the Metropolitan Seminary in Buenos Aires where in 1956 Jorge Bergoglio met them.

By then the Jesuits were again one of the largest and most important of the religious orders in Argentina. In 1961, when the Uruguayan Jesuits split to create their own province, there were 407 members in the Argentine province—a number not far off what it had been before Carlos III expelled them. But compared to its earlier, eighteenth-century self, the Society of Jesus was in many ways an emasculated animal. Missions were geared less to the frontier than to manning the fortress that protected the Church from the modern world.

Within that fortress, there was little room for uncertainty or innovation. The *Exercises* were given as group retreats, with talks and exhortations, rather than the personal individual encounter that Saint Ignatius had designed. The foundational texts were buried in a mound of commentaries. Contrary to the original spirit of the order, Jesuit trainees were infantilized by summaries and manuals that stipulated how many shirts a Jesuit should have and what he should eat for breakfast. In his interview with Father Spadaro in September 2013, Francis recalled the environment in which he was formed as one of "closed and rigid thought, more instructive-ascetic than mystical."

Bergoglio's vocation survived the deficiencies of this formation because he was able to penetrate beneath the scholastic layers to the sixteenth-century "primitive charism" of the early Jesuits, which would be his model for reform. Sinking his roots deep into Ignatius's sixteenth-century loam enabled him to survive the post–Vatican Council chaos within the Society of Jesus. Above all he learned the capacity for spiritual discernment that would become second nature to him.

It meant not just learning to distinguish good from bad but striving to do great things for God—the Jesuits' motto is *Ad Maiorem Dei Gloriam*, "For the Greater Glory of God"—yet usually in ways that were humble and unseen. What Bergoglio learned as a Jesuit was the capacity to "do the little things of every day with a big heart open to God," as Francis told Father Spadaro.

⚘

JORGE began as a novice in Córdoba alongside twenty-five young men ranging in age from eighteen to twenty-six. Saint Ignatius had conceived the novitiate as a series of six core experiences known as "experiments," based on the lives of the early Jesuits. The most important was the month-long silent retreat, the *Exercises*, where novices discerned the presence of God in their lives and confirmed (or not) their call to be Jesuits. There was also a month of work in hospitals, cleaning and emptying bedpans, spending time alongside people in severe pain and suffering. The third "experiment" was a month on pilgrimage, when the novices were sent off in threes with very little money and had to depend on the kindness of strangers. The fourth was an experience of "low and humble tasks" built into the daily timetable—cleaning, sweeping, waiting on tables, washing clothes—which for aristocrats in Ignatius's time would have been seen by their families as deeply demeaning. The last two—teaching faith to children in local schools and practicing giving talks—helped novices prepare for their lives as Jesuits.

When not out on an "experiment"—the retreat, hospital, or pilgrimage— the daily timetable was formal, penitential, and tightly regulated. From rising at 6:20 a.m. through to lights-out at 10:30 p.m., virtually every quarter hour was assigned. Except for meals, cleaning, Latin and Greek, and study of the *Rules*, time was absorbed in periods of prayer, either alone or as a group. As well as the Office (recital of the Psalms four times a day) there were meditations, Mass, the Angelus, Rosary, spiritual reading, the lives of the saints, and eucharistic adoration. Of these, the most important for Ignatius was the thrice-daily *examen*, when the novices would examine their consciences. To encourage penitence and humility, there was also the *culpa*, when the novice-master would pick out a novice and invite the others to criticize him.

In common with other religious orders before the Vatican Council, the novices were invited to mortify the flesh in order, as Saint Ignatius put it, "that one's sensual nature may be obedient to reason, and all the lower parts of the self may become more submissive to the higher." Novices were invited to use the *cilice*—a prickly metal band worn for a few hours a week around the upper leg—as well as the *discipline*, a small whip for self-flagellation. These were to encourage chastity: the apostolic freedom to love others without being attached to them, and to embrace the poverty of not owning others. But in the early 1960s this idea was confused by a prevailing nervousness about sexuality, reflected in a number of rules: the novices had to address each other using the formal *usted* form, and to avoid so-called particular friendships there had always to be at least three (*numquam duo, semper tres*) in any group. If there was an unhealthy aspect to this—mortification of the flesh would disappear almost everywhere after the Second Vatican Council—there was also an important insight: that too much exclusivity in friendship can cause divisions and separation in the wider group.

Bergoglio has not spoken of his novitiate, but there are glimpses of him in a memoir by his contemporary, Jorge González Manent, known as "Goma." A colleague from his Catholic Action days in Flores, Goma had followed Bergoglio into the Jesuits but had spent his first novitiate year in Montevideo, Uruguay. When he joined Jorge for the second year in Córdoba, he found it strange to have to address him as "Brother Bergoglio." He recalls that Jorge's Latin was better than anyone else's because of his eighteen months at the seminary, and that his bookshelves already revealed his future passions: Romano Guardini's *The Lord*; a biography of Ignatius's companion, Peter Favre; Thérèse of Lisieux's *Story of a Soul*; and a book about Saint Francis of Assisi. If Bergoglio was bookish, the explanation was partly his health: his damaged lung led him to be excused from the pilgrimage and from more onerous cleaning tasks. But his piety clearly annoyed some of the novices. Goma recalls how in one *culpa* where it was Bergoglio's turn to be criticized, "many of the comments were about the pious long faces which he puts on when he takes Communion or when you meet him in the corridors with his head tilted to one side."

In 1959 the novices had a distinguished visitor: Father Pedro Arrupe, then provincial in Japan, who would be elected superior general six years later. He showed them a documentary about the atom bomb falling on Hiroshima, which Arrupe had experienced firsthand, and described the extraordinary story of the Jesuits in east Asia since the days of Francis Xavier and Matteo Ricci. Both Bergoglio and Goma were enraptured and asked him, separately, to be considered for mission there. Arrupe told them to wait until after philosophy, and to write to the general in Rome.[15]

JORGE took his simple vows of poverty, chastity, and obedience on March 12, 1960 and was now a Jesuit, with the right to put SJ (for "Society of Jesus") after his name. The vows would be key to his calling. Poverty meant not being controlled by possessions and identifying with the poverty of Christ. For Jesuits it brings flexibility and simplicity, availability for the mission, and acts as a vaccine against what Jesuits refer to as "riches to honors to pride"—the desire for preferment and wealth that in the *Exercises* Ignatius imagines the devil using to lure people from their true calling. The second vow, chastity, was also about apostolic freedom: to be available to love and serve others without seeking to possess them. Obedience, the third vow, was also linked to freedom for mission: to boldly go where Jesuits were most needed, at the service of God's will rather than their own. It meant trusting your superior, and sometimes knuckling down—a mortification not of the flesh but of the ego.

Until the late 1960s the Jesuits in the southern cone of South America shared formation houses: although each did the novitiate in their own country, the Jesuit students of Chile, Argentina, Uruguay, Paraguay, and Bolivia all did their juniorate in the Chilean capital, Santiago, and their philosophy and theology at the Colegio Máximo in Buenos Aires province. In Bergoglio's case—because the Jesuits took into account his secondary education and time at the seminary—the juniorate was only a year. Together with Goma and others, Jorge traveled by truck to Mendoza, then by plane across the cloud-piercing mountain range of Aconcagua, landing in the improbable strip of land between the Andes and the Pacific that is Chile.

The Casa Loyola was a purpose-built formation house twelve miles outside Santiago in a village then called Marruecos. The setting was rural and healthy: large gardens with almond trees and artichoke plants gave way to huge pear and apple orchards reached by rose-lined paths. There were farm animals, a wine-making bodega, and vegetable patches tended by Jesuit brothers. Like the novitiate, it was a monastic existence: self-sufficient, self-contained, bound by silence and prayer, with neither radio nor newspapers. Inside the house there were 130 simple small rooms (bed, cupboard, basin, desk) off long corridors at the end of which were the communal bathrooms, with hot water twice a week. The juniors dressed in cassocks outside the house and for Mass, but inside they wore ordinary clothes.

The timetable was less micromanaged than at the novitiate, to allow time for studies. After getting up at 6:00 a.m., there was personal prayer until 7:30 a.m., Mass (in Latin), breakfast at 8:00 a.m., followed by house-cleaning tasks. Classes were from 9:00 a.m. to 1:00 p.m. Apart from Sundays and feast days, when talking was allowed, lunch was in silence at long tables, listening to an edifying book or fifteen-minute practice talks by juniors over the clatter of plates. After lunch there was time for rest before beginning classes again, from 2:30 p.m. until 8:00 p.m., with a break at 5:00 p.m., when the students gathered in groups under the trees to take tea and chat, supposedly in Latin, but in Chile the rule was seldom enforced. Twice a week there was time in the afternoon for sports—basketball and volleyball—and for the garden, clearing paths or picking apples. Outside the brief recreation periods, juniors were asked to keep silence, to pray and meditate constantly, and to study hard.

The studies gave a grounding in humanities: Latin, Greek, literature, oratory, rhetoric, art, and culture. Because the grades were never posted on the board—it was an atmosphere that encouraged conformity rather than competition—it was impossible to know who stood out academically; the classes were formal, large (usually about fifty students), and passive, usually in the form of a lecture. Yet "although the times were still quite conservative, there was in the Chilean province a vision of change that would develop in the years following the Council," recalls Juan García-Huidobro, a contemporary of Jorge's at the Casa Loyola. His classmates all remember, for example, Father José Donoso, SJ, in whose interactive classes on art "we learned to savor the beauty and mystery of the world, what it was to be human, and the depth of God," recalls Francisco López, a Uruguayan junior at the time. Goma, too, remembers Donoso's blackboard packed with quotes and symbols that he spent the class unwrapping with "astonishing erudition."

One part of the juniors' formation especially impacted Jorge: the weekend apostolic visits to the poor of the area. The Casa Loyola had been built by Father—now Saint—Alberto Hurtado, SJ, a Jesuit pioneer of social projects such as the Hogar del Cristo that continue to this day. Like most of the Chilean Jesuits of his time, he came from the upper class but began to question, in the 1940s, the Church's place in society: for Father Hurtado, poverty was a scandal that undermined Chile's claim to be a Catholic country, and he famously said that charity should only begin where justice ends.

Father Hurtado had wanted direct contact with the poor to be a necessary part of Jesuit formation, and for the Casa Loyola to have a mission to the people of Marruecos. It was a model that Bergoglio, as provincial, sought to imitate in Argentina more than ten years later.

The village was the hub of a district of poor tenant farmers who lived on the edge of destitution. Argentina and Uruguay were at the time far wealthier than Chile, and the sight of the very poor wandering the street was a new sight for Jorge and his Uruguayan contemporary, Francisco López. Jorge was assigned to teach religion in a basic little school in Marruecos, the Escuelita No. 4, where the children arrived dirty and often without shoes. In a May 1960 letter to his sister María Elena, Jorge sought to connect the poverty he saw in Chile with her eleven-year-old prayers. After congratulating her for her letter and diligent studies, he turned to her spiritual growth. "I want you to be a little saint," he wrote. "Why don't you try it? We really need so many saints."

Let me tell you something. I give religion classes in a third and fourth grade school. The boys and girls are very poor, some even come to school without shoes on their feet, and very often they have nothing to eat and in winter they feel the harshness of the cold. You don't know what that's like because you've never wanted for food and when you're cold you just get close to the stove. But while you're happy, there are many children who are crying. When you sit at the table there are many who don't have more than a piece of bread to eat, and when it rains and it's cold many of them are living in tin shacks and they have nothing to cover themselves with. The other day a little old lady said to me, *padrecito*,[16] if I could get hold of a blanket how good that would be, *padrecito*.

And the worst of it is that they don't know Jesus. They don't know Him because they've got no one to teach them. Do you see now why I say to you that we need many saints? I want you to help me in my apostolate to those children—you'd do it really well. For example, what would you say to making the effort of praying the Rosary each night? I know it's an effort, but your prayer would be like the slow drizzle of winter that, when it falls on the land, makes it fertile, makes it bear fruit. I need my apostolate to bear fruit and that's why I'm asking for your help.

I'll wait now for you to write soon and tell me what plan you have for helping me in my apostolate. Don't forget that on that plan a child's happiness depends.[17]

Jorge's companions remember him as quiet and studious, and a good conversationalist. His lungs continued to exclude him from sport—in the Casa Loyola it was basketball—and for the same reason he did not go camping in the mountains with the other juniors in the summer. But he did swim—a habit he would keep up, for the sake of his lungs.

Unlike Chile's juniors, who were almost all the products of the Jesuit-run fee-paying upper-class Santiago schools, the Argentine juniors were socially more mixed, and divided politically. "Those who came from the popular classes were staunch Peronists, while those came from the upper class who had come through the Colegio del Salvador were strongly anti-Peronist," recalls Raúl Vergara, a Chilean contemporary. "You really noticed that among the Argentines, that lack of togetherness."

Jorge was not from the privileged world of Jesuit private schools, and his sympathies were increasingly with Peronism—although his fellow juniors do not recall him taking a stand in these arguments. In 1956, a first cousin of his—Lt. Col. Oscar Lorenzo Cogorno—was one of eighteen officers killed by an army firing squad after taking part in a failed uprising against the anti-Peronist president, General Aramburu.[18]

That uprising had been in protest against *gorilismo*, or fanatical anti-Peronism, something Bergoglio, too, opposed. He was part of a generation of young Catholics who were increasingly angered by the veto exercised by the army over Peronism, which prevented it taking part in elections and in countless other, often petty, ways sought to humiliate its supporters. The bishops, who after the overthrow of Perón deplored what it called a "totalitarian régime that, invoking God, deceived and disoriented the masses, and persecuted the Church with the aim of replacing it," had thrown in their lot with the army as the guarantor of a Christian nation, which associated the Church, in the popular mind, with *gorilismo*. When Jorge voted in 1958, it was very probably for Arturo Frondizi, a Radical close to the nationalists and Christian Democrats, who came to power on the promise of lifting the ban on Peronists taking part in elections.

The Jesuit students at the Casa Loyola lived, says the Uruguayan Francisco López, between two eras: "on the one hand, a way of life and daily practice of what we understood to be the daily life of a Jesuit, and on the other a feeling that this could all be done another way." The tensions between what was and what could be would lead almost all of Jorge's contemporaries leaving religious life. But in his case, it produced a determination to stay and lead the change. Those who knew him at this time were struck by his focus. Even in that early stage of his formation, Jorge clearly saw his path ahead. Vergara recalls that during one afternoon's tea recreation, "someone asked Bergoglio what future he saw for himself and he said, 'what I'm really interested in is being in charge of the formation of future Jesuits.' In other words, he saw himself as a novice master or provincial."

In March 1960 Jorge entered the Colegio Máximo, an hour's drive from the Argentine capital, in the province of Buenos Aires, which would be his base for twenty-three of the next twenty-six years. Set in a 120-acre estate, it had rooms for 180 Jesuits, a cavernous church, and endless little chapels for the priests to say their daily Mass on their own, for there was a large community of priests and brothers there, in addition to the students. The college also had a retreat house for guests—known as the "Mínimo"—as well as various offices coordinating local pastoral and evangelization initiatives.

Its main purpose, however, was study. The Máximo was one of the most important Catholic centers of teaching and research in South America: researchers and doctoral students came to use its immense world-class library and archive. Next door was the Jesuit-run National Observatory, and three buildings were dedicated to scientific research. There was an active printing press, which ran off the highly respected theology journal *Stromata*. Although only Jesuits were resident, the classes were full of members of other religious orders that had formation houses in the vicinity of San Miguel in order to take advantage of the Máximo. The Jesuits' mother college was at the heart of a network of houses belonging to various orders that made San Miguel a hub of religious life in Argentina.

A few months into his first year of philosophy, Jorge lost his two fathers—one biological, the other spiritual—within weeks of each other. Mario died on September 24, 1961, in his early fifties, of a heart attack at the Old Gas Meter stadium. Father Enrico Pozzoli, by now frail, came to the wake, and soon after was taken to the Italian Hospital.

When Jorge went to see him there the Salesian was asleep, so he left the room and chatted to a priest in the corridor outside. Soon another priest came out of the room to tell Jorge that Father Pozzoli had woken and was expecting him. Jorge then did something strange: he told the priest to inform Don Enrico that he had already left. Days later, the Salesian died without saying good-bye to the young man whom he had guided over many years.

His action tormented him for a long time. "I assure you, Father Bruno," he wrote to the head of the Salesians in 1990, "if I could have that moment again I would." Even twenty-eight years after the event, his letter shows that Bergoglio's reaction remained mysterious even to himself: he had not wanted the priest woken up, he explained, because "I felt bad, I didn't know what to say," and lied because "I don't know what happened to me, if it was shyness or what." He was clearly wrestling with emotions he could not fathom or express.

In the Church, too, there was a dying. New winds were blowing in the era before the Second Vatican Council, which opened in Rome in October 1962. There was a growing generational divide between the young clergy and lay people who had come of age in the 1950s, on the one hand, and the Argentine bishops, who belonged to the previous generation of the 1930s and 1940s, on the other.

They made up at that time the largest episcopate in Latin America— sixty-six bishops representing forty-six dioceses. Argentina's was the tenth-largest group of bishops at the Council. But they were mostly unprepared for what was about to happen there and were largely bystanders. They had been tightly linked to Pope Pius XII, had close ties to Italy, and identified with the Roman Curia, much of which resisted the Council's reforms. With the exception of a number of new young bishops committed to renewal, most of the senior Argentine bishops took the Curia's view in expecting the Council to be a brief gathering that would anathematize modernity and allow them to return home. When it took off in another direction, the Argentine bishops would find themselves burdened with implementing changes they had not sought, while clinging to a model of public engagement that was ever less credible to young Catholics.

For that new generation, however, there were great expectations. They read the Buenos Aires Catholic magazine *Criterio*, edited now by a brilliant young priest, Father Jorge Mejía (made a cardinal in 2001, along with Bergoglio), who channeled through its pages the new streams of thinking from France. Also in its pages were articles by two seminary professors who would later be cardinals who shaped Bergoglio, Eduardo Pironio (a future collaborator of Paul VI) and Antonio Quarracino (who would persuade John Paul II to make Bergoglio a bishop and his successor as archbishop of Buenos Aires). These were the bright lights of a new generation.

Goma, who had caught up with Jorge at the Máximo after staying on in Chile, remembers that the Council there "was like a personal devotion: some people barely knew it was happening, while others of us followed it closely." He and Jorge, firmly in the latter group, set about publicizing the Council at the entrance to the Máximo with short texts mounted on exhibition boards answering questions about what the Council was and what it was setting out to do. The exhibition was a great success, and requests began to arrive to put it up in chapels and convents in the area.

The Council was also followed in discussions between Jorge and the future provincial of Chile, Fernando Montes. They met over mate in the grounds, always in the same place under the trees, while others played sport: "He had his lung problem, and I just wasn't very keen. I liked to chat," Montes recalls. They became friends. "He wasn't overwhelming, like other *porteños*," says Montes, referring to the famed brashness of people from Buenos Aires. "Compared with them, he was more like someone from Santa Fe or Córdoba. He seemed to me more refined." They didn't just discuss earnest matters. They also laughed about the endless stream of nonsense spoken by an old Jesuit in the house who had lost his memory.

But the Council occupied more and more of their conversations. He and Jorge were very aware, Montes said, "of being on the side of those who wanted a more open Church, not a Church of resistance to the world." They had grasped that the objective of the Council was to redefine the Church's presence in the world in order to speak to it better. Like the bishops in bed with the anti-Peronist military, defending the myth of the Catholic nation, distant from the poor, the Church had become, in its structures, disincarnate, absent from the contemporary world, responding primarily to itself. It lived by its own, often splendid light—the glory and logic of its timeless truths, the complex grammar of its ancient liturgies—and less by the *mysterium lunae*, God's light.

In that sense it was like much of the philosophy they were now studying—dry commentaries that offered elaborately sophisticated answers to questions no one was asking. "I studied philosophy from textbooks that came from decadent or largely bankrupt Thomism," recalled Francis to Father Spadaro.

> When does a formulation of thought cease to be valid? When it loses sight of the human or even when it is afraid of the human or deluded about itself. The deceived thought can be depicted as Ulysses encountering the song of the Siren, or as Tannhäuser in an orgy surrounded by satyrs and bacchantes, or as Parsifal, in the second act of Wagner's opera, in the palace of Klingsor. The thinking of the Church must recover genius and better understand how human beings understand themselves today, in order to develop and deepen the church's teaching.

For the Chilean Jesuits, accustomed to the more open and affectionate regime of the Casa Loyola, the Máximo was a cold shower. Rules about modesty and particular friendships—the *numquam duo* principle—were more tightly observed, as was the encouragement to speak only Latin to each other during recreation. Classes, too, were in Latin, as were the essays and theses. But during matches—in the best Argentine tradition, the Máximo's sport was soccer, and its pitch was legendary—yelling in Spanish was the norm.

There were some spring shoots of renewal. Jacinto Luzzi gave classes on Pierre Teilhard de Chardin, the French Jesuit author of *The Phenomenon of Man* and *The Divine Milieu*, who was a forbidden theologian prior to the Council. Teilhard not only reconciled faith with the natural world and science but posited an optimistic, evolutionary, incarnate kind of thinking that was at odds with the neoscholastic philosophy taught at the time. But for Jorge the most important professor at the Máximo was the dean of philosophy, Miguel Fiorito, who was a master of Ignatius's discernment rules. As Bergoglio's spiritual director, Fiorito was key to his development. "Spiritual discernment is one of the great dimensions of Pope Francis," recalls a Bergoglio contemporary, Father Fernando Albistur, "in large part learned from Father Fiorito in this house."[19]

But these were the exceptions. "It was an era of change that the Máximo responded to with a certain resistance and formalism," recalls Jorge's Uruguayan contemporary, Francisco López. Most of the professors were old, foreign, and unprepared for the engagement with the contemporary world—"The joys and the hopes, the griefs and the anxieties of the men of this age, especially those who are poor or in any way afflicted," as the opening of the 1965 document *Gaudium et Spes* famously put it—to which the Council was inviting the Church. The real action at the Máximo in those years was in the small groups who formed to discuss what it meant to be a Jesuit in these new times. It was a process of self-questioning that would lead many to leave; for Bergoglio, it shaped his ideas about the Society's renewal.

Jorge's cycle of philosophy studies ended, in 1963, with the *periculum*, the oral defense of three years' study. It was an intimidating exam: it lasted two hours, and was conducted in Latin in front of a panel of at least ten Jesuits. On the basis of the results, the scholastics were divided into sheep and goats. The more intellectually gifted in the upper stream would go on to teach and research, while those in the lower were destined for more practical pursuits, such as communications. Jorge entered the upper stream.

At the end of philosophy, Jorge, along with the other graduates, received his minor orders, a stage toward priesthood. He wrote to Father Arrupe, who had just been elected general, to offer himself for the mission in Japan, but he received the answer back that his lung disease made him unsuitable.

He was now a regent, meaning a Jesuit bound to teach for the next two (or, in his case, three) years in a school. Jorge, along with Goma, was assigned to teach literature at the Colegio de la Inmaculada Concepción in Santa Fe, one of the Argentine Jesuits' oldest and best-loved institutions.

BEFORE he died in 1999, the last novel published by Morris West, author of Vatican potboilers such as *The Shoes of the Fisherman*, was about an Argentine cardinal who was elected pope. Apart from the Italian surname, there is almost nothing in common between Luca Rossini, the main character of *Eminence*, and Jorge Bergoglio.[20] But what is surprising is how little of Argentina there is in the Rossini character. Perhaps West thought it would seem ridiculous to have an Argentine pope who loved tango, drank mate, and followed San Lorenzo. No doubt he would have also strained credulity to the breaking point if he had imagined that his character also knew the great short-story writer Jorge Luis Borges.

But truth is stranger than metafiction: Bergoglio did know Borges, after inviting him in 1965 to give classes on gaucho literature to the sixteen- and seventeen-year-olds he was teaching at the time. The link was María Esther Vázquez, Borges's secretary, who had taught piano to the Bergoglio children. At that time she presented a radio program on the Radio del Estado and invited Jorge—who in turn invited Goma to join him—to be interviewed about Jesuits teaching literature.[21]

La Inmaculada, which occupies a whole block on Santa Fe's main square, is Argentina's first and oldest secondary school, and can claim to be its most prestigious, the alma mater of many of Argentina's best-known public figures. It was in the college—founded in 1610 to educate the colonial elite and restored to the Jesuits in 1862—that the then rector had persuaded the chiefs of the local Mocobi and Abipone peoples to be reduced, and where, in 1636, a Jesuit brother's painting of the Virgin of the Immaculate Conception, hung in the chapel next to the college, began giving off little streams of healing water.

When Jorge arrived there in early 1964, he came through a formidable colonial entrance leading to a patio with orange blossom trees. From here the school led off to the right, the Jesuit community to the left, with the movie theater directly ahead—a huge atrium, where the school assemblies were held, but which on Sundays became the Cine Garay. It was the best cinema in town, with room for fifteen hundred people and the latest movies on 70mm projectors. In summer the movies were projected onto huge screens hung between the orange trees, while smoke from mosquito coils curled up between the chairs.

When Jorge taught at La Inmaculada, at the ages of twenty-eight and twenty-nine, about half of the pupils boarded. It was disciplined, and with a strict dress code—jackets and ties at daily Mass—but it was not as severe as English boarding schools at the time. Two days a week, the pupils did community work, building wooden houses in the poor parish that the Jesuits ran in Alto Verde, or playing sports and camping.

"From the first moment, he seemed to be mature," recalls one of the Jesuits at the time, Father Carlos Carranza, who describes Bergoglio as "discreet, serene, peaceful, someone for whom the students cared a lot." Goma, who took over Jorge's literature course, also recalls his "very special relationship" with the students of the literature academy, who remember their teacher as demanding, generous, and brilliant, yet gentle and reserved. They were won over by his humor and directness, touched by how hard he worked for them, and aware of his sophisticated mind. "On the blackboard there were always arrows linking facts and ideas inside circles," recalls Rogelio Pfirter, later an ambassador to London. "He encouraged questions of all kinds and his answers were rapid and precise. I never saw him hesitate." Rogelio's brother Eduardo recalls Bergoglio's self-effacing nature: "He behaved with great simplicity, never seeking to dominate or stand out, which wasn't very common in the Jesuits in those days." Many have also commented on the quality of his talks, which a former pupil, Guillermo Venturi, remembers as engaging and entertaining. "Besides his natural speaking qualities, he added a literary knowledge that gave him the ability to explain things in a very beautiful way," recalls Father Carranza.[22]

But his popularity didn't save him from the inevitable nicknames. Jorge Milia remembers him being called Carucha—"Long Face"—because of his mournful expression. He was also known as Irma la Douce, after the French hooker played by Shirley MacLaine in the 1963 comedy, because as sub-prefect of discipline "he handed out harsh punishments with an angelic face."

Roberto Poggio, a student there, will never forget one of those punishments. After Poggio slapped a younger boy during a sports match, Bergoglio asked him to come to a classroom at a particular time. When he got there, he saw ten of his friends sitting in a circle and Bergoglio sitting off to one side. "He told me I should tell my friends in detail what happened, and it became something that stuck with me for life. They were understanding, they gave advice, and somehow I felt as if a load been lifted from me—I felt no reproach or criticism from them." The pupils' jury decided the punishment: Poggio was suspended from sports for two weeks and had to apologize to the younger student.[23]

Jorge Milia also remembers Bergoglio's unique way of punishing. Milia was given an oral examination on literature—the result of his failing to hand in his work on time—as part of his final exam by three Jesuits, including Bergoglio. After giving it his all, Milia reached his conclusion and waited. After a long silence, Bergoglio began speaking.

> We all know there is no grade for an exam like this and we also know that Señor Milia should never have had to undergo it, that if he had to do so it is because he did not hand in his practical work on time, because he supposes that for him rules do not exist, because he does what he wants at whatever cost, as is his custom. Therefore, although the grade that should correspond to him is ten, I believe we should give him a nine, as a final reminder of his time here in this college. Not to reprimand him, but so that he remembers always that what matters is the duty carried out day by day, the work that is done systematically yet which should never become routine, the patient building, brick by brick, rather than the impulsive improvisation to which he is so attached.

"Nine," agreed the other Jesuits. Milia, who was overwhelmed by the justice of his teacher's decision, has never forgotten that lesson.[24]

The subjects assigned to Jorge—literature, psychology, and art—were not the obvious ones for a chemical technician, but it was typical for Jesuits to be stretched by teaching subjects not their own. Jorge was in any case an avid reader of the classics, and it made sense to put him in charge of the school's prestigious literature academy. The Inmaculada academies, specializing in different subjects, were a distinctive part of the school tradition: pupils applied to join, making the case for why they should be admitted, and the teachers in charge of the academies decided whether to accept them.

Jorge taught the literature of Spain in his first year at the college, and of Argentina in the second. Detecting a desire in his pupils to go straight to modern texts, he rearranged the syllabus so that they read the medieval classic El Cid at home and began in class with the twentieth-century poet Federico García Lorca. As they discovered a taste for literature, he moved them back through the Spanish Golden Age authors such as Cervantes, Quevedo, and Góngora in an order that, he later said, "came naturally." The experiment worked; as the boys became more engaged, he encouraged them to pursue their passions, offering tutorials. "The great thing about Bergoglio," wrote Milia in his school-days memoir, "was that no doors were closed. Whoever wanted to explore that monument that is the Spanish language could do so in whatever depth he wished, without conditions or euphemisms."

Milia recalls Jorge introducing them to the late-medieval *Danza de la Muerte*, macabre Spanish recitals in which a personification of Death invites people in different stations in life to dance around a tomb, reminding them, in poetry, of their mortal end. To aid their understanding, Jorge arranged a Cine Garay showing of the 1957 Ingmar Bergman movie *The Seventh Seal*, which tells the story of a medieval knight's chess game with Death. Milia and the others were then asked to write film critiques, commenting on the use of scenery, characters, music, and so on.

It was Jorge's idea to invite writers to the school, so that his pupils could learn not just about the fruits but also the craft of authorship. The first was María Esther Vázquez, who subsequently arranged for Borges to visit La Inmaculada for five days in August 1965 to speak on gaucho poems. It was an extraordinary coup, which the local university jealously regarded—recalls Milia—as "being like the Berlin Philharmonic coming to play 'happy birthday' at a children's party."

The poet, essayist, and master of the short story, precursor of what would soon be an international explosion of 1960s Latin-American literature, was at this time in his sixties, an icon in Argentina who was recognized wherever he went and whose distinctive voice was widely imitated. His growing fame coincided with the rapid loss of his sight—God gave him, Borges once poignantly said, "books and the night at the same time"— and was at this time dependent on his librarian-like memory to source his playful, cerebral fictions.

Borges, Bergoglio said in 2010, "had a genius's knack for talking about any subject without ever showing off." He knew and loved Borges's stories, which take place in a kind of hyper-reality, where the characters move as ciphers in a labyrinthine world of libraries and ideas. There is much in Bergoglio's own style of speaking and writing—crisp, witty, and playful, relishing paradoxes and wordplays—that suggests an affinity.

John Baptist–like, Jorge prepared for the great man's coming by giving a crash course in his oeuvre, so that when Borges arrived, by bus, in the chill of August 1965, he was amazed to find the boys so well acquainted with his works. During those days, almost blind and walking with a cane, he was feted, spoke to appreciative audiences, and enjoyed both students and the Jesuits. Looking back, Milia realized that Bergoglio's great gift to his pupils was precisely the time they had been able to spend with that unseeing guru who could spin the most trivial object or event into a marvelous tale.

Jorge made sure it bore fruit. He had been encouraging his pupils to write, and now he asked them to create some tales, the best of which would be sent to be read to Borges. He and Goma selected the eight best and dispatched them in a file labeled "Original Stories." Soon after, the rector of the college, Father Ricardo O'Farrell, received a letter from Borges thanking him for the Jesuits' hospitality and offering to write a prologue to "that book," whose title he said he liked very much. It was the first time it had occurred to anyone that the stories *were* a book, let alone that they could be published. But with Borges's offer, a publisher was easily found.

Borges returned to Santa Fe in November for the launch of *Cuentos Originales*, which, buoyed by his praise, became a local success in the city. Bergoglio sent the book to a poet he knew, Sofía Acosta, to ask what she thought of it, then deftly sent her letter praising the stories to the editor of a newspaper in the neighboring city of Paraná (where his great-uncles' palazzo was now a restaurant). "Our wish is to highlight the achievements and values of this work, which has become a bestseller in Santa Fe," Jorge wrote, asking him to make the book better known "by means of your distinguished newspaper." It was an early display of political savvy.

In the prologue to *Cuentos Originales* Borges writes: "It is likely that among these eight writers will be one who becomes famous, and bibliophiles will seek out this short volume in search of this or that name which I do not dare to predict." The book *was* sought out, but not until 2013; by journalists rather than bibliophiles; and not because of the names that appear in it, but because of one that does not. Borges, the great ironist, would have been delighted.

One of the contributors to the volume was the journalist Jorge Milia. Forty years later, he published his memoirs of his school days at the urging of Bergoglio, with whom he has stayed in touch. The then cardinal arch-bishop offered to write the prologue to the memoir, which came out as *De la Edad Feliz* (Of Happy Times) in 2006. Milia, who these days pens online columns explaining Francis's *bergoglismos*, can safely claim to be the only author who has had prologues written by two of Argentina's most famous sons—Jorge Luis Borges and Pope Francis.

Borges considered himself agnostic, yet had been taught to read the Bible by his English Protestant grandmother, prayed the Our Father each night because he had made a promise to his mother, and died in the presence of a priest. Yet he was also a lover of Jewish wisdom, who wrote about Buddhism and knew the Qu'ran well enough to declare that there wasn't a single camel in it (a point he used to criticize a certain kind of nationalist writer who stuffs his books with "local color"). In his last fantasy, *Los Conjurados*, he imagines the founding miracle of a nation in which "men of diverse tribes, professing diverse religions, and speaking diverse languages, have taken the strange decision to be reasonable. They have resolved to forget their differences and stress their affinities." It sounded much like what Cardinal Bergoglio would later promote as the culture of encounter.

THREE

STORM PILOT

(1967–1974)

V OCABOR FRANCISCUS. "I will be called Francis." It was a breathtaking choice. Because no pope had ever taken the name, it needed no Roman numerals but stood stark and simple as *il poverello* in a hair shirt, the cast-off silks at his feet.

No one ever thought a pope could be called Francis; it would be like taking the name Peter, or Jesus. They were one of a kind.

"I was astonished at the boldness of it, because the name Francis is a whole program of governance in miniature," the Vatican commentator John Allen told Boston Radio. "He is this iconic figure in the Catholic imagination that awakens images of the antithesis of the institutional church. . . . That's an awful lot of weight to put on your shoulders right out of the gate. If you're not prepared to walk that talk, then you're going to be in real trouble."[1]

Bergoglio had walked that talk over a lifetime. Right now it mostly meant saying no, like keeping his old black shoes, his silver pectoral cross (a pope's is normally gold), and his faithful black plastic watch, or refusing the limousine waiting to take him back to the guesthouse for dinner ("May God forgive you for what you have done," he joked with the cardinals). After Mass with the cardinals the next day, he left the Vatican in a Ford Focus—the security guards had better cars than the pope—to pray at the shrine of Saint Mary Major, returning via the priests' hostel where he had stayed before the conclave. There he collected his bag, paid his bill to a shocked clerk ("I checked in under another name" was the caption on a widely tweeted photo), and chatted and joked with staff. There wasn't much to collect. He had been washing his clothes at night, letting them dry on the radiator.

Meeting with the press corps two days later in the modern audience hall next to St. Peter's, he put down his prepared text and told them how some of the cardinals had come up with other names: Adrian, for example, after the sixteenth-century Dutch pope ("he was a reformer, we need a reform"), or perhaps Clement XV to take revenge on Clement XIV who suppressed the Jesuits. At the end of the audience, having charmed six thousand journalists from eighty-one countries, he greeted a selection of media people, one by one, up on the proscenium. He didn't receive them sitting but came forward to greet them. Among them was a blind man working in the Vatican communications office, with his guide dog in a harness. Francis embraced the man, and while they talked he placed his hand on the golden retriever's head.

It was lots of those little things. They weren't mere gestures, nor were they calculated messages. They flowed from his identification with the Christ of the Gospels.

In the weeks and months that followed, Francis used the authority inherited from Saint Peter to step free of the monarchic papacy, trying to eliminate, as far as he could, what separated him from ordinary humanity. He wasn't against the things themselves, only if they were obstacles or distractions. But a media narrative of pauperism began to take hold, according to which everything he did was a refutation of wealth and privilege. He chose to stay in the Vatican guesthouse where the cardinals had billeted during the conclave, not, as was reported, because the Apostolic Palace was lavish (it is not) or because the Casa Santa Marta was simple and humble (it cost $25 million to build and is lined with marble), but so that people could have direct access to him: he didn't want the bottlenecks of intermediaries that had kept Benedict XVI—in spite of his own humility and accessibility—distant and isolated.

In the Santa Marta Francis created a whole new means of papal communication: brief, three-point homilies delivered off the cuff at the 7:00 a.m. Mass each day in the modern chapel, the fruit of his dawn contemplation of that day's readings, mate in hand.

"We must learn to be normal!" he told his Jesuit interviewer, Father Antonio Spadaro, in August that year, and he put it into practice, collecting his tray of food in the Santa Marta dining room like anyone else, making his own phone calls and many of his appointments, keeping his own diary, and making visits—always in the blue Ford Focus, without any kind of entourage—to parishes and charities around Rome, to spend time with the old and the homeless and the foreign-born.

Stories of Francis's personal kindness, impossible to verify, began to make their rounds, like the time he left his room to find a Swiss Guard standing outside his door and brought him a chair. "But Holy Father, I cannot sit down. My boss does not allow it," the guard told him. "Well, I'm the boss of your boss, and I say it's fine," Francis told him, before going back inside to fetch him the Italian equivalent of a Twinkie.

He wasn't afraid to *hacer lío*, to create a little havoc, such as the September 2013 visit he made to a refugee center in Rome, where he said empty convents should not be turned into hotels but should be used to house immigrants, "the flesh of Christ." Or the time he phoned a woman in Argentina and appeared to suggest she should receive the Eucharist even though her priest had said she couldn't ("Some people are more papist than the pope," she said he told her). Or the time he told delegates of the Latin-American and Caribbean Confederation of Religious Men and Women (CLAR) not to worry if they received a letter from the Vatican pulling them up for some doctrinal infraction or other, that it was better to have a Church that made mistakes and got dirty to one that stayed inside.

"We've got to flip the omelet," he told the CLAR delegates: why was it world news when the Dow Jones was up or down a few points, but not when an old man died of cold in the street? "We've got to turn this around," he told them. "That's the Gospel."

In his daily homilies and speeches he gently but with total focus led the charge against what the theologian Henri de Lubac called "spiritual worldliness." It was a sickness with many symptoms: high-spending prelates, "airport bishops" often absent from their dioceses, bishops who flitted from one gala dinner to the next, Catholic laymen who used chivalric orders to advance their business interests, dioceses that idolized efficiency and put plans before people, elite groups with theological or liturgical agendas, self-appointed inquisitors who combed priests' homilies in search of heterodoxy, church organizations that were so professional that they were indistinguishable from those of the world—the list was long. The Church, Francis endlessly pointed out, was not an NGO but a love story, and the men and women were links in this "chain of love." "If we do not understand this," said Francis, "we have understood nothing of what the Church is."

The choice of name began to make deeper sense, for Francis of Assisi was the great enemy of spiritual worldliness. Back in 1205 he had made himself a beggar for Christ's sake, spurning a life of comfort and privilege to be among lepers and the trees and wild animals of his beloved Umbria. His infectious joy flowed from making room, all the time, for what came first: God, Christ, His creation. "He loved nature, animals, the blade of grass on the lawn and the birds flying in the sky," said the pope of his namesake in an interview on the eve of his Assisi visit on October 4, 2013. "But above all he loved people: children, old people, women."

In naming himself after the *poverello*, Francis was identifying not just with a saint but with an underground stream that had often in history bubbled up in moments of crisis but had just as soon vanished. Times had changed since the saint of Assisi, said Francis, "but the ideal of a missionary, poor Church is still more than valid. This is still the Church that Jesus and his disciples preached about." This was his vision: a Church shaped by the periphery, which put the poor first, that was ambulant, materially simple, boundary-leaping, and lived from the sweet joy of evangelizing. It was a Church that, in the words of Bergoglio to his fellow cardinals prior to the conclave, rejected spiritual worldliness in order to live by not its own light but by the *mysterium lunae*, the light of the divine.

Francis's twelve-hour Assisi visit on October 4, 2013, allowed him to teach this vision of the Church in a tour of all the places linked to the *poverello*'s life. He had speeches to give, and scheduled stops to make, yet to those watching him that day it seemed as if he was being led from one place to another by God's holy faithful people, eager to show him their pretty hilltop earthquake-shattered town. "They dragged him to every cave, every altar, and every crypt," Cardinal Seán O'Malley of Boston, a Capuchin Franciscan who was with him, later recalled. "Everywhere he would go, someone would stand up and say, 'This is the first time a pope has ever come here.' I kept thinking, 'He shouldn't be here this time! He's not a young man.'"

When he was "in his sins," Francesco di Bernardone had been afraid, even disgusted, by the sores of lepers, and ergo by them; but later, as he cleaned their bodies and dressed their wounds in the leprosarium, the omelet got flipped: those whom he had recoiled from now gave him delight and joy. It was a rebirth, a healing, a way of seeing the world now with God's eyes. Pope Francis began his visit to Assisi among today's lepers, the profoundly disabled, at the Seraphicum Institute. For an hour he was theirs: they clasped his hand, took him aside to confide their thoughts and feelings, played with his pectoral cross, shouted and grunted and screamed. "We are among the wounds of Jesus," Francis said in a quiet voice, visibly moved. "These wounds need to be recognized, and listened to."

The following month Francis stunned the world by caressing the sores of Vinicio Riva, a fifty-three-year-old man whose facial disfigurement was so grotesque it caused people to get off buses to avoid looking at him. When Francis kissed his painful growths, a symptom of a genetic disease called neurofibromatosis, Riva's heart beat so fast that he thought he would die. "He didn't even think about whether or not to hug me," he later said. "I'm not contagious, but he didn't know that. But he just did it: he caressed me all over my face, and as he did I felt only love."

Francis was the nineteenth pope to visit Assisi but the first to go to the so-called stripping room in the archbishop's palace, where Francesco di Bernardone, in front of his family, took off his nobleman's silks and renounced wealth and power. "Worldliness brings us to vanity, arrogance, pride, and these are idols," Pope Francis said. "All of us have to strip ourselves of this worldliness." Otherwise, he said, "we become pastry shop Christians, like beautiful cakes and sweet things but not real Christians."

That afternoon, in outdoor meetings with clergy and young people, speaking in his fluent Argentine-accented Italian, he was at his colloquial best. At San Rufino Cathedral he told priests to resist giving "interminable and boring homilies where no one understands anything" and reminisced about bygone days when parish priests knew the names of all their parishioners, "and even the name of the dog in each family." He told clergy that couples that separated didn't know how to forgive each other in time. "I always said to newlyweds: argue as much as you want. If the plates fly, let them. But never let the day end without making peace, never!" Urging them to reach out to the marginalized and the disregarded, he told them: "Do not allow yourselves to be obstructed by prejudices, habits, mental or pastoral rigidity—the famous 'it's always been done this way.' You can reach the peripheries only if you carry the Word of God in your heart and walk with the Church, like Saint Francis."

Even after countless visits, a Mass, and five speeches, he drew energy from the crowd of twenty thousand young people waiting for him outside the Basilica of St. Mary of the Angels at the end of the afternoon. Speaking of how hard it was to marry in a culture dominated by the provisional, he told them how a woman in Buenos Aires had complained to him that her son was in his thirties, had a girlfriend, but wouldn't get married. "I said, Signora, stop ironing his shirts!"

Francis's visit was intensely followed in the Italian media. They knew he was fun and bold, but it was easy to get this wrong, to see him as some kind of rebel or iconoclast. He was restoring what had been lost: not spurning the Church and its doctrines but seeking to recover their meaning and purpose, which were to reveal Christ. That meant being against some things, and offending some people, but only in order for the Church to be more like it is, not to turn it into something else.

What people loved about Francis—just as they had about the man from Assisi—was precisely his Christ-likeness: his authenticity amid the phoniness, his simplicity in a world of materialism, his spontaneity amid the stuffed cassocks, his preference for the poor in a world vying to be rich. He was humble in a world of celebrity, a sinner in a world of self-justification, a leper-kisser in a world obsessed with beauty.

That made him—although this didn't suit the media narrative of rupture—a direct successor of Benedict XVI. The more astute observers could see that Francis's freshness and honesty and directness rested on something solid and unchanging, that he was, in a sense, changing everything at the same time as he was changing nothing. What he had succeeded in doing was making the delivery of the message match its content. The syllabus—humility, prayer, dependence on Christ—was the same, but Benedict XVI's finely honed, crystalline texts, delivered in a quiet voice by a remote figure, were now being spoken and acted by a man who jumped out of a chair to make off-the-cuff remarks in physically affectionate encounters. Benedict clarified who was Christ, what it meant to live in and through Him; Francis recalled Christ. The widespread attraction to him showed that even inside the staunchest Western agnostics there lurks a long-buried remembrance of the God-made-man.

It was like Francis's friars in the 1300s reaping what the monks had sown over the previous seven hundred years. As G. K. Chesterton's much-loved biography of Saint Francis describes it, referring to the sixth-century founder of Western monasticism, "What St. Benedict had stored, St. Francis scattered . . . what had been stored into the barns like grain was scattered over the world like seed."[2]

Now another Francis was taking another Benedict on the road.

THE Second Vatican Council, which ended in 1965, the year he taught in the Colegio del Salvador in Buenos Aires, was Jorge Mario Bergoglio's reference point. In the late 1960s and early 1970s, when the Church was being pulled apart, Bergoglio was a newly formed Jesuit, and then a young provincial. It was a time when religious orders like his were undergoing their own reforms, debating what it meant to return *ad fontes*, to their origins, as the Council asked them to do. Within the Society of Jesus, which took the lead in implementing the Council worldwide, the turbulence had been particularly intense, above all in Latin America, because the post-conciliar changes came at a time not just of a cultural explosion, as in Europe and America, but of political revolution.

It would be because Jorge Bergoglio clung to the idea of reform rather than rupture, of reform not revolution, that his fellow Jesuits urged Rome to name him provincial, and why he became unpopular with the avant-garde intellectuals within his province. It was they, subsequently, who spread the false idea of Bergoglio as a conservative, and the myth that he wanted to take the Jesuits back to before the Council. His decisions and his writings tell the opposite story.

The Council broke a dam, unleashing pent-up streams of a long-overdue renewal. The faithful could pray in their own language. Scripture could be directly engaged. Up went the bridges, especially to Jews, now seen as elder siblings rather than obdurate foes. Out went the monarchical society—pope and bishops ruling over a great mass of people via the clergy and religious—in favor of the People of God, marked off from one another by role, not rank. A new tone was struck, of dialogue and participation, engagement and hope. Catholics would no longer recoil from modernity but would be its midwives, helping to bring to birth a more human world. Through the documents agreed in the bishops' titanic three-year meeting there ran again a new, almost Franciscan stream. The Council committed its bishops and clergy to a greater simplicity of life, "to be poor, simple, humble and lovable, in her speech and attitude," as Pope Paul VI put it.

The Council's sixteen documents remain the Magna Carta of modern Catholicism, rich in biblical and scriptural insights, recapturing the vitality and engagement of the early Church. Properly absorbed, they would make the Church more missionary—more credible and convincing—by purifying it of worldliness. Renouncing the attachment to power and prestige in favor of a new dependence on the Holy Spirit would release new energies for the evangelization of the world.

Yet the documents were not always well absorbed. The Council's purpose was to equip the Church to transform the modern world, pointing it outward, for mission. Yet the very notion of the Church changing—after so long resisting the idea of the *world* changing—was unsettling. The Council was an *aggiornamento*, an updating, of the Church to meet the needs of the times, but that was often mistaken—by both progressives and reactionaries—as a mandate for modernization, that is, adapting the Church to the modern world by making it more like the modern world.

The problem, as Benedict XVI pointed out in one of his last speeches as pope in February 2013, was that "the Council that got through to the people was that of the media, not that of the Fathers." The changes were filtered through a political lens, as a struggle between different factions, with the media taking the side of those perceived to be wanting a rupture. Before the Council, many in the Church had confused what was essential and unchanging—what Jesus had entrusted to the Church to preserve— with what was in reality traditional, or contingent on a particular age. After the Council, the danger was reversed: what was essential could come to be seen as empty custom, and what was new to be seen as per se good. Hence the rows: some blamed the Council for changing too much, while others fumed that it had changed too little. As the Church divided, the authority of the papacy shrank. Groups of Catholics acquired their own magisteriums, by which they judged others.

In the late 1960s, the crisis crystallized around the issue of birth control. When Pope Paul VI opted to uphold the ban on artificial contraception, after electing to ignore the findings of an expert committee he had appointed, his encyclical letter *Humanae Vitae* sparked a rebellion and furious debates about authority versus individual conscience. An exodus began, especially among the Western middle classes, as huge numbers joined a new and expanding congregation known as "nonpracticing Catholics."

The crisis was felt not just in declining church attendance but in priesthood and religious life. If the growing numbers of men and women leaving orders to marry speeded trends already evident in the pre-conciliar Church, the sharp drop in numbers of entrants showed the damage from post–Vatican II turbulence.

The Society of Jesus, which went out first and fastest to implement the Council, was hit hard by declining numbers. Worldwide, the thirty-six thousand Jesuits in 1965 made up the largest, best-organized, and most expert body of priests in the Church, a third of whom taught over a million students in almost five thousand schools, colleges, and universities across the world. By the 1970s Jesuit numbers had dropped by a third. New vocations—men entering the Society—in some places dried up altogether.

The loss of vocations reflected, at least in part, the Jesuits' uncertainty about their new mission. Like other orders, the Jesuits were invited to drink again from the wells of their founders—a process described as "returning to the sources," or *ressourcement*. But there were intense disagreements about what that meant.

The Jesuit renewal worldwide was led by Father Pedro Arrupe, elected general for life at the close of the Council in 1965 by a gathering of the world's Jesuit provinces (a mixture of elected delegates and provincials) in Rome. General Congregation 31 (GC31) agreed that "the entire government of the Society must be adapted to modern necessities and ways of living" and that the spiritual heritage of the Jesuits was "to be purified and enriched anew according to the necessities of our times." The passionate, visionary Don Pedro was a Basque medic, had Ignatius's hook nose and warm smile, and, having seen the atomic bomb drop on Hiroshima, Japan, was no stranger to crisis.

As the Council ended, Father Arrupe asked the provincials to carry out a belt-and-braces survey of the purpose of the Jesuits in the modern world. Three years and four hundred responses later, the mission was clear: they were called to stand with the poor in their desire for justice and peace.

Traveling the world over the next years, trying to hold the Society together amid defections and threats of splits above all in Spain, Arrupe urged his brethren to go back to the sources of Ignatian spirituality. *The Spiritual Exercises* were rediscovered afresh, not as hoops to jump through but as a school of prayer; Ignatius's *Autobiography* was revealed for the first time in its authentic text; and the nineteenth-century rulebooks could finally be shelved to make space for the original *Constitutions*. Discernment would no longer be something Jesuits read about but something they practiced for themselves.

Jorge Bergoglio became closely involved in this renewal while reading theology at the Colegio Máximo between 1967 and 1970. There he formed a close bond with Father Miguel Angel Fiorito, the pioneer of Jesuit spiritual renewal in the Argentine province, who restored the original method of doing the *Exercises* as an individually guided retreat. As well as being dean of philosophy, this introverted, white-haired metaphysician, at that time in his late forties, became Argentina's leading authority on Saint Ignatius's rules for discerning spirits. "In one way you could say he was the spiritual director of the Argentine province," says Father Miguel Yáñez, SJ, who these days teaches in Rome.

A dry, rigorous man of disconcertingly few words, Fiorito was much loved by those who managed to get close to him, including the future provincials of Argentina and Chile. As their spiritual director, he "made us go back to the Ignatian sources of discernment," recalls the Chilean Fernando Montes: "It was Fiorito who sparked it all off." The Argentine province's future leaders (novice masters, rectors of the Máximo, and provincials) of the 1970s and 1980s—above all Jorge Bergoglio, Andrés Swinnen, and Ernesto López Rosas—formed a group around Fiorito, helping him produce his new *Boletín de Espiritualidad* ("Bulletin of Spirituality") off the college presses.

The third issue in 1968 contains the first of many articles by Bergoglio, "The Theological Meaning of Election," which treated the struggle between God's choosing and the one chosen. It showed how deeply he had absorbed Saint Ignatius's discernment rules, as well as his focus on the renewal of Jesuit formation. Jorge was a deeply committed pupil of Fiorito's and was closely linked to him. His Uruguayan contemporary, Francisco López, recalls Bergoglio telling him that he was preparing with Fiorito to be novice master. When, in 1968–1969, the novice house—now down to just one or two newcomers—was moved from Córdoba to San Miguel, it was set up in a rented house, the Villa Bailari, and Bergoglio became the assistant to the new novice-master, Father Alfredo Estrella.

The Fiorito group took seriously the idea of *ressourcement*, a renewal that involved a return to the "primitive charism" of the first Jesuits and adapting it to modern times. This was very different from another version of renewal that involved rejecting that heritage as passé and uncritically embracing contemporary ideas. Bergoglio's understanding of the difference between the two was shaped by a French theologian Yves Congar, who had influenced Pope John XXIII's decision to call the Second Vatican Council. Congar's classic 1950 text, *True and False Reform in the Church*, looked back over Church history to work out why some reformers who usually started out with good aims—to counteract abuses and corruption, restore holiness and zeal—spun off into schism and division, while others produced great fruits in renewed holiness and unity. What was the difference?

Congar found that true reform was always rooted in pastoral concern for ordinary faithful people: it was oriented to, and shaped by, the periphery, not the center. In other words, it valued tradition—the Catholic constants such as eucharistic worship, a teaching magisterium, devotion to the saints, and so on—which were valued by the ordinary faithful, rather than the avant-garde elites. True reform sought to make the Church more true to itself and was on guard against attempts to align it with contemporary secular movements (such as nationalism in the sixteenth century or Marxism in the twentieth). Its fruits were a greater zeal and fidelity, as well as unity. True reform attacked the spiritual worldliness that stopped the Church from looking like and acting like Christ. This, in Bergoglio's reading, was the early Jesuit story—a reform that had revitalized the Church by restoring its poverty, holiness, missionary focus, obedience to the pope, and unity—and it would be what, as a Church leader from his thirties on, he dedicated himself to.

That meant combating false reform, the converse of the true reform and its abiding temptation. False reform was driven by ideas in self-enclosed groups distant from the ordinary faithful. It rejected links and tradition, and was vulnerable to or aligned with contemporary ideologies, producing reactions that ended in division and sometimes schism. This was the story of avant-gardism: enlightened elites who saw themselves entitled to impose or lead reforms according to particular ideas or ideologies, which always produced a reaction, either from those with other ideas, or from defenders of the status quo. With false reform, the Church became a battleground of competing elite projects, and what followed were disunity and the loss of identity.

This was close to being a description of the Argentine Jesuits in the late 1960s and early 1970s, divided between a "progressive" group of theologians living out in base communities and committed to Marxist versions of liberation theology, whose actions and views horrified another group of (generally older and more conservative) members of the province. The divisions reflected broader Jesuit debates over identity. But they also mirrored splits in the Argentine Church generally in the wake of the Council, fueled by a growing political divide.

BERGOGLIO's other inspiration was the application of the Second Vatican Council to Latin America by its bishops meeting in Medellín, Colombia, in 1968. The declaration by the Latin-American bishops' confederation (CELAM) gave the Church in the continent its own distinctive voice, above all in what it called the preferential option for the poor.

The Medellín document expanded the Christian understanding of liberation as freedom not just from sin but also from sinful social structures that kept the majority poor. This was the origin of the term *liberation theology*. At a 2010 inquiry, Bergoglio explained:

> The option for the poor comes from the first centuries of Christianity. It's the Gospel itself. If you were to read one of the sermons of the first fathers of the Church, from the second or third centuries, about how you should treat the poor, you'd say it was Maoist or Trotskyist.

The Church has always had the honor of this preferential option for the poor. It has always considered the poor to be the treasure of the Church. During the [third-century] persecution of the deacon Lawrence, who was the administrator of the diocese [of Rome], they told him to bring all the treasures of the Church. A few days later he appeared with a throng of poor people and said: "These are the treasure of the Church." At the Second Vatican Council the Church was redefined as the People of God and this idea really took off at the Second Conference of the Latin-American bishops in Medellín.[3]

There were political implications of this new stance. The Church no longer had permission to be politically aligned with social and economic elites. But while it deplored institutionalized violence and unjust social structures, the Medellín document warned against both Marxism and liberalism as contrary to the dignity of the human person, and categorically opposed armed revolution, which it warned "engenders new injustices." Medellín also took a strong stand, with *Humanae Vitae*, against artificial methods of birth control, which the document saw as a neo-Malthusian attempt by the rich to curb the numbers of poor.

Argentina's bishops took the Medellín program and adapted it to Argentina in their 1969 Declaration of San Miguel. The declaration lamented the collapse in priestly vocations, the questioning of authority, as well as the mounting social protest, but it embraced the new direction set by Medellín, calling for a Church that "honors the poor, loves them, defends them, and embraces their cause" while offering a mea culpa for the way the Church often "appears wealthy."

One part of the document, written by Father Lucio Gera, was the genesis of a peculiarly Argentine version of post-Medellín theology that strongly influenced Bergoglio and other Jesuits around him. While it called for justice, deplored oppression and exploitation, and stood up for the rights of workers, the document rejected Marxism as "alien not only to Christianity but also to the spirit of our people." This was certainly not a conservative, pre-conciliar view. But nor did it frame *el pueblo* in sociological or Marxist terms, as liberation theology was then doing. The San Miguel declaration saw the people as active agents of their own history; startlingly, it asserted that "the activity of the Church should not only be oriented toward the people but also primarily derive *from* the people." The vision of San Miguel was of a Church with a clear option for the poor, but understood as a radical identification with the ordinary people as the subjects of their own history, rather than as a "class" engaged in a social struggle with other classes. Bergoglio shared that San Miguel vision.

In the late 1960s and early 1970s, however, the other version of liberation theology proved attractive to many post-conciliar Catholics, especially in educated middle-class milieux where the Marxism was dominant. Marxist dependency theory had a clear account of why Argentina and other countries remained poor despite foreign investments and exports: the more closely third-world economies are tied to foreign capital, wrote Eduardo Galeano, author of the wildly popular 1971 anticolonial epic *Open Veins of Latin America*, the more dependent and impoverished they become. The alternative to the export-led, developmentalist model of growth promoted by Latin-American governments of the time was a Cuban-style socialism that, so the theory went, could insulate a developing economy from the harsh winds of international capitalism and distribute in favor of the poor.

In Argentina, that narrative was taken up by a new Peronist left, which sought to blend this Marxist analysis with the broad worker base of Peronism. Still the largest party, and still excluded from the ballot box, its leader, Juan Domingo Perón, was quick to spot the shifting political wind, and from his exile in Spain he recast his movement now as a form of anticolonial revolutionary struggle. Although he never actually endorsed the revolutionary version of Peronism, Perón did little to discourage attempts by activists like John William Cooke, leader of the Peronist "Resistance" in Argentina, to turn his movement into an Argentine version of Cuban socialism.

At the same time that socialism and Peronism were getting into bed with each other, increasing numbers in the Church were seduced by Marxism. A 1967 manifesto by a group of developing-world bishops called on the Church to reject the market economy, describing wage labor as slavery and socialism as Christian love in practice. The "Manifesto of Third World Bishops" was taken up at once in Argentina, where it was signed by 320 priests, among whom were nine Jesuits. From that ferment emerged the Third World Priests' Movement or MSTM, which at its height in the early 1970s had a membership of around 10 percent of Argentina's clergy and perhaps a quarter of young priests, while hundreds more sympathized without being affiliated.

The best known of its members was Father Carlos Mugica, a charismatic, tennis-playing priest from a wealthy, conservative family who ministered in a shantytown alongside Retiro station in downtown Buenos Aires. Like many well-to-do Catholics at the time, Mugica embraced Peronism out of intense guilt over the Church's ties to the anti-Peronist post-1955 regimes, which led many working-class Argentines to loathe the Church. "Many of us priests felt that we were marginalized from the people and we made the decision to act 'from the people and with the people,' walking with the people," he wrote. "That's how the process began, with priests in the slums, with the priest directly present in his people." [4]

Mugica and the Third-World priests had a messianic view of Peronism as a force of popular liberation, while seeing politics through a socialist prism. For the MSTM, the people were Peronist, and therefore the Church, in order to be with the people, should be, too. Yet the political agenda was more Castro's than Perón's. The MSTM's aim, it declared in 1969, was "the socialization of the means of production, of political and economic power, and of culture." Two years later the MSTM said that Peronism was the means to achieve that. "The revolutionary Peronist movement," it declared in 1971, "will necessarily lead to the revolution which will make possible an original and Latin-American socialism."[5]

The MSTM mixed this socialist discourse with a call for changes in Church doctrines and practices such as obligatory priestly celibacy. This put them at odds with most of the bishops on both counts. The Church hierarchy in the 1960s was, if anything, closer to the armed forces than before, each seeing the other as guardians of the common good. Faced with protest in both society and Church, they tended to close ranks.

The Argentine Church soon reproduced within its ranks the broader political divisions of the country. Catholics were increasingly divided between those backing social revolution and those who looked to a military government as a defense against communism. The split would lead, in the mid-1970s, to one group of priests appeasing the consciences of guerrillas who killed for the sake of the revolution, while another group reassured those who captured and tortured the guerrillas that they were defending Western Christian civilization.

Argentina's decadelong cycle of violence began in 1969, when students and workers were killed by the army during a protest in Córdoba. The *cordobazo,* as it became known, was the catalyst for the Argentine guerrilla groups, which had begun two years earlier following a meeting in Havana, Cuba. There Castro's socialist government agreed to supply funds, arms, military training, and intelligence support for guerrilla armies, as well as sanctuary for fugitives of these "armies of national liberation" across the continent. The guerrilla cadres each organized by the four Argentine delegates eventually coalesced into the two that were responsible for most of the mayhem in the 1970s: the Trotskyite ERP (Popular Revolutionary Army) and the Montonero Peronist Movement (MPM), known as the "montoneros". Between them the ERP and the montoneros had around six thousand active members by the mid-1970s and an urban terrorist strategy that became deadlier over time. In the decade between 1969 and 1979, the guerrillas carried out more than eight hundred murders and 1,748 kidnappings, let off hundreds of bombs in the middle of cities, and carried out dozens of assaults on army and police bases.

The montoneros were mostly male students or graduates from upper- and middle-class families who had been radicalized by Marxism but tutored by MSTM priests. The three original founders, former Catholic Action militants, had been taken by Father Mugica to the shantytowns, introduced to liberation theology, and led by stages into revolutionary Peronism.

Mugica himself balked at the use of violence, but the young men were taken to that next step by Juan García Elorrio, an upper-class ex-seminarian who had been one of the Argentine delegates in Cuba in 1967. His journal, *Cristianismo y Revolución,* mixed a Marxist power analysis— the army's exclusion of Peronism was designed to maintain the oligarchy in exclusive privilege—with the nationalist idea of a second war of independence, this time against international capital and its local lackeys, "the oligarchy." But the key radicalizing factor was faith. García Elorrio held out the figure of Camilo Torres, the Colombian ex-priest guerrilla who died in 1966 with a rifle in his hands, as the model of messianic sacrificial love.[6]

Father Mugica and the Third-World priests did not assist the guerrillas or actively support their violence, but regarded their actions as justified or inevitable. The montoneros launched themselves in 1970, on the anniversary of the *cordobazo,* with the brutal kidnapping and execution of the former president, General Aramburu, who had led the purge of Peronism in 1955. When the first montoneros were killed, Mugica disobeyed his bishop by presiding at their funerals. Father Hernán Benítez, ex-Jesuit and former confessor to Eva Perón, praised the montoneros in the pages of *Cristianismo y Revolución*. Violence was per se neither good nor holy, Benítez wrote, but nor was it unbiblical. "We must fight for the liberation of the oppressed even if it means assuming the sin of violence."

Over the next three years, as the kidnappings and murders stepped up in pace and intensity, the army engaged in complex negotiations with Perón over lifting the proscription of his party and preparing for civilian rule. Hundreds of young militants in Catholic Action circles and the Peronist Youth signed up with the montoneros for training, convinced that their hour had come, while thousands of others pledged their support.

As long as the armed forces were in power and Peronism was proscribed, it was possible to justify guerrilla violence as a means of securing democratic elections. But by the time those elections were finally called, in 1973, political violence no longer needed a justification: it was hitched to a runaway train.

Not long after the *cordobazo*, just as the guerrillas and the Third World Priests' Movement were beginning their period of militancy, Jorge Bergoglio was ordained a priest in the chapel of the Colegio Máximo by a retired bishop. It was December 13, 1969, five days shy of his thirty-third birthday.

There were only a handful of others being ordained with him. Almost all of those with him in the busy novitiate in Córdoba a decade before had fallen away. A dozen had left in 1969 alone—to marry, or join the social struggle, or both—and even more would leave the following year, when the province had no new entrants at all.

Watching him that day sprawled facedown in a white vestment on the stone floor of the chapel were his brothers Alberto (who had also tried a Jesuit vocation but left) and Oscar; his sister María Elena; his first-grade teacher, Estela Quiroga; and his mother, Regina, who surprised her son by coming forward at the end of the Mass to kneel for his blessing. Also present was his grandmother Rosa, by now thin and frail, who handed him a letter she had written in case she died before this moment, which Pope Francis has kept to this day folded in his Breviary. "On this beautiful day in which you can hold in your consecrated hand Christ our Savior and on which a broad path for a deeper apostolate is opening up before you," she wrote, "I leave you this modest gift, which has very little material value but very great spiritual value." It was her "testament," written in a mixture of Spanish and Piedmontese, part of which reads:

> May my grandchildren, to whom I gave the best of my heart, have a long and happy life. But if one day pain, illness, or the loss of someone they love should afflict them, let them remember that one sigh before the Tabernacle, where the greatest and most venerable of the martyrs is kept, and one glance at Mary at the foot of the Cross, will cause a drop of balm to fall on the deepest and most painful wounds.[7]

To prepare for ordination Bergoglio had gone on an eight-day retreat. It was a chance to scroll through his life thus far and meet God hidden in it all, to give thanks for the graces received and to ask pardon for those he had refused. In one prayer session of, he later recalled, "great spiritual intensity," he penned a personal *credo* (meaning "I believe").

> *I want to believe in God the Father, who loves me like a child, and in Jesus, the Lord, who infused my life with his Spirit, to make me smile and so carry me to the eternal Kingdom of life.*
>
> *I believe in the Church.*
>
> *I believe in my life story, which was pierced by God's loving gaze, who on that spring day of 21st September, came out to meet me to invite me to follow Him.*
>
> *I believe in my pain, made fruitless by the egotism in which I take refuge.*
>
> *I believe in the stinginess of my soul, which seeks to take without giving.*
>
> *I believe in the goodness of others, and that I must love them without fear and without betraying them, never seeking my own security.*
>
> *I believe in the religious life.*
>
> *I believe I wish to love a lot.*

I believe in the burning death of each day, from which I flee but which smiles at me, inviting me to accept her.

I believe in God's patience, as good and welcoming as a summer's night.

I believe that Dad is with the Lord in Heaven.

I believe that Father Duarte is there, too, interceding for my priesthood.

I believe in Mary, my Mother, who loves me and will never leave me alone.

And I believe in the surprise of each day, in which will be manifest love, strength, betrayal, and sin, which will be always with me until that definitive encounter with that marvelous face which I do not know, which always escapes me, but which I wish to know and love. Amen.[8]

The quirky credo showed how deeply ingrained, by now, was his sense of identity as a Jesuit, one who was both—as the Jesuits put it—"flawed and called." On the eve of ordination he had the three things a person most needed to thrive: the knowledge he was loved, activity that was meaningful, and a future in which to hope. He was in a state of what Saint Ignatius called consolation, with direct heart-knowledge of God's presence and a sense of the essential goodness of the world.

Jorge's awareness of his sinfulness—a core egotism and stinginess—had led him not to self-loathing but to a deep confidence in God's tender care for him. Nor was there any doubt in his mind that, fifteen years after the event, he had been chosen on that spring day in 1953. Despite the loss of his father and his confessor, he did not feel alone. From a decade of daily prayer, attendance at Mass, immersion in Scripture, examining his conscience, and sitting before the Eucharist had come a deepening awareness of being carried by those he could no longer see or touch. And he had learned, in that time of turbulence in the Catholic world, to trust the Church and religious life, confident that the Holy Spirit was working through them to bring him home, eventually, to God.

Following graduation in theology at the end of the following year, 1970, he went to Spain for his tertianship, the last stage in a Jesuit's formation that would prepare him for final vows. Bergoglio spent his in Alcalá de Henares, a turreted city to the east of Madrid where Ignatius had spent time in the 1520s studying and giving spiritual exercises. For five months, between September 1970 and April 1971, Bergoglio lived with a dozen recently ordained Jesuits from Spain, Latin America, the United States, and Japan in a college considered an early-Jesuit jewel. There he studied the newly rediscovered *Constitutions*, and for the second time in his life he sank into the monthlong *Exercises*: it had been twelve years since he had done them in the novitiate, but this time both he and the Society as a whole understood so much more about how they should be done. Outside the retreat, they visited patients at the small Antezana hospital, where Saint Ignatius had once acted as cook and infirmarian, and a women's prison known as La Galera.

It was Jorge's first time in Europe, and a chance to encounter in the flesh places he knew well from books, not just those linked to Saint Ignatius and the early Jesuits but also the Castilian frontier towns whose cobbled streets still spoke of Golden Age mystics, saints, and playwrights. One of his fellow tertians, Jesús María Alemany, accompanied him on many of these excursions to Madrid, Salamanca, Segovia, and Avila. The Spanish Jesuit was struck by the Argentine's simplicity, love of soccer, and spiritual depth, and remembers him as self-effacing, affable, austere, yet sociable, with firm convictions.

He spent Christmas in Pamplona with the family of another of the Spanish tertians, José Enrique Ruiz de Galarreta, who remembers the Argentine as formidably clever and engaging company. From Pamplona they went exploring the Roncal Valley in the Pyrenees, close to the French border. Afterward, Bergoglio spent some weeks on pilgrimage to two landmarks in Saint Ignatius's journey: his birthplace of Loyola and the Benedictine monastery of Montserrat near Barcelona.

Back in Argentina he was now "considered apt to be a Jesuit," but did not take his final vows until two years later, on April 22, 1973. In a chapel in the Colegio Máximo, in the presence of the provincial, Father Ricardo O'Farrell, representing the general, he renewed the vows of poverty, chastity, and obedience he had taken at the end of his novitiate thirteen years earlier, promising to remain forever in the Jesuits "according to the manner of life established in the Apostolic Letters of the Society of Jesus." He went on to take the fourth vow promising "a special obedience to the sovereign pontiff in regard to the missions." He then moved to a side chapel in order to make further private vows added by Saint Ignatius to forestall ecclesiastical careerism and spiritual worldliness. Bergoglio promised never to amend the *Constitutions* in respect of poverty, except to make them more strict; never to "strive for ambition" for any high office in the Church or the Jesuits; and made a final promise that, even if made a bishop, he would still take advice from the Jesuit general. The vows had been designed in the sixteenth century, thinking of the centuries ahead and anticipating that Jesuits might be tempted to be bishops. But not even the farsighted Ignatius contemplated one being made pope.

Two years earlier, shortly after his return to Argentina from Spain, Bergoglio was made novice master, a key role in the province. After the drought of 1970, the trickle of vocations that followed—three in 1971, four in 1972—needed nurturing. His experience as assistant to the previous novice master and his work with Fiorito on the spiritual renewal of the province made him an obvious candidate. But entrusting the care of novices to a thirty-five-year-old was still unusual.

Bergoglio's new novitiate, unlike his own before the Council, gave the novices space to become aware of their inner spiritual motions, while having a strong apostolate among the poor. He was inspired by the Jesuit French mystics, especially the seventeenth-century Louis Lallemant who, like Bergoglio, had a gift for spiritual direction and formation. As had Fiorito and Bergoglio in the late 1960s, Lallemant sought in his own time to retrieve the "interior spirit" from the more regimented strain of formation that won out in the century after Ignatius's death, which stressed obedience to rules and human effort to cultivate the virtues. Lallemant saw this as a distortion of Saint Ignatius who, he writes in his *Spiritual Doctrine* of 1665, "lays greater stress on the interior law which the Holy Spirit writes in the heart, than on the constitutions and exterior rules." Bergoglio believed, like Lallemant, that "the sum of the spiritual life consists in observing the ways and the movements of the Spirit of God in our soul, and in fortifying our will in the resolution of following them."

The interior freedom that Bergoglio encouraged was supported by an austere and humble environment: the wearing of cassocks, work in the gardens, ministering to the sick, and apostolate among the poor, as well as the regular practice of the *examen* and a timetable punctuated by prayer. Father Angel Rossi remembers his novitiate at this time with great fondness. It was austere, prayerful, and purposeful, "very serious, but not closed in any way," he says. "There was a certain discipline, but in no way was it conservative."

Bergoglio lived with the novices at the Villa Bailari until his nomination as provincial in July 1973. It was not far from the Máximo, where at this time he was also made vice-rector and professor of pastoral theology—the most practical kind, designed to equip priests in their ministries, which included topics such as the administration of the sacraments, homiletics, pastoral care, and ethics. He was now, as he had foreseen he would be all those years ago in Chile, a *formator* of young souls, who had the solemn task of projecting an idealized version of a Jesuit.

TOGETHER with his fellow Jesuit, the theologian Father Jacinto Luzzi, Bergoglio in 1971 began giving spiritual support to leaders of a Peronist movement called the Guardia de Hierro ("Iron Guard"), in the Jesuits' Salvador University (USAL). When this link came to light after Francis's election, it was assumed that the Guardia was inspired by a Romanian fascist organization of the same name. In fact, it was named after the Puerta de Hierro ("Iron Gate") in northeast Madrid where Perón lived in exile. And far from being right-wing, it was committed to keeping alive the original, worker-based, social-justice Peronist platform of the 1940s.

Originally part of the Peronist Resistance formed in the early 1960s to coordinate responses to the army's anti-Peronist purges, the Guardia objected to the leftward lurch of the Resistance under John William Cooke. Its leaders went to Madrid in 1967 and 1968 to meet Perón, who convinced them to become political foot soldiers, building up cadres and leaders by organizing in the barrios and teaching Peronist doctrine. By 1973, the Guardia had around four thousand fully formed members and some fifteen thousand activists, mostly in Greater Buenos Aires and Rosario. From around 1970, as part of the tidal wave of support among young people for Peronism in those years, the Guardia acquired many adherents in the USAL.

The Guardia was one of almost twenty different organizations that in the late 1960s made up the huge network of militants known as the Juventud Peronista ("Peronist Youth"), which was mobilizing for Perón's return. Within the JP, there were both large left-wing revolutionary groups (dominated in the 1970s by the montoneros) and small right-wing ones, and others in the intermediate, or "orthodox," area in between, of which the Guardia was the largest and most important.

Unlike the upper-middle-class montoneros, the *guardianes* came from the organic Peronist milieux of working-class and lower-middle-class Argentines, and could therefore claim, unlike the guerrillas, to be a genuine people's movement. The Guardia were highly critical of the montoneros' Marxist and violent deviations from authentic Peronism, which they saw as not just immoral but a strategic political error that would cost lives for no purpose. But in 1971, when Bergoglio got to know them, they were coming to terms with the painful truth that the montoneros' wild popularity among young people was a result of Perón's strategic blessing.

Within the Salvador University, there were three political groupings, each with their own Jesuit chaplain. The conservative one, favorable to the Onganía military dictatorship, seen as a bulwark against communism, was close to Father Alfredo Sáenz; a second, linked to Father Alberto Sily, was the montonero group, which favored armed revolution; while the third group, who looked to Bergoglio and Luzzi, was made up of the *guardianes*: traditional or orthodox Peronist activists and intellectuals preparing the ground for Perón's return.

Julio Bárbaro, one of the Guardia's leaders at the USAL who went on to be a Peronist deputy, recalls that Bergoglio and Luzzi were among the few priests who understood the Guardia and supported its commitment to an authentic, nonviolent, *pueblo*-oriented Peronism. "Bergoglio was completely different from the Third World [MSTM] priests," he recalls. "While they went into politics to make up for what was lacking in their faith, he stayed close to his faith and from there sought to enrich politics. He said what mattered was not ideology but witness." While he shared intellectual interests with the *guardianes*, he was always a pastor, Bárbaro adds. "If you were Peronist and you approached him, he supported you, gave you catechesis, sought to deepen your faith. It wasn't a political involvement as such. He was a priest who happened to be Peronist, rather than a Peronist priest."

The *guardianes* offered a natural political and intellectual home for Bergoglio, who both influenced and was influenced by them. He introduced them, for example, to the French novelist and radical essayist León Bloy, whom Francis quoted in his first homily ("He who does not pray to the Lord prays to the devil") and whose purist, radical, and orthodox Catholicism was a good fit with the Guardia's Peronism. Among other books on the Guardia's reading list were classics on political and military strategy, including ones by the British military theoretician Basil Liddell Hart, pioneer of the so-called indirect approach. Some of his precepts help to explain Bergoglio's own tactics: avoiding direct confrontation, while gradually weakening the enemy's resistance in indirect ways, then moving suddenly, when least expected.

The most influential Guardia intellectual in the USAL was Amelia Podetti, whom Bergoglio met in 1970, and who introduced him to left-wing nationalist thinkers like Arturo Jauretche and Raúl Scalabrini Ortiz. She taught the ideas of both at the university and later at the Colegio Máximo, while editing *Hechos y Ideas*, a Peronist political journal that Bergoglio read. Until her premature death in 1981 she was one of a group of thinkers—among them the Uruguayan philosopher Alberto Methol Ferré—who saw the Church as key to the emergence of a new Latin-American continental consciousness, *la patria grande*, which would take its place in the modern world and become an important influence on it. This was Bergoglio's intellectual family—a Catholic nationalism that looked to the *pueblo*, rather than to the state, and beyond Argentina to Latin America; and which saw Medellín as the beginning of a journey to the continent becoming a beacon for the Church and the world.

❧

BERGOGLIO was given another major responsibility in 1972 when he was appointed a consultor, one of five Jesuits named to advise the provincial, Ricardo O'Farrell. A year later, Bergoglio was made provincial after O'Farrell was forced to stand down early in the midst of a crisis in the province. The crisis had many dimensions, but one very clear symptom. In the early 1960s, there had been more than 400 Jesuits in the Argentine province, including more than 100 in formation, 25 of whom were novices. By 1973 the province had 243 Jesuits including 9 in formation and only 2 novices. Those numbers were bad even in relation to other Jesuit provinces at the time.

The Argentine province was unsure of its identity, and increasingly divided. Progressive experiments and reforms under O'Farrell had exposed divisions among the Argentine Jesuits over how to implement the renewal called for at the 1965 Jesuit gathering in Rome, General Congregation 31. Father Orlando Yorio recalled taking part in many provincial meetings between 1969 and 1972 "in which there appeared major insoluble problems arising from positions and expectations that were opposed to each other."[9] Yorio, a friend of Father Mugica's, was the unofficial leader of a group of Third-Worldist Jesuits. O'Farrell allowed Yorio, together with Franz Jalics, who was among the first signatories of the MSTM declaration, to live in a new kind of "insertion" community in the barrio of Ituzaingó, initially with six theology students.

O'Farrell's encouragement of the Third-Worldist group was scandalous to a religious order that was deeply embedded in the Argentine establishment. The Society ran two of the country's most prestigious schools whose graduates occupied leading positions in society, or themselves became Jesuits, linked by blood and natural affinity to judges and generals and business leaders. Many of the Jesuits were from army families, and there were four Jesuit military chaplains resident in the observatory behind the Colegio Máximo. They did not take kindly to the idea of Jesuits in the *villas miseria* encouraging or theologically justifying the guerrillas, and regarded the MSTM's criticism of the Church hierarchy as intolerable.

Another point of contention was the Salvador University in Buenos Aires, created by the Jesuits in 1956. O'Farrell had named a commission of five Jesuits to reform the USAL administration, but with little success. A generous grant scheme to allow poor people to study had resulted in low attendance, and the professors were on meager salaries, creating a further social justice dilemma. As well as hemorrhaging money—the university had a debt of US$2 million—it had become ungovernable. There were complaints about laxity—a number of Jesuits had left to marry students—while its student body was dominated by the Marxist and Peronist left, which organized repeated sit-ins and strikes. A number of the professors—including the two liberationist Jesuits, Sily and Yorio—were close to the MSTM and the guerrillas, while two priests who acted as chaplains to the montoneros—Mugica and Alberto Carbone (on whose typewriter the montoneros wrote their first communiqué)—gave courses there.

O'Farrell's reform of the Jesuit formation syllabus, which he entrusted to the group led by Yorio (after appointing him vice-dean of theology at the Máximo in 1969), was for many the tipping point. Yorio's mélange of philosophy and theology, known as the curriculum, was heavy on sociology and Hegelian dialectics, and suppressed the juniorate period of humanities studies, considering it bourgeois. Yorio's many critics—among them Bergoglio—saw this reform not as a return to Ignatian sources but an ideological assault on them.

In 1972, a group of senior Jesuits in the Argentine province petitioned Father Arrupe to remove O'Farrell as provincial, and he agreed: O'Farrell would step down in 1973 after just four years of his six-year term. The consultors were tasked with drawing up a *terna*, a list of three names, of who might succeed him. In the course of Bergoglio's travels and discussions with 184 priests and 46 brothers in more than fifteen Jesuit communities, many of them reached the conclusion that it was the young consultor himself who should be elected. O'Farrell's natural successor, Father Joaquín Ruíz Escribano, had been killed in a car accident when returning from Córdoba, and the generation above was too divided—hence the desire to skip a generation. Among the depleted ranks of the younger Jesuits, Bergoglio was the standout leader.

The province's sage, Father Fiorito, was Bergoglio's promoter. In his work on the *Exercises*, Fiorito had been promoting a renewal that was true to the original charism of the Jesuits, one that could unite the province following years of experimentation and division and attract new vocations. Fiorito was not himself a natural leader, but he knew one who was. He had seen Bergoglio's natural gifts—wisdom, astuteness, courage—firsthand, as well as his knowledge of Jesuit primary sources and his capacity for spiritual discernment.

The province turned to Bergoglio, recalls Father Ignacio Pérez del Viso, because they perceived that "too much promotion of social justice could lead us to forget the religious dimension" and that "his solid roots in spirituality would allow him to keep a balance." It was his first mandate for reform. Yet Pérez del Viso was not the only one concerned about Bergoglio's inexperience. Not only was he young, but he had never even been the superior of a Jesuit house. Only in mission territories would Jesuits ever choose a provincial who had never been a superior. Being in charge of novices was one thing, but what experience had he of neurotic people, sick people, alcoholics, or relationship conflicts? It was too much to put on one so green. Yet people insisted that "we were in a special moment that required a young and decisive helmsman like Bergoglio," he recalls.

"Bergoglio was our *piloto de tormentas* ('storm pilot')," is how another Jesuit, Father Fernando Albistur, puts it.[10]

"I was only thirty-six years old," Pope Francis later told his interviewer Father Spadaro. "That was crazy."

To draw up the *terna*, the consultors in June 1973 went on a retreat in La Rioja led by its bishop, Enrique Angelelli.

A few weeks before, on May 25, the military regime had abdicated, turning over the government to civilian rule, after the Peronists obtained more than 50 percent of the votes in the March elections. The way was now set for Perón's return in June and elections in October, which he won with a massive majority. As part of the army's relinquishing of power, 370 prisoners detained for terrorist offenses were set free—part of a fruitless bid to draw a line under the growing guerrilla violence.

With Perón's return, the montoneros temporarily abandoned their armed struggle, but the ERP only intensified its campaign. In the same month that the Jesuits were on their retreat in La Rioja, sensing that the moment was ripe for revolution, the ERP carried out three murders, five kidnappings of businessmen, and a number of major arms seizures. Perón's return on June 20, meanwhile, showed just how violently split his movement had become: right-wing Peronists fired on left-wing Peronists at Ezeiza airport, resulting in the deaths of 16 and 433 wounded. It was a mild skirmish compared with what was to come. By early 1974 the Triple A (Argentine Anticommunist Alliance) death squad had begun its activities, a covert attempt by the Peronist government to meet guerrilla violence with mayhem of its own.

Tensions were also running high in La Rioja, where there were a number of Jesuit missionaries. The Jesuits were close to Bishop Angelelli and wanted to support him in his increasingly fraught support for landless workers. The day before the consultors' retreat the bishop had gone to say Mass for the missionaries and people in one of his parishes, Anillaco, where he was met by a lynch mob of angry farmworkers sent by local landowners. The bishop had backed a bid by unions to take over water reservoirs on land vacated by a family who had returned to Italy, which led to the landowners denouncing them as communists. Although Angelelli escaped on this occasion, he was a marked man and would be killed by the army not long after the coup in 1976.

Recalling the consultors' retreat thirty years after that murder, Cardinal Bergoglio in 2006 described "unforgettable days, in which we received the wisdom of a pastor who dialogued with his people" during which they had learned of "the stoning which that people and their pastor endured, simply because they followed the Gospel."

Later that year, when Bergoglio was in Rome to take a course, he accepted an invitation from the Israeli government to go on pilgrimage in early October to the Holy Land. Yet almost as soon as he arrived in the American Colony Hotel in Jerusalem's Arab quarter, the Yom Kippur War (when Egypt and Syria invaded Israel) broke out. He spent a day and a half visiting the Old City, including the Holy Sepulcher, Ein Kerem, and Bethlehem, but was afterward confined to his hotel. There he spent six days reading books on Saint Paul's letters to the Corinthians he borrowed from the library of the Jesuits' Pontifical Biblical Institute in West Jerusalem, as the air filled with the drones of planes and sirens. The rector of the Institute at the time was Father Carlo Maria Martini, the future cardinal archbishop of Milan, whom Bergoglio probably met here for the first time.[11]

IN the early 1970s, Bergoglio began to use an expression that captured a key and enduring element in his thinking. In his 2012 radio interview with Father Isasmendi, the then cardinal recalled that in the events of 1970 and 1971

> There was a lot of talk at that time about "the people," *el pueblo*, but you didn't know what they meant when they used the term. The politicians talked about *el pueblo*, the intellectuals talked about *el pueblo*, what *el pueblo* was calling for . . . but what did they mean? We priests must talk to a "people," but a very special people. In the Bible we appear as a "holy people"; Saint Peter talks about a "holy people rescued by the blood of Christ" and invites us to be faithful to that call. . . . The people who follow Jesus always look to Jesus, and

the Virgin, and have a basic fidelity pointing in that direction, and so little by little I started to talk about the holy people of God, the faithful people. The expression that I really like is *santo pueblo fiel de Dios*, "God's holy faithful people."

While reading Denzinger's *Enchiridion*—a widely used compendium of church traditions—Bergoglio had been struck by an early-church formula of Christian faith: that the faithful people was infallible *in credendo*, in its believing. The Vatican II document, *Lumen Gentium*, had recast the Church not as an institution so much as a people, the "People of God"; from Denzinger he had grasped that the "people" was also a repository of faith. As Bergoglio later wrote: "When you want to know *what* the Church teaches, you go to the Magisterium . . . but when you want to know *how* the Church teaches, you go to the faithful people. The Magisterium will teach you who is Mary, but the faithful people will teach you how to love Mary."[12]

In his first talk as provincial, Bergoglio would use this notion to reject ideologies. From now on, the idea would appear constantly in his writings. The *pueblo fiel* were both vaccine and antidote, the hermeneutic of a true reform.

Although this was his own thinking, it is also redolent of a specifically Argentine post-conciliar strain of liberation theology known as the *teología del pueblo*, or "theology of the people." For many years it was little known, and not seen as a liberation theology at all outside Argentina, where it was associated above all with three priests: Lucio Gera, Rafael Tello, and the Jesuit Juan Carlos Scannone.

Gera was the pioneer. A teacher at the Villa Devoto seminary in Buenos Aires, he was one of the official invited theologians at Medellín and was a key contributor to the bishops' San Miguel declaration in 1969. He and Tello were initially part of the discussions that led to the MSTM but left over what they regarded as its unacceptable embrace of Marxism.

In the years 1972 and 1973, before he was made provincial, Bergoglio, along with Scannone, was on the editorial board of the Jesuits' widely respected theology journal *Stromata*, which in the early 1970s held a series of important symposia at the Colegio Máximo on the big themes of the day: dependency, socialization, and liberation. Because spirituality, rather than theology, was his specialist area, Bergoglio did not contribute to the journal or to the discussions following the papers, but these two streams of liberation theology were swirling around him. Both started from the Church's reflections at Medellín on the historic quest for liberation, but whereas liberation theologians at the time used Marxist categories for analyzing and transforming reality, the Argentine theologians around Gera started with the culture and religiosity of *el pueblo*, which naturally resisted both Marxist and liberal ideologies.

Who is *el pueblo*? In a 1973 article that ran in *Stromata* the following year, Gera defined it in terms of the despised and marginalized majority, from whom comes the desire for justice and peace. For Gera, *el pueblo* is an active agent of history, not, as liberals and Marxists view it, a passive mass needing to be made aware. "The people have a rationality," wrote Gera. "They have their project; we don't give it to them." The role of theologians was not to impose categories, he argued, but to interpret the people's project in light of its salvation history. Gera put it starkly. "Either theology is the expression of the People of God or it is nothing."[13]

Scannone elucidated other key differences between a Marxist-influenced liberation theology and the *teología del pueblo*. Where the first saw the people as an essentially socioeconomic or class category (the proletariat, the landless peasants) in opposition to a dominant class or bourgeoisie, the second saw the people as a historic and cultural, even symbolic category, that includes those who share in the common project of liberation, whatever their status. The first saw the history of the Latin-American people as one of oppression until the socialist revolution appeared on the scene; whereas the second sees in its culture and history a process of liberation that began long ago, even if awaiting its full expression. The "sapiential rationality" of this "popular culture" is not that of the Enlightenment, "nor does it correspond with the canons of modern technological and instrumental reasoning," Scannone argued. "But that does not make it any less human, rational, and logical, nor any less usable for theology."

Scannone and Gera's theology was suspicious not just of enlightened elites seeing history through the prism of their ideologies, but wary of elitism of any sort. Whether in liberalism, Marxism, or clericalism, Gera saw an elite attempt to arrogate the power to determine how the "people" should think or act, and therefore a denial of the "prophetic charism" that a Christian people has by virtue of their belonging to Christ. "Renouncing elitism in the area of possession and ownership is not enough," wrote

Scannone. "We must also renounce the elitism in the area of knowledge that we now find among the enlightened elites of both the left and the right."[14]

Bergoglio did not take direct part in these debates; he was not a theologian and was wary of being ensnared by labels. But his own view of history, both national and Christian, pointed him in the same direction. In the idea of "God's holy faithful people" Bergoglio had what theologians call a hermeneutic—an interpretative key, or yardstick—that would allow him to reform and unite the province, beyond ideology, by focusing very directly on the poor. It was neither conservative—he did not share the pro-elite Catholic nation stance of the pro-Onganía bishops—nor clerical: he did not believe that the clergy, or the bishops, or Rome were in possession of the truth that they distributed downward, but that the Holy Spirit was revealed through a dialogue between the *pueblo fiel* and the universal Church. It was a radical stance, an option for the ordinary people, the fishermen and shepherds to whom God revealed Himself in Jesus Christ two thousand years ago.

Although a non-Peronist could in theory support people theology, its adherents were natural Peronists. They identified with the popular Catholic nationalist tradition, as opposed to a liberal, conservative, or socialist viewpoint, and saw their task as walking with the Peronists as the expression of the people. Typical of the people-theology Jesuits was Ernesto López Rosas, the author of an important work on the Christian values of Peronism.[15]

Not only was Bergoglio close to the Guardia, but in February and March 1974—via a friend, Colonel Vicente Damasco, who was a close collaborator of Perón's—he was one of a dozen experts invited to contribute his thoughts to a draft of the *Modelo Nacional*, a political testament that Perón conceived as a means of uniting Argentines after his death. (It was finished before he died, but then ignored by his widow Isabel, who sidelined Colonel Damasco.)[16] When Perón died in July, Bergoglio celebrated a Mass, and sent a letter to the province mourning the general, pointing out that he had been democratically elected three times and was therefore "anointed" by the people. Yet Bergoglio's respect for and identification with Peronism as the vehicle for the popular values of the *pueblo fiel* did not make him a party activist. The *pueblo fiel* preceded Perón, indeed had shaped him and his movement, and delegated to him the task of government; the *pueblo fiel* was therefore a standpoint also from which to critique Peronism—whether the revolutionary version of it created by the middle-class guerrillas or its later incarnations.

In the highly politicized Church of the early 1970s, however, the pro-Peronist people-theology Jesuits inevitably clashed with liberals and Radicals in the Society, and with Marxist liberationists like Yorio. In a 1974 *Stromata* article Yorio took it for granted that socialism was the political expression of the Gospel, and Marxism its partner in bringing it about, while the ERP and the montoneros—middle-class students or graduates engaged at this point in large-scale terrorist operations—were the means by which the "poor" defended themselves from unjust oppression. Yorio noted approvingly that "the Peronist special formations and other armed groups inspired by Marxism are an attempt to respond to this need of an armed force that can guarantee the reality of a popular socialism."[17]

The irony was that the embracing or justification of revolutionary warfare by middle-class Catholics like Yorio was nothing if not elitist. As Richard Gillespie notes in his classic study of the montoneros, *Soldiers of Perón*, "The launching of the urban guerrillas was an initiative 'from above,' the decision of small groups of militants rather than a response to a widespread popular demand." Despite their initial success in attracting recruits in the early 1970s, the guerrillas were never able to transform their "special formations" into anything close to a mass movement, while representing—to a far greater extent than the Red Brigades in Italy or the Bader Meinhof in Germany—a major threat to the peace and stability of Argentine society. Their campaign of terrorism and the genocidal policy with which the armed forces responded to it after 1976 look, in retrospect, like a civil war between two middle-class factions, which the poor, the ordinary folk—Gera's ignored majority, Bergoglio's *pueblo fiel*—watched as bystanders from the sidelines.

SHORTLY after the new provincial moved into the Jesuit curia on Bogotá Street in the geographic center of Buenos Aires, Bergoglio had a visit from the general, Father Arrupe. In August 1973 they went to La Rioja, where Bergoglio had been just four months earlier, to visit the Jesuit missionaries there—they ran four parishes, tending to the destitute in remote areas—but had a secondary mission, entrusted to them by Pope Paul VI, to lend public support to Bishop Angelelli. Their arrival, heralded in the press, was not easy. Arriving by plane from Córdoba, pilot and passengers were told to stay on the runway. After what seemed an eternity, the bishop eventually arrived in a car to take them off the plane and out by a back entrance. It turned out that the same thugs hired to stone Angelelli in Anillaco had been sent to the airport to jeer at Arrupe.[18]

Pope Francis—who spent a long time praying before Arrupe's tomb in September 2013—told his interviewer Father Spadaro that Don Pedro "had the right attitude and he made the right decisions." During many hours on that visit they formed a close bond that would last over the difficult years ahead. Arrupe encouraged him to carry through the renewal of Jesuit formation, to focus on priorities at a time of dwindling resources, and to encourage vocations by giving the province a sense of unity and identity.

Carlos Pauli, then a young teacher at La Inmaculada school, recalls a weekend in 1974 when Bergoglio came to give the staff a retreat in a local farmhouse belonging to the college. They were amazed at his youth, but also at his pep talk, which explained the distinction between ideology and Christian hope, and how the latter was incarnate in the ordinary, "non-enlightened" Argentine *pueblo fiel*. "He showed how ideologies instrumentalize the poor, and seek a kind of total explanation of reality, whereas Christian hope is beyond all ideologies because it makes room for God to act," Pauli remembers. "It was a very tense time politically, and it was incredible to hear this kind of language from a senior churchman."

That was also the message in his first address to the province in February 1974, when Bergoglio invited the Jesuits to overcome their "sterile intra-ecclesiastical contradictions" in order to embark on "a true apostolic strategy." It was a robust speech that warned against fruitless conflicts with the bishops, enervating conflicts between "progressive" and "reactionary" wings, and of Jesuits pursuing their own ideas rather than God's plans. He deployed the subtle discernments of the Second Week of the *Exercises* to teach that the will of God is not to be identified with a person's own vision or project of the good. "The only real enemy," he told the Jesuits, "is the enemy of God's plan. The real problem is the problem raised by the enemy in order to impede God's plan. This is the key that will enable us to distinguish what is essential from what is secondary, what is authentic from what is false. This is the foundation on which our unity and our apostolic discipline depend."

Bergoglio went on to identify their temptations as Jesuits as a certain "avant-gardism" and "elitism" as well as "a fascination for abstract ideologies that do not match our reality." In a veiled reference to Gera and Scannone's "people's theology" he welcomed "a healthy allergy" developing among Argentine Jesuits to "theories that have not emerged from our national reality." And he laid out his God's-holy-faithful-people hermeneutic as a vaccine against the prevailing ideologies and political violence, inviting the Jesuits to see that if they were sincere about putting the people first, they would align themselves with its values.

> This believing people neither separates its religious faith from its historical aspirations nor does it confuse the two in a revolutionary messianism. This people believes in the resurrection and the life: salvation, work, bread, everyday understanding in their families. For their country, what they believe in is peace. There are some who think that this is not revolutionary. But the people themselves, who are asking for peace, know full well that this peace is the fruit of justice.[19]

Bergoglio's first reform had three key elements: integrating and consolidating people and property, redeploying Jesuits to the periphery, and encouraging vocations while renewing formation. Each objective served, in its way, his overall goal of depoliticizing the province and refocusing it on the Jesuits' pastoral mission.

The first priority was to integrate a scattered and disunified province. Valuable properties in Mendoza and Córdoba—including the building where he had spent his novitiate—were sold to cover the USAL debt prior to its handover. The decision to relinquish the USAL was encouraged by Father Arrupe, who believed that at a time of diminishing manpower it made little sense to run two Catholic universities in Buenos Aires (the Jesuits also had the Catholic University, UCA) in addition to those in Córdoba and Salta.

The lay people to whom the provincial handed over the USAL were former leaders in the Guardia de Hierro, which had disbanded following Perón's return and election in October 1973 and would be officially dissolved after his death in July 1974. Not only did Bergoglio trust them— they were charged with creating a university on Jesuit principles, in tune with Argentine popular values—but his close relationship with them smoothed the transition. This was a time for "creative courage" and for "wisdom to know how to detect the real enemies and their plans," he told USAL's newly established civil association during the handover in May 1975, before praising them as "the only possible guarantee of the preservation of the Universidad del Salvador's identity."

The handover took until March 1975. The Jesuits would continue to offer pastoral support but would neither teach in nor run the USAL. But they supplied the vision. At the request of the new directors, Bergoglio drew up a charter committing the university to a three-point mission statement, "History and Change," which is unmistakably his: the prime mover of change must be the faith of the people, "despised by the arrogance of the enlightened, which has characterized it as credulity and alienation," while the future is brought about by "deepening the path already traveled" rather than the "servile imitation of foreign models or the abandonment of what is ours."

Yet what Bergoglio saw as depoliticizing the USAL others saw as politicizing it in a different way. Both the Jesuit left—priests like Yorio and Sily—and liberal establishment Jesuits such as Father Fernando Storni, a Radical Party sympathizer, regarded the USAL handover to Bergoglio's "friends in the Guardia" as a betrayal for which they never forgave him.

Another decision that provoked opposition was the closure of the Jesuit "insertion" communities that had sprung up in O'Farrell's period as provincial. Bergoglio wanted to consolidate the existing residences, but he also believed in the young and old mixing; by dissolving the small communities, he sought to bolster the life of residences and increase the Jesuits' sense of belonging at a time of decreasing numbers. But it was also a way of bringing back into the fold the outliers—Third-Worldists who were critiquing bishops and egging on guerrillas—whose priesthood and religious life were at risk. By the end of 1974 he had dissolved all but the one led by Yorio, who was challenging his decision.

The second objective was to deploy Jesuits to Argentina's outlying areas to evangelize among the poor in line with the vision of Medellín. In some respects this was the counterpart of the closing of the insertion communities—to send out to the periphery those who had grown too comfortable in the residences. He expanded missions in far-flung places of desperate poverty, such as the five parishes in La Rioja, and opened others in San José del Boquerón, in Santiago del Estero, where Jesuits had been missionaries before their expulsion in the eighteenth century. He also sent men to the native village of Santa Victoria in Salta, in the far north of the country along the Bolivian border, and to remote missions in Jujuy and Tucumán—in each case, working among the very poorest. In order to reach more places, he created a roving team of a dozen priests who would "mission" together in one place for some months before moving to the next. As novices began to arrive, they would be sent to those missions for their "experiments."

In the late 1970s, he sent young Jesuits to shore up the Society's ministries in Ecuador. When this met with the objection that the Argentine province was short of men, Bergoglio's response, recalls Father Albistur, was, "We Jesuits are not about holding on to people; we're about sending people on mission to wherever the need is greatest."[20]

Closer to home, Bergoglio created a new apostolate in the worker barrios surrounding the Colegio Máximo, which expanded in the late 1970s as new vocations began to arrive. He also gave his support to the work of Jesuits in the *villas miseria* of Buenos Aires—Yorio in Bajo Flores, as well as Father "Pichi" Meisegeier, who worked with Mugica in Villa 31 next to Retiro station—despite the fact that, as he would tell a 2010 inquiry, "at that time it was assumed that priests who worked with the poor were *zurdos* ('commies')." Even when the Triple A death squad began picking off shantytown priests, Bergoglio did not pull them out. But after Mugica was gunned down outside the church of San Francisco Solano in May 1974, Bergoglio told them not to go around alone and to stay in after dark.

The third priority was vocations. Bergoglio formed a team under Father Jorge Camargo to organize discernment retreats for young people, going from school to school. The results were soon apparent. The 1970s were a time of rising vocations in the Argentine Church in general, as young people turned away from politics, but the Jesuits were especially favored: five novices in 1975 rose each year to reach fourteen in 1978, after which they oscillated between twenty-eight and thirty-four a year, levels exceeding even the early 1960s. As the pipeline filled back up, Father Camargo was asked by the Jesuit curia in Rome to share the province's secrets.

At least part of the recipe was Bergoglio's articulation of a renewed vision of Jesuit life based on the early, missionary days of the Society. He not only attracted new vocations but kept them: annual departures in the late 1970s and 1980s dropped to just a trickle. He named as novice master another close Fiorito collaborator, Father Andrés Swinnen, and visited the novices at least once a week, encouraging them to pray for vocations—something he urged on the whole province. He also asked them to say novenas—a traditional Catholic prayer cycle—for vocations of Jesuit brothers, who were at that time dying out: there were about thirty, mostly in their seventies. By the 1980s, twenty-three had joined.

Bergoglio relied not just on his own strategic efforts, but on the Lord of Miracles—a popular Salta devotion—to whom he pledged that once new vocations reached thirty-five in a year, he would send them on pilgrimage to the shrine. When that number was reached in September 1979, just as Bergoglio's time as provincial was coming to a close, he dispatched to Salta a platoon of shiny new novices.[21]

BERGOGLIO was one of 237 delegates from ninety provinces in five continents summoned to Rome for the 32nd General Congregation of the Society of Jesus. Unlike almost all previous such assemblies, GC32—held over thirteen weeks between December 1974 and March 1975—had been called not to elect a new general but to consolidate the Jesuits' post-conciliar renewal.

Father Arrupe hoped thereby to quell the rebellions in Spain, where restorationists had lobbied Rome to create a new autonomous province dependent directly on the Holy See that looked much like the nineteenth-century Society. Pope Paul VI had rejected their petition, but the *ultras* continued to be active, especially in Rome, where they had the ear of senior officials and a presence in the Jesuit-run Gregorian University. On the eve of the general congregation, they had created a new network, Jesuitas en Fidelidad ("Jesuits in Fidelity"), which was lobbying against both GC32 and Arrupe.

Arrupe chose Bergoglio to head them off because he was in Church law the superior of their leader, Nicolás Puyadas, a Spanish Jesuit who had joined the Argentine province in the mid-1960s. As soon as he became provincial Bergoglio—who had as little patience with restorationists as he had with Marxists—dispatched Puyadas to Europe, where in early 1974 he published an anti-Arrupe tract. In the run-up to GC32 the Jesuits in Fidelity were distributing the book in preparation for a planned protest. In the presence of two witnesses, Bergoglio ordered Puyadas under pain of obedience to leave Rome, which the Spaniard was forced to do in order to remain a Jesuit. Together with his old Máximo colleague and now Chilean provincial, Father Fernando Montes, Bergoglio then headed to Termini rail station, where they successfully persuaded other *ultras* arriving from Spain to return home.

A more important challenge came from Pope Paul VI, who addressed the delegates at the opening of GC32 on December 3, 1974, with what was essentially a love letter with an emphatic warning. Paul VI was close to the Society, admired it, and saw it as key to implementing the Second Vatican Council. Much in his passionate speech is a reminder of the Jesuits' charism. "Wherever in the Church—even in the most difficult and extreme fields, in the crossroads of ideologies, in the social trenches—there has been and is now conversation between the deepest desires of human beings and the perennial message of the Gospel, Jesuits have been and are there," he told them. Bergoglio would later describe it as "one of the most beautiful addresses ever made to the Society by a pope."[22]

Yet it contained an urgent plea for the Jesuits not to abandon their core mission as apostolic priests under obedience. They must adapt to the age, he said, without succumbing to its temptations—skepticism, individualism, rationalism, love of novelty—nor losing their identity. Expressing alarm at the way the Jesuit renewal had in many places gone off the rails, he passionately underlined the importance and urgency of the decisions facing their future and urged them to get back on track.[23]

Some of the delegates were mystified by the address, others distressed that, while they had come to Rome to discuss poverty and justice, the pope seemed obsessed with discipline and doctrine. But for some of those present, including Bergoglio, it struck a chord. He recognized in the pope's analysis an accurate discernment of what had gone wrong in the Argentine province as well as elsewhere. In Congar's terms, Paul VI had been laying out a vision of true reform and warning them against a false version of that reform that would only lead them down blind alleys. Paul VI's allocution "in many ways shaped how Bergoglio saw the Society," says Father Swinnen, novice master at the time.

Pope Paul's warnings were prophetic. Although GC32 consolidated the Jesuit renewal, the agreement for which it is best remembered took the Society down a new and divisive track. Decree Four incorporated the pursuit of social justice as a key part of everything Jesuits did. The original purpose of the Society of Jesus in the sixteenth century had been the "defense and propagation of the faith." Now, at GC32, this became "the service of faith, of which the promotion of justice is an absolute requirement."

The decree had been driven not, as many supposed, by the Latin-American delegates, but by a group of French-speaking Europeans and Canadians, for whom it was vital to see the struggle for justice not as something outside religion but integral to it. For the Latin-American delegates, who had lived with the idea at least since Medellín in 1968, the decree offered, in that sense, little new. But unlike Medellín, Decree Four appeared to have few safeguards against being turned into an ideology; it was the fruit of a last-minute amalgamation of two texts, and vulnerable to a selective reading. Bergoglio saw two risks with it: one was of forcing Jesuits into bed with political movements pursuing justice (by what other means or agency were "unjust structures" to be tackled?); the second was the loss of identity of which Pope Paul had warned. Where did evangelization and priesthood fit in? Which came first? What stopped a Jesuit from being merely a political campaigner or social worker?

Whatever the other Latin-American delegates made of it, "Bergoglio did not have much sympathy for that Decree Four," recalls Father Swinnen. "When he was speaking to the novices he didn't quote it."

The Jesuits spent the next twenty years working out the ambiguities: in the deaths of Jesuits at the hands of right-wing dictatorships in Latin America as well as in the sudden closures, especially in Spain and Mexico, of "privileged" schools. Jesuits came to be seen as rebels, identified with the "loyal opposition" within the Church, standing with the left in politics and often against Pope John Paul II, always in the name of justice.

Three years after he was elected, John Paul II dramatically intervened in the Society, for a time suspending its constitution. After admitting at GC33 in 1983 that the interpretation of Decree Four had often "reduced the concept of justice to too-human dimensions," at GC34 in 1995 the Society amended its purpose once again, this time to make clear that there could be no promotion of justice without the promotion of faith. By that time Bergoglio was a bishop.

During his provincial address in 1978, Bergoglio made many references to GC32, but none to Decree Four. What he did quote was Paul VI's historic teaching document on evangelization, *Evangelii Nuntiandi*, issued a few months after the end of GC32 in December 1975. In it Paul VI makes clear—in line with Medellín—that there can be no proclamation of the Gospel without also attending to the liberation of people from "concrete situations of injustice." But Paul VI also warns about the Church reducing its mission to a "mere temporal project," leaving it open to "manipulation by ideological systems and political parties." That was the discerning nuance lacking in many of the applications of Decree Four.[24]

Evangelii Nuntiandi would be Bergoglio's favorite church document, the one he would cite throughout his time as provincial, rector, and later bishop. Not long after his election, Francis described it as "the greatest pastoral document ever written." Its great purpose was to reconcile eternal Church teaching with the diversity of cultures.

Considering some of the hidden hands involved in its drafting, it is easy to see why he identified so closely with it both in 1975 and since. The sections on faith taking flesh in a people (Paul VI preferred the term *culture*) as well as those valuing popular religion, were effectively an Argentine contribution, drafted by Father Gera. The insights reached the document via another Argentine, Eduardo Pironio, the former bishop of Mar del Plata who, as secretary-general of CELAM in 1967 and 1968, had been the moving spirit at Medellín. A collaborator and confessor of Paul VI, he had recently chaired the synod of bishops in Rome from which *Evangelii Nuntiandi* sprang.

That synod marked another coming-of-age moment for the Latin-American Church. Bergoglio's future collaborator, Professor Guzmán Carriquiry, has written that the synod marked the end of the "iconoclastic" phase of the post-council, which had been dominated by a "north-Atlantic crisis of authority, the failure of the Guevarist revolution, and the growing disorientation of the intellectuals."[25] The stage was now set for the second CELAM gathering at Puebla, Mexico, in 1979, whose leading light would be Gera. The way Bergoglio and his people-theology and USAL/Guardia colleagues saw it, the failure of ideology and the intellectuals was leaving history open to the advent of the *pueblo fiel*.

Cardinal Pironio can in some ways be seen as Bergoglio's precursor. His mission was the implementation of Vatican II in Latin America. He had a clear option for the poor but a wariness of ideology, and believed the Gospel offered the basis of a new model of society that transcended the capitalist-communist debate. Just as Bergoglio later would, Pironio alienated conservatives by his commitment to social justice and the left by his failure to endorse Marxist versions of liberation theology. Like Bergoglio, Pironio was no revolutionary, but something deeper: a Gospel radical with a pastoral strategy that prioritized the poor. As rector of the Máximo after 1980 and later as bishop and archbishop, Bergoglio would take that strategy—Pironio's vision, and that of *Evangelii Nuntiandi*—onto the street.

Remembering him in 2008, ten years after his death, Bergoglio described Pironio as "a man of open doors you wanted to be with." When you went to see him, "wherever and however busy he was, he made you feel as if you were the only thing that mattered." It could be many people's description of Bergoglio.[26]

They had something else in common. When Paul VI died in 1978, there was talk of Pironio—an Argentine born of an Italian family, with a Franciscan spirituality—as a possible pope. He was virtually Italian, some reasoned, so if the cardinals wanted to look to the developing world, why not this Argentine?

FOUR

CRUCIBLE

(1975–1979)

MANY COMMENTATORS SAW the day when the Vatican was hauled before the United Nations over clerical sex abuse as Francis's first major test. It was in mid-January 2014, shortly before the first anniversary of his election, and he had enjoyed spectacular media ratings. But in the weeks leading up to the Holy See's appearance before the Committee on the Rights of the Child in Geneva, Switzerland, it looked increasingly as if the Vatican was going to be given a rough ride.

On the day of the hearing, at his daily 7:00 a.m. Mass in the chapel of the Casa Santa Marta, Francis spoke of "corrupt priests" who "instead of giving the Bread of Life, give a poisoned meal to God's holy people." He stopped and shook his head in disbelief. "Are we ashamed? *So many scandals!*" Some "have led to us paying out huge sums of money," he said, adding: "Well that's good, that's how it should be. *But the shame of the Church!*" He went on to attribute "those failings of priests, bishops, lay people" to their lack of relationship to God and their worldliness. "They had a position in the Church, a position of power, even of comfort. But the Word of God, no!"

Over in Geneva, the Holy See delegates—Archbishop Silvano Tomasi and the Vatican's former top prosecutor on abuse, Bishop Charles Scicluna—were unflappable in the face of a grilling from the eighteen-strong UN committee. If there was a time when the Vatican was slow to face up to the reality of the abuse crisis, said Scicluna, today it very much "gets it." In hours of question and answer, the delegates spelled out in great detail the complex juridical relationship of the Holy See to the global Catholic Church and described the sea change in accountability and transparency over the previous decade at both the diocesan level and in the Vatican.

No other institution had been, in this area, more criticized or litigated for its historic failures, and no organization had traveled so far and so fast in ensuring they could not be repeated. The failures were well known and documented, and had been the basis of many claims, leading to payouts of millions of dollars in the United States alone. Between the 1960s and the 1980s, in common with other institutions, the Catholic Church had no proper mechanisms to understand or deal with abuse: victims were silent or were silenced, and in line with the scientific view of the time, offenders were sent off for treatment, declared "cured," and sent to new parishes and ministries, where they often abused again. In the 1990s, victims—adults now, with therapists and lawyers—began bringing lawsuits, but not even then did the issue properly surface, because compensation settlements contained confidentiality clauses. Not until the 2001 US crisis in Boston, Massachusetts, when diocesan files were turned over to the courts, did screaming headlines document the whole sad history of collusion, cover-up, and moral blindness.

What followed was wholesale change: external monitoring of strict guidelines to prevent cover-up ever again taking place; massive payouts to victims; review of files stretching back decades; the removal and defrocking of dozens of priests. The changes were not perfect or universal—there were still dioceses in Africa and Asia that lagged behind the Church elsewhere, procedures that could be sped up, bishops who had not been made to resign over their mishandling—and the issue was by no means closed. Victims continued to step forward claiming abuse decades earlier, and the healing of deep wounds inflicted by men who used their spiritual authority to violate adolescents would take generations. But in its handling of the issue the Catholic Church was—in Western countries, at least—a transformed institution whose procedures had become models for other organizations.

The Vatican, too, had moved on from its position of defensiveness and denial in the late 1990s. Rome had direct control only over the 1,000 clergy who worked in the Vatican city-state; almost all of the world's 410,000 priests were under the control of their bishops or religious orders. But the Vatican could tell bishops to take action. From 2001 Cardinal Joseph Ratzinger, later Pope Benedict XVI, had asked local bishops to send him details of each case so he could see they were not being brushed under the carpet but had been referred to police and social services. After his election in 2005, Benedict XVI asked all bishops' conferences across the world to introduce rigid guidelines that ensured past and present allegations were acted upon. At the heart of those rules was deference to local law, ensuring that police and social services were brought in as soon as an allegation was made, and that the safety and welfare of minors were paramount. The Vatican also amended its own regulations to make the process of laicization—stripping a man of his priesthood, a power reserved to the Vatican—faster and easier. Of the 3,400 cases reported by local dioceses to the Vatican between 2004 and 2011, 848 priests were laicized, while 2,572 were punished with other, lesser penalties—usually old men who had spent time in prison for their crimes, whom the Vatican told to spend the remainder of their lives in prayer and penance.[1]

Yet when the UN released its report on February 5, it was as if the Vatican had never been in Geneva and none of this had ever happened. The committee spoke as if the Church were a retrograde institution, characterizing the Holy See as a kind of corporate head office of a global corporation that subverted local laws. The report demanded that the Vatican "immediately remove" all priest abusers, accused the Holy See of imposing a "code of silence" on clergy to prevent them from going to the police and of shuffling priests within parishes, and deplored the Vatican's "policies and practices which have led to the continuation of the abuse by and the impunity of the perpetrators." Amazingly, the report went on to lecture the Vatican on policies in other areas, telling it to erase what it called gender stereotyping from the curricula of Catholic schools, alleging that its teaching on sexuality was homophobic, and declaring that the idea of male and female sexes as complementary was incompatible with modern gender theory. It even called for the Church to change its teaching on abortion, which, as some Catholics pointed out, would hardly advance the rights of the child.

Vatican spokesman Father Federico Lombardi did not hide his amazement, saying it appeared as if the report had been "practically already written, or at least already in large part blocked out before the hearing." Indeed, it looked a lot like a report sent to journalists weeks before the hearing by a little-known London-based NGO, the Child Rights International Network, or CRIN, which worked closely with the UN committee. Its director had told the media that "child abuse happens in other closed institutions, but what's unique about the Catholic Church is that the Holy See is a state that's voluntarily signed up to the UN Convention on the Rights of the Child." (She did not seem to mind that a "closed institution" would hardly be likely to make itself accountable to a UN committee.)

On its website, it was clear where CRIN was coming from, describing religious institutions as "arcane" with "entrenched power structures." Its report rehashed a fantastic series of *Da Vinci Code*–like myths: that the hundreds of thousands of priests worldwide were employees of the Vatican, and local bishops its agents; and that priests accused of abuse were being secreted in the Vatican beyond the reach of law-enforcement agencies. These myths in turn rested on a single grand idea: that the Church remained an unreformed institution, which in 2014 handled abuse no differently from the 1990s—or even from the 1960s and 1970s, when most of the abuse happened—and that the Church put its reputation above justice, sacrificing innocent lives in the process, following policies set by the Vatican.[2]

An ideological narrative had captured a UN committee and made it impervious to reason and evidence.

Francis stayed quiet, but a month later, when nobody had expected a reaction, he quietly challenged the UN's assault without mentioning it by name. He said statistics showed clearly that most abuse happens in the family and left deep wounds. The Catholic Church was "perhaps the single public institution to have moved with transparency and responsibility" on the issue, he said, adding, "No one has done more, yet the Church is the only one to have been attacked." He also praised Pope Benedict XVI, who he said had been "very courageous" in confronting the Church's abuse scandals and "opening the way" to reform.

Francis had gently exposed the scapegoating of the Church, and he wasn't afraid to lose popularity in pointing it out. Among many furious reactions was that of the Survivors' Network of those Abused by Priests (SNAP), which had been delighted by the UN report. It now said that

Francis's comments showed he had "an archaic, defensive mindset that will not make kids safer."

Francis had by then appointed a commission to advise him on safeguarding policies and specifically the pastoral care of abuse victims. Its members included Cardinal Seán O'Malley of Boston, the US bishop who had led a radical reform of the Church's handling of the issue, as well as an abuse victim and campaigner for the rights of Irish survivors, Marie Collins. Of the five lay people in the commission, four were women, including a former Polish prime minister and leading British and French psychologists.

In April 2014 Francis made impromptu remarks, speaking softly and in Spanish, to a French child protection group, saying he took personal responsibility for "all the evil that some priests—many, many in number, though not in proportion to the totality" had done, and promised to be "strong" in imposing sanctions. The words *many, many* were important: Vatican comments had often focused on how proportionally small the number of abusers were rather than on what struck most ordinary people, which was that the overall number was staggeringly high. The reference to "sanctions" also sent a message that the days of bishops' impunity for mishandling were over. In an airborne press conference on the papal plane back from Tel Aviv at the end of May, Francis said a priest who abused was like one who performed a satanic Mass. "We must proceed with zero tolerance," he said.

In early July he met six abuse survivors for one-on-one meetings at the Vatican. Leaders of abuse-victims groups described the event as a meaningless public relations stunt, but that was not how the survivors who met Francis experienced it. "He seemed genuinely frustrated at what he was hearing. He listened and seemed genuine," said an Irish survivor, Marie Kane, who added: "There was a lot of empathy. There was no looking at watches. I was the one who ended it as I had said all I wanted to say."

The survivors stayed over at the Santa Marta and met Francis informally at dinner the night before. In the morning, they attended Mass in the chapel, where in a searing homily Francis begged their forgiveness. "Before God and his people I express my sorrow for the sins and grave crimes of clerical sexual abuse committed against you. And I humbly ask forgiveness," he told them, before asking for their help in improving the Church's response to the issue.

One of those he met was a British survivor of abuse by Jesuit priests, and founder of a helpline for victims, the National Association for People Abused in Childhood (NAPAC). Peter Saunders, an enthusiastic cyclist, gave Francis a cycling cap, telling him jokingly it had been hard to choose between watching the Tour de France leave from London or come and meet the pope. While Cardinal O'Malley translated, Saunders told Francis that the Church in all parts of the world had to introduce procedures at the level that now existed in the United Kingdom and the United States and should put more resources into helping and healing survivors. Saunders was with Francis for at least half an hour, and could carry on talking as long as he needed. Francis nodded continually. "I know I was listened to," said Saunders. "He gave me his total attention. We had eye contact. I told him I wasn't interested in being part of a public-relations exercise, but it was clear that's not what it was." Saunders was struck by the pope's genuineness. "There's no guile in him."

After the meeting, he was bombarded with e-mails from angry survivors criticizing him for meeting the pope. Many claimed Francis had been mixed up with the Argentine dictatorship and was complicit in the cover-up. "It's hard to read stuff like that," says Saunders.[3]

IN the mid-1980s Bergoglio was accused by a small number of Argentine human-rights activists of complicity with the 1976–1983 military dictatorship. The indictment was first contained in a 1986 book by a widely admired Argentine Catholic lawyer and former Peronist government official, Emilio Mignone, founder of a human-rights organization, the Center for Social and Legal Studies (CELS). In his book *Church and Dictatorship*, Mignone claimed that two Jesuits had been abducted from a shanty town in Buenos Aires after Bergoglio had given a "green light" to the security forces to arrest them. It was a shocking claim.

After Mignone died in 1998 his CELS colleague, Horacio Verbitsky, a Marxist journalist who had acted as intelligence chief for the montoneros, spoke to one of the two Jesuits prior to his death in 2000. The interview with Father Orlando Yorio, who had left the Society of Jesus in 1976, led to

Verbitsky elaborating on Mignone's charges in a series of articles that generated headlines after Bergoglio became archbishop in 1998. Like a drummer toy with long-life batteries, the allegations kept being repeated: in a book by Verbitsky in 2005, in a dossier sent to cardinals in conclave that year, and in a judicial inquiry to which Bergoglio gave evidence as cardinal in 2010. Finally, when Francis was elected, the claims went viral.

Francis had not yet finished his address from the balcony overlooking St. Peter's Square on the night of his election on March 13, 2013 when the British daily the *Guardian* tweeted: "Was Francis accessory to murder and false imprisonment?" It reprinted a 2011 article with several errors, two of which the newspaper retracted. But the allegations were by then taking wing. As journalists clicked through his copious online archive, Verbitsky, now aged 71 and glorying in the global attention, offered his own verdict of the new pope. Francis, he pronounced, was "an *ersatz* version of himself, like the water mixed with flour that indigent mothers use to cheat their children's hunger." And he tried to attach a moniker to him, as the "Pope of the Dictatorship."[4]

The Vatican's spokesman, Father Federico Lombardi, told journalists that the accusations came from "anticlerical left-wing elements." Given Verbitsky's background this was accurate, but it had a defensive ring. Equally inconclusive was an initial statement by the other Jesuit concerned, Father Franz Jalics. From his retreat house in Germany, Jalics, who was still a Jesuit, said he and his former provincial had long since been reconciled, that he considered the matter closed, and that he was "unable to comment on the role of Father Bergoglio in these events." But that only begged questions. If Jalics had forgiven Bergoglio, what had he forgiven—and why could he not comment on his former provincial's role? A few days later, Jalics issued a second statement. "The fact is: Orlando Yorio and I were not denounced by Father Bergoglio."

A week after Francis's election, therefore, the media found themselves caught between two contradictory narratives: "the slum pope" versus "the pope of the dictatorship." Because the two stories were hard to reconcile, a myth began to take hold: that in the early 1990s the "conservative" Jesuit provincial Bergoglio had become a "progressive" Cardinal Bergoglio as result of a conversion. The myth allowed liberal Catholics above all to praise Pope Francis effusively while retaining the right to wag fingers over his supposedly dubious past.[5]

In almost every media report of the Yorio/Jalics allegations it was assumed that in the mid-1970s the armed forces had ousted a popular democratic government and imposed a horrific regime against the wishes of the people. The truth was very different. The deposed Peronist government was by then deeply unpopular, and the coup was broadly welcomed. If there were ever a clear mandate for the armed forces to take the reins in Argentina, it was in March 1976, when Argentines had been living with escalating internecine violence for the previous five years.

The recent phase of that violence had begun with the montoneros' decision to break with Perón in May 1974 and resume their armed struggle. The general died two months later, leaving his third wife, María Estela (known as Isabelita), in charge of what became a disastrous presidency. The montoneros denounced her government in the name of Perón's previous wife. *Si Evita viviera, sería montonera*, was the catchy cry of the time: "If Evita were alive, she would be a montonero."

Faced with a tide of bombings and kidnappings, Isabelita declared a state of siege, unleashing covert death squads to wage war on the guerrillas. In the first seven months of 1975, the so-called Triple A (Argentine Anticommunist Alliance) carried out 450 assassinations and two thousand "disappearances," yet its actions only legitimized the guerrillas, whose leaders were convinced now that they could seize the state. The ERP and montoneros began to deploy heavy weaponry against army bases and regiments, paid for by millions of dollars earned from kidnappings of businessmen. Foreign capital was in flight, inflation reached 600 percent, and unemployment was soaring. By 1975, politics had been reduced to an escalating violent fratricide between two factions of Peronism. The media concluded that a coup was both inevitable and necessary, and all the main newspapers were calling for the tanks to leave their barracks.

Although the armed forces did not move into the Casa Rosada until March 1976, the so-called dirty war had begun the year before, when Isabelita gave the military free rein to pacify the northeast province of Tucumán. Between three hundred and four hundred Trotskyite guerrillas belonging to the Popular Revolutionary Army (ERP) were carrying out a series of major attacks there, battling the army in the mountains, destroying police stations, and hoping to create a liberated territory. Bergoglio in 2010 recalled that the attack "frightened and disorientated many people." Isabel's decree, which ordered the security forces to use all and every means to "annihilate subversion" in the province, was followed by a second decree in response to a major October 1975 montonero assault in Formosa. That decree gave a legal basis for spreading those methods—abduction, torture, and summary executions—to the entire country. These methods would become all too familiar after the coup a year later.

The decrees authorizing those methods were approved by a democratically elected government and had the support of all main parties. Those same parties—Radicals, socialists, conservatives—strongly backed the coup when it came. The politicians accepted the military analysis that extraordinary measures were needed to combat the guerrillas, and they had good reason for doing so. The ERP and the montoneros in the mid-1970s had around 6,000 trained members, and the active support of perhaps 150,000. As a percentage of the population it was small, but they were organized, equipped, technologically capable, flush with money, ruthless, supported by Havana, and focused on taking power. It was, at the time, the largest guerrilla force in the Western Hemisphere.

The ERP attack in Tucumán and the montoneros' offensive in Formosa were part of an insurrection strategy straight out of the handbook of the Argentine doctor turned Cuban revolutionary, Ernesto Guevara, known as "Che." Once a society had reached an objectively revolutionary situation, his theory went, guerrillas could seize control of territory, and the people would gradually come out in their support. Over time, the liberated territory would expand, altering the balance of power. The guerrillas believed after Perón's death that that moment had come, and the memoirs of the generals show that they, too, believed it was a real possibility. Even after the coup, when the state could wage war without due process, it took two years to defeat them: from 1976 to 1978, the guerrillas managed 748 murders, and the montoneros alone carried out more than two thousand "operations."

It is arguable in retrospect that both guerrillas and the armed forces were deluded in believing that revolution was around the corner. Yet understanding how close to that point the country was perceived to be explains why Argentine civil society—political parties, trade unions, the

Church—supported military intervention, tolerated a police state, and justified to themselves and to each other the extraordinary measures the armed forces deployed. Most people did not have a clear picture of what those measures involved, for the junta was highly effective in concealing its methods. Indeed, secrecy was a key part of the military strategy: Argentine military planners had learned the lessons from the 1973 coup of General Augusto Pinochet across the Andes in Chile, which had provoked international outrage by shooting hundreds of alleged left-wing militants.

The Argentine junta, led by General Jorge Videla, believed that to eradicate the guerrillas it would be necessary to eliminate five thousand people and that killings of civilians on this scale would be unacceptable to a Christian society and to international opinion. Furthermore, only secret operations could achieve the shock-and-awe immediacy needed to break the guerrillas' highly effective cell structure. The junta's strategy, therefore, was to conduct torture and interrogations in clandestine military centers, and to dispose of the prisoners in secret, denying all knowledge of them: they would be "disappeared." This way, they could act so swiftly that the guerrillas would be too disoriented to regroup or fade into the civilian population. Meanwhile, the junta would carry out a thoroughgoing reform of the state and the economy, hoping that peace and prosperity would over time lead the population to consider the armed forces their saviors.

The repression was massive, rapid, and secret. Most Argentines knew something—there were almost-daily reports of abductions—but years of living with Triple A and guerrilla violence meant they took time to grasp that something new and systematic was afoot. "I knew that something serious was happening and that there were a lot of prisoners," Bergoglio recalled in 2010, "but I realized it was much more than that only later on. Society as a whole only became fully aware of events during the [1980s] trial of the military commanders. . . . In truth I found it hard to see what was happening until they started to bring people to me and I had to hide the first one."

Only after the dictatorship fell in 1983 did Argentines discover the full scale of what had been carried out in their name: 340 secret detention centers that practiced routine torture by electric cattle prods; prisoners drugged and killed by dropping them from helicopters into the sea, or shooting them and burying them in unmarked graves. The best contemporary estimate is that during the dictatorship (1976–1983) the state killed 7,201 people, all but 754 through "disappearances." Added to the 1,167 (half disappearances, half executions) during the seven years previous to the dictatorship makes a total of 8,368 killed by the state between 1969 and 1983. A little more than half were active guerrillas, the rest unarmed civilians. Most were young people, between fifteen and thirty-five years old.[6]

As the death toll mounted in 1976 and 1977, grieving and confused relatives of the *desaparecidos*—a ghostly noun that the foreign media left in Spanish—found themselves stonewalled by the police, and many turned to the Church. The bishops initially sought to maintain relations with the junta, only to find that they had very little influence over it. While they managed to get some prisoners released, their policy of engagement— born of decades of identification with the state—gave the junta legitimacy and the bishops a reputation for pusillanimity: twenty-five years later they used Pope John Paul II's millennium repentance initiative to ask forgiveness for their "indulgence of totalitarian postures" and their failure to do more to prevent the killings.[7]

That acknowledgment came with the benefit of hindsight. At the time the choices were complex. The bishops had heard that torture was being used and condemned it in their May 1976 statement, yet the same statement recognized the need for exceptional measures and for the army to be cut some slack. Jorge Casaretto, at the time the young bishop of La Rafaela, says the regime "admitted to us that excesses had been committed, but they never told us they had created an apparatus of torture and disappearances." In May 1977, the bishops were bolder and clearer, speaking out in emphatic terms to condemn the atrocities. But the day after the statement was made, the guerrillas killed an admiral in a spectacular car bomb attack. "So the armed forces said to us: 'Look what happens when you issue a condemnation,'" remembers Casaretto. "It was a heavy psychological blow."

The bishops were also too divided to give a concerted response. The fifty-seven members of the conference split between rightists, moderates, and progressives. The rightists were numerically small—half a dozen— but they had some big dioceses such as La Plata and Rosario, and, more important, they included the military vicariate, a separate church jurisdiction that included more than two hundred armed forces chaplains.

The vicariate's bishops, Adolfo Tortolo and Victorio Bonamín, saw the dictatorship as salvation from the horrors of democracy, and the repression as a holy war that would save Argentina from communism. They knew what was happening, and justified it.

On the opposite wing were about a dozen progressive bishops, who from the start nudged the main body of bishops toward a firmer public line in favor of human rights. Because they headed peripheral dioceses and had many members of the Third World Priests' Movement (MSTM) among their clergy, they learned before most of their colleagues what the repression involved, spoke against it, and paid the price: by 1983 three of these bishops had been killed in mysterious traffic accidents. In each case, they had faced increasing hostility from security forces, and in two cases were carrying files on the disappeared that then vanished from the scenes of the accidents.

The main body—about two-thirds—of the bishops shared the junta's objectives of restoring order and peace. "We thought that the 'inorganic' violence could only be dealt with by an 'organic' violence," recalls Bishop Casaretto. That made them, like most Argentines, inclined to be supportive of the junta and therefore slow to wake up to the ferocity of its measures. The bishops condemned torture from the start, but in 1976 and 1977 did not publicly break with the regime or denounce it; in that sense the bishops were bystanders, rather than complicit. By 1980, the pro-dictatorship bishops had been sidelined, and the bishops' conference worked actively for a return to democracy.

In the mid-1970s, however, the Church was itself a theater of war. La Rioja, the poor northwestern diocese where Bergoglio had gone with the general, Father Arrupe, was the most obvious example. Shortly after the coup, the head of the air force in La Rioja accused Bishop Enrique Angelelli of preaching politics and refused to allow his appointed chaplain to enter the Chamical air force base. When Angelelli in protest banned religious services at the base, the army bishop, Victorio Bonamín, overrode him and installed his own chaplain. Bonamín was close to the army chiefs who arranged for the abduction of two of Angelelli's priests, whose bodies were found days later, tortured and riddled with bullets, together with a list of "subversive" priests who were warned they were next.

Because anyone who worked with the poor in the shantytowns was considered a *zurdo* ("commie"), priests and nuns were even more of a target than they had been before the coup. During the dirty war some twenty priests and members of religious orders were killed, eighty-four disappeared, and seventy-seven exiled, and many hundreds of lay activists shared their fate. In 2010 Bergoglio told the judicial inquiry:

> There were some [at the time] who did theology with a Marxist hermeneutic [i.e., interpreting through a Marxist lens] that the Holy See did not accept, and others who didn't, who sought a pastoral presence among the poor using a Gospel hermeneutic. The leaders of the dictatorship demonized *all* liberation theology, putting in the same basket both those priests who used a Marxist hermeneutic—who in Argentina were few compared with other countries—as well as those priests who were simply living their priestly calling among the poor.[8]

Some of those who were killed were connected to Bergoglio. On June 4, 1976, two Colegio Máximo students belonging to the Assumptionist order were disappeared from the nearby parish of Jesús Obrero in La Manuelita by uniformed guards looking for Father Jorge Adur, an MSTM priest who was for a time chaplain to the montoneros. A month later, five members of the Irish branch of the Pallottine order were horribly murdered at the church of San Patricio in Buenos Aires. One of them, the seminarian Emilio Barletti, was a student at the Máximo, and another, Father Alfredo Kelly, had Bergoglio as his spiritual director.

Because of the strong Jesuit presence in La Rioja, Bergoglio was immediately informed in July that the bodies of two of Angelleli's priests had turned up by a railway track, having been tortured, and a Catholic lay worker gunned down in front of his children. Angelelli had told many people he would be next. Bergoglio was abroad when, on August 4, 1976, the bishop was driven off the road on which he was returning from a Mass he had held for his two murdered priests. On the backseat was a dossier of evidence naming those responsible, which was removed from the scene. Even though Angelelli had clearly been clubbed to death, the death was reported as an accident. Bergoglio, who knew it wasn't, returned to Argentina at once.

Later, as pope, he supplied documents which assisted the prosecution, finally, of two senior military officers in Angelelli's murder.[9]

As provincial, Bergoglio had two objectives during the dirty war, both of which had been set by the general in Rome. The first was to protect the Jesuits. The second was to assist the victims of the repression. The two objectives were, obviously, in tension with each other: if it had been known that their provincial was abetting subversives sought by the state, all Jesuits would have been suspect. It was a high-wire act, but Bergoglio pulled it off. Not one Argentine Jesuit lost his life in the dirty war, and he managed to save dozens of people. What he did not do was speak out publicly against the regime, but he could hardly have done so without sacrificing his objectives, for no obvious gain.

He succeeded for two main reasons.

The first was the breadth and depth of his relationships. His main links were with the deposed Peronists, but he had contacts in the montoneros as well as in the armed forces, and a line to the navy chief, Admiral Emilio Massera. More important, he had the confidence of the three Jesuit army chaplains living in the Colegio Máximo, as well as a senior Jesuit, Father Enrique Laje, who was influential in Argentine military circles. Bergoglio also had good links with bishops in both the moderate and the progressive camps, and with the Vatican's representative to Argentina, the apostolic nuncio, Pío Laghi; last, as a provincial close to Arrupe, he had access via the Jesuit curia to the Holy See.

The second reason was his ability to play his cards very close to his chest. Only someone with Bergoglio's legendary inscrutability could pull off the extraordinary feat of sheltering in the Máximo dozens of people fleeing the dictatorship, under the noses of the army chaplains (who never guessed) and the soldiers outside. They were known only as "students" or "people on retreat," and not even his secretary, who drove many of the refugees to airports and train stations, knew who they were. For this reason, only Francis can say exactly who, and how many, he helped to escape. Beyond vague references in his judicial witness statements and remarks in his 2010 interview, *El Jesuita*, that he assisted people by sheltering them in the Máximo, he has given few details.

Until his election most of those whom Bergoglio helped respected his silence with their own. But in March 2013, angered by the injustice of the

Verbitsky accusations, many felt compelled to step forward or were truffled out by journalists. Among those most surprised by the stories were the Argentine Jesuits themselves—especially those living in the Máximo at the time. Bergoglio had given nothing away. It was easy to see where he earned his nickname among the Jesuits, "La Giaconda," the title of da Vinci's painting of the Mona Lisa, with her famously impenetrable expression.

Even though not all have shared their stories, enough former escapees now have to create a clear picture of how Bergoglio saved dozens of people, above all in the years 1976 to 1978, by sheltering them in the Máximo and filtering them abroad via a Jesuit-run international network of escape routes. Most went to neighboring Brazil or Uruguay, and from there to Europe. Bergoglio picked up many of the refugees himself, installed them sometimes for weeks or months in the Máximo, arranged false identity papers, drove them to the airport, and saw them safely onto the planes. In one case, "because he looked quite a bit like me," he said in 2010, he gave a young man his identity card and clerical clothes, and smuggled him out through the Brazilian border town of Foz do Iguaçu.[10]

Although Bergoglio got some people out of Argentina via boat to Uruguay, the most common route was through the Argentine-Brazilian border—the old Jesuit mission lands among the Guaraní. The escapees made their way to Misiones in northern Argentina, where missionaries ferried them over the River Paraná from Puerto Iguazú. On the other side they were met by Brazilian Jesuits who sheltered the refugees in Rio de Janeiro, arranged money and tickets for their escape to Europe, and, when it was safe, put them on flights. Each person involved at each stage of the journey knew only about the part for which they were responsible—the bus journey, or the lodging, or the papers—in case they were caught.

This sophisticated and audacious network was all the more remarkable because the military dictatorships at the time in all the Southern Cone nations—Argentina, Uruguay, Brazil, Paraguay, and Chile—had mutually agreed in the so-called Condor Treaty to hunt down and hand over so-called subversives fleeing neighboring countries. The way in which the Jesuits of South America mirrored that counterinsurgency cooperation with their own cross-border refugee-smuggling network is one of the great untold stories of the time.

On March 24, 1976, the day the army deposed Isabel Perón, Bergoglio was moving the province headquarters from 327 Bogotá Street to the Colegio Máximo in San Miguel. Now that vocation numbers were on the rise, "it seemed right for the provincial to be close to the formation house," he explained in a 1990 letter to the head of the Salesians in Argentina, Don Cayetano Bruno. Formation remained Bergoglio's main priority, and he needed to be close to the students.

Even though a coup had been long expected, the Jesuits had no idea it would be that day, and they found themselves shifting furniture and files into a van as helicopters thudded overhead, tanks blocked roads, and soldiers jogged through the streets.

The new military government announced what it called a National Reorganization Process, known to Argentines simply as *el proceso*. Some of the tunes were familiar: Congress and courts were closed, political activity was suspended, and strikes were banned. But many were new. The government would be led this time by a three-man junta representing each branch of the armed forces, which between them divided up the cabinet posts: although the army commander in chief, General Jorge Videla, was president, he would make no executive decisions without consulting the naval chief, Admiral Emilio Massera, or the head of the air force, Brigadier Orlando Agosti. Also new was the degree of social control: newspaper editors were told what to publish, and the state took charge of all TV channels.

The ambition of the new government was to "restore the essential values which serve as the basis for the integral direction of the state" and—according to its communiqué that day—to "eradicate subversion and promote economic development." The economic plan was monetarist shock therapy: shrink the state, freeze wages, and open markets to foreign competition. It didn't work. After an initial spurt of growth and investment, Argentina plunged into yet another economic crisis, this time with sharp rises in unemployment.

By then, however, the country was entombed in an eerie political silence. Not until 1978 did some Argentines begin to emerge from their sepulchers, encouraged by relatives of the *desaparecidos* who the year before began their sad vigils in front of the Casa Rosada. The sight of the Mothers of the Plaza de Mayo, with their white kerchiefs and ghostly pictures of their vanished children, endlessly circling the square under the surly gaze of soldiers, caught the attention of the world. By then, the junta had changed its leaders, and the new ones sought to distract that attention by the 1982 invasion of British-occupied islands off Argentina's southern coast. Argentina's defeat in the ensuing Falklands War (Guerra de las Malvinas) triggered the dictatorship's collapse and the return to democracy in 1983.

ONCE installed in the Máximo in 1976, Bergoglio set about reforming the formation program of the Jesuit students, a key element of his wider strategy of refounding the province after years of chaos, experimentation, and division.

Speaking that year about the welcome upturn in new entrants, he said it was vital for them to find in the province a spirit of consolation that was the result of the union of souls, mutual trust, apostolic zeal, and obedience. The serpent in the Jesuit garden, he said, was "a certain avant-gardism." The devil's subtlest tactic was to make them believe that the Church needed saving (by the Jesuits) from itself. Behind this temptation was a lack of faith in God's power present in the Church. Noting that "just as there are tempted Jesuits, so there are tempted communities" of Jesuits, he listed the signs to watch out for: where conflict is more important than unity, the part more important than the whole, and personal ideas more important than reality.

To combat these temptations, Bergoglio had a three-point strategy. The first was a revision of the study program. He reintroduced the juniorate (the one- or two-year grounding in arts and humanities) and restored the separation of philosophy and theology to replace what he described in his 1990 letter to Don Bruno as "the mélange of philosophy and theology called 'curriculum' in which they began by studying Hegel [sic]." Bergoglio's new juniorate was a chance to root students in Jesuit and Argentine traditions, rather than foreign models. The studies included not just the European classics but also courses in Argentine literature—from El Gaucho Martín Fierro to Borges. History was revisionist, restoring the Catholic, Hispanic, and early-Jesuit elements in Argentina's past that were ignored or scorned in liberal history. Bergoglio wanted the Jesuits to value popular religious traditions alongside high culture, to know about gauchos and caudillos as well as railways and telegraphs.

The second element was a pastoral outreach among the local population, an enterprise that would grow spectacularly over the next ten years as the Máximo filled up with students, but which also aroused an opposition to him within the Jesuits that would come to a head in the 1980s. In the same letter to Don Bruno he recalled:

> When I was in San Miguel I saw the neighborhoods lacked pastoral care. This bothered me, and we started to attend to the children: Saturday afternoons, we taught catechism, then they played, etc. I realized that we professed Jesuits had taken a vow to teach doctrine to children and the uneducated [*niños y rudos*], and I began to do that myself together with the students. The thing grew: we had five churches built, we organized in a very systematic way the education of the children of the area on Saturday afternoons and Sunday mornings. This led pretty soon to the accusation that this was not the proper apostolate of the Jesuits, and that I had "Salesianized" [*sic*] the formation.

The concrete service of the poor in weekend missions in the local neighborhoods would connect the Jesuit students to the *santo pueblo fiel de Dios* and keep them rooted in reality. "The faithful people tire us because they ask concrete things of us," he noted in one of his talks at this time. "In our minds we are kings and lords, and whoever dedicates himself exclusively to the cultivation of his fantasy will never come to feel the urgency of the here-and-now. But the pastoral work in our parishes is the opposite."[11]

The third prong of his formation reform was the deepening of their Ignatian spirituality, as ever under the guidance of Father Fiorito, who lived in the Villa Bailari with the novices and was spiritual director to many of the students in the college—both Jesuits and non-Jesuits. Bergoglio's many talks and writings of the time, published in the *Boletín de Espiritualidad*, are master classes in Ignatian discernment, many of which are concerned with the subtle temptations that lead to rejection of Church authority and divisions in the Jesuit body. He makes particular use of Paul VI's *Evangelii Nuntiandii*, lamenting the emergence of certain "base communities" that reject Church authority and become ideological. ("Perhaps it would do us good to suffer a while before the Lord," says

Bergoglio, "asking forgiveness for the times that, in our work as pastors, we have sinned in this area.")[12] But mostly his references are to Saint Ignatius's own writings—and above all the *Exercises*—that combat the devil's many and subtle attempts at dividing the Jesuit body.

In the talks he gave to the Jesuits as provincial, his diagnosis of the province's challenges merged with his view of what had gone wrong in the country and the Church at large. Christianity in Argentina had been taken hostage by violent ideologies. His generation had succumbed to the temptations of the revolutionary messianism of the guerrillas or the anti-communist crusade of the men in khaki, and the result was diabolic: the Body of Christ had been split along temporal lines, and orders such as his own had seen their members dwindle and disperse. In reforming the Society of Jesus in Argentina, Bergoglio wanted the Jesuits to surrender their all-too-human schemes and be shaped by the "periphery"—the pastoral needs of the poor.

In this, Bergoglio was following the wisdom of Yves Congar's 1950 text *True and False Reform in the Church*. True reform came about through the periphery being allowed to shape the center; "reforms that have succeeded within the Church are those which have been made with concern for the concrete need of souls, in a pastoral perspective, aiming at holiness," the French Dominican had written. What upset reform, leading to division and schism, was ideology—a partial interpretation in which some values are extolled and others demonized. The post-conciliar Jesuit changes showed all the signs of a "false" reform, not least because it had led (on both left and right) to a greater alignment with secular ideologies. True reform meant returning to the sources, reaffirming essential Catholic traditions.

Bergoglio's talks show him developing two major vaccinations against the lure of ideology. The first was the God's-holy-faithful-people idea: following Congar, God's power was to be discerned not in elite schemes but in the ordinary believing poor. The second was a series of governing "Christian principles," a kind of sapiential wisdom captured in a series of criteria for discernment. In 1974, when he addressed the provincial congregation, there were three: unity comes before conflict, the whole comes before the part, time comes before space. By 1980, he had added a fourth, anti-ideological principle: reality comes before the idea. They were principles deduced from various of his heroes—the early companions of Saint

Ignatius, the Paraguay missionaries, even the nineteenth-century caudillo Rosas—and one major source: what he called "the special wisdom of the people whom we call faithful, the people which is the people of God."[13]

Those four principles, said Bergoglio, "are the axis around which reconciliation can revolve." They would constantly appear from now on in his writing and speeches—and were shared with the world in *Evangelii Gaudium* (*The Joy of the Gospel*), Pope Francis's first authored document, released in November 2013.

Bergoglio's 1980 talk argued that elite projects "deny their own brothers and sisters the power to make decisions, to move a process forward, and to organize themselves: the right to form their own institution." They "do not desire to form a body" but instead "aim to hold on to a privilege of power." That power divides, unlike like the power of God. The unifying power of God is located outside the schemes of the elites—in God's faithful people.

> Restorationists and idealists, conservatives and revolutionaries will always be fighting to get power, get control, run the institution. The argument remains put in such a way that there are just two possible alternatives: our institutions have to be either restoration workshops or antiseptic laboratories. In the meantime, while we argue and waste time on these arguments, we do not see the real movement going on among God's faithful people. It is with these people that effective power, wisdom, real problems, serious suffering, all move forward—and here, too, is the movement of salvation. Then, as always, the restorationist and idealistic ideologues, incapable of smelling the sweat of the real advance, will get left behind. They are cut off in their elitism and hold on to their tired, gray, cartoon-book narratives. Thus they fail to join in the march of the history where God is saving us, God is making us a body, an institution. God's power enters history so as to make of human beings one single body.[14]

SAINT Ignatius of Loyola's dictum that love is known more in deeds than words was especially true of Bergoglio during the dirty war. His silence was not just caution, and it wasn't just his character. It was key to his objectives. The Jesuits were being watched—the telephones were tapped and the post searched—and the province mirrored the divisions in the Church and the country. There were Jesuits who sympathized with the guerrillas, and others who identified with the military, and any number of others in between with Radical, liberal, or Peronist sympathies.

The three Jesuit military chaplains living in or next to the college were under obedience to Bergoglio as provincial and he had their trust. Their tip-offs and influence in military circles gave him space to maneuver; he could warn those at risk of being targeted, and get information on those who had been taken. He was able to tell his fellow Jesuit Julio Mérediz, for example, who slept in a room with a corrugated-iron roof in a youth center, that he was on an air force list of possible subversives. "He ordered me to go and live in the Colegio Máximo," Father Mérediz recalls. "I went there and hid and that saved my life."

Bergoglio took considerable risks. In 1977, for example, he took a truck to the house of his old laboratory boss, Esther Ballestrino de Careaga, whose daughter Ana María was being watched, and removed their library of Marxist books to hide in the college. And he regularly went to collect another dear friend, the human rights judge Alicia Oliveira, from her place in hiding, so she could meet her young children at the Colegio del Salvador in Buenos Aires.

Oliveira offers a valuable window onto Bergoglio's thoughts and actions at the time. She was an anticlerical left-wing Peronist, a single mother of three, and Argentina's first female criminal judge. She met Bergoglio in 1972 when the provincial went to consult her on a legal matter. Finding themselves on the same wavelength, they became friends. Oliveira was one of the founders of the Center for Social and Legal Studies, CELS, a human-rights monitor that in 1975 was becoming an increasing annoyance for the security forces, and which later included Bergoglio's first accuser, Emilio Mignone. With coup rumors circulating, and concerned for her safety, Bergoglio invited her to live in the college—an invitation she laughingly turned down, saying she'd rather go to prison than live with priests.

Following the coup she was considered ideologically unsuitable and lost her court position (Bergoglio anonymously sent her flowers; she recognized the handwriting on the card praising her qualities as judge). Shortly afterward the CELS office was raided and she went into hiding, lodging with a friend but leaving her children with others. Bergoglio brought her to meet her children twice a week in the college. There they discussed the appalling friend/foe military logic, and the inability of the junta to distinguish between political, social, and religious commitment—or between varieties of liberation theology.

Oliveira also saw firsthand Bergoglio's anxiety for the safety of the Jesuits, especially those in the *villas miseria* where the guerrillas and their front organizations were based. He confided in her about the efforts he was making to find detainees, both before and after Yorio and Jalics were taken in May 1976; and he invited her to farewell lunches for people he was helping to escape, at the Jesuit retreat house in San Miguel as well as the Jesuit residence of San Ignacio de Loyola close to the Plaza de Mayo. "When someone had to get out of the country, there was always a lunch," she recalls. "He never missed them."

Rescuing people from the clutches of the armed forces once they had been taken was an almost impossible task, but Bergoglio had some successes. One of them was a student of Father Juan Carlos Scannone's. Bergoglio found out where he was being held and convinced the commander that he was innocent. But the young man, whose surname was Albanesi, had been tortured; worse, he had seen the face of his torturer. That meant, the officer informed Bergoglio, that he could not be freed. "Bergoglio told him that it was a serious sin to kill an innocent man," remembers Scannone. "He said: 'If you believe in hell, you should know you'll get sent to hell for a serious sin.' He saved the boy's life."

Another success was Sergio Globulin, who had been a lay theology student at the Máximo in the late 1960s. Bergoglio had celebrated his wedding in 1975 and went to visit Sergio and Ana more than once in the *villa miseria* where they taught. After Sergio was abducted in October 1976, Bergoglio found a safe house for Ana and energetically set about getting her husband released. After eighteen days, he succeeded. By then Sergio had been so badly beaten, he needed to be hospitalized for a month.

Bergoglio came to see him there, and told Sergio and Ana that they had to leave the country, which they did with the help of the Italian vice-consul. "He told us about his various attempts to get us freed and to demonstrate my innocence, attempts that had required meetings with various high-ranking members of the Armed Forces," Sergio Globulin recalls. "That's why he kept telling us to get out. He knew other groups in the army were looking for me." They went to live in Friuli, Italy, where Bergoglio visited them in 1977 on a visit to Rome.[15]

Miguel La Civita, at that time a theology student at the Máximo, witnessed the effect on Bergoglio of one of the meetings the provincial held to get Globulin released.

> I was present when [Bergoglio] met a military officer from the Morón Air Base. I was asked to bring him and the soldier some food, to his office. [Bergoglio] was telling him that the kid had to reappear. When the meeting was over, he rang the bell for me to go and collect the trays. When I got there he asked me to see the officer out. I thought that was unusual, because he always saw guests out himself. When I went back to his office to get the trays, he was vomiting. He said: "Sometimes when you're done talking to those people, you've got to throw up." He told me it was a chess game: one bad move and you're toast. Three days later, Sergio showed up, really badly beaten.

Along with "Quique" Martínez Ossola and Carlos González, La Civita was one of three of Bishop Angelelli's seminarians from La Rioja studying at the Máximo. After they fell under suspicion from the military, Bergoglio agreed with Angelelli in 1975 that they should complete their studies in the college.

When news reached him of Angelelli's suspicious death, Bergoglio cut short a meeting of provincials in Central America, arriving back at the college late at night some days later. He went straight to see the three seminarians, who were distraught and afraid. "We heard the footsteps and nearly died of fright," remembers La Civita. "We had already been thinking how we could escape. He knocked on the door, said, 'It's Jorge, don't be scared.'" After consoling them, he gave them a series of instructions: always to walk around together; not to use the main staircase, but the elevator; and if they saw people they didn't know, to make their way to a particular room and phone him.

For their safety, Bergoglio did not let them join the other students doing apostolic work in the barrios of San Miguel but enlisted their help in what they came to realize was a refugee-hiding operation. "We helped Bergoglio attend to people who presented themselves as students or as young people on retreat, but who we guessed were fleeing from persecution," recalls Quique. He remembers handfuls of people being hidden at any one time, perhaps thirty in total. They never knew much about them, because Bergoglio told them not to ask questions, but the *riojanos* worked it out. "We knew because we were asked to take meals up to such-and-such a person, who was in a part of the college where people weren't allowed, because that's where people on silent retreat stayed," says La Civita. "There was a whole floor. On one side people were actually doing retreats, on the other side were the ones in hiding."

A number of the refugees were Paraguayan and Uruguayan. Gonzalo Mosca, a radical on the run from the Uruguayan dictatorship, went to Buenos Aires but discovered that the police had orders to arrest him. He called his brother, a Jesuit in the Argentine province, who contacted his provincial. Bergoglio collected Mosca from the center of Buenos Aires and drove him out to the Máximo. "If they stop us, tell them you're going on a spiritual retreat," he told him. Mosca stayed for four days; Bergoglio came to his room each afternoon, armed with a radio and Borges stories. He fixed a flight to Puerto Iguazú—"Father Jorge not only accompanied me to the airport, but actually saw me onto the plane," Mosca recalls— from where he was taken over the River Paraná and looked after by the Jesuits in Brazil, who arranged his papers and flight to Europe. Looking back, Mosca is astonished at his courage. "If they had caught us together, we would both have been put away."[16]

La Civita remembers the provincial taking in a priest who had been threatened by a right-wing group called Tradition, Family and Property after he spoke out in a homily against the killing of the Pallottine fathers. "One day before lunch Jorge came and told us that Vicente had to get out of the country because there was an order to arrest him. He said the one who had received the order would not act on it for forty-eight hours, but then he would have to. He said he had to get Vicente out to Uruguay."

These operations took place under the nostrils not just of the army chaplains, but of the army itself. A military base was close by the Máximo; from 1977 the air force owned the observatory inside the college grounds; and just outside the iron gates, the soldiers patrolled. Sometimes they would camp close by and carry out operations in the area. Angel Rossi, a Jesuit novice at the time, remembers a 1977 raid on the novitiate house—which was a few streets from the Máximo—by soldiers claiming to have heard shots; the novices were held at gunpoint against the walls while the rooms were turned over.

The Máximo itself was never raided, although one night it came very close. It was toward the end of 1977, when around twenty soldiers passed through the iron gates and surrounded the college with trucks. Father Scannone, seen as a liberation theologian and therefore suspect, had his heart in his mouth as he heard the boots in the corridors outside. But the soldiers didn't go inside the rooms. Bergoglio gently, but with impressive self-confidence, told them to go back to their barracks, that they had no right to be in the college. They left.

Inside the college, there was a group of around thirty priests, including the military chaplains, who could be described as conservative Jesuits sympathetic to the dictatorship. Professors such as Yorio linked to the Third-World priests had been removed, and the faculty was by 1976 firmly in the anti-Marxist "theology of the people" school of Fathers Gera and Scannone. But the political tensions remained strong, and an atmosphere of caution had reached into the classrooms. La Civita was taken aside after theology class one time after making a reference to John's Gospel that smacked of Marxism. "Look, Miguel," the professor told him, "when you want to talk about that come to my room: I think the same as you but watch what you say in class, because there are *botones* [snitches]."

La Civita describes Bergoglio as an "eel" because "he had this amazing ability to maneuver in that environment."

In the judicial evidence he gave in 2010, Bergoglio said he went to "people who could make things happen: some of them linked to human-rights organizations, some not," and "to priests who I supposed to have links to the police and the armed forces." Pressed a number of times to say who they were, the cardinal avoided giving names: "friends, acquaintances," he said, adding later, "some were Jesuits, some lay people, some were friends of Jesuits."

Bergoglio's contact with Admiral Emilio Massera came through the ex–Iron Guard leaders in the Salvador University (USAL). Massera, who had been appointed navy chief by General Perón before Perón's death, had political ambitions to succeed him as the movement's leader. In 1976 and 1977 he sought to co-opt former leaders of Peronist groups to build a political base, among whom was Francisco "Cacho" Piñón, the USAL rector. Piñón took advantage of the approach to secure an agreement from

Massera to protect the university and its personnel. The quid pro quo was an invitation from USAL to Massera to give a speech and receive an honorary degree on November 25, 1977, at which the Jesuits were represented by the Máximo's rector, Father Víctor Zorzín.

Although some of the ex-Guardia leaders would later be seduced by Massera, Piñón was not one of them; he had no more sympathy than Bergoglio for the admiral's tedious political theories, which he shared at length in his lecture that day. The *honoris causa* degree was purely to protect the USAL. "Bergoglio totally understood that keeping a university from being 'intervened' in the dictatorship was not a little girls' game," says the ex-*guardián* Julio Bárbaro. Bergoglio did the same for the Jesuits. Miguel Mom Debussy, a Jesuit student in the Máximo in the 1970s who occasionally drove Bergoglio's car, says the provincial told him he met Massera to discuss the sale of the Jesuit observatory next to the college, which had become a financial drain. There was no deal—in the end the air force bought the observatory—but the meeting enabled a vital contact. "He did it to protect the students and the novices," says Debussy, who later left the Jesuits.

Massera's role in the dirty war condemned him, after the fall of the dictatorship, to life imprisonment. The fact that Bergoglio had met with him was seized on by the left as evidence that the former provincial had been a "collaborator." But as those close to him at the time, such as Alicia Oliveira, point out, he was as appalled by the national-security ideology of the dictatorship as he was by the Marxist-nationalist ideology of the montoneros, despite each dressing in Catholic clothes. On the other hand, Bergoglio would have a relationship with anyone—especially if it could save lives.

Without those relationships, he could achieve none of his objectives. For the same reason, the nuncio lunched with General Videla, and the head of the bishops' conference arranged Admiral Massera's 1977 audience with Pope Paul VI. Many said afterward that the bishops should have spoken out instead. The bishops say they saved more lives by keeping these links. It is arguable either way, but in 1976 and 1977 the dictatorship still had popular legitimacy and the most common assumption was that to be arrested you had to be involved with the guerrillas. No one at that time was asking bishops to issue statements against the regime, while hundreds were begging them to intercede with the authorities through private channels to save lives. A public repudiation of the regime would have made that advocacy impossible.

Every life saved was precious but overall the results were meager. The papal nuncio, Pío Laghi, in 1977 lamented to a US diplomat how each branch of the armed forces passed off inquiries to another, and how it was almost impossible to find anyone to claim responsibility for a disappearance. The bishops, he said, had asked for explanations about thousands of cases, but had been given information on just a few dozen. Tracking down *desaparecidos* was no small task. For the first two weeks, while the prisoners were in police stations or army bases being "sorted" according to the threat they were reckoned to represent, there was a chance of springing them—if you could find out soon enough where they were. But once they had entered the clandestine detention centers, that chance became vanishingly small. Of the five thousand prisoners thought to have passed through the largest detention center, the Navy Mechanics School, known as ESMA, only a few hundred survived (among them Yorio and Jalics). When the survivors later told what had gone on there, it was clear why the army had not wanted to let them live.

Apart from Globulin, Albanesi, and Yorio and Jalics, and possibly one or two others, Bergoglio had few successes in rescuing the victims of this butchery. His old friend Esther Ballestrino de Careaga once brought to him a woman whose two sons had been abducted—both were communist militants who were involved, as were Esther's children, in the ERP. "She was a widow, and her sons were all she had left," Bergoglio recalled in 2010. "How she cried! It was a scene I will never forget. I made some inquiries but got nowhere, and I often reproach myself for not doing more."

Nor could Bergoglio save Esther herself. She was one of the three founders of the Mothers of the Plaza de Mayo, who held their first rally in front of the Casa Rosada in April 1977. In June, Esther's daughter Ana María was disappeared, but amazingly was returned alive in October. Esther took her and her other two daughters to live in Sweden. But once there, she felt guilty at abandoning the Madres and returned to Buenos Aires, saying she would carry on until all the others were returned alive. The Madres group—which had expanded to include two French nuns and relatives of the disappeared, among them a young man called Gustavo Niño—met each week at the church of Santa Cruz. In December they were planning to make public their first list of eight hundred *desaparecidos*.

Niño's real name was Lt. Col. Alfredo Astiz. He was one of Massera's thugs who had infiltrated the group by feigning to have a *desaparecido* brother. After joining the Madres in the square, and attending a number of meetings at the church, he arranged the death squad that took them away. It was one of four army stings between December 8 and 10, 1977, which included the abduction of the two other Madres founders, Azucena Villaflor and María Ponce.

Bergoglio was devastated. He tried without success to reach members of Esther's family, and desperately sought help from human-rights organizations as well as the archdiocese, who told him they had no news. He went with fellow members of the nuns' congregation to the French embassy, who made energetic representations to the junta.

Years later they learned that, even as they pleaded for information, the tortured corpses of the Santa Cruz dozen, as they became known, were floating in the south Atlantic.

UNLIKE "Pancho" Jalics, Oswaldo Yorio never reached a place of peace or forgiveness before dying of a heart attack in Montevideo in the winter of 2000. When the journalist Olga Wornat interviewed the sixty-five-year-old former Jesuit in the Uruguayan capital just weeks before his death, she met a man in broken health whose face still crumpled with hurt. "I have no reason to think he ever did anything to free us," Yorio had told Horacio Verbitsky in 1999, "but rather the opposite." To Wornat, Yorio made a far more appalling accusation: "I am sure that he gave the list with our names to the Marines."[17]

Yorio was still broken not just by the five months he spent chained and blindfolded in a cell twenty-five years earlier, not knowing if each day would be his last, but by an enduring bitterness against his former provincial, whom the year before he had lived to see made the archbishop of Buenos Aires. To Catholic friends in the left-wing, human-rights world such as Professor Fortunato Mallimaci, he insisted to the last that Bergoglio was devious, power-obsessed, and duplicitous. It was a narrative that had developed over twenty years, with encouragement from Mignone and Verbitsky, and revolved around the same premise: Yorio as innocent victim, and Bergoglio as a dangerous reactionary engaged in a double game.

Yorio's specific grievance—plugged with relish by Verbitsky after

Yorio's death—was that Bergoglio had willfully or at least knowingly left Jalics and him "unprotected" in the months after the coup. No one today claims, as Yorio did to Olga Wornat, that Bergoglio actively betrayed the two priests; the evidence, as Jalics came to see, was that the priests were seized on May 23, 1976, because of their links to a catechist-turned-guerrilla who had under torture identified them as people she had worked with. Yet Yorio's relatives and Verbitsky insist that Bergoglio's sins prior to the abduction were those of omission. Through a series of actions, they claim, he left the Jesuits prey for the ESMA squad that descended that day on their house in the Bajo Flores area of Buenos Aires. Those actions include, they allege, Bergoglio failing to defend them from false accusations that they were connected to the guerrillas, and arranging their departure from the Jesuits just at the moment that they were most exposed. "He put them in a risky position and didn't try to avoid it," claims Orlando's brother, Rodolfo Yorio.[18]

To foreigners, this sounds like, at worst, a crime of negligence, but in Argentina the allegation has a dark resonance. Emilio Mignone's 1986 book *Church and Dictatorship*, which made public Yorio's allegations, had an authority deriving not just from his highly respected work in CELS but his experience of having a disappeared daughter. Mónica Mignone was a catechist in the same *villa* as Yorio and Jalics, and was abducted just a week before they were. While searching for her, Mignone père was distraught that the many bishops he knew well from his Catholic Action days were unable to secure his daughter's release; and the book is an angry denunciation of the Church's failure to speak out against the regime on behalf of victims. Mignone finds the reason why in a cozy connivance between Church and army built up over many years. Bergoglio's alleged behavior toward the two Jesuits is part of a long litany of sins of complaisance or connivance used by Mignone to buttress his book's central claim that the armed forces "took charge of the dirty task of cleaning the Church's inner patio, with the acquiescence of the prelates."[19]

This charge—that bishops took advantage of the dirty war to extirpate liberation theology by acquiescing in the deaths of its exponents—has offered the Argentine left a satisfying explanation of why the bishops didn't take a firmer line against the junta. As many left-wing narratives do, it places the Church (with the exception of "good" bishops like Angelelli) on the side of the regime against the people.

The evidence, however, doesn't support it. One wing of the clergy—the military-chaplain vicariate led by Bishop Tortolo, along with Bishop Bonamín and certain military chaplains, such as the sinister Cristián von Wernich, later indicted for murder and kidnapping—certainly saw the eradication of Medellín-type theology as part of a wider crusade against subversion, and were complicit. But this was never true of most bishops or Church leaders, and it does not explain their initial reluctance to break with the regime. The evidence points, rather, to a gradual awakening, and an increasingly coherent opposition by the bishops, in the late 1970s, to the junta's ideology and methods.

In Bergoglio's case, the specific Mignone/Verbitsky accusation is that he gave a "green light" to the marines to abduct Yorio and Jalics because—although this is never stated directly—he wanted them dead because he disagreed with their theology. The evidence for this claim, which was always rejected by Mignone's CELS colleague Oliveira and many others in the world of human rights such as Adolfo Pérez Esquivel, was picked over by a judicial inquiry in 2010 and, following Francis's election, by journalists and his Argentine biographers. All have come to the opposite conclusion: that Bergoglio's actions had no impact on the arrest of Yorio and Jalics, that they had knowingly exposed themselves to considerable risk despite his pleading and offers of protection, and that following their arrest he (among many others) went to extraordinary lengths to secure their release. Reviewing all the documents and oral testimonies relevant to the case, a long roll call of eminent judges, jurists, and human-rights organizations such as Amnesty International have reached similar conclusions.

So how did Yorio come to the view that Bergoglio had betrayed them, and die believing it?

BERGOGLIO had known Orlando Yorio and Franz Jalics since the early 1960s. Jalics, a Budapest-born naturalized Argentine who belonged to the Chilean province, in the late 1960s taught Bergoglio fundamental theology and was, for a time, his spiritual director, which Bergoglio later described as his special gift. Yorio, who was from Buenos Aires, entered the Jesuits in 1955, was ordained three years before Bergoglio, in 1966, at the age of thirty-four, and taught him Saint Augustine's *De Trinitate*. In the 2010 judicial inquiry Bergoglio described Yorio as having an "exquisite sensitivity linked to an above-average intellect" and remembers his theology classes as *sabrosas*—lively and enjoyable. He also described Yorio and Jalics as "good religious" who had a balanced, orthodox position on liberation theology, within the parameters set by the Holy See.

That was not the whole truth. Yorio was a politically committed theologian, active in the Third World Priests' Movement (MSTM), a friend of Father Carlos Mugica, and a revolutionary Peronist who believed in the montonero cause. Nor did Bergoglio mention that Yorio was part of the group around the previous provincial, Ricardo O'Farrell, which had fostered egalitarian living-out experiments and had been directly responsible for the redesign of Jesuit formation so that it no longer included "bourgeois" humanistic studies. In short, Yorio represented the postconciliar Jesuit chaos that Bergoglio had been elected to supersede.

In 1970 a mix of theology students and professors, led by Yorio and Jalics, went to live in a base community in a poor area of Buenos Aires. The Ituzaingó community was an avant-garde experiment in nonhierarchical, politically *engagé* living that was highly controversial at the time in the Argentine province: some had subjective interpretations of their celibacy vow, while others were said to be involved with the guerrillas. In Yorio's twenty-seven-page 1977 letter to the Jesuit curia in Rome giving his account of the years leading up to their abduction, he acknowledged that "for a number of the theologians [the Ituzaingó experiment] led to them rethinking their vocations and leaving the Society," but always, he said, after proper reflection and with the agreement of the provincial.

The provincial, O'Farrell, ordered the community to close and gave Yorio a role researching theology and politics. Yorio moved to the Jesuit community in the Buenos Aires neighborhood of Belgrano, which housed the Jesuits' institute, the Center for Social Research and Action (CIAS), where he was often invited to give talks on liberation theology to religious orders. Unhappy with Jesuit residential life, however, Yorio at the end of 1972 persuaded O'Farrell to allow him, with Fathers Jalics, Dourrón, Rastellini, and Casalotto, to create another base community, this time in an apartment on the calle Rondeau.

Again there were rumors about their links to the guerrillas and breaking their vows. Following his election as provincial in mid-1973, Bergoglio for the time being approved the mission and told them not to worry about the rumors. In November 1974, a Jesuit student who had been with Yorio in the Ituzaingó community, Juan Luis Moyano, was arrested and tortured for suspected guerrilla links after being "disappeared" from a *villa* in Mendoza in western Argentina. Bergoglio managed to get him out and sent him abroad for study.

At the end of 1974, Bergoglio had a series of meetings with the four Jesuits (now minus Casalotto, who had left to join the diocesan priesthood), which included a two-day retreat that Yorio recalled in his letter as being "very fruitful." Bergoglio had decided to close the community as part of his provincial restructuring and asked if they would accept, under obedience. The Jesuits said they were *available*—the word has a technical meaning in the Society of Jesus of an interior disposition for mission, one of the key tests of obedience—but wanted to challenge the decision to dissolve the community, arguing that it was an apostolic success. It was agreed that Bergoglio would send Rastellini on mission to Jujuy, that Yorio would make a representation to Rome arguing against the decision to dissolve the community (it would take over a year to get a verdict from the general, Father Arrupe), and that in the meantime the three Jesuits would move to another community. Yorio made another decision at this time—to accept Bergoglio's invitation to take his final vow, which he had postponed, in mid-1976.

In early 1975, Yorio, Jalics, and Dourrón moved to a house in the Barrio Rivadavia, alongside Villa 11.14 in Bajo Flores where Yorio had begun working. There, Jalics ran retreats while the other two acted as *curas villeros*, managing a team of catechists, one of whom was the woman who later that year joined the guerrillas. At this time montonero violence and the death squads were each stepping up their operations, and the *villas miseria*—the guerrillas' base—had become extremely tense places.

The Argentine bishops in February 1975 ordered liberationist professors to cease teaching in the Villa Devoto and other seminaries, and the Colegio Máximo followed suit: in March, Yorio was relieved of his teaching post there in a letter from the rector, which in 1977 he described as curt and disrespectful.

There was a group of senior Jesuits in the Máximo with right-wing political convictions who remained highly critical of Yorio and his colleagues. "In the Colegio Máximo there were rumors that I was a montonero chief and I had women," Yorio recalled to Wornat. "Francisco Jalics various times told the Jesuits in writing what they were exposing us to." Bergoglio knew the rumors were untrue, but the senior Jesuits had the ear of the bishops and of the Jesuit curia in Rome, and Bergoglio—as Yorio acknowledges in his letter—was under pressure from many quarters to dissolve the community and pull the Jesuits out of the *villa*.

Bergoglio, however, continued to support the Barrio Rivadavia Jesuits. The problem came to a head with Yorio's final vow. A Jesuit is invited to make the vow once Rome has received a recommendation from his provincial with the support of the consultors, who have in turn received favorable written evaluations (called *informationes*) about their suitability from Jesuits who know him well. In July 1975 Bergoglio told Yorio that the *informationes* he had received had been negative: at the root of the objections, the provincial told him, appeared to be a false impression in many people's minds of what had gone on at the time of the Ituzaingó community. He had commissioned other Jesuits to write a new *informatio* on him, but it, too, had come back negative. The consultors could not agree to recommending Yorio.

This was a major blow. If Yorio had made the final vow, it would be far easier to protect both him and the community from the fierce criticisms. Yorio's 1977 letter shows his provincial at this time under enormous strain and unsure what to do next.

> Father Bergoglio told us . . . that the pressures were very great, and that he could not resist them. . . . He asked us to pray, to think, and that he would do the same, and that we should keep meeting. We had two or three meetings. He spoke to us about dissolving the community. . . . He told us he didn't know what to do, and that he feared committing an injustice. . . . He asked us not to speak with other Jesuits in the province (still less with the consultors) because the province was in a very delicate situation and that this would create a problem of division. . . . He told us to be patient and that for the good of the province we should keep all this confidential and that together we should seek a solution.

Yorio, Jalics, and Dourrón began to see that it was going to be hard to remain both in their base community and in the Society of Jesus. They wrote to Bishop (soon to be Cardinal) Eduardo Pironio, former arch-

bishop of La Plata and now head of the Vatican's Congregation for Consecrated Life in Rome, giving an account of their community and offering
what Yorio described as "a sketch of a structure of religious life in the
event we were unable to continue in the Society." What he proposed was
a new kind of avant-garde Ignatian institute that explicitly rejected the
idea of obedience to religious superiors. According to Bergoglio's deposi-
tion in 2010, the two Jesuits had also sent the draft constitutions to three
bishops they thought might be sympathetic to them.

In December 1975, Yorio recalls, "the forces of the extreme right [Tri-
ple A] had machine-gunned one priest, and they had abducted, tortured,
and left for dead another one. They both lived in *villas miseria*. We were
receiving warnings to take care." Jalics went to see Bergoglio, who promised, says Yorio, "to speak with people in the armed forces to tell them we
were innocent."

Yorio also sought support for his position within the Jesuits from his
former CIAS colleagues in Belgrano, many of whom shared his liberationist views. This was precisely what Bergoglio had sought to avoid—a
confrontation between left and right within the Society at a moment of
high political tension in the country. In February 1976, in a tense meeting, Bergoglio told them that the general, Father Arrupe, wanted a solution, and that they needed to decide either to leave the Society or obey,
which meant dissolving the community and going to live in the residences. The issue was not their work in the *villa*, as some later claimed;
Bergoglio supported their work among the poor, just as he backed the
work of another Jesuit, Father "Pichi" Meisegeier, who had replaced Father
Mugica in Villa 31 next to Retiro station. Bergoglio wanted Yorio and
Jalics in a Jesuit residential community (as Father Pichi was), not to give
up their work in the slum.[20]

Yorio said they needed time for a proper discernment. Bergoglio suggested they apply to Rome for a leave of absence. They agreed, and gave
him the papers to hand directly to Father Arrupe when he left for Rome a
few days later.

Ten days after the meeting, Bergoglio returned from Rome with a letter
from Arrupe ordering that the community be dissolved within fifteen
days, and the three Jesuits be removed from Argentina—Jalics to the United
States, and Yorio and Dourrón to another province. It was a dramatic
order, one that suggested that Arrupe believed the rumors about their

involvement with the guerrillas. Bergoglio told Yorio that "he had told the general that this order was tantamount to expelling us from the Society, but that the general's mind was firm in the matter."

Aggrieved, the Jesuits took three days to decide to leave the Society and set up their own religious institute. Their dismissal was approved on March 19. With talk of an imminent coup, Bergoglio urged them again to leave the *villa* for their own safety—they were "too exposed to the paranoia of the witch hunt," as he put it years later—and offered them rooms in the provincial curia on Bogotá Street until they found a bishop. They thanked him but refused. "He told them they had to leave, that it was very risky," recalls Alicia Oliveira. "But they wouldn't budge. They wanted to stay." It wasn't just Bergoglio warning them, but Father Rodolfo Ricciardelli, who coordinated the priests in Villa 11.14. He had heard the same rumors, and asked everyone doing social and pastoral work to leave the *villa*, for their own sakes and for the sakes of the people there. Yorio, Jalics, Dourrón, and a group of catechists chose to remain.

The three priests now found themselves passed between bishops like hot potatoes. Yorio had earlier shown his idea for a new religious institute to an old friend of the Jesuits, the archbishop of Santa Fe, Vicente Zazpe, but he hadn't wanted to get involved. Now they found that other bishops took the same view. Bergoglio asked another friend, a Salesian bishop, to take them, but Miguel Raspanti of Morón would only take Dourrón alone.

At this point it dawned on them what to others might have seemed obvious: that on the eve of a military coup, three ex-Jesuits suspected—however falsely—of guerrilla connections, who had disobeyed their provincial and wanted to create a new, nonhierarchical community in a shantytown, were unlikely to have bishops falling over each other to invite them to their dioceses. In Yorio's own words, they realized "it would be impossible to get a bishop unless the problem of the secret accusations could be clarified, and that in the meantime our priesthood and our lives were now in great danger."

Yet still they stayed in the *villa*, even after four women catechists who worked there—among them Mónica Mignone, Emilio's daughter—were abducted from there in mid-May, never to reappear. They even stayed when Archbishop Aramburu, learning on his way to Rome to be made a cardinal that the three had left the Jesuits, withdrew their licenses to practice as priests in his diocese. (When they informed Bergoglio, he told them they could still say Mass in private with the faculties he had given them.) A week later, on May 23, dozens of marines descended on the *villa* and arrested Yorio and Jalics along with eight catechists—Dourrón was on his bicycle, and just avoided being caught.

THE catechists were released after questioning, but Yorio and Jalics were taken to the clandestine ESMA center. For a number of days they were held in cells with hoods over their heads, their hands tied behind their backs, and their legs chained to a cannonball. They were given no food or water, and left to urinate and defecate over themselves while being insulted, threatened with the electric cattle prod, and interrogated after being injected with a serum.

Outside, Bergoglio moved fast. He notified Bishop Tortolo, Cardinal Aramburu, the nuncio, and the general in Rome, and from his army chaplain contacts worked out where Yorio and Jalics were being held. Bergoglio was convinced that the army would realize their mistake and release them. "We moved straightaway, but I didn't think it would last so long," he recalled in 2010.

Inside the ESMA, the army had indeed realized their mistake. After the interrogation was over, the officer in charge came to speak to the priests. They were told, recalls Yorio, that "there had been serious charges made against us. That imprisoning us had created a big problem for them, because there had been a very strong reaction in the Church and in many sectors of the country. That I was a good priest. But that I had made a mistake: to have gone to live with the poor. That this was a materialist interpretation of the Gospel. That when Christ spoke of the poor, he meant spiritual poverty."

They were told they would soon be released, recalls Jalics in his memoir, yet "despite this commitment we were then for some inexplicable reason kept in custody for five months, blindfolded and handcuffed." The publicity surrounding their capture had made it impossible for them to be "disappeared," but equally impossible for them to be released. Yorio and Jalics were moved to a house in the barrio of Don Torcuato, where they remained until October. They were not tortured and there were no further interrogations; they could go to the bathroom, and were fed. But they remained blindfolded and in chains through five long months, powerless over their fate.

Once it was clear that they were not going to be released soon, Bergoglio sought to apply pressure from many different directions to ensure they did not "disappear." A large number of people were witnesses, at this time, to his anxiety for them and his efforts on their behalf. To Jalics's family Bergoglio wrote on September 15, urging them not to give up hope. Alluding to his disagreements with Jalics, the provincial reassured them that "the difficulties that your brother and I have had between us concerning the religious life have nothing to do with the current situation." He added, in German: "Franz is a brother to me."

How Yorio and Jalics came to be released remains unclear. Mignone claimed it was Pope Paul VI's direct calls to the commander in chief of the army, General Jorge Videla. It may have been Jalics's brother in the United States personally contacting Jimmy Carter, at that point campaigning for president, who called Videla. Or it may have been the Jesuit general, Father Arrupe—whom Bergoglio had contacted at once following the kidnappings—leaning on the Argentine embassy to the Holy See; or Cardinal Aramburu speaking three times to Videla. Most likely, it was a combination of all of these. The 2010 judicial inquiry concluded that their release was "a consequence of steps taken by the religious order to which the victims belonged and the interest shown in them by leading members of the Catholic Church."

Bergoglio's efforts on behalf of the priests were considerable. He managed to arrange two interviews each with the navy chief, Admiral Emilio Massera, and with General Videla. Convinced, by piecing together various bits of evidence, that the navy held them, "I told [Massera] those priests were involved in nothing at all strange," Bergoglio told the 2010 inquiry. But the naval chief on that occasion gave nothing away, promising only to investigate. After two months, having heard nothing, Bergoglio succeeded in getting another interview. It lasted less than ten minutes and was "very ugly," he recalled. By now certain Massera had them and was lying, Bergoglio was exasperated. He told him, "Look, Massera, I want them to appear." He then got up and left. It went better with Videla:

I don't remember the exact date, but I calculate that the first audience was about two months after the kidnapping. He was very formal: he made a note, and said he would find out. I told him that it was said the navy had them. The second time, I found out which military chaplain was going to say Mass at his house, the residence of the commander in chief. I asked [the chaplain] to tell [Videla] that he was ill, and that I would be replacing him. That Saturday, after Mass, I asked to speak to him. There he gave me the impression that he was going to be more concerned and take things more seriously. It wasn't violent, like with Massera.

Yorio and Jalics were eventually released in October 1976 after a drugged ride in a helicopter that left them asleep on a remote stretch of ground outside Buenos Aires. "They had had to set us free because it was common knowledge that the navy had abducted us," Jalics recalled. "But now that we were free, they could kill us in the street to stop us talking."

When Bergoglio took Yorio's call, he took precautions in case the line was tapped: he told them not to say where they were but to send someone who knew their location.

Jalics was sent to join his mother in the United States. Meanwhile, Bergoglio met Yorio at his mother's apartment with Bishop Jorge Novak of Quilmes, who agreed to accept Yorio as a priest in his diocese. Bergoglio then paid for Yorio to be sent to Rome to take a course at the Jesuit-run Gregorian university. All of this, Yorio recalled, the provincial carried out "with great diligence and care" and "my bishop was very grateful." Yet "he could give me no explanations of what had occurred before [my arrest]. He made haste to ask me please not to ask him because at that moment he felt very confused and wouldn't know what to say. Nor did I say anything. What could I say?"

THERE, but for Yorio's interior crisis, the story might have ended. It didn't because he entered a vortex of posttraumatic grief and stress that got worse with the passing of the years. The long incarceration was the final stage in a gradual stripping of his sense of self. He had lost his identity as a Jesuit and theologian; he had lost the community that incarnated his theological ideals; he had been, as he saw it, forced to leave the Jesuits because of false rumors that the general in Rome appeared to believe. Then he had been spurned by bishops and deprived of his license as a priest, before losing his human dignity and freedom in a cell over many months, after which he was exiled. As existential displacements go, it was extreme. "I think it was conditioned by the suffering he had to undergo," Bergoglio told the 2010 inquiry, when he was asked about Yorio's belief that he had been betrayed.

In Rome, Yorio reconstructed the events to try to make sense of them, and over time came to pin his anger on his provincial. Yet the criticisms he makes in his long 1977 letter to Father Moura in the Jesuit curia in Rome are a very long way from the accusations in the Mignone book. What frustrates Yorio in that letter is the injustice of being driven out of the Society by false accusations made by faceless opponents, and finally an order from the general without the chance to defend themselves. In all of this, says Yorio, "the provincial did nothing to defend us and we had begun to question his honesty. We were tired of the province and feeling totally insecure." They were upset that Bergoglio "told us about pressures, but not what they were, and without him actually accusing us of anything and without offering us a concrete way out." Those are the worst charges Yorio makes against Bergoglio in the letter, which ends with a series of pleas to try to understand what had happened. Yorio was bewildered, and saw himself, at that stage, as a powerless victim.

Over time, that bewilderment was turned to anger by the narrative later emerging from human-rights circles. The investigations into disappearances ordered by President Raúl Alfonsín in the mid-1980s had exposed the complicity of some of the bishops and military chaplains, and a simplistic dualism had entered the discourse of the left. The narrative split the Church, and Argentine society, between sheep and wolves, between angels and demons. On the side of "good" were those brave martyrs like Angelelli and the bishops who had spoken out, while the other bishops were tarred, to different extents, with the crime of betraying their flock, of acquiescence and collaboration. In this scheme, there were only opponents and guilty bystanders.

This narrative allowed former guerrilla sympathizers to keep alive the illusion of a popular revolution frustrated by the forces of reaction, and to shirk their own role in the chaos and carnage. It was also an account that left no space for those who—like Bergoglio and most bishops—had no sympathy for the dictatorship and had worked quietly, and sometimes heroically, to save lives. Living in Montevideo after the fall of the Argentine dictatorship, Yorio saw his own story reflected in Mignone's angry tale of betrayal. "What will history say of those shepherds who handed over their sheep to the enemy, without defending them or rescuing them?" Mignone had asked. Yorio now saw Bergoglio as an *entregador*, a betrayer. Like Verbitsky after him, Mignone never questioned Yorio's evidence for this assertion. And Bergoglio never at the time sought to defend himself.

Mignone's account was taken up by some of the liberationists within the Jesuits who saw Bergoglio as a reactionary. Juan Luis Moyano, who died in 2006, had been a Jesuit student in Yorio's base community in Ituzaingó in 1972 and was tortured and imprisoned in Mendoza in 1974. Bergoglio sent him to Germany to study, from where he went to Peru for many years, nurturing resentment against his provincial. He remained in contact with Yorio and assumed his account of Bergoglio. Brought back to Argentina in 1991, he became one of Bergoglio's detractors, supplying quotes to Verbitsky as the "anonymous Jesuit" who backed Yorio's accusations by citing Bergoglio's meetings with Admiral Massera as evidence of his sympathy for the dictatorship. By the late 1990s, the demonization of Bergoglio had reached the point where Yorio came to believe something quite preposterous—that his provincial had actually put his name on a list that he gave to the torturers.

That is certainly not what he believed at the time. But in Yorio's 1977 letter you can see the idea taking shape. The letter elicits sympathy, but also reveals the narcissism that suffering can induce. His headstrong conviction of the rightness of his base community and his work among the poor appeared to blind him to the headache he was causing for his provincial. The letter shows no understanding of Bergoglio's efforts to do the right thing for them in spite of huge opposition to them from within the Jesuits and the bishops, and from Rome. To blame his provincial for not offering them a "concrete way out" seems rich, when the option to obey their provincial was there all along. It would have meant recognizing that they were Jesuits under obedience and living in the residences with others whose views they did not share—but they could have continued their work in the *villa*. Even when that concrete option was no longer available, when they had chosen to leave the Jesuits but had not yet found a bishop, Bergoglio offered them a refuge and place of safety.

To paint Bergoglio as an angel, however, would be to reverse the scheme. His confusion both before Yorio's detention and after his release shows a man troubled by self-doubt and weighed down by huge conflicting pressures; he is very far from the authoritarian, decisive figure he himself has painted. It would be extraordinary if, in navigating the elaborate tangle of conflicting loyalties and allegiances in the province at the time, he had made no mistakes. But whatever they were, he neither betrayed the two Jesuits nor did anything to facilitate their capture; even in Yorio's own account, he is a diligent, caring provincial trying to move them in the best direction while respecting their freedom; and who, after their capture, moved heaven and earth to secure their release.

Jalics took a different path from Yorio. For some time he, too, was convinced they had been betrayed, and blamed Bergoglio for failing to defend them. In spite of his angry feelings, he prayed intensely to forgive the Jesuits he thought had betrayed him. In the United States he decided to remain a Jesuit after all, and beginning in 1978 he went to live in a retreat house in Wilhelmsthal, Germany, where since then he has given *The Spiritual Exercises*. In 1980, on a thirty-day retreat, realizing that his healing was being held back by a desire for vengeance, he burned a store of documents he had been keeping from the era. It was an important step. Eight years later, at a meeting in Rome, he broke down sobbing in front of his superior. Released at last from the past, all bitterness left him.

Then came a further realization: *no one* had betrayed them. On visits to Buenos Aires in the late 1990s to give retreats, he met with Bergoglio several times. By then it was clear that he and Yorio had been abducted on that day because the catechist who became a guerrilla had given up their names during torture.

In 2000 Father Jalics and Archbishop Bergoglio celebrated Mass publicly together, and, report those present, fell into each other's arms in a heartbreaking act of reconciliation. Thirteen years later, the world's media beat a path to Wilhelmsthal, looking for comment from a white-haired eighty-six-year-old Jesuit on events that had occurred in a far-off country nearly forty years before. A few months later, in October, Jalics met Francis in the Casa Santa Marta.

FIVE

THE LEADER EXPELLED

(1980–1992)

I T WAS 10:15 A.M. on the second morning after Francis's election, and the young man at the reception desk at the Jesuits' headquarters on the Borgo Santo Spirito in Rome, a few hundred yards from St. Peter's Basilica, was dealing with what he assumed to be another hoax call. This one had said, "Good morning, it's Pope Francis, I'd like to speak with the father general," and rather than say, "Sure, and I'm Napoleon," Andrea asked curtly, "May I ask who's calling?"

Ever since Francis's election, said Father Claudio Barriga, SJ, who recounted this episode in an e-mail to fellow Jesuits, the phone had been ringing incessantly, and a few of the callers were lunatics. "There's no problem," this caller assured Andrea. "Seriously, I am Pope Francis. Who are you?" The young man gave his name and the pope asked how he was this morning. Fine, fine, said Andrea breathlessly, but pardon me, *un po' confuso*. It now dawned on him that the caller was who he said he was. When Francis gently asked again to be put through to the father general ("I would like to thank him for the beautiful letter he sent me"), Andrea relented. "Forgive me, Your Holiness, I will connect you right now."

Brother Alfonso, Father Aldolfo Nicolás's Brazilian secretary, took the call. "Holy Father, congratulations on your election!" he said. "We are all praying very much for you!" At the other end of the phone Francis was laughing. "Praying for what? That I carry on or go back?" "That you carry on, of course!" Brother Alfonso answered, as he entered Nicolás's office and passed him the phone, hissing: "It's the pope!" The general, almost as thrown as Andrea downstairs, switched helplessly between calling him "Pope," "Holiness," and "Monsignor" as Francis thanked him for his letter, said he was looking forward to meeting, and promised to call again to make a date.

He did, and that Sunday afternoon at 5:30 p.m. the first Jesuit superior general ever to meet a Jesuit pope found Francis at the door of the Casa Santa Marta. Francis gave Nicolás a fraternal hug, insisted on him using the informal Spanish *tú* form, and made the affectionate if improbable request that Nicolás should treat him like "any other Jesuit." "There was calm, humor and mutual understanding about past, present, and future," Nicolás said afterward in an internal communiqué, adding: "I left the Santa Marta convinced that it will be worth collaborating fully with him in the Lord's Vineyard."[1]

The healing had begun.

In a letter a week later to the 17,200 members of his order worldwide, Nicolás told them Pope Francis "feels deeply Jesuit" and this was evident in his papal coat of arms and his letter to Nicolás. The Society of Jesus, he said, needed to affirm its support for the holy father and offer him all their assistance. Then came a curious paragraph:

> We are aware that our efforts are limited and that we all carry the burden of a history of sin that we share with all humanity (GC 35, D. 1, n.15). But we also experience God's radical call inviting us to consider all things and look to the future in a new way, as Ignatius did in Manresa. This is the time to appropriate the words of mercy and goodness that Pope Francis repeats so convincingly and not to allow ourselves to be swept away by distractions from the past, which may paralyze our hearts and lead us to interpret reality with values that are not inspired by the Gospel.[2]

Distractions of the past? Nicolás knew how deep the wounds ran. In all the years Bergoglio had been coming to Rome as bishop, archbishop, and cardinal, he had never stayed at or even visited the Borgo Santo Spirito, as Jesuit bishops usually do, nor spoken to Nicolás's predecessor as general, Father Peter-Hans Kolvenbach. Nicolás knew that there were

Jesuits of a certain vintage—both inside Argentina and elsewhere—who mistrusted Bergoglio, saw him as a retrograde, divisive figure; and he knew that this toxicity could damage the Jesuits' relationship with the new pope, giving journalists a major story. He needed to build bridges with Francis and heal the wounds, beginning with an effusively warm letter that he had made sure reached him on his first day. To Nicolás's obvious delight, Francis's immediate, personal response by phone, letter, and their meeting on March 17 showed that the pope wanted the same.

Francis's opportunity for reconciliation with the Society of Jesus took place on July 31, 2013, the Feast of Saint Ignatius of Loyola, when he celebrated Mass with two hundred Jesuits at their awesome baroque church in Rome, the Gesù. Nicolás spoke afterward of "the simple reality of a gathering of brothers, 'friends in the Lord,'" which the event evoked. Francis lit a votive candle to Saint Ignatius, and stopped at the altar of the great missionary Saint Francis Xavier. He also visited the chapel of Our Lady of the Way, patroness of the Jesuits and the title of a fresco that was dear to Saint Ignatius and his early companions. But what really moved those present was his visit after Mass to the tomb of Father Arrupe, the Jesuit general who had died in 1991, ten years after being paralyzed by a stroke and losing his speech. John Paul II had seized the opportunity at that point to intervene in the Society of Jesus, and Francis was one of those who knew how much Arrupe had suffered in the years that followed. "It was an intense moment of deep prayer and gratitude," Nicolás wrote to the Jesuits. "It was obvious that the pope would like to have remained longer."[3]

But what neither he nor most of the press reports mentioned was the penitential tone of Francis's homily. He prayed that he and all of them would receive "the grace of shame" for their failures, adding that Jesuits are taught to look upon the crucifix and "feel that very human and very noble sentiment that is shame for not measuring up." It was both a personal reflection and a universal message for all Jesuits; but maybe there were old men whom he particularly wanted it to reach. Some were in Argentina, others were in Rome, a few were elsewhere. Some were dead.

In August, after the Vatican had emptied in advance of the tourist tsunami, Francis met the forty-seven-year-old editor of the prestigious Jesuit journal *Civiltà Cattolica* at the Casa Santa Marta for a six-hour interview over three meetings. Father Antonio Spadaro was taken up in the lift, and shown into Room 201, where there was a sitting room with desk and chairs adjacent to the pope's little bedroom. Francis waved him in. "You have to be normal," the pope told him, smiling. "Life is normal."

Spadaro had to set down his notebook to rely on the recorder. Switching seamlessly between Italian and Spanish, roaming over a huge range of topics, Francis was a volcano of ideas, concepts, and references, yet serene and rooted. Spadaro found almost everything about him to be a surprise: "his way of speaking, his availability, his openness, his immediacy, his depth, his politeness." In one of the meetings, as they went over his answers, taking it in turns to read each paragraph out loud, Francis brought him an apricot juice and poured it for him. Spadaro never much liked apricot juice, "but from that moment it has been dear to me."[4]

"A Big Heart Open to God," a twelve-thousand-word interview published simultaneously in fifteen Jesuit journals across the world in September 2013, was by far the most significant interview ever given by a pope. The only comparable precedent was Benedict XVI's book-length interview, *The Light of the World*, which had briefly dominated the news when it came out in November 2012, when Benedict XVI had said the use of a condom can be "a first step in the direction of a moralization, a first assumption of responsibility" in the context of AIDS in Africa. But the rest—even his saying very clearly that he would resign if he felt physically unable to continue—had been ignored as predictable, because that is how the media saw him. The Jesuit interview with Francis, on the other hand, was a bombshell, in part because the media had decided that everything he did or said spelled change. The *New York Times*, which had an advance copy, honed in on Francis's comment that the Church had become too "obsessed" with "too few things"—contraception, homosexuality, and abortion—in a story that went viral within minutes. "A lot of people felt the Church had been focusing on those things, but to hear a pope say it so bluntly and so candidly was a real shock to people," says Father James Martin, SJ, of *America* magazine, which published the interview in the United States.

The pope was recasting the Church as tender mother rather than harsh judge. In its most quoted part, Francis said he "saw clearly that the thing the Church needs most today is the ability to heal wounds and to warm the hearts of the faithful; it needs nearness, proximity." He then used a startling image.

I see the Church as a field-hospital after battle. It is useless to ask a seriously injured person if he has high cholesterol and about the level of his blood sugars! You have to heal his wounds. Then we can talk about everything else. Heal the wounds, heal the wounds. . . . And you have to start from the ground up.

The Church sometimes has locked itself up in small things, in small-minded rules. The most important thing is the first proclamation: Jesus Christ has saved you. And the ministers of the church must be ministers of mercy above all. . . . In pastoral ministry we must accompany people, and we must heal their wounds.

How are we treating the people of God? I dream of a church that is a mother and shepherdess. The church's ministers must be merciful, take responsibility for the people and accompany them like the good Samaritan, who washes, cleans and raises up his neighbor. This is pure Gospel. God is greater than sin. The structural and organizational reforms are secondary—that is, they come afterward. The first reform must be the attitude. The ministers of the Gospel must be people who can warm the hearts of the people, who walk through the dark night with them, who know how to dialogue and to descend themselves into their people's night, into the darkness, but without getting lost.

Francis's metaphor of the Church as a battlefield hospital almost certainly came, consciously or not, from the lazaretto in Manzoni's *The Betrothed*, the Italian epic his grandmother Rosa used to read to him as a child, which was on the pope's desk when Spadaro interviewed him.

The lazaretto was a hellish, makeshift place outside the walls of Milan where thousands of plague-stricken patients were brought to recover or mostly die, following a war-induced famine. Run by intrepid, self-denying friars who cared for throngs of sick in appalling circumstances, the lazaretto is used by Manzoni to great effect as a backdrop to the novel's heart-rending scenes: it is where the lovers are reunited, and where Father Cristoforo—a humble, tender, fearless son of Saint Francis—is found at the novel's end, plague-weakened yet expending his remaining energies in the service of others. As a metaphor for the Church as channel of mercy, rather than regulator and rule maker, it was extraordinarily powerful.[5]

Those were the parts of the interview that generated—as they were intended to—the main news coverage. But while Francis was capable of communicating in the simplest of terms to the broadest range of people, he could also use a coded language for internal consumption. Parts of the interview were designed specifically for the readers of those Jesuit journals.

Noting that "now more than ever" Jesuits were called to work closely with the whole Church, he told Spadaro that this required "much humility, sacrifice and courage, especially when you are misunderstood or you are the subject of misunderstandings and slanders." He went on to give examples: "Let us think of the tensions of the past history, in the previous centuries, about the Chinese rites controversy, the Malabar rites and the Reductions in Paraguay." Jesuits knew what he meant: these were historic examples of "inculturated" missionaries adopting practices at odds with Rome but which history showed to be on the side of right. Francis was demonstrating that he understood, as a Jesuit, the price that obedience to the Church sometimes demanded, while stressing that living in that tension produced what he called "the most fruitful attitude."

The interview also contained another olive branch to the Argentine Jesuits who continued to be suspicious of him: he confessed to governing the Argentine province in an authoritarian manner, not consulting enough. But he firmly rejected the injustice of the accusation many Jesuits had made of him that he was right-wing. "My authoritarian and quick manner of making decisions led me to have serious problems and to be accused of being ultraconservative," he told Spadaro, "but I have never been a right-winger."

Asked what it was about being a Jesuit that shaped his papacy, the pope did not hesitate: "Discernment." He described the Jesuit means of distinguishing good and bad spirits as "the instrument of struggle in order to know the Lord and follow him more closely." Discernment, he said, "guides me in my way of governing." Decision making included discussion and consultation, but was about "looking at the signs, listening to the things that happen, the feelings of the people, especially the poor." It meant sometimes waiting and assessing, taking the necessary time to decide on a course of action; or doing something now that you had thought you would do later. His choices as pope—living in the Casa Santa Marta, using a humble car—were the result of a discernment that followed from "looking at things, at people, and from reading the signs of the times." Ordinarily, the way of making decisions was the one Saint Ignatius in *The Spiritual Exercises* described as the "Second Time," "when sufficient light and knowledge is received through experiences of consolations and desolations, and through experience of the discernment of the different spirits."

Spadaro noted that Francis's Jesuit model was Peter Faber (1506–1546), Saint Ignatius's first companion, a Savoyard Frenchman who, unlike Ignatius and Xavier, was of peasant stock. Bergoglio, who was a lower-middle-class boy from Flores while most of his companions were graduates of prestigious Jesuit private schools, may have identified with Faber for that reason. But the two were alike in other ways. Faber was gentle, open-minded, with a great capacity for dialogue—he had a particular mission to the Calvinists—yet was a leader and reformer who was capable of decisive government. On his birthday that year, December 17, 2013, Francis had breakfast at the Casa Santa Marta with four homeless men and their dog, before later that morning declaring Faber a saint by means of an "equivalent canonization"—entering his name in the calendar of saints without a formal ceremony. He called Nicolás to tell him. "I just signed the decree," he told him.

In the New Year, Francis celebrated Faber's canonization with 350 Jesuits at the Gesù. In his homily he described the new saint as a "modest man, sensitive, with a deep inner life and endowed with the gift of making friends with people of all kinds," as well as being "a restless spirit, indecisive, never satisfied." On July 31, 2014, the Feast of Saint Ignatius, Francis joined the Jesuits for lunch. Photos were later posted on the website of the Jesuit Curia that showed Francis laughing uproariously, at home with his brothers again.[6]

Not only had the relationship healed, but Francis's desire to be seen as a Jesuit pope meant the Society was basking in his reflected popularity. Ever since Paul VI in 1974, Jesuits had felt chill winds from Rome. In less than a year, Francis had brought the Society back into the fold, modeling a whole new papal relationship with the Jesuits that was almost the exact reverse of John Paul II's. Meanwhile, Francis had set about building bridges with his Jesuit critics in Argentina, sending them affectionate handwritten letters that some read with tears in their eyes.[7]

Not long after Bergoglio stood down as provincial in December 1979, he had a second brush with death. Dr. Juan Carlos Parodi, then a thirty-seven-year-old surgeon, was called out to the San Camilo Clinic in Buenos Aires to treat a Jesuit priest who years later he realized was Bergoglio. His patient was suffering from gangrenous cholecystitis, a severe inflammation that cuts the blood supply to the gallbladder, a fatal condition if not treated. Dr. Parodi, who remembered only that his patient had been "very ill," removed the gallbladder and drained the affected area. Bergoglio recovered in a few days and, when the doctor refused to be paid, gave him a book on Saint Ignatius, who had also suffered agonizing cholecystitis.[8]

Bergoglio was now rector of the Colegio Máximo, one of three positions (the others are provincial and novice master) appointed by the general in Rome. His successor as provincial was Father Andrés Swinnen, who in turn was replaced by Father Ernesto López Rosas as novice master. All three were part of the group around the province's spiritual guru, Father Miguel Angel Fiorito, in the late 1960s, and shared a similar outlook. That made for a smooth transition. Swinnen kept Bergoglio's innovations—the team of roving missionaries, the vocations group, the expansion of discernment retreats—while raising funds to cover the costs of the dozens of new vocations.

As rector, Bergoglio was director of the philosophy and theology faculties, and in charge of the formation of close to one hundred Jesuit students, which would double by the time he stepped down in 1986. He had exercised a de facto role as *formator* after moving into the college as provincial in 1976, but could now, as he turned forty-three, focus wholly on the calling he had first recognized in Chile twenty years earlier. The college was filling up with dozens of new Jesuits—young men needing to be formed—and Bergoglio had a compelling model of missionary priesthood and Ignatian spirituality to impart. Swinnen's policies continued Bergoglio's priorities: in order to improve formation, the college retained the best students as professors in the Máximo rather than let them be sent to universities abroad, as happened in the 1960s and early 1970s.

Bergoglio's reorganized studies of philosophy and theology were at the heart of the study cycle at the Máximo. The curriculum was national and popular, with the juniors receiving solid doses of Argentine history and literature. The philosophers and theologians imbibed the *teología del pueblo*, with its emphasis on popular religiosity, as dominant at that time in the Máximo as it was in Argentine diocesan seminaries. But the Máximo was not parochial. In 1985 the college hosted a four-day international conference on the evangelization of culture and inculturation, and Bergoglio invited Jean-Yves Calvez, the French Jesuit expert on Karl Marx who had been one of Arrupe's four chief advisers, to give a course each year at the Máximo. Spirituality remained key: the rediscovered *Exercises*, and Ignatian discernment, were a major part of student life, and the articles (many of them by Bergoglio) in the spirituality journal edited by Fiorito, the *Boletín de Espiritualidad*, continued to shape the province's renewal.

Bergoglio's formation program, however, had an extra, radical element seldom found in Jesuit training at the time, which he took from the early missions that so inspired him. It was an option for the poor expressed in manual labor, hands-on pastoral care, and a deep respect for popular culture and values, especially a religiosity of pilgrimages, shrines, and devotions. It was a radical *inculturation* into the lives of God's holy faithful people.

Over the years this format met with increasing opposition from older Jesuits in Argentina, elsewhere in Latin America, and eventually from the Jesuit curia in Rome. Within Argentina, the hostility came from senior Jesuit intellectuals in the Center for Social Research and Action, or CIAS, who took advantage of the change of general in Rome in 1983 to lobby against the rector and his followers, arguing that Bergoglio's model of formation was backward and out of step with the Society of Jesus in Latin America. When the new superior general, Father Kolvenbach, imposed the CIAS's candidate as provincial in 1986, the move met with opposition from the younger Jesuits angry at what they saw as the dismantling of Bergoglio's apostolate. The Argentine Jesuits entered a tense period that eventually split the province and led to Bergoglio's internal exile.

At heart those tensions echoed unsettled questions over Jesuit identity and mission that so vexed all three popes of the 1970s. Soon after his election in August 1978, Pope John Paul I scheduled an address to the Society of Jesus that his sudden death five weeks later prevented him from giving. His successor, Cardinal Karol Wojtyla of Krakow, elected John Paul II in October of that year, gave Arrupe the scolding his predecessor had prepared, and said he agreed with it. Arrupe did, too—in part. He told Jesuit leaders in Rome that after fifteen years of searching and experimentation it was time to restore some traditional values that had been jettisoned in the process. But he was old and ill, and believed another should now take the helm, and in 1980 he asked permission of John Paul II to resign and call a new general congregation.

John Paul II ordered him to wait; he wanted to reform the Society before it chose his successor. But then came the shooting of the pope in St. Peter's Square, and in August 1981 Arrupe was felled by a cerebral thrombosis that left him hemiplegic and increasingly without speech. In accordance with the Jesuit constitutions, the general's responsibility should have passed to an interim administrator who would call a general congregation to elect a successor. But the convalescent John Paul II overrode the constitutions and imposed his own personal delegate, the octogenarian Italian Jesuit Paolo Dezza, who had been Paul VI's confessor.

The eighteen-month papal intervention sent shock waves through the Society and turned many Jesuits into lifelong opponents of John Paul II. Others saw it as a chance to take stock after the heady Arrupe years of experimentation and innovation. In February 1982 Swinnen joined eighty-five other provincials in Rome to hear John Paul II tell them things Bergoglio would have agreed with: that Vatican II needed to be authentically interpreted, that the Jesuits needed a distinctive "priestly" engagement in the quest for justice as well as a rigorous formation that was "spiritual, doctrinal, disciplinary, and pastoral." He asked them to take up four tasks: ecumenism, interreligious dialogue, dialogue with atheists, and the promotion of justice. At the end of the address, the pope gave permission for the Society to elect Arrupe's successor.

In September the following year, Bergoglio and López Rosas were elected to accompany Swinnen as delegates to GC33 in Rome. The election of a Jesuit general has similarities with a papal conclave. Before the voting, there was a report about the state of the Society and discussions of the necessary requisites of the future general. There was also a prayerful time for *murmurationes*, during which the two hundred delegates could discreetly discuss and get to know candidates. Just like the cardinal electors in a conclave, they weighed candidates' prayerfulness, leadership, and organizational skills, as well as their capacity to tackle the challenges of the moment; anyone showing any sign of ambition was automatically disqualified. Then, after a prayer to the Holy Spirit and oath of secrecy, the voting was carried out by secret written ballots.

On September 13, 1983, Father Peter-Hans Kolvenbach was elected on the first ballot, a shy, soft-spoken Dutchman with a goatee beard and the diplomatic skills to restore relations with the Holy See. Although GC33's main purpose was his election, it issued a statement that echoed reservations (which Bergoglio shared) about Decree Four, lamenting "deficiencies . . . essentially linked to the tendency to reduce the concept of justice to too-human dimensions." The decree was reaffirmed, but the statement stressed the need to integrate justice into the service of faith.

Back home there was regime change, too, triggered by the military junta's disastrous invasion in April 1982 of barren islands in the South Atlantic claimed by Argentina but occupied by Great Britain since the nineteenth century. The six-week Falklands War was devastating in its cost in lives—649 Argentines and 255 British died fighting over islands with a population of just eighteen hundred—but for Argentines it was doubly traumatic because of the tortuous mix of emotions involved. On the one hand, Argentines believed passionately that the recovery of the islands was a matter of justice; on the other, they came to see that the military junta had used the invasion in the hope of avoiding accountability for the crimes of the dirty war.

There were many Jesuits from army families, and prayers and Masses were said at the Máximo for the beleaguered troops. During the war, in May, Pope John Paul II made a long-planned pastoral visit to the United Kingdom. To maintain balance, he paid a two-day visit to Argentina on June 11, just as its ten thousand soldiers were fighting a desperate losing battle in Port Stanley (they surrendered days later). Bergoglio went with the staff and students of the Máximo to a huge outdoor Mass celebrated close to the Monument to the Spaniards in Buenos Aires where John Paul II prayed for a rapid end to the war, and to hear the pope speak to religious and priests in Buenos Aires cathedral.

Bergoglio shared the mixed emotions of his compatriots. Like them he believed the islands were part of Argentine territory, and British occupation a colonial injustice. What he said at the time of the war has not been recorded, but as cardinal archbishop he spoke often at Masses for the veterans, deploying the quasi-mystical language of Argentine nationalism that jars so strongly with the British focus on the right to self-determination of the island's occupants. Blessing relatives of fallen soldiers on their journey in October 2009 to the islands to erect a cenotaph in Darwin cemetery, for example, he told them to "go and kiss that land which is ours and which seems so far away," and that their sons, husbands, and fathers "fell there in an almost religious gesture of kissing with their blood the soil of the fatherland." And in 2012, on the thirtieth anniversary of the conflict, he spoke of those who died as "sons of the fatherland who went out to defend their mother, the fatherland, to claim what belonged to the fatherland and had been usurped."

Yet he was appalled by the war, and the recklessness of the invasion, describing it in 2008 as "a sad story, a dark chapter in Argentina's history." But he was determined that the veterans and their families not be burdened with the nation's shame, constantly demanding that they be honored and remembered, and their sacrifice acknowledged. "Society owes them a great debt," he said in his homily that year, pointing out their psychological as well as physical scars, and the challenges the traumatized veterans faced in finding work and forming relationships. Among those at the Mass that day was a group of veterans whom the government did not recognize as such and whose cause Bergoglio had backed, arguing that everyone involved in the war, on or off the theater of combat, bore its scars and deserved to be recognized.[9]

The Falklands defeat, and the revelations of incompetence and corruption that followed, permanently destroyed Argentines' historic faith in the armed forces as national saviors. Even before the troops came home, the dictatorship had begun to unravel. As journalists uncovered the first mass graves of *desaparecidos*, the junta began negotiating with the political parties a pathway to elections. The victory of the Radical Party candidate, Raúl Alfonsín, in the October 1983 presidential elections marked a decisive break with the past. Among his first moves was the creation of a commission led by the writer Ernesto Sábato to probe human-rights abuses during the dictatorship. Its report, *Nunca Más* (Never Again), led to a landmark trial and the imprisonment of a number of former junta leaders—an extraordinary achievement. But as the scope of the trials widened, restlessness in the ranks of the armed forces led Alfonsín to a put a stop to them in the interests of consolidating democracy. Argentina would continue for the next twenty years to be caught between the need and desire for both justice and reconciliation.

The economy proved harder to restore than democracy. Alfonsín failed to deal with the soaring budget deficit, vast foreign debt, and shrinking economy he had inherited from the dictatorship, and despite a new

currency, by the end of the decade the country was in a major hyperinfla-
tionary crisis. For working-class Argentines living in the barrios around
the Colegio Máximo in San Miguel, the 1980s were a time of great hard-
ship, as rising prices and unemployment pushed thousands of families
into destitution.

"WITHIN four or five years we were two hundred in the college, all Jesuits, all Argentines," remembers one of its former students, Angel Rossi.
The Máximo was "a real powerhouse of energy" at this time, recalls another,
Leonardo Nardín. Its growth could be glimpsed in buildings: a large new
novice house had sprung up to replace the Villa Bailari, and a new library
opened in October 1981, boasting one of Latin America's largest theology
collections.

Work also began in 1980 on a new church. From the early 1970s the
Jesuits in the college had served the parish of Our Lady of Perpetual Help
together with its five chapels, three schools, and an adult education
center. After he became rector, Bergoglio secured permission from the
Bishop of San Miguel to build a new parish church, St. Joseph the Patriarch, on land donated by the college. The parish covered three barrios of
simple dwellings on unpaved roads that turned to mud in the rains.
Bergoglio's first baptism at the church—a baby called Griselda on February 24, 1980—took place a month before the inauguration of the parish
on the Feast of Saint Joseph, March 19, the same day Francis would begin
his papacy thirty-three years later. In 1980 the church was little more
than a shed but, through the efforts of students and parishioners, soon
acquired bricks and a roof. Within a couple of years, it was a huge church
at the center of a busy pastoral operation including a children's kitchen,
and two schools next to the Máximo offering job skills workshops and
adult education. The Patriarca San José parish eventually spawned four
new large chapels spread over the three barrios.[10]

One day Bergoglio appeared with four cows, four pigs, and six sheep.
He had many more mouths to feed at a time of rising prices and squeezed
donors, and had twenty-five empty fertile acres around the college. Trees
were pulled up behind the college to make way for sheds and barns. The
land was fenced off and dug for vegetables, and shelters were built to house
livestock: eventually there were (according to one of the students whose

job was to keep a tally) 120 pigs, 50 sheep, 180 rabbits, 20 cows, and a number of beehives.[11] A Jesuit brother took a jalopy to the market each afternoon to collect products past their sell-by date. On their return, the students chose what was fit for humans and what went to the pigs.

The farm, born of need, served a higher end. It brought students from middle-class backgrounds into the lives of workers. They had taken a vow of poverty, Bergoglio told them, and poor people worked: "it is the law of all, which makes us equal to others." Only by sharing the lives of the poor, he said, could they discover "the true possibilities of justice in the world" as opposed to "an abstract justice which fails to give life."[12] In addition to six hours of classes a day and studies, the students had manual tasks most weekdays. Inside were the kitchen, the laundry, and the endless corridors and bathrooms that needed cleaning. Outside, they took on tasks under the supervision of the Jesuit brothers who ran the farm day to day. Students collected honey, milked cows, and cleaned out the pigsty, where they often met the rector in his plastic boots. "It was a mucky job and many objected," recalls Guillermo Ortiz, who today runs the Spanish-language section of Vatican Radio. "But they couldn't complain against Bergoglio because he would put his boots on like the rest of us to get down in with the hogs."

The hours spent on work during priestly formation were very important to their rector, recalls Gustavo Antico. "He went over each of the jobs he gave us and helped us with them, completely naturally." Manual work helped students develop a fundamental Ignatian principle: "not to be limited by the greatest and yet to be contained in the tiniest—this is the divine."[13] It meant, Pope Francis explained years later to Father Spadaro, "being able to do the little things of every day with a big heart open to God and to others" and "being able to appreciate the small things inside large horizons, those of the Kingdom of God." It was about avoiding both pusillanimous obsession with detail and grandiose, unrealistic projects.[14]

The farm was also key to the Jesuits' local apostolate. It helped to feed not just the college but the poor of the surrounding barrios. As the 1980s economic downturn bit into local jobs and salaries, Jesuit students sent out by the rector on house visits reported many families eating barely once a day. "Bergoglio said, 'We can't sit around with our arms crossed while people are hungry and we lack nothing,'" recalls Alejandro Gauffin.[15] They commandeered a huge cooking pot, gathered an army of volunteers, and lit a fire in a field under a tarp, which grew into the Casa del Niño, feeding four hundred children a day, and a similar-sized operation next door in San Alonso. Most of the food came from the college farm and was the same as that served in the Máximo's dining room. "We never went hungry because there was a lot of it, but it was the same food, mostly a kind of *guiso* ('stew') that the simple people around us ate," recalls Miguel Yáñez, who saw this as totally consistent with their option for the poor. But some of the professors grumbled: "they were used to another standard."

The farm was also an aid to contemplation. "He took me outside where the community kept sheep and pigs," remembers María Soledad Albisú, later a nun, who had Bergoglio as her spiritual director at this time. "He told me this was a good place to pray and that God is to be found in the lowliest things."[16] Working with the animals and the land taught patience, tenacity, and humility, and opened up the many Scripture stories involving herds of hogs and flocks of sheep, while for the novices and scholastics—many of whom were graduates of prestigious Jesuit schools— being knee-deep in pig muck brought alive the startling meditation at the beginning of *The Spiritual Exercises*: "Thus for our part," writes Saint Ignatius in the "Principle and Foundation," "we should not want health more than sickness, wealth more than poverty, fame more than disgrace, a long life more than a short one . . . desiring and choosing only what conduces more to the end for which we are created."

The days of class and manual work were framed by prayer. Early mornings were cordoned off for individual contemplation, followed by Mass in the morning and community prayer in the evening. Twice a day, noon and evening, the bell summoned everyone to the chapel for a fifteen-minute silent *examen*, or review of the graces and sins of that day, seeing where God was present, giving thanks, and saying sorry. Like Saint Ignatius, Bergoglio set great store in the *examen*, describing it as "the way for us to seek the truth about ourselves before God."[17] The spirituality of the *Exercises* permeated the Jesuits' life in other ways: in talks and retreats led by Bergoglio, Fiorito, and others, and in regular meetings with spiritual directors. "We were all formed in the conviction that there is great power in prayer and that as Jesuits we can help others through *The Spiritual Exercises*," recalls Ortiz. "Every decision or choice had to be prayed over and discerned," agrees another of the Jesuit scholastics at the time, Fernando Cervera. "He taught us that every decision had a consequence, which had to be weighed."

It was a missionary spirituality, in which the concrete needs of people often interrupted the schedule of prayer. When Rossi was on his annual eight-day retreat one year he was summoned by Bergoglio on the fourth day. "He said to me, 'You're very comfortable praying, eating and sleeping, but outside the college there is a woman with four children who is homeless, so leave the retreat and get her a roof over her head, and when they have a home, you can go back to the retreat.'" Rossi had no idea how to do that, but over the next few days he learned—with Bergoglio's help. "He knew what doors to knock on," says Rossi, who never forgot the lesson. "I went back once I had completed the 'mission.'"

DOZENS of students fanned out over the barrios of the town on Saturday afternoons and Sunday mornings, going from house to house in San Miguel, collecting children for Mass and giving catechesis in the fifteen chapels run by the Jesuits. Yáñez recalls a typical weekend:

> Saturday morning I was in charge of the bees, someone else had the vegetable garden—we each had our tasks: the sheep, the pigs, whatever. That was the morning. In the afternoon, we had lunch and then went to the barrios to gather up the children for the catechism. We usually had a lot of organizing to do—the summer camps, for example, or the Day of the Child celebrations when we got three thousand children together and each one got a toy, mostly new ones. There were a lot of us; we were very organized and highly motivated. For example, two of us during the year were assigned to talk to the toy manufacturers to ask for donations—they saw what we were doing and they wanted to help. For the summer camps, we took about five hundred young people—first the boys, later the girls—to the seaside at Mar del Plata, where the fishmongers gave us a whole load of food for free. Sunday mornings, we had Mass in the different communities, then catechesis, house visits and then back to the college for a longer siesta, sport, study—our time was free. And in the evening we got the guitars out, played cards, with Bergoglio there, just like anyone else. It was a very intense, very organized week. I had a great time.

Patriarca San José embodied Bergoglio's vision of a radical apostolate geared to the peripheries. Rather than put up a sign with Mass times outside the church and wait for people to come, he sectioned the area off into zones, assigned dozens of Jesuit students to each one, and sent them out through dusty or muddy streets to visit households ("no corner was left untouched," says Rossi). "It was a Copernican revolution," recalls another student, Renzo De Luca. "We had to go and really knock on the doors and say: 'Look, here's the *Catechism*. Send us your young people.' You had to have a lot of nerve to invite them to church while it was obvious that they had the bare minimum to eat. Yet people responded to our call."[18]

Bergoglio told the students to "get into the barrio and walk it," starting with the young people—the others, he said, would follow in their own time—and to spend time with the elderly and sick, paying close attention to the needs of the poorest, whether for food, medicine, or blankets. The Jesuits still recall their rector's many exhortations. "Our vocation asks that we be pastors of large flocks, not strokers of a few preferred sheep," was one. "It is better that on the Lord's Day he should find us with war wounds from having gone to the frontier than pudgy and pale from having stayed behind" was another.[19] On Sundays, Bergoglio waited outside the church, greeting people and hearing their confessions before Mass. His homilies were simple, direct, funny, and engaging: penetrating, never too long, based on three points, and punctuated by back-and-forth banter with the congregation.

Bergoglio built institutions to improve the lives of the people in the barrios of Manuelita, Constantini, and Don Alfonso. Through donations, the Casa del Niño came to occupy a building capable of feeding two hundred children at a time in the dining room and fifty at a time in the crèche, and gave food, medical care, and schooling for more than four hundred children daily. Other buildings went up: there was a night school for adults who had not finished high school, a technical school to learn trades, and scholarships to enable children to go on to college. "We really made a difference," recalls Yáñez. "Today those kids are teachers and doctors, or they've got degrees and have really got on in society." The summer camps for children near Mar del Plata were paid for with donations that the Jesuits gathered during the year. "To take a child who has never seen the ocean and who has never had a vacation was a way of giving them dignity, of treating them as a human person," recalls Fernando Albistur. "Even today there are those young people who are now married who have children who come up to you in the parish and say, 'Thanks to you I saw the ocean, I saw the beach, I had a vacation once in my life.' "[20]

Bergoglio told the students how, in meeting the concrete needs of the poor, Christ was teaching them something important. He had learned this, he said, from a woman called Marta, who had a large, penniless family and was the kind who survived by asking for things; it was easy to tire of her requests. One Sunday evening, when she approached Bergoglio and said her family was hungry and cold, he told her to come back the next day to see what he could do. "But Father," said Marta, "we're hungry *now*, and we're cold *now*." He went to his room, took a blanket off his bed, and found her food. The point Bergoglio had learned was that Christ spoke through the poor, and meeting their needs was not something that could be deferred for one's own convenience.

When the students returned to the college, Bergoglio would be waiting for them, tapping his plastic watch if they were late—he valued punctuality—and checking the soles of their shoes for evidence of barrio dust. The students reported on people's needs and he would organize help. "He used us as bridges," recalls Rossi. "Mostly when we went back with what they needed they had no idea he was behind it."

During the week, in pastoral theology classes and meditations, Bergoglio asked the students to reflect on their experiences. He insisted that they were not going to teach, but to be taught by, the *pueblo fiel*; the Jesuits' capacity for inserting themselves into the culture they were sent to evangelize was "the decisive test" of their faith. "How difficult it is, and how lonely it can feel, when I realize I must learn from the people their language, their terms of reference, their values, not as a way of polishing my theology but as a new way of being that transforms me," he told them.[21] A major part of that learning was to respect and understand popular forms of piety: asking the saints to intercede, praying the Rosary, going on pilgrimages to shrines, reverently touching statues. Bergoglio encouraged his students to do the same. His idea, recalls Rossi, was that "here we have poor people, and because they are poor they rely on faith, and because they have faith, they are our center. Their faith, their culture, their way of expressing their faith—that's what we must value."

In October and November 1985, two more chapels were inaugurated in Patriarca San José parish: one in San Alonso, the other not far from the college. A journalist sent to cover the second—a vast church in the colonial style named for the Jesuit Paraguay martyrs—described processions of joyful people carrying flower-decked wooden images and flags, listening to speeches under umbrellas. She was astonished by the transformation of a neighborhood that had been notorious for its poverty, street gangs, and neglect. Newcomers were no longer pelted with stones; children were nourished and schooled; the elderly and the sick were cared for; the parish's chapels overflowed; all was clean and tidy. Around the church, "instead of ditches full of garbage, you saw flowers and cut lawns, painted doors, and baskets to hold rubbish bags; not a single defaced wall, or signs of aggression—just a fraternal human family, proud of itself, and celebrating." She was struck by the "intelligent and serious" Jesuit students she met who had catalyzed this makeover, so different from the ones she had known a decade earlier who had idolized Che Guevara and scorned the Church's past as bourgeois. The article was headlined: "The Miracles of Father Bergoglio."[22]

In a lengthy article in 1980, referring for the first time in his writings to GC32's Decree Four, Bergoglio laid out the "criteria of apostolic action" for Jesuits promoting justice. The action, he wrote, must be rooted in the concrete demands, as well as the culture and values, of the *pueblo fiel*, and so avoid the approach of the enlightened classes (whether liberal, left-wing, or conservative) who were "for the people, but never with the people." Their action must fit within the history and spirituality of the Jesuits. And it must start from a direct contact with the poor, seeing concrete acts of mercy as acts of justice, and then reflecting on that encounter.

The new awareness that resulted, says Bergoglio, would eventually bring about structural change, avoiding the sterile "we-should-ism"[23] of those who pursue justice in the abstract. The specific Jesuit task, he said, was to train and encourage lay people through *The Spiritual Exercises*, and to create institutions of belonging. A sign of the vitality of a project was its capacity for bringing together lay people committed to it. Above all, said Bergoglio, Jesuits must bring about change through inculturation. That meant never acting on the poor, as ideological elites did: in converting hearts and structures, they must not commit the injustice of betraying the culture of the people, nor their legitimate values and aspirations.

> The example of Our Lord saves us: He became incarnate in the people. Peoples have habits, values, cultural references which are not easily

classified. . . . To adjust our ears to hear their desire for change requires humility, affection, the habit of inculturation, and, above all, a rejection of any absurd pretension to be become the "voice" of the people, imagining perhaps that they don't have one. . . . The first question any pastor seeking to reform structures must ask is: What is my people asking of me? What is it calling on me to do? And then he must dare to listen.[24]

☙

BERGOGLIO's ideas about inculturation echoed an emerging theme within Latin-American theology. He had been part of the preparations for the third continent-wide Latin-American bishops' council (CELAM) meeting at Puebla in 1979, whose concluding document had affirmed the option for the poor while definitively rejecting the Marxist-influenced version of liberation theology. One account of Puebla, which passed into media reports at the time, saw only an attempt by conservatives led from Rome (Pope John Paul II and his ally, the secretary-general of CELAM, Colombian archbishop Alfonso López Trujillo) to clamp down on liberation theology, resisted by the Latin-American bishops defending Medellín. But that missed the other, more important story of Puebla: the recognition that an option for the poor meant an option for their distinctive popular culture and religiosity.

Bergoglio saw Puebla as a huge breakthrough. It now became possible to look at Latin America through its own cultural tradition, preserved above all in the spiritual and religious resources of the ordinary faithful people rather than through the lens of imported or elite ideologies. If those resources were liberated, Bergoglio believed, Latin America could free itself from those ideologies as well as from the economic imperialism of money, both of which held Latin America back by destroying "the Christian originality of the encounter with Jesus Christ which so many of our people still live out in their simplicity of faith."[25]

The story of Puebla is partly, then, the story of the rise of the Argentine school of post-Medellín theology. The document's rich passages on the evangelization of culture and popular religiosity were drafted by the pioneer of the *teología del pueblo*, Father Lucio Gera, as well as a Chilean theologian in the same line of thinking, Father Joaquín Allende. At Puebla they took Paul VI's *Evangelii Nuntiandi*—which had itself been influenced by Gera—and applied it to Latin America, citing it ninety-seven times in the concluding document.

Another key contributor to the redaction of the Puebla document was Alberto Methol Ferré, a Uruguayan thinker on the CELAM staff who would have a major influence on Bergoglio's ideas about the historic destiny of the Latin-American Church. Bergoglio first met Methol Ferré in 1978 at a lunch with the USAL rector, Francisco Piñón. These River Plate theologians and intellectuals—including the current head of the Vatican's Commission for Latin America, the Uruguayan Guzmán Carriquiry—formed a short-lived group called Juan Diego de Guadalupe, which met regularly in Argentina in the run-up to Puebla. Bergoglio, recalls Carriquiry, "came and went" from these meetings but followed them closely.

Liberation theology was still equated in most people's minds with the Marxist edition prevalent in Central America and the Andean countries, one that implied that a "people's Church" of base communities at odds with the "institutional" Church. But there were at least two post-Medellín liberation theologies, both committed to liberation and the option for the poor but with different roots: one nourished by post-Enlightenment liberalism and Marxism (which Latin-American theologians brought back from their studies in Europe), the other by national, popular, and Catholic traditions. Gustavo Gutiérrez, the Peruvian priest who authored the founding text of liberation theology in 1971, would revise his own thinking under the latter influence. By the 1990s he had come to accept that the "historical force" of the poor was through culture and faith rather than merely political struggle.

The German theologian whom in 1980 John Paul II named to head the Vatican's doctrine watchdog, the Congregation for the Doctrine of the Faith (CDF), took a strong interest in these developments, and in the distinction between these two strains. From 1982 Cardinal Joseph Ratzinger hosted meetings of Latin-American theologians at the Vatican to look at what was good and true in liberation theology and what was incompatible with core Christian understandings. The *Instruction* issued by the CDF in 1984 condemned the use of Marxist hermeneutics in some strains of liberation theology, as well as their reduction of the rich biblical concept of liberation to political categories; but the CDF was careful to acknowledge that there were different versions of liberation theology, and only some contained these errors. Two years later, the CDF issued a second *Instruction* that praised the theology of liberation, especially its affirmation of popular piety and the option for the poor—the key Latin-American theological insight that John Paul II so valued.[26] The first *Instruction* was reported in the media as a blanket condemnation of liberation theology, while the second was ignored by the media because it contradicted that story. Thus two myths were forged: that all liberation theology was Marxist, and that the Vatican condemned all liberation theology. Argentine *teología del pueblo* disproved both.

In between the two instructions, in September 1985, Bergoglio hosted at the Colegio Máximo a major conference of 120 theologians from twenty-three countries on the topic of "the evangelization of culture and the inculturation of the Gospel," in order to mark the four hundredth anniversary of the arrival of the Jesuits in Argentina. His opening address was pure Puebla, identifying both faith and culture as "privileged places where divine wisdom is manifested." The first was the Gospel, which revealed God's saving plan through His visible image, Jesus Christ; the second was "the different cultures, fruit of the wisdom of peoples" that reflected "the creative and perfecting Wisdom of God." At the end of his address he paid "filial homage" to Father Arrupe "who in the Synod on Evangelization of 1974 pronounced what was then the novel word 'inculturation.'"[27]

The conference was opened by the Argentine bishop, Antonio Quarracino, who was reaching the end of his term as CELAM's president. Quarracino, who knew and admired Bergoglio since they had first met in the mid-1970s, would soon be named archbishop of La Plata and, in 1990, archbishop of Buenos Aires. Once there, he would work to get Bergoglio made his auxiliary bishop.

✑

BECAUSE he would never again be so visible at such close hand to so many, the Jesuit students' recollections of Jorge Bergoglio as he neared fifty have a special value. Even those who later critiqued aspects of the Bergoglio era agree that he was a demanding but loving father figure, a brilliant teacher, a spiritual master, and a captivating leader. He prayed for two to three hours a day, ran a college of two hundred resident students and hundreds more nonresidents, plus a vast parish; he taught pastoral theology, gave retreats, organized conferences, raised money for the college, and was mentor and spiritual director to dozens of Jesuits. Yet his students remember him as always there for them. "He went from giving spiritual direction to speaking on the phone with a bishop to washing clothes in the laundry before going to the kitchen and the pigsty and then back to the classroom," remembers Cervera. "He was involved in every detail with each one of us."

Bergoglio's hands-on management extended to the kitchen, where on Sundays—when the staff was off—he took charge. His mother had taught him well; he was a good cook (his sister María Elena says his pièce de résistance was stuffed calamari). A friend at the time remembers organizing a meeting of thirty theology students at the Máximo but, close to the time of their arrival, had nothing to give them to eat. Bergoglio wasn't fazed. "Go into the center of San Miguel and buy four spit-roasted chickens, four *panes de manteca* (lard bread), and four cans of cream," he told him. When he came back, he found Bergoglio had organized a team of students to peel and boil the potatoes. Bergoglio told him: "This is one of my mother's recipes. You cut the bread in two. One half you use to cover the cooked chicken; the other half you use to stuff it. The same with all four chickens. You put them in a hot oven for ten minutes, take them out, add the cream, and you turn off the oven. You serve it with the potatoes, and that's it—everyone happy" (they were).[28]

Bergoglio expected much and gave much, too; he was always out there in front, *primereando*. He sought excellence, quoting Saint Ignatius's Latin adage, *age quod agis*, which English-speaking Jesuits summarize as "do what you're missioned to do and don't let other things, even very good ones, distract you, because that's how the devil makes sure you blow it." He was sensitive to different students' needs. Tomás Bradley, a novice who had studied agronomy and loved the outdoors, was given a summer duty managing the college's reception desk to encourage him to find God in the boredom and stillness of a desk job.[29] In keeping with the austere habits of a lifetime, Bergoglio never took vacations himself, but sent the students away in the heat of January for two weeks to the mountains of Córdoba, where first the novices and then the scholastics stayed in an old school hut.

He was tough and demanding, but never harsh. When Nardín got back from one of the summer camps with the children to begin his annual eight-day retreat, "he saw I was exhausted and said, 'Have a siesta until five, and instead of four prayer sessions, do three.' He had that kind of personal care." Cervera recalls how often, after they had been working hard, "he would appear with a bottle of wine and something to eat, and we ate together in a family atmosphere."

He wanted them to develop as mature Jesuits, alive to the temptations of the ego. Ortiz remembers trying desperately to impress him over a number of weeks by gathering ever-larger numbers of children for the Sunday Mass Bergoglio celebrated at San José. But each week the rector told him, *pocos, muy pocos* ("not many, not many at all"). When, on the third week, Ortiz proudly came with fifty noisy children, and Bergoglio again told him *muy pocos*, the young Jesuit exploded and told him to go to hell, at which point the rector took him to the side of the church and gave him a hug. "It's not about the numbers you've managed to bring," Bergoglio told Ortiz. "It's the kids themselves that matter. Your vanity stopped you seeing that. Now, finally, you've got it."

Ortiz learned to be straight with Bergoglio, to express his feelings and frustrations, whereas some who were tested and probed by their rector resented it. "He treated you like a father, and like a father you could unburden to him," says Ortiz. Rossi recalls:

> The people that could expect a dressing down from him were those who wanted people to know how good and perfect they were, or who were legalistic. Conversely, he responded to fragility with a sensitivity I don't think I've ever seen in anyone else. If you could apply some kind of mathematical rule to Bergoglio, I'd say it was, the greater the fragility, the greater the response from him. I've always said: if you hit rock bottom, even if you're his biggest enemy, just go and see him— he'll be there for you, not just with time, but whatever you need: a house, food, work, whatever. Human fragility brings out the best in him. That's why those who have most enjoyed his papacy are not the poor in the abstract but the huge numbers of poor people he has helped. They know who he is. On the one hand they've seen this mercy and forgiveness, and on the other this exquisite charity, the kind of giving that the Gospel describes as an unrestrained outpouring.

His students found Bergoglio's vision deeply attractive. He offered a model of what it meant to be a twentieth-century Jesuit based on what he saw in the early Society of Jesus. They admired his deep grasp of Ignatian spirituality, which he had a born teacher's ability to communicate. He was well read and had a penetrating, systematic intellect, but proceeded as much from the gut as from the mind. Where Rossi describes him as "a mix between a desert ascetic and a brilliant manager," Nardín says he was a "very astute saint—very able, and streetwise: it's an unusual combination." His authority was innate. "He was born to lead," says Gómez. "His whole thinking is that of a leader." He offers an example: Bergoglio's skill in tailoring the qualities needed for a task to the abilities of those available to him, working out how the different qualities and temperaments in them could collectively add up to what was needed. "It's what people who govern know how to do," says Gómez, who used to be Argentine provincial.

Despite his tenderness, there was an inscrutable, disconcerting side to Bergoglio. His was an intuitive, sapiential kind of knowing, an ability to read a person's hearts that monks call *cardiognosis*. "He just knew you," recalls Rossi. "He heard what you hadn't said." Rossi adds that Bergoglio "is an intuitive discerner, which can be disconcerting. He can help you decide in two minutes what you hadn't even begun thinking about. He's not infallible, but he usually gets it right." He liked to step outside categories: Gómez says Bergoglio sought either a midpoint between extremes or a position outside dichotomies, and stressed certainties that guaranteed a shared belonging: he recalls him after a conference at the Máximo being happy because he had equally challenged both the "left" and the "right." Others describe him as having an irreverent and mischievous streak, which was always checked by the boundaries of Church tradition, which he never overstepped.

Bergoglio's care for the Jesuits in formation, and their devotion to him in return, gave him enormous influence over them. It was a charismatic, personalist style of leadership, the kind Latins (and especially Argentines) respond naturally to, yet which Anglo-Saxons can regard as suffocating or demagogic. Nardín gives an example of Bergoglio's charismatically authoritarian leadership: one time he called on students who smoked (Bergoglio, with his weak lungs, never did) to give it up out of solidarity with the workers in San Miguel who were unable to afford cigarettes. "He said, 'And if anyone thinks they can't, come and see me.' It wasn't an invitation, or a suggestion," says Nardín. "It was like, 'We are going to do this.' And we did."

Bergoglio was decisive. "He discerned a lot, consulted, and sought consensus in some things," recalls Cervera. "But when he had to decide, he decided on his own account." He usually saw what needed to be done but, back in the 1970s and 1980s, often failed to invest time in allowing others to see it that way, too. As provincial and rector, "I did not always do the necessary consultation," Francis, looking back, told Father Spadaro, adding: "My authoritarian and quick manner of making decisions led me to have serious problems."

Bergoglio's spectacular success as provincial and rector turned out to be also his weakness. As he pushed ahead rapidly, transforming both the Jesuits and the lives of the people of San Miguel, he was creating a problem: the sheer pace and extent of the changes would provoke resentment. He had created, in just a few years, a thriving institution, deeply embedded in Argentine culture and in the lives of the poor, based on a radical and compelling vision of primitive Jesuit missions, and a charismatic, inspiring leadership. The continued high numbers of vocations, the transformation of the neighborhoods, and the seriousness and dedication of the young Jesuits told their own story. The difficulty was that provincials and rectors are supposed to serve single terms, then stand down and fade into the background. Bergoglio as rector, however, had become a "provincial without portfolio" whose personal authority exceeded his official one, and whose term didn't end, in practice, with the naming of his successor. Even after Bergoglio stepped down as provincial, Swinnen and López Rosas saw themselves as the executors of his vision; and in many different ways he had more influence by the end of his time as rector than he had had as a provincial.

The Argentine Jesuits today wryly joke that Bergoglio becoming pope was the obvious solution they never thought of at the time.

✎

WHEN Father Ignacio Pérez del Viso returned from studies in Europe in 1978, he found almost everyone in the Argentine province happy with Bergoglio's rule as provincial and subsequent role as rector. The grand exception was Pérez del Viso's own community in the wealthy north of Buenos Aires, in the barrio of Belgrano, where Jesuits worked in the province's social sciences institute, the Center for Social Research and Action, which in the 1980s became the locus of a campaign against Bergoglio.

The Argentine CIAS was founded in 1960, after the Jesuit curia in Rome had asked each of the Jesuit provinces to establish a study center to use the emerging social sciences to highlight and analyze structural injustice. In their 1968 letter, the Jesuit provincials of Latin America defined CIAS's mission as "helping to raise awareness, stimulating and guiding mentalities and actions, through research, publication, teaching, and advice."[30]

During the ferment of the late 1960s and early 1970s, many of the Jesuits in the Argentine CIAS were among the original signatories of the Third World Priests' Movement (MSTM) around Father Mugica. At least one CIAS employee was involved in the guerrillas and was later killed by the armed forces. Many of the Jesuits in the institute were close to Ricardo O'Farrell, the provincial before Bergoglio, and backed Yorio and Jalics against Bergoglio in the conflict over the community in Bajo Flores. There were some—particularly Father Fernando Storni, one of the CIAS founders who was President Alfonsín's religious adviser—who had not forgotten the handover of the Salvador university, which they saw as a betrayal. Others, such as Father Enrique Fabbri, took an avant-garde view of sexuality and marriage, which troubled Bergoglio.

Such disagreements are normal, especially among articulate and educated Jesuits, and do not by themselves account for the animosity of the CIAS community toward Bergoglio. Nor is it enough to look through a political prism. In his 1986 book *Church and Dictatorship*, Emilio Mignone, for example, wrote of CIAS that "the dominating role played by Father Jorge Bergoglio and his faction within the Jesuits lessened the center's vitality." This reflected a view taken by the left at the time: that Bergoglio had in some way muzzled the CIAS, which might otherwise have played a prophetic human-rights role in the dirty war. This was the view of Father Michael Campbell-Johnston, for example, an English Jesuit liberationist who liaised with the CIAS institutes across Latin America on behalf of the general. He was appalled that "our institute in Buenos Aires was able to function freely because it never criticized or opposed the government," and he berated Bergoglio in 1977 for being "out of step with our other social institutes in the continent." Campbell-Johnston found unconvincing Bergoglio's explanation that Argentina was not Peru or El Salvador.[31]

That was not, however, the view of the CIAS Jesuits in Argentina, says Pérez del Viso. They accepted, first, that provincials have a duty to censor Jesuit publications, and second, that all media were muzzled under the dictatorship. They knew that the CIAS journal could never have carved out a role for itself criticizing human-rights abuses. After it published a December 1976 article critical of torture, for example, the junta came close to shutting the journal down, and only relented after its author, Father Vicente Pellegrini, left the country. When the Buenos Aires newspaper *La Opinión* republished the CIAS article, the government closed it. Only the English-language *Buenos Aires Herald* had any freedom of expression under the dictatorship, audaciously printing a daily record of the disappeared—although its editor and chief news editor were exiled.[32]

There was a specific liberationist charge against the Bergoglio-Swinnen regime: that it was too concerned with feeding the poor and not enough with asking why they were poor. In this view, Bergoglio's vision was "sacramentalist, a-critical, and assistentialist," as the Jesuit Juan Luis Moyano would later put it to Horacio Verbitsky—attacking symptoms of poverty, not causes; helping the poor but not confronting politically what made them poor. But most of the CIAS Jesuits were not liberationists, and the CIAS critique did not come solely from the left.

The tension between Bergoglio and the CIAS Jesuits went deeper and was more visceral: the latter resented what they saw as an attempt by Bergoglio to claim and impose a particular notion of Saint Ignatius and Jesuit identity. They perceived—and in this they were not wrong—that Bergoglio had replaced their own "progressive" model of Jesuit renewal with another, which they saw—and in this they were constrained by their prejudices—as a throwback. As José María Poirier, the editor of *Criterio*, puts it, "he was criticized for presenting a very personal version of Ignatius's legacy, and there were not a few who criticized him for distorting that legacy."[33] Bergoglio had come, it seemed, from nowhere—a youthful provincial, from a lower-middle-class background, and not even a doctorate in theology—and turned everything on its head. The mostly older, academic, upper-class Jesuits of the CIAS resented this, not least because of his success in fostering huge numbers of vocations, thereby threatening to reshape the whole future of the province.

Jesuits recall a tribal rivalry at the time between the Colegio Máximo and the CIAS, behind which were two opposing narratives of what it meant to be a son of Saint Ignatius. To the younger Jesuits at the Máximo, the CIAS were whiskey-drinking leftists, armchair socialists who preached about poverty but avoided contact with the poor, "all for the people but nothing with the people," as Bergoglio's parody slogan put it. Before stepping down as provincial, Bergoglio wrote to the CIAS citing Father Arrupe's 1977 message in which he spoke of the importance of contact with the reality and life experiences of the poor: "If this does not happen we then run the risk of being abstract ideologists or fundamentalists, which is not healthy," Arrupe had written.[34]

Viewed from the CIAS, conversely, Bergoglio's Máximo looked like an old-fashioned boot camp for parish priests, with a whiff of anti-intellectualism about it, like one of Peronism's plebeian slogans, "Sandals yes, books no." It is striking how often the criticism of Bergoglio was expressed in enlightenment terms of progress-regress. Consider, for example, a former director of the CIAS in Buenos Aires, later a provincial, describing with horror the Máximo under Bergoglio:

> It was a very closed regime. You can't believe it, he introduced Argentine Jesuits to popular religiosity. He took them all to the barrios, and turned the Máximo into a parish, even though we already had a parish nearby. As rector of the Máximo he was an academic but he managed also to be a parish priest. He created a whole load of chapels. And he encouraged a style of popular religiosity among the students, who would go to the chapel at night and touch images! This was something the poor did, the people of the *pueblo*, something that the Society of Jesus worldwide just doesn't *do*. I mean, *touching images* . . . what is that? And the older ones, praying the Rosary together in the gardens. Look, I'm not against that, but I'm not in favor either. It's just not typical of us. But it became normal at that time.

An American Jesuit based in Peru, whose view of Bergoglio was informed by leftist CIAS Jesuits such as Juan Luis Moyano (who also spent many years in Peru) and Oswaldo Yorio, claimed in a history of the Society of Jesus in Latin America that Bergoglio had taken the Argentine province "back to pre–Vatican II values and lifestyles." As a result, wrote Father Jeffrey Klaiber, SJ, "the Argentine province did not march in unison with the rest of the Society of Jesus in Latin America." However, "not all Jesuits shared Bergoglio's conservative views," he went on, citing the CIAS. The remark is revealing of the reputation that in some Jesuit circles remained fixed long after Bergoglio had become a bishop: both province and provincial as irredeemably conservative, with only the CIAS holding out bravely on behalf of the forces of enlightenment and progress.[35]

The Argentine province *was* out of step with the Jesuits, both worldwide and in Latin America. "We were very aware that elsewhere Jesuits lived differently, were more politicized," recalls Yáñez. Bergoglio sent Jesuits on mission abroad—among them, for example, was Renzo De Luca, whom Bergoglio dispatched to Japan and visited in Nagasaki—but those in formation were kept in San Miguel, and the best minds stayed to teach there rather than abroad. The Argentine juniors, for example, did not take part in the meeting of the Southern Cone Jesuits organized by Father Fernando Montes, the Chilean provincial who had studied with Bergoglio at the Máximo in the 1960s. Montes was typical of how other Latin-American provincials viewed the Argentine Jesuits at the time. As rector, says Montes, "Bergoglio privileged popular religiosity and the work of the young people in popular parishes while neglecting the research centers, in particular the CIAS. . . . It was a kind of popular religiosity very close to the people, to the poor, very Latin American, but more Peronist than modern."

Whether or not this was an express aim, the effect of the Bergoglio-Swinnen provincialate was to insulate the Argentines from the turbulence of GC32's Decree Four, which in Latin America was used to justify Jesuits backing socialist movements and speaking out against dictatorships that defended the interests of the wealthy. In Chile, for example, where Salvador Allende's socialists had been ousted by a conservative military dictatorship, the Jesuits followed the example of the Chilean bishops' Vicariate of Solidarity in opposing the regime of General Augusto Pinochet in favor of human rights—a stance they were able to take, in part, because of the Church's constitutional separation from the state. In Central America, where military regimes defended landowner interests, Decree Four meant Jesuits sympathizing with revolutionary struggles seeking to overthrow them—and in some cases losing their lives in the process. But Argentina in the 1970s was not El Salvador or Chile; only a dogmatic observer could claim that the "people" were represented by the guerrillas, or that the military dictatorship, despite the horrors it committed, did not have, at first, widespread popular support.

Yet in the mid-1980s, following the collapse of the military junta and the Sábato commission revelations, it was all too easy to forget that context. The simple view, promoted by human-rights groups in Argentina and the international media, was that the military junta had killed thousands of innocent people and that the Church had stood by and let it happen or encouraged it. If there was a strong sense of shame among Catholics about the Argentine Church's role in the dictatorship, for Jesuits in Latin America and elsewhere, who saw themselves as part of a prophetic social justice/human-rights vanguard, the idea that their Argentine confrères were "complicit" in a genocidal regime was mortifying. This is why the specific accusations against Bergoglio in Mignone's book *Church and Dictatorship* were so damaging. "Mignone's claims about Bergoglio had a great impact," agrees Pérez del Viso.

The book was devastating because Mignone's personal credibility and integrity were beyond question: he was a deeply Catholic human-rights activist with strong international ties, especially in the United States, whose daughter had been disappeared while working as a catechist in a slum. Yet Mignone's *J'accuse*, aimed at the Church in general and certain individuals in particular, for failing to speak out against the atrocities, assumes that had the Church done so, the tortures and the abductions could have been prevented. It was a simple, appealing narrative that spoke to the moment. But the book itself was undermined by its ferocity and crudeness. Mignone's stance was that of courtroom lawyer rather than historian, mixing half-truths with facts, and simplistically splitting the world into complicit or heroic. As a result, the book played well to the gallery but failed to provoke the wider debate about the links between Church and state that Mignone wanted to see.[36]

It was nonetheless effective in increasing the opprobrium directed at the time at the Argentine Church in general and Bergoglio in particular, and helps explain why the CIAS critiques were accepted so uncritically in Rome and elsewhere in Latin America. Argentina's "difference" was a problem to the Jesuits, and especially to the general's regional assistant for Latin America, a Spanish-born Jesuit who had been Peruvian provincial in the 1970s, Father José Luis Fernández Castañeda. The prejudices of Kolvenbach's advisers were obvious when they visited the Máximo during the 1980s. "There was a real difficulty outside in understanding the Argentine model," recalls Velasco. "They said, 'Those guys are right-wing,' so they were expecting us all in soutanes and saying Mass in Latin, which we weren't."

Rome's view of the Bergoglio-Swinnen regime had been shaped by constant complaints by the CIAS Jesuits—Father Fabbri, for example, wrote often to Rome—that the Máximo regime was "un-Jesuit" and that Swinnen was Bergoglio's puppet. Swinnen in March 1983 tried to move the CIAS community to the Jesuits' house in the center, close to Congress, so that it could have a role lobbying politicians, but the CIAS Jesuits said they had not been consulted and complained to Rome. The newly elected general, acting on the advice of Fernández Castañeda, backed the CIAS against the provincial. It was a sign of what was to come next.

As Swinnen's period as provincial drew to a close, Kolvenbach decided to intervene in the Argentine province to impose a new direction. He sent out an adviser to oversee the consultation process that produced a *terna*, or three-name list of potential provincials. When the consultors' *terna* reached Kolvenbach, he rejected all three names. He then summoned Swinnen and Father Víctor Zorzín, the Jesuit who at that point headed the Conference of Argentine Religious, to Rome. Zorzín's name was not on the *terna* but had been suggested to Rome by the CIAS Jesuits. When they reached the Borgo Santo Spirito, Kolvenbach interviewed them separately. He told Swinnen that Zorzín would be provincial. "There was no other issue discussed on our visit," Swinnen recalls.

Zorzín, who had been *socius*, or assistant, to the provincial before Bergoglio, Father O'Farrell, now named as his *socius* Father Ignacio García-Mata, CIAS director until stood down by Swinnen, and one of Bergoglio's fiercest critics. Rome was imposing the status quo ante.

"It may sound crazy," says Father Rafael Velasco, until recently rector of the Jesuit-run Catholic University in Córdoba, "but you can read this as Peronist versus anti-Peronist: the *gorilas* [fanatical anti-Peronists] were in the CIAS, and the *pueblo* was with Bergoglio and the others." The parallel is intriguing. When Perón was ousted in 1955, a progressive elite—a mixture of liberals, conservatives, and the left—overturned in the name of progress and modernity a charismatic leader considered a demagogue. There is even a parallel between what followed under Zorzín and the *gorila* military governments of the late 1950s: a cleansing, in which everything associated with the deposed regime was reversed. "It was an emphatic shift," recalls Nardín, "which out of immaturity sought to destroy what came before in order to assert itself." Another Jesuit contemporary describes how "the new line was to do everything now contrary to what you did before" and describes how the pastoral mission to the barrios around the Máximo was gradually dismantled.

> The messages we received from above went wholly against what we had been living and doing in the Máximo: there was to be no more regular discipline, no more manual work.... This disorder soon translated into the parish: they no longer went to look for the children, the apostolic horizon was lost, and some Jesuits in formation began going out with catechists. Little by little the apostolate was abandoned, and in just a few years the churches were reduced to the bare minimum, among other things because there was a policy of "cleansing" the *bergogliano* Jesuits. And once there were no more of them, they sacked the lay people who remained faithful to Bergoglio's project—that was the most painful and scandalous thing of all.

That sad scene suggested another, even more uncomfortable parallel, from two centuries earlier. At that time, too, there was a thriving inculturated Jesuit apostolate among the poor in Argentina that increased the dignity of human lives and produced great fruits, but whose independence was resented, and that was eventually suppressed on the orders of the general in far-off Rome.

⚜

IN order to create space for the new provincial regime, Bergoglio agreed with Zorzín in May 1986 to take a sabbatical in Germany to explore a doctorate on Romano Guardini. He first spent two months learning German in the Göethe Institut in the Rhine town of Boppard, lodging with an elderly couple. Then he went on to the Jesuit Faculty of Theology near Frankfurt, Sankt Georgen, which boasted an excellent Guardini collection. With the professors there, he planned to work up a thesis topic.

Guardini (1885–1968) was one of the twentieth century's most creative Catholic minds, a German priest-philosopher influential on the Second Vatican Council whose deep thinking about modernity had fascinated Bergoglio ever since he read *The Lord* as a novice. Guardini was a huge figure in the 1950s who influenced American Catholic luminaries such as the monk poet Thomas Merton and the novelist Flannery O'Connor, as well as the great German-speaking theologians of the twentieth century such as Hans Urs Von Balthasar, Karl Rahner, and Walter Kasper. He was also widely quoted and admired by Pope Paul VI (who tried to make him a cardinal) and Pope John Paul II, and especially by Guardini's compatriot Cardinal Ratzinger, the future Benedict XVI, who knew him personally. Guardini saw the drama of the modern age as a pendulum swing between heteronomy (placing authority outside oneself, in another human being or institution) and autonomy (placing authority in oneself), and proposed that true happiness and freedom were only possible in theonomy—recognizing God as the authority for human life, setting each human being free to become a whole person in "I-thou" relationships.

There were affinities: Guardini was the son of Italian émigrés who studied chemistry, and who remained faithful—despite intense pressures, not least from Nazis—to his "inner authority." Bergoglio's specific interest was in Guardini's early (1925) text *Der Gegensatz* ("Contrast"), a critique of Marxist and Hegelian dialectics that Bergoglio believed could be useful for conceptualizing the dynamics of disagreement. Guardini's discussion drew on the work of a nineteenth-century Tübingen theologian, Johann Adam Möhler, who argued that in the Church contrasting points of view (*Gegensätze*) are fruitful and creative, but can become contradictions (*Widerspruch*) when they fall out of the unity of the whole and develop in opposition to the body. This was precisely the distinction drawn on by Yves Congar in his discussion of true and false reform in the Church that had so influenced Bergoglio. His desire to explore Guardini's *Gegensatz*, in other words, was of a piece with his core underlying interest in politics and institutional reform, and helped to shape what as cardinal he would promote as a "culture of encounter."

For three months Bergoglio lived in the Jesuit community at the university of Sankt Georgen, reading deeply and widely in a way he had been unable to do since his student years. He applied himself assiduously during the next four months in intense study that later bore fruit. But he was miserable. The prospect of this man of action embarking on doctoral research at the age of fifty was anyway improbable, but, more to the point, Bergoglio was a deeply rooted and connected person who needed community. Lonely and homesick, he would stroll in the evenings to the cemetery, from where he could see the Frankfurt airport, and wave to the planes bound for Argentina. He was filled with *nostos algos*, the yearning for his place—not just his geographical home of Buenos Aires, but his place as a

Jesuit leader and reformer that had been his life for the previous fifteen years. His displacement ran deep, and by December he would be home again.[37]

A profound experience in prayer had encouraged him to return. He had made a pilgrimage to the Bavarian city of Augsburg where, in the Jesuit church of Sankt Peter am Perlach, he contemplated a Baroque-era painting from the early 1700s known as *Maria Knotenlöserin*, "Mary, Untier of Knots," which was the object of a local devotion. The painting's story goes back to a feuding married couple who had been on the verge of a bitter separation. The husband, Wolfgang Langenmantel, had sought help from a local Jesuit priest, Father Jakob Rem, who prayed to the Virgin Mary "to untie all the knots" in the Langenmantel home. Peace was restored and the marriage was saved; and to give thanks for the miracle their grandson commissioned the painting and donated it to the church.

At first glance, it is nothing out of the ordinary: the painting shows the Virgin, surrounded by angels and protected by the light of the Holy Spirit, standing on a serpent. But the middle of the painting is striking: an angel to Mary's left is passing her a silk thread full of knots that she unties, handing on the unknotted thread to an angel on her right.

Father Rem's prayer to the Virgin had been inspired by an ancient formula of Saint Irenaeus: *The knot of Eve's disobedience was loosed by the obedience of Mary.* Obedience was precisely Bergoglio's knot. It is the key vow for Jesuits, and one he strongly believed in; it was what made mission and unity possible. Yet what he had been given was not a mission, but a means of getting him out of Argentina because he was an obstacle. What obedience did he owe?

Obedience comes from the Latin *obaudire*, to "hear" or "listen to." The vow is meant above all to free the heart from the ego in order to listen to God, and to submit freely to His will: the Virgin is the perfect model of such obedience. What was God's will, now, for Bergoglio, in the middle of his life? He knew it wasn't to sit in a library for three years, tweaking footnotes. He was a leader, a reformer, a pastor, a missionary. But how could he obey that call and his superiors at the same time? In Guardini's terms it was a conflict between heteronomy—placing ultimate authority in the Society of Jesus—and theonomy: looking to God as his Superior. The challenge, as ever, was to discern what was of his ego—what in 1969 he had named as that broken, stingy part of him, that sought to control and to cling—and what was of God, in whose obedience lay his true freedom.

During those hours in the bare stone church chilled by the coming Bavarian winter, he passed in prayer his knot to the angel, who passed it to the Virgin, who gently untied it and passed it to the other angel, who took it to Buenos Aires, where Bergoglio followed.

It would cause tension, but he had to return. Beyond the call to be a Jesuit was the deeper call, that primordial obedience. God, as ever, was running before him, *primereando*, like blossoms on almond trees.

He took back with him a load of *Maria Knotenlöserin* prayer cards. In the 1990s, after a local copy of the painting—known in Spanish as *María Desatanudos*—was hung in a church in Buenos Aires, it took off in an extraordinary way, leading Bergoglio later to say he had never felt so much in the hands of God.

"HOWEVER interested he was [in Guardini], deep down he knew he had to serve in other ways," says Father Gómez, who was in the Colegio del Salvador when Bergoglio suddenly returned in December, his arms full of photocopies. The *socius*, Ignacio García-Mata, had earlier received a call to say he was coming back; surprised, the provincial, Víctor Zorzín, assigned Bergoglio a room in the Colegio del Salvador, the prestigious school that occupied a whole block of Callao Street in the noisy heart of Buenos Aires where he had taught for a year after his two years at La Inmaculada. Bergoglio would teach some classes while pursuing his doctoral research. Guillermo Ortiz, who as a novice had tried to impress Bergoglio by his children-gathering abilities, was at this time doing his own regency at the Salvador and found himself on the same floor and sharing a bathroom with his former rector. "He was cheerful or at least appeared to be," he recalls. "But I felt they were punishing him for something."

Zorzín had moved the Jesuit curia from the Máximo back into the city. López Rosas, one of the Fiorito group who had been novice master under Swinnen and who was now rector of the Máximo, invited Bergoglio to give classes on pastoral theology on Mondays. Bergoglio would stay over the previous Sunday night, dining with the students, for whom he was an awesome figure. Rafael Velasco, one of the students at the time, recalls their "huge admiration" for Bergoglio. His two book collections of articles were considered essential reading for the students, and they looked forward to these weekly visits.

This was Bergoglio's most fertile intellectual period. As rector, he had published an article a year in the journal he had helped to found in 1968, the *Boletín de Espiritualidad*; but after stepping down in 1986, he published an average of three articles a year over the following three years. He also published sporadically in *Stromata*, the Jesuits' theology journal. *Meditaciones para Religiosos* (1982), his first collection of articles and talks, was followed by *Reflexiones Espirituales* (1987) and *Reflexiones en Esperanza* (1992).

No one had relationships, within the province, as deep and wide as Bergoglio's, and no one had anything close to his authority. His third collection of addresses and articles, *Reflexiones en Esperanza*, which came out in 1992, shows that even in the late 1980s Bergoglio was called on to make presentations at major provincial events: he gave, for example, a long and moving speech on the occasion of the canonization of the Jesuit martyrs of Paraguay in May 1988.[38] Even officially demoted from all positions of authority in the province, he remained for most Jesuits their guiding light.

⚗

ON April 11, 1987, at the instigation of the Argentine curial cardinal, Eduardo Pironio, the first World Youth Day outside of Rome was held in Buenos Aires. Pope John Paul II, donning a poncho, was greeted by uproarious crowds, preaching reconciliation amid the storm of mutual recriminations and accusations over the dirty war. Bergoglio met the pope for the first time at a meeting organized by the nuncio with Christians of different denominations. "I had a brief exchange with the Holy Father," he recalled in 2005, "and I was impressed especially by his gaze, which was that of a good man."[39] Bergoglio was one of hundreds of priests who heard confessions and distributed Communion on the Avenida de Mayo: the city had seen nothing like it since the iconic days of the International Eucharistic Congress that Bergoglio had heard so much about from his grandmother Rosa.

But Argentina was more fractious and restless in the late 1980s than in 1934. Young army officers staged a series of rebellions that Easter in protest at the treatment of the armed forces by the courts, while former ERP militants attacked a military barracks eighteen months later, leaving dozens dead. It was obvious by the elections of May 1989 that President Alfonsín was fast losing grip: hyperinflation wiped out salaries and mobs sacked supermarkets. The Peronist candidate that year, Carlos Menem, was a son of Syrian immigrants from the impoverished province of La Rioja. He sported sideburns and paraded on horseback with a vague promise to make things better. Following Menem's victory in the May 1989 elections, Alfonsín ignominiously departed, months ahead of schedule, in the hope of averting further chaos.

On the eve of those elections Bergoglio gave the inaugural lecture of the 1989 academic year at the Universidad del Salvador on the need for a new "anthropology of politics." It was the skeleton of what would have been, had he written it, his doctoral thesis: a sophisticated, if at times to a layman impenetrable, exploration of Guardini and Saint Ignatius. It is possible to find in this lecture the basis of his future addresses as cardinal at the Te Deum services in the cathedral on Argentina's national day, May 25, which he would use to help build a new civic culture.

The lecture argued that Argentina was highly politicized yet lacked a narrative of what politics was for—to improve lives and harmonize different visions and interests, using power as service for the building-up of the common good while avoiding the temptations of utopianism and nostalgia. His deep reading of Guardini—especially *Contrast* and *The End of the Modern World*—had clearly paid off: the lecture sought to supplant a Hegelian dialectic of clashing opposites by what he calls "a mutual interaction of realities." It ended with a quote from Fyodor Dostoyevsky's *The Brothers Karamazov*: "Whoever does not believe in God will not believe in the people of God. . . . Only the people and their future spiritual power will convert our atheists, who have severed themselves from their own land."[40]

By the time of his lecture tensions were building over Kolvenbach's attempt to detach the province from Bergoglio. The problem was twofold: first, Bergoglio remained the reference point for the entire younger generation of Jesuits; second, the way that the new direction was being imposed caused resistance among the younger Jesuits, which in turn only made them more devoted to Bergoglio—rather in the way that *gorilismo*, or fanatical anti-Peronism, embedded support for Perón in the 1950s. The province's problem, says Rafael Velasco, was that "almost everything turned on its identification or not with a particular model, which was in turn identified with a person, who was Bergoglio." Like Argentina's politics, reduced to the Peronist/anti-Peronist dichotomy, the Argentine Jesuit province was paralyzed by a dispute between two visions, one of which was embodied in a person.

The challenge the provincial, Zorzín, faced in implementing Kolvenbach's unpopular policies became clear soon after Bergoglio returned from Germany.

A meeting of Jesuit procurators in Rome was due to take place in September 1987. A procurator is elected by his own province with a specific mandate: to report on the state of the province, to reflect with the other procurators on the state of the Society, and to vote on whether to call a general congregation. The election of a procurator does not involve a Jesuit standing, or even offering himself as a candidate (which would be seen as quite inappropriate): he is simply elected by the provincial congregation, whose members are themselves elected by a vote of at least two-thirds of the province.

To the fury of the provincial leadership, Bergoglio was elected procurator in March. The CIAS Jesuits suspected he had returned early from Germany precisely to make himself available for the ballot. Whether or not that is true, the vote showed that Bergoglio continued to enjoy the popularity and esteem of the province, while signalling the unpopularity of Kolvenbach's intervention and the policies of the new provincial. Bergoglio's election as procurator "was a clear protest against Rome," says Velasco. "It was saying to them: 'you put who you want, we will continue do our own thing.' It was a very clear signal." As procurator, Bergoglio was tasked with writing a report on the state of the province to the procurators' congregation, which gave him a platform from which to critique his opponents. He would also have had, once in Rome, time with the general to discuss the report. It was the best opportunity Argentine Jesuits had to try to change the direction of their province. But Rome wasn't going to be deflected.

THE sudden adoption of foreign formation models—especially the texts and approaches of the Spanish Jesuits—was causing unhappiness. "We got given a lot of the language of *indigenismo* when we hardly have any native peoples," recalls Nardín. "That wasn't our drama. Ours was the inclusion of immigrants from the interior." *Indigenismo* was the next wave of liberation theology applied now to native peoples. Bergoglio criticized it in his 1988 talk on the Jesuit martyrs, when he referred to "*indigenista* Marxism that denies the importance of faith in the transcendent sense of the culture of a people, while reducing culture to a battlefield."[41]

The Spanish approach now being imposed at the Máximo had no time for the *teología del pueblo* or popular religiosity. It was foreign, rationalist, and sub-Marxist—the opposite of what Puebla represented. The fact that these materials patronized and misunderstood Argentina served only to illustrate, for the younger Jesuits, Bergoglio's warnings about detached ideologies.

Despite the new orthodoxy there was also an incoherence, a lack of purpose and clarity, in the provincial government. Whatever Bergoglio's limitations, the Argentine Jesuits say that he at least had a vision around which they could rally, whereas what followed was incoherent, uninspiring, and poorly implemented. "We had a province myth, then we didn't," recalls Velasco. "We had a project, then suddenly we didn't. . . . We needed an identity, a project, to know our own horizons."

In September 1988, the general, Father Kolvenbach, visited Argentina for a week's meeting with the Latin-American provincials in San Miguel at the end of which he celebrated his fortieth year as a Jesuit by lunching with the CIAS community. That evening he concelebrated Mass at the church of El Salvador, next to the college, before returning to Rome the following morning. Remarkably, he never even met with Bergoglio. Whatever took place between Kolvenbach and Bergoglio at the procurators' meeting the year before, it had not brought them closer.

Over the next two years, 1988 to 1990, the province increasingly polarized and turned in on itself. As tensions mounted over the new formation and the abandonment of the apostolate, a frustrated provincial leadership began to see discontent as dissent. Bergoglio was increasingly blamed for stirring this up, although he did and said little. His supporters say the provincial was seeking to make him the scapegoat for the widespread unhappiness in the province. This reading appears to be supported by the CIAS Jesuit who kept the minutes of the consultors' meetings at the time, who recalls that "in every one of them we spoke about him. It was a constant worry, what we were going to do with this man." It was a painful period, involving the kind of breakdown that can occur in families, even religious ones. Father Juan Ochagavía, a Chilean Jesuit who was one of Kolvenbach's key advisers, recalls that "there were many wounded sensibilities" in the Argentine province at the time.

Eventually, the expulsion of Bergoglio and those seen as his devoted followers came to be seen as the solution to the tensions. In April 1990 the rector of the Máximo, Bergoglio's former collaborator Ernesto López Rosas—presumably acting on orders—suddenly turned on him, removing him from his teaching post. Students in Bergoglio's popular pastoral theology class were told he would no longer be teaching it. He was asked to surrender his Máximo room key. Thereafter he would never return to the college which had been his home for most of the previous twenty-five years.

Those identified as his close followers were now sent abroad. "All the Jesuits who in their moment had strong ties to Bergoglio, who tended to be very able people, were sent to Europe to do, if possible, a degree or doctorate," recalls Zorzín's associate, García-Mata. Among the "exiles" was Miguel Yáñez, who these days teaches moral theology at the Gregorian University in Rome and sits on Pope Francis's commission on sex abuse.

Bergoglio himself was sent to the Jesuit residence in central Córdoba. His supporters were told not to contact him. By ostracizing him, the province's leaders hoped to unite the province, but that is not what happened. In the 1990s, vocations plummeted again to single figures and departures in some years returned to double figures, as in the crisis days of the early 1970s.[42] The divisions within the province deepened during García-Mata's period as provincial (1991–1997), for which Bergoglio, who was made a bishop in 1992, could no longer be blamed. After García-Mata's term ended a provincial was brought in from Colombia in a bid to heal the divisions. When Father Alvaro Restrepo, SJ, was asked many years later what had gone wrong, he said with great diplomacy but accurately that "it was a problem of leadership. Argentines are very affectionate, they like to offer themselves, they need a leader. And at a certain point there were different leaderships."[43]

BERGOGLIO spent two years—June 1990 to May 1992—in Room 5 of the Jesuit Residencia Mayor in the heart of the pretty colonial mountain town of Córdoba. There he said Mass, heard confessions, gave retreats, read books, and penned letters—some of which, like those he wrote to the Salesian Don Cayetano Bruno, were long reminiscences—as well as the many meditations that in 1992 were published as *Reflexiones en Esperanza* ("Reflections in Hope"). His main day-to-day role was as confessor. He spent many hours listening to the pain and shame of students and professors of the university, as well as the people from the barrios who came to the city center because their own priests were too busy saying Mass on Sundays to hear their confessions. Bergoglio had never before given so much time to being a channel of forgiveness and mercy. It softened him, kept him close to the *pueblo fiel*, and put his own troubles in perspective.

Yet this was a sharp time, a purgative time, he later told Father Spadaro, "of great interior crisis." He had entered a midlife suffering, a stripping-back to the bare branches of his being. As Carl Jung might put it, his ego was being fried, and he had to wait until it was over. Saint Ignatius describes this as desolation: the sadness of abandonment, when the presence of God is barely palpable, when *one finds oneself thoroughly listless, lukewarm, sad, and as though cut off from one's Creator and Lord*, as he puts it in *The Spiritual Exercises*. For a time Bergoglio slept badly and ate little; he grew agitated and fragile, and spent hours staring out of a window. "We thought he was sick," recalls Father Carlos Carranza. Concerned, the doctor who tended to the Jesuits brought him a medal of the Virgin of Guadalupe from the basilica in Mexico City. "When I gave it to him," recalled Selva Tissera, "Bergoglio got so emotional his eyes filled with tears and he put it round his neck."[44]

In powerful people—leaders like Bergoglio—desolation teaches what the *Exercises* describes as "true knowledge and understanding" that of our own power we can do nothing "but that all this is a gift and grace from God our Lord." Desolation is visited on us, said Saint Ignatius, "so we are not to build our nest where we do not belong."[45] Bergoglio knew these rules better than anyone, but knowledge of the spiritual purpose of what he was enduring was of no help at all in escaping its pain. He could only watch the province he loved be dismantled and implode into factionalism, and the next generation of its leaders—men he had nurtured and guided—scattered to the four winds. It was an experience of powerlessness that brought him like nothing before in his life into the perspective of the poorest.

Like them, he could only be patient, trust in the Lord, and take each day as it came, allowing himself to be molded, trusting that it would one day bear fruit. In 2003, he told a politician who needed to stand down and was terrified of the decision: "Manuel, you've got to live your own exile. I did. And afterward you'll be back. And when you do come back, you'll be more merciful, kinder, and you're going to want to serve your people more."[46]

After six months in Córdoba he wrote down a series of notes, published later as "Silencio y Palabra" (Silence and Word), intended to assist "the discernment of a religious community that was passing through difficult circumstances." The community was obviously the Argentine Jesuit province, and what makes the discernment doubly fascinating was that the spiritual forces he saw at work in its crisis were the same as Pope Francis would later seek to combat in the Church as a whole.

Bergoglio began by recognizing the impossibility of human solutions to some crises, the way "visceral impotence" imposed the "grace of silence." He noted that Saint Ignatius identified the temptations of ambition and lack of poverty as the main causes of intra-Jesuit division, the temptation being to filter God's plans through one's own predetermined schemes and methods. These two causes were in turn accompanied by attitudes of mistrust and suspicion, descending into triumphalism and spiritual worldliness. Triumphalism, wrote Bergoglio, is a way of avoiding the Cross through attachment to "progress (or the appearance of it), the technification of the Spirit, the 'Coca-Cola-ization' of religious life." Allied to this was the temptation identified by the theologian Henri de Lubac of spiritual worldliness—the most insidious temptation of all for religious people ("more disastrous," wrote De Lubac, "than the infamous leprosy that disfigured the dearly beloved Bride at the time of the libertine popes"). Spiritual worldliness was putting oneself at the center. It was what Jesus saw the Pharisees doing, when they gave glory to themselves.

In the second part of the article Bergoglio considered how to respond to a temptation that appears *sub angelo lucis*—the bad spirit in the guise of an angel. Only Jesus can force a bad angel to show itself, and create room for God's light; and the means of his doing so are the ones he showed: "keeping silence, praying, and humbling ourselves." It was a reflection rooted in the Third Week of the *Exercises*, which contemplates Christ's Passion and specifically *how the divine nature goes into hiding, that is to say, how Christ as divine does not destroy his enemies, although he could do so, but allows himself in his sacred human nature to suffer most cruelly.*[47]

Bergoglio considers how this means enduring the "primordial rage" unleashed against those perceived to be weak, when the guilt and inadequacies of the accusers are off-loaded onto a scapegoat; and how it means taking up the Cross like Jesus, voluntarily embracing it and acknowledging our sins, yet avoiding the self-pity and pride of victimhood. The Cross would eventually oblige the devil to reveal himself, because the devil mistakes gentleness for weakness. "In moments of darkness and great tribulation," writes Bergoglio, "when the 'tangles' and the 'knots' cannot be untied and nothing is clear, then we must say nothing: the gentleness of the silence will make us look even weaker, and it will be the same devil who, emboldened, will show himself and his true intentions, no longer disguised as an angel of light but boldly and shamelessly."

The final section was entitled "God's War." There were often times, he observed, when God went into battle with the enemy of humankind, and it was a mistake to get involved. At such times, "in the silence of situations of the Cross, he asks us only to protect the wheat, and not to try to weed out the darnel." He referred to an image on the ceiling of the Jesuits' residence in Córdoba that showed novices protected by Mary's cloak under the inscription: *Monstra te esse matrem* ("Show yourself to be a mother"). When God went into battle, he wrote, it was important not to interfere, not to engage in factionalism or divide the world into good and bad, but to go "under the cloak of the Holy Mother of God" and there "to live in the holy tension between the memory of the Cross and the hope of the Resurrection."[48]

The cognizance of the role cast for him as a suffering servant may not have lessened his pain, but it charted for Bergoglio a path through his anguish, and perhaps stiffened him for the next blow. In August 1991, Zorzín's assistant, the former CIAS director García-Mata, a fierce critic of Bergoglio, was made provincial. He appointed as his *socius* the CIAS director at the time, Juan Luis Moyano, who had recently returned from Peru. Moyano would be one of the key sources for Horacio Verbitsky's campaign to indict Bergoglio over Yorio and Jalics, supplying the journalist with vehement quotes. For the American Jesuit Jeffrey Klaiber, "appointing Moyano to that position, a man who worked for the poor and who had been expelled by the military, was a clear sign that the General wanted changes in the province."[49] It was equally a clear sign that Bergoglio no longer had a future with the Jesuits.

In December 1991, Bergoglio gave a meditation on the Third Week, following Jesus from the Last Supper to the Crucifixion and his burial. In contemplating the corpse of Jesus, Bergoglio noted how it was easy to take spiritual refuge in what was or might have been, or to demand a resurrection straightaway, or to refuse in different ways to accept that the corpse really was a corpse.

> And yet it is a corpse, and divinity is hidden in it, and will be resurrected. That is how, throughout history, the Church's true reforms, those that bring life to parts of it that are dead, are born from within the entrails of the Church itself, and not from outside. God's reforms happen right there, where there is no other solution but to hope against all hope.[50]

SIX

A BISHOP WHO SMELLED OF SHEEP

(1993–2000)

TRUTH, BERGOGLIO TOLD a Caritas retreat in 2012, is like a precious stone: offer it in your hand, and it draws others to you; hurl it at someone, and it causes injury. Pope Francis's *Evangelii Gaudium* (*The Joy of the Gospel*), which came out in November 2013, was a gem-in-the-hand document that never cajoled or hectored, preferring to dazzle and bewitch. But it was tough, holding nothing back, lashing out at worldliness and corruption in all its forms, while urging the Church to learn to live from the energy of missionary love. Evangelization was not a crusade, or a marketing campaign; it was not about proselytizing. The Church grew, said Francis, by embodying the loving mercy of God.

It was the first papal declaration to apologize for its own length. Francis said he knew that people didn't read long documents anymore, that some might find the detail excessive: at two hundred pages, it was far longer than either of Paul VI's great 1975 exhortations, *Gaudete in Domino* (*On Christian Joy*) and *Evangelii Nuntiandi* (*Evangelization in the Modern World*) to which *Evangelii Gaudium*, even in its title, paid homage. But then, Francis packed in an astonishing range of topics, as if his first teaching document—or at least, the first he had mainly authored—might also be his last.

Francis paid only lip service to Benedict XVI's synod on the new evangelization the year before to which this was scheduled to be the pope's response, while demonstrating in every paragraph what it meant to evangelize. If that synod had been dominated by the tired, timid, inward-looking spirit of the European Church, *Evangelii Gaudium* was an eruption of the energy and insights from Latin America, stuffed with references to the Aparecida document of 2007: a Church of and for the poor, rooted in the Second Vatican Council, geared to mission, focused on the margins, centered on God's holy faithful people, in confident dialogue with culture yet bold in denouncing what harmed the poor. It presented a Church that was tender and maternal, a big, borderless lazaretto of healing and love.

Francis had made the world sit up with his by now iconic question about gay people on the papal plane from Rio—"who am I to judge this person?"—and had done so again with the Jesuit interview, with its battlefield hospital and his complaint about "obsessing" over certain doctrines. Many had assumed that these were off-the-cuff comments in interviews, and that a papal document would rein it all back into the comfort zone. But *Evangelii Gaudium* proved that his airborne remarks reflected deep thinking about the way the news media's focus on neuralgic questions—especially the so-called pelvic issues—had had the effect over the years of overemphasizing the moral and judgmental dimension of the Church's teaching. "The biggest problem is when the message we preach then seems identified with those secondary aspects which, important as they are, do not in and of themselves convey the heart of Christ's message," he observed in *Evangelii Gaudium*, before calling for the Church not to bury the news about God's saving merciful love but to put it on a flagpole.

The document paid tribute to the Church's modern popes. At times it echoed the joyful, spirit-filled reformism of John XXIII, at others the prudent discernment of Paul VI; elsewhere it echoed the prophetic ardor of John Paul II, or the serene lyrical clarity of Benedict XVI. Yet for anyone familiar with his voice, the document was unmistakably *bergogliano*, treating favorite themes such as the holy-faithful-people hermeneutic and the perils of spiritual worldliness. He even managed to include his four principles—"time is greater than space," "unity prevails over conflict," "realities are more important than ideas," "the whole is greater than the part." Perhaps because sapiential wisdom was not considered appropriate for a papal document, *Evangelii Gaudium* linked these for the first time explicitly to the Gospel.

Also thoroughly *bergogliano* was the way he combined a direct, everyman's language with phrases of enormous complexity. The lyricism, too, was his. Francis, who endlessly reread the classics of literature, had a novelist's gift for linking ideas and getting them to point beyond themselves. "Thanks to our bodies," he wrote in *Evangelii Gaudium*, "God has joined us so closely to the world around us that we can feel the desertification of the soil almost as a physical ailment, and extinction of a species as a painful disfigurement." (In January 2014 that phrase was set on a plaque in Rome's Biopark, next to an image of Francis in St. Peter's Square supporting a parrot on his outstretched fingers.) Or, speaking of the Resurrection, he wrote that "each day in our world, beauty is born anew, it rises transformed through the storms of history."

The document was at its most powerful when it captured his vision of what he called the Samaritan Church, the Church that heals by direct personal contact. "Jesus wants us to touch human misery, to touch the suffering flesh of others," he wrote. "Whenever we do so, our lives become wonderfully complicated and we experience intensely what it is to be a people, to be part of a people." To grow in the spiritual life, he said, was to become missionary, to come out to meet others; and when we do, "we learn something new about God. Whenever our eyes are opened to acknowledge the other, we grow in the light of faith and of knowledge of God." As usual, the invitation was accompanied by a warning about the alternative: "We do not live better when we flee, hide, refuse to share, stop giving, and lock ourselves up in our own comforts. Such a life is nothing less than a slow suicide." And he warned that being a missionary was not a part-time activity but required surrender to a new kind of existence—a soul-filled other-centeredness:

> My mission of being in the heart of the people is not just a part of my life or a badge I can take off; it is not an "extra" or just another moment in life. Instead, it is something I cannot uproot from my being without destroying my very self. I am a mission on this earth; that is the reason why I am here in this world. We have to regard ourselves as sealed, even branded, by this mission of bringing light, blessing, enlivening, raising up, healing, and freeing. All around us we begin to see nurses with soul, teachers with soul, politicians with soul, people who have chosen deep down to be with others and for others.

The part of the document that attracted most media headlines was the least original. When Francis critiqued free-market "trickle-down" theories that trusted the market to set wages and conditions, he was speaking out of a long papal tradition of teaching stretching back, in modern times, to Leo XIII in the late nineteenth century. In *Rerum Novarum* (1891), Pope Leo, too, had damned the enrichment of the few at the expense of the many and the idolatry of markets that justified it, while calling for state intervention to protect and succor its victims. Most recently, Pope Benedict XVI in 2007 had built on the same tradition in his sophisticated social encyclical, *Caritas in Veritate*.

Yet when Francis in *Evangelii Gaudium* said trickle-down didn't work ("the excluded are still waiting") and deplored "the laws of competition and the survival of the fittest, where the powerful feed on the powerless," it caused shock in many quarters, as if the pope were proposing to resurrect socialism just at the time everyone could agree that capitalism had created the best of all possible worlds. Former US Republican nominee Sarah Palin fretted that some of the pope's statements "sound kind of liberal," American talk radio host Rush Limbaugh called it "pure Marxism," and Fox News's Stuart Varney complained that Francis was mixing religion and politics, that the Church wasn't competent to pronounce on economic matters, and that, in any case, the free market had delivered huge prosperity across the world. On the left, conversely, many were delighted, declaring Francis the new anticapitalist pinup.

Yet Francis wasn't critiquing the market in the sense of the free exchange of goods and services and ordinary human economic activity, which had indeed generated wealth since the beginning of time; and even less was he proposing a collectivist or any other alternative "system." He was unmasking an idolatrous mind-set that had surrendered human sovereignty to a hidden deity, a deus ex machina, which demanded to be left alone to function unimpeded. What Francis deplored were "ideologies that defend the absolute autonomy of the marketplace," the attitude that justified or tolerated inequality and poverty by arguing that they were necessary or tolerable by-products of the ordinary functioning of the market. Thus was created "a new tyranny . . . which unilaterally and relentlessly imposes its own laws and rules."

Francis spoke not from the point of view of an alternative economic theory, but from that of the poor, and their need. If societies could regard stupendous wealth and at the same time grinding misery (long-term unemployment, wages insufficient to keep families, malnutrition) as inevitable by-products of a normally functioning market, then something had rotted in both the human soul and the mind.

> Just as the commandment "Thou shalt not kill" sets a clear limit in order to safeguard the value of human life, today we also have to say "thou shalt not" to an economy of exclusion and inequality. Such an economy kills. How can it be that it is not a news item when an elderly homeless person dies of exposure, but it is news when the stock market loses two points? This is a case of exclusion. Can we continue to stand by when food is thrown away while people are starving? This is a case of inequality. Today everything comes under the laws of competition and the survival of the fittest, where the powerful feed upon the powerless. As a consequence, masses of people find themselves excluded and marginalized: without work, without possibilities, without any means of escape.

A Catholic columnist on the *Forbes* magazine website who said he was "spitting with rage" over the pope's remarks perfectly illustrated the mindset Francis had identified. After posting statistics charting the *embourgeoisement* of millions of peasants over the past century, Tim Worstall wrote that "everything is moving in the right direction, even if not as gloriously fast as we would like it to be. . . . The market based economic system that he is complaining about is exactly the economic system that is in the process of solving the problems that he identifies."[1] By imagining that one day poverty would be magically solved by the market, it was an attitude that justified inaction in the here and now. Anyone who knew poor people, rather than read about them in econometric theory, understood immediately what Francis meant: waiting for the market to generalize prosperity was a different experience for the poor than for the wealthy.

Behind this mentality Francis saw "a rejection of ethics and a rejection of God," one that, like all idolatries, increased its hold on human hearts and minds through addiction (consumerism) while demanding a constant supply of human lives (the impoverished, the unemployed) for sacrifice on its altar, while claiming the autonomy to continue operating unimpeded by laws and state regulation. Challenging the idea that states should interfere as little as possible with the workings of the market, Francis called for "a vigorous change of approach on the part of political leaders" aimed at "a return of economics and finance to an ethical approach that favors human beings."

The most startling and original part of the document was the least discussed in the media: an unprecedented attack by a pope on his own Church. No modern pope had ever given his fellow believers such a tongue-lashing. In an early section entitled "No to spiritual worldliness," he named and shamed "adulterated forms of Christianity" in which pious Catholics glorified themselves rather than Christ, and self-appointed elites lorded over ordinary mortals in the Church, deploring them either for their backwardness (in the case of liberal Catholics) or their lack of doctrinal purity (in the case of conservatives). Francis deplored the "dour judges bent on rooting out every threat and deviation" as well as "querulous and disillusioned pessimists" afflicted by "the evil spirit of defeatism," which is "the fruit of an anxious and self-centered lack of trust." Quoting Pope John XXIII's famous words at the start of the Second Vatican Council criticizing the "prophets of doom who are always forecasting disaster," he lambasted the "self-absorbed promethean neopelagianism" and "narcissistic and authoritarian elitism" of self-appointed guardians of orthodoxy who spend their time "inspecting and verifying" rather than evangelizing. He also deplored those with "an ostentatious preoccupation for the liturgy, for doctrine, and for the Church's prestige, but without any concern that the Gospel have a real impact on God's faithful people" and the way liturgical backwoodsmen turned the Church into "a museum piece, or something which is the property of a select few."

It was hard not to see this as a response to those who, during his first Easter as pope, had criticized him for washing the feet of twelve juvenile detainees at the Casal del Marmo, a young offender institution in Rome, on Holy Thursday. One of them was a girl from Serbia, who became the first Muslim and the first woman ever to have their feet washed by a pope. The inclusion of women was technically a violation of a 1988 edict from the Vatican's Congregation for Divine Worship and the Discipline of the Sacraments, which held that because the rite reenacts Jesus washing the feet of his apostles, only men should participate. But most dioceses in the world (including Buenos Aires) had long ignored that rubric. Francis, as he always did as archbishop, was restoring an early-church practice when bishops washed the feet of the poor.

His attack on spiritual worldliness went beyond particular mind-sets to include—although he did not mention them by name—bishops and others prominent in the Church. Deploring "a fascination with social and political gain" and "an obsession with programs of self-help and self-realization" (meaning, presumably, the kind of self-centered therapy workshops found in certain retreat centers), he also criticized "a concern to be seen," "a social life full of appearances, meetings, dinners, and receptions," as well as "a business mentality, caught up with management, statistics, plans, and evaluations whose principal beneficiary is not God's people but the Church as an institution."

In this way, Francis was extending the holy-faithful-people hermeneutic, using it now not to attack Argentine armchair revolutionaries but self-referential church leaders. The symptoms were the same: "spiritual masters and pastoral experts who give instructions from on high," who "indulge in endless fantasies" and "lose contact with the real lives and difficulties of our people." The Jesuit provincial who once lambasted left-wing Catholic ideologues in Argentina now deplored bishops and prominent lay people in almost exactly the same terms:

> Those who have fallen into this worldliness look on from above and afar, they reject the prophecy of their brothers and sisters, they discredit those who raise questions, they constantly point out the mistakes of others and they are obsessed by appearances. Their hearts are open only to the limited horizon of their own immanence and interests, and as a consequence they neither learn from their sins nor are they genuinely open to forgiveness. This is a tremendous corruption disguised as a good. We need to avoid it by making the Church constantly go out from herself, keeping her mission focused on Jesus Christ, and her commitment to the poor.[2]

THE story of how Bergoglio came to be made bishop begins with Pope John Paul II wanting Antonio Quarracino, the archbishop of La Plata, to replace Cardinal Juan Carlos Aramburu of Buenos Aires when the latter reached retirement age in 1987. Quarracino was a gifted churchman who after attending the sessions of Vatican II went on to play major roles within the Church both in Argentina and continent-wide. As president of CELAM, he had formed a bond with the Polish pope.

Quarracino was John Paul II's sort of bishop: close to workers, solid in doctrine, pro-life, and pro–social justice. An articulate polemicist with a strong sense of irony, he had great gifts of clarity and a Peronist's capacity to connect with ordinary folk. But he could be crude, and his tendency to shoot from the hip led him to be seen as more reactionary than he was. A fierce critic of President Alfonsín's attempts to separate Church and state, introduce divorce, and ban religious education from schools, Quarracino in 1987 tried to claim that an address by John Paul II to the Argentine ambassador to the Holy See was an indictment of the Radical government's policies. Alfonsín asked the Vatican if this was true; the Vatican said no; and the Radical president thereafter had a perfect excuse to use his presidential powers under the *patronato* to veto Quarracino's appointment to Buenos Aires. Cardinal Aramburu was now asked to stay on, and not until Carlos Menem became president at the end of 1989 could Quarracino finally be named to Argentina's mother diocese. He was installed in July 1990—shortly after Bergoglio was moved to Córdoba—and made a cardinal the following year.

Quarracino was close to President Menem whom he had gotten to know when the then governor of La Rioja was imprisoned under the dictatorship. As Quarracino had urged, and possibly at his behest, Menem shortly after taking office issued an indult for the dirty war criminals who had been tried and imprisoned under Alfonsín: some 220 military officers, including former junta leaders, were set free, along with seventy civilians, among whom were former guerrilla leaders. Alfonsín had passed laws circumscribing the scope of criminal responsibility for the dirty war, restricting those serving jail sentences to those who had either given orders or grossly exceeded them. But Menem now set the prisoners free, arguing that it was time for the national reconciliation John Paul II had called for on his 1987 visit. The move was supported by industry, the agro-export sector, as well as the bishops, but deplored by the Mothers of the Plaza de Mayo. Alfonsín called it the saddest day of his life.

Menem's 1989–1999 two-term administration, the first Peronist government since the general and his widow fifteen years earlier, mixed a classically Peronist alliance of the usual interest groups—small business, trade unions—with a radically neoliberal economic and foreign policy. He forged an unexpected bond with the very part of Argentine society that had always been at odds with Peronism: the financial and agro-export sector. Their talented leaders served in Menem's administration, crafting his economic policy and carrying out his reforms, persuaded that only a Peronist government had the political legitimacy to deliver the necessary shock therapy to Argentina's bloated and state-dependent economy.

That shock came in the form of a mass sell-off of public-owned enterprises and a so-called convertibility law that replaced the national currency with a new one, the peso, making it convertible to the US dollar at a rate of one to one. It was a radical attempt to kill off hyperinflation and spark economic growth. By limiting the money supply to dollar reserves, the government denied itself the right to print money, leading to an upsurge in confidence, a sudden inflow of foreign investment, and inflation reduced to almost zero. Argentina at last had some stability after the devastation of hyperinflation. In the early 1990s, the economy grew by a third and middle-class Argentines enjoyed a bonanza of conspicuous consumption.

However, the government's failure to build a social-security network alongside the free market left the poor unprotected, and statistics showed an alarming increase in poverty and unemployment despite economic stability and growth. The architects of the policy—led by Domingo Cavallo, the economy minister—put their faith in the workings of markets, confident that investment and growth would eventually trickle down to the poor; but at the end of the Menem decade they were still waiting. Rather than overflowing the glass once the glass was full, the glass just got bigger: the rich got richer and the poor either stayed poor or got poorer. When it all began to unravel in the crisis of 1998, what made Argentines especially furious was the revelation of corruption on an eye-watering scale: the fusion of state, market, and judiciary, and the impunity of a new, fantastically wealthy class of Menem millionaires.

In keeping with their new policy of distance from the state, Argentina's bishops were consistent critics of the government's neoliberal policies and their social effects, especially of corruption and impunity. Menem, however, adopted strong pro-life policies and vigorously defended the Church on the world stage (Argentina publicly sided with the Holy See, for example, when it was left isolated in the 1994 population conference in Cairo). Menem could offset the criticism from his bishops through a warm relationship with both Quarracino and the Holy See, oiled by both direct and indirect financial assistance.

After he was made a cardinal in February 1991, Quarracino took advantage of his relationship with the pope to get Bergoglio appointed as his auxiliary, a bishop who assists the metropolitan bishop of a large diocese. He had wanted to do this since at least 1988, when he told the Jesuit general, Father Kolvenbach, that "the Argentine Church has great expectations of Father Bergoglio." This was confirmed in mid-1990 when the apostolic nuncio to Argentina, Archbishop Ubaldo Calabresi, warned the provincial, Father Zorzín—who had decided at that point to send Bergoglio to Córdoba—that the Church had a mission for the former provincial. "When he's given that mission, he'll go where he has to go," Zorzín testily told Calabresi.

Archbishop Quarracino invited Bergoglio in January and April 1990 to give retreats to dozens of his clergy in La Plata. In the first, "Our Flesh in Prayer," Bergoglio reflected powerfully on Jesus's parable of the Good Samaritan, the story of the foreigner who comes to the aid of a traveler beaten by brigands. He showed that those who passed by on the other side—symbolized in Jesus's telling by the priest and the Levite—used a series of distancing techniques, which were all temptations: either they intellectualized the suffering they saw, or evaded responsibility for it by reassuring themselves that this is how life was. The Samaritan, on the other hand, got on his hands and knees to get close to the victim, opened his heart to him and bound his wounds, shouldered him and spent his money on him. "That is what we will be judged on," Bergoglio told the priests, adding that this proximity was at the heart of the Incarnation. Jesus, far from "passing on the other side," paid the ultimate price in sacrificing his own flesh for those who suffer; and God's closeness to humanity is the reason why "prayer touches our flesh in its very nucleus, it touches our heart."

Prayer, he told the priests, meant enduring the possibility of change; it meant a willingness to suffer. When a person ceases praying and starts complaining, "he ceases to serve the Gospel and becomes a victim. He canonizes himself." Making oneself the victim, rather than Christ, was blasphemy; "and a flesh that is used to blasphemy, which does not know how to ask for help for its own wound and sin, is a flesh incapable of helping the wounds of others." Even if he dedicates his life to God he will only ever be able to come close to himself. "It is the asepsis of the Pharisee," Bergoglio warned: "neither virus nor vitamin."[3]

Bergoglio was impressing on the priests of La Plata a model of Church that would be key to his teaching and leadership as bishop and cardinal: one that was intimate, physically close, looks the poor in the eye, and speaks to the heart. He showed that Catholicism was a fleshly business; it was how God saved humanity—by coming close, and embracing reality as it was. Yet too often the Church was tempted to flee that reality, taking refuge in bureaucracy, ideology, or rationality. Salvation can only happen, he suggested, one person at a time, through direct personal engagement. Unless love was incarnated, it was not love; meanwhile, the poor could be lifted from poverty if they were treated and loved as individual human beings.

The retreats only made Quarracino more determined to secure Bergoglio for the diocesan Church. He had seen the way Bergoglio's pastoral operation had transformed San Miguel and was shocked at how the Jesuits had ostracized him. Temperamentally, the Jesuit and the bishop were wholly unalike. Where Bergoglio was quiet, discreet, and austere, Quarracino was a wordy extrovert who relished the limelight and the trappings of his office. But there was a natural affinity in their common background and their political and cultural inclinations. They were both sons of 1920s Italian émigrés who shared a similar theological outlook—pro-Medellín, anti-Marxist—in the "national and popular," Peronist tradition of the *teología del pueblo*. Both were committed to CELAM, and to the idea of a transnational Catholic unity for Latin America. And both were admirers of the Uruguayan philosopher Alberto Methol Ferré. But at a deeper level, Quarracino saw Bergoglio as what both he and the Church needed. Despite his bluffness, Quarracino was in humility aware of his own shortcomings. He was also in awe of Bergoglio's spiritual depth and leadership qualities, recognizing in his prudence and discernment—he referred to him affectionately as *el santito*, "the little saint"—precisely what he lacked.

Shortly after the second retreat, Bergoglio left for Córdoba and Quarracino began making moves to have him named bishop. It took another eighteen months. Appointments of Catholic bishops follow a lengthy consultation within the local Church organized by the nuncio, who sends a *terna*—a list of three names—to the Congregation of Bishops in Rome, which decides whether to appoint, to refuse, or to delay pending further

Jorge's grandparents Giovanni Bergoglio and
Rosa Margarita Vasallo with their eldest son,
Jorge's father, Mario.

Jorge's parents, Mario and Regina,
on their wedding day in 1935.

Jorge as a teenager, late 1940s.

Jorge (*left*) and his brother Oscar in their First
Communion outfits in the 1940s.

Jorge with classmates and the Salesian priests who ran the Wilfrid Barón de los Santos Angeles primary school he attended between 1948 and 1949. Jorge is fourth from the left in the third row from the top.

Jorge on parade at the school. He is the second boy. (G. PIKO/ARGENPRESS)

The Bergoglio family in 1958. Jorge (*in cassock*), who that year entered seminary, with (*back row, left to right*) his brothers and sisters Alberto, Oscar, and Marta and (*seated*) María Elena, with their parents, Regina and Mario.

Argentine Jesuits studying at the Casa Loyola, outside the Chilean capital, Santiago, in 1960. Almost all would leave before finishing their formation. Bergoglio is in the back row, fifth from the right. Andrés Swinnen, who would succeed him as Argentine provincial, is back row, fifth from left. Bottom row, far right, is Jorge González Manent ("Goma"), author of a memoir about their novitiate.

Bergoglio the teacher in 1964. *Right*: with the writer Jorge Luis Borges in 1965, when he invited him to talk to his students at the Colegio de la Inmaculada Concepción in Santa Fe, Argentina.

A view of the 200-bedroom Colegio Máximo in the Buenos Aires province town of San Miguel, where Jorge Bergoglio spent most of his life as a Jesuit: as a student of philosophy and theology (1966–71), as lecturer in pastoral theology and novice-master (1971–72), as provincial (1973–79), and as rector (1980–86).

Above: Pope John Paul II made Bergoglio a cardinal in February 2001 along with a large number of Latin-American diocesan archbishops. *Below*: Cardinal Bergoglio entering the Sistine Chapel for the first time in the April 2005 conclave. Cardinal Cormac Murphy-O'Connor, then the archbishop of Westminster, is on the left of the picture.

María Desatanudos—"Mary, Untier of Knots"—the Argentine copy of the German picture that Bergoglio gave out on prayer cards at his ordination as bishop in 1992, sparking a popular devotion.

Cardinal Bergoglio welcomes President Néstor Kirchner and the First Lady, Cristina Fernández de Kirchner, to the cathedral for the traditional Te Deum on May 25, 2006, Argentina's national day. After taking offense at the cardinal's address, President Kirchner opted in subsequent years to celebrate the Te Deum outside Buenos Aires.

When this picture of Bergoglio being prayed over by evangelical pastors at a 2006 ecumenical gathering was published in *La Nación*, traditionalist Catholic groups declared he had "apostasized." On the left of the picture, in a friar's habit, is the papal preacher Father Raniero Cantalamessa.

The cardinal on fire: preaching at the CRECES gathering in 2006.

Cardinal Bergoglio was a regular user of the Buenos Aires subway, the subte. Line A took him from the Plaza de Mayo, where he was based, to his childhood barrio of Flores.

Bergoglio the street preacher.

ENRIQUE CANGAS

MARCELO GENLOTE/ARCHIVO CLARÍN

Speaking after a Mass in Villa 21 in December 2010 to thank Padre Pepe Di Paola, who after fourteen years of service to the slum and surviving threats from drug traffickers, was taking time out.

"The handover." With Pope Benedict XVI on February 28, 2013, the day his historic resignation from the papacy took effect and the Diocese of Rome was *sede vacante*. The pope, who made the decision to resign in Mexico in March 2012, saw Latin America as the new source for the universal Church.

A thoughtful Cardinal Bergoglio arrives for the general congregations of cardinals prior to the conclave in March 2013. His brief but powerful speech convinced many of the cardinals that the new pope had already been chosen.

In the Sistine Chapel at the conclave that elected him. To his left his friend Cardinal Claúdio Hummes, the Brazilian cardinal who told him: "Don't forget the poor."

Francis shocked Vatican staff by joining them in their canteen on July 25, 2014. He waited in line with the rest of the employees for his lunch of pasta, cod, and grilled tomatoes. The cashier didn't have the courage to charge him when he appeared at the register.

At lunch in the Jesuit General Curia on the Feast of Saint Ignatius, July 31, 2014. On the left of the photo (*seated*) is Father Alfredo Nicolás, the Jesuit superior general, who after the election of Francis, acted swiftly to heal the wounds of the past. To the pope's right (*standing*) is Father Attilio Sciortino, minister of the Curia, and to his left (*seated*) is Father Joaquín Barrero, superior of the Curia and regional assistant for Southern Europe.

Building bridges through bonds of trust: *above*, with British abuse survivor Peter Saunders in July 2014, who gave Francis a cycling cap; *above right*, in Jerusalem with old friends Omar Abboud and Rabbi Abraham Skorka; *right*, with Bishop Tony Palmer, tragically killed in July 2014.

"If the Church is alive, it must always surprise us." At his general audience in St. Peter's Square at the Vatican, November 20, 2013.

information. In Bergoglio's case, there were hurdles: the negativity toward him of the new Jesuit provincial, Ignacio García-Mata, and his *socius*, Juan Luis Moyano. But Quarracino managed to bypass the Vatican's Congregation of Bishops to speak directly to John Paul II, who signed the nomination on May 20, 1992.

Bergoglio found out only the week before, when the nuncio asked to meet him at Córdoba Airport on his way back from Mendoza to Buenos Aires. Archbishop Calabresi, who like Quarracino rated Bergoglio highly, often telephoned him to consult him about candidates for bishops. This time, however, the nuncio asked for a face-to-face meeting. At the airport they spoke about "serious matters," Bergoglio later recalled, until it was time for the nuncio to board. "Ah, one last thing," Calabresi told him as he made to leave, "you've been named auxiliary bishop of Buenos Aires and the designation will be made public on the twentieth."

"My mind went blank," Bergoglio recalled in his 2010 book-length interview, *El Jesuita*. "Whenever something really unexpected happens, whether good or bad, my mind always goes blank."[4]

Any priest invited to be ordained a bishop has the right to refuse if asked (ordinations are sacraments, which cannot be forced). Professed Jesuits have a particular reason not to accept: they have taken a special vow not to seek ecclesiastical office. But when the pope himself makes the request of a Jesuit, he usually agrees, accepting episcopal ordination as a fulfillment of his fourth vow to go on mission wherever (and however) the pope needs him. In accepting, like other Jesuit bishops at the time—most prominently the archbishop of Milan, Cardinal Carlo Maria Martini—Bergoglio remained a member of the Jesuit order; and like Martini, he would always put the letters "SJ" after his name. But it was a nominal belonging. Being made a bishop released him from his Jesuit vows of obedience and poverty: the first because he was no longer under orders from the general, the second because under church law a bishop must own property. In all practical senses of the word, in other words, he ceased to be Jesuit.

The appointment amazed Church observers. The only Jesuit ever to have been made a bishop in Argentina was Joaquín Piña, a Spanish missionary who in 1986 was asked to lead the small diocese of Puerto Iguazú in Misiones. It was also surprising because Quarracino would now have six auxiliaries, when only four in the past had been needed. But mostly it was surprising because, outside a few small circles, most Argentines had no idea who Bergoglio was. It was neither the first nor last time that, amid general astonishment, he would appear seemingly from nowhere to take up senior office.

Together with twenty others receiving their mitres on June 27, 1992, the fifty-five-year-old Bergoglio was ordained a bishop in the metropolitan cathedral of Buenos Aires by Cardinal Quarracino, together with the nuncio and the archbishop of Luján, Emilio Ogñénovich. Asked to address the congregation briefly, Bishop Bergoglio drew on his La Plata retreat. "There are brothers and sisters," he said, "who with their lives ask us please not to cross over to the other side but instead discover in their wounds those of Jesus Himself."

Bergoglio stood out from the other bishops in two respects. Father Carlos Accaputo, who would later become one of Bergoglio's closest collaborators, had heard negative things about the new auxiliary. At the ordination, however, he "was struck, when it was over, by the large number of very poor people who went to greet him—they were all people from the margins. At which I thought: *aha*. There's something going on here I need to find out about." The second curiosity was the prayer card which Bishop Bergoglio handed to well-wishers. Where the other bishops' cards portrayed favorite saints, his was a German painting of the Virgin Mary unraveling a silken thread. ("We had no idea what it was about," remembers another priest present, Father Guillermo Marcó.)

Every new bishop chooses a coat of arms. Bergoglio's was a blue shield, on which was imprinted the Jesuit symbol—the monogram IHS, (the first three letters of the name of Jesus in Greek) against the background of blazing sun—and below it a star, standing for the Nativity, alongside a spikenard, representing Saint Joseph. Underneath was the motto he had chosen: *Miserando atque eligendo*, the phrase used in a homily by the Venerable Saint Bede describing Jesus recruiting Saint Matthew: *And looking at him mercifully, he chose him.* That homily is in the Church's daily prayer readings for Saint Matthew's feast day, September 21— the spring day in 1953 when the young Jorge Mario was "mercy'd" by God in the confessional of the basilica in Flores.

The basilica was in the area Quarracino had entrusted to Bergoglio, one of four districts that made up the huge archdiocese of Buenos Aires, with a stable resident population of three million that more than doubles by day. Compared to the others—Belgrano in the north, the Center in the east of the city, and Devoto in the west—the vicariate of Flores in the south was by a long shot the poorest: it included forty-five parishes in five lower-middle-class or working-class barrios, most of the city's large shantytowns, including the one where Yorio and Jalics had been abducted, and almost all of its popular shrines. Quarracino wanted Bergoglio to take charge, above all, of the ten-strong slum priests' team, and to do for Flores what Quarracino had seen him achieve in San Miguel.

He was allocated an office and residence in the clergy retirement house in the calle Condarco, a few blocks from the basilica of Flores. The Divine Mercy sisters who had played such a role in his infancy were still close by, among them Sister Dolores. But the house he grew up in on Membrillar Street had been sold after his mother's death in 1981, and his brothers and sisters had long since married and had families of their own.

While the Condarco rooms were being made ready, Bergoglio spent nearly three months at the Jesuit curia house, Regina Martyrum, in the center of the city, going to his office each day. Father Kolvenbach had told the new Jesuit provincial, Father García-Mata, to place himself at the service of Bishop Bergoglio, and the provincial had invited him to live there after his nomination was announced in May. But it wasn't an easy relationship. Bergoglio blamed García-Mata for defaming him in a report the provincial had written to Rome—the report was secret, but one of the consultors had informed Bergoglio—while García-Mata felt threatened by Bergoglio's popularity among the younger Jesuits. As the weeks went by the provincial began to be irritated by what he regarded as Bergoglio's "interfering" presence. Things came to a head at the end of July 1992, on the feast of Saint Ignatius, when García-Mata asked him when he was leaving.

"But I'm very comfortable here," Bergoglio told him.

"Jorge," the provincial answered, "it's not right for an auxiliary bishop of Buenos Aires to be living in a Jesuit community. There's no province where that happens."

If he wanted him out, said Bergoglio, he should inform him formally. So García-Mata wrote to Father Kolvenbach, who backed the provincial, who left the general's letter in Bergoglio's room. García-Mata received a written response in return, in which Bergoglio gave the date of his departure.[5]

Thus, painfully, did Bergoglio leave his Jesuit life.

Most Jesuits who become bishops retain strong links with the Society, often staying in Jesuit residences while traveling, and looking in on the Borgo Santo Spirito when in Rome. But over the next twenty years, on many trips to Rome, Bergoglio never once stepped inside the Jesuit curia, nor spoke to Father Kolvenbach; and although he had good relations with Father Alvaro Restrepo, the Colombian who replaced García-Mata as Argentine provincial in 1997, he severed most of his links with the Argentine Jesuits until after his election as pope.

BERGOGLIO was not the kind of bishop the clergy were used to. He was un-clerical, straightforward, humble, austere, and effective. He had endless time to give the faithful and their pastors, and was always available. He had no secretary, was easily reached on the telephone after his morning prayer (he woke at 4:00 a.m. and could be reached after 6:00 a.m.), and if unable to answer would call back within a couple of hours. Problems were solved swiftly, often by him directly. "It was a way of being a bishop that was much physically closer than we were used to," recalls Father Fernando Giannetti, parish priest of Our Lady of Mercy in Mataderos, a sprawling parish where the streets once stank with the offal from the city's slaughterhouses. "He came to see you and he listened. That created a very close bond between him and the priests of the area as well as with the faithful."

The clergy liked his personal approach. When he wanted to talk, he took the trouble to visit. He was still decisive and a good decision maker, but the torment of Córdoba had softened him: he dialogued more, and consulted. He went from parish to parish, spending time with clergy, drinking mate, asking about the time they gave to prayer, and finding out what they needed. Priests who were ill found him by their bedside, or moving in to say Mass and hear confessions for them, sometimes cooking and cleaning for them. When a priest couldn't find another to replace him during their vacations, Bergoglio—who never took vacations—would supply for him, sometimes for weeks. There are many stories of the help he gave to priests struggling with vows or addictions or simply pastoral challenges.

Many bishops are teachers or administrators, whose natural home is their desk, but Bergoglio was a practiced pastor. He began as he would continue as archbishop and cardinal: without a driver or assistant, keeping his own diary, making his own calls, and moving around the city on the bus and the subway, or by foot. He spent much of his time in the *villas miseria*, building up the team of slum priests, and procuring funds and resources for their projects. The priests could see he knew parish life, says Giannetti, by the way he tenderly, patiently guided teenage candidates for confirmation. "He was teaching us a style of pastoral outreach that is not about pointing out to people what they're doing wrong but bringing them in, enabling their encounter with God," he recalls. It was what Bergoglio meant by the Church as facilitator rather than regulator.

Early on, Bergoglio asked Father Guillermo Marcó, then a young curate in a parish in Flores, to accompany him on his walkabouts. With a Protestant mother and atheist father, Marcó was interested in interreligious dialogue and communications, and had a radio program on a commercial channel. Bergoglio was intrigued by him, and years later would recruit him to manage his press relations. For his part, Marcó was struck by the new bishop's "way of being, his simplicity. He was quite captivating."

Another young priest who would be a key future aide was Father Accaputo, who gave a course in a Flores parish on Catholic social teaching. Impressed, Bergoglio asked him to come and work in the Church's charity agency, Caritas, in Flores. But the priest first wanted the bishop to know his views. Accaputo explained that he was orthodox, neither conservative nor progressive, that conservatives wanted to put faith inside a box whereas progressives talked so much they emptied faith of its meaning. And he went on to share his views on the universal as well as the local Church, including some areas of disagreement with Cardinal Quarracino. "At the end of it Bergoglio said great, no problem, and we started to work together," recalls Accaputo. "I felt for the first time that I had a met a man with authority in the Church with whom I could speak person to person, as an equal."[6]

After eighteen months, just before Christmas 1993, Cardinal Quarracino put Bergoglio in charge of administering the archdiocese. Naming him vicar-general on top of the Flores vicariate meant a significant increase in his responsibilities and brought him into regular contact with the whole clergy of the diocese.

He became the cardinal's right-hand man, his stand-in, and the hidden hand behind many of his speeches and homilies. Quarracino, who as president of the bishops' conference until 1996 was the public face of the Argentine Catholic Church, came increasingly to depend on his vicar-general's advice and industriousness. But Bergoglio wasn't always able to save Quarracino from himself. Although the cardinal was a pioneer of dialogue with Jews and progressive in many respects, he was viscerally homophobic, proposing in 1994 on his regular live television slot that gay people should be sent to live in a "large zone" with its own media and laws in order to avoid "a stain on the face of society." The remark— the worst of a series he had made over the years—led to the threat of a lawsuit and a task force of lawyers was needed to defend him. Bergoglio, horrified, would try to make amends later, as archbishop.[7]

Bergoglio also disliked Quarracino's closeness to Menem and the way he allowed the Church to be absorbed into the government's patronage network. When Quarracino stood down as bishops' conference president in 1996, Bergoglio supported attempts by his successor, Archbishop Estanislao Karlic of Paraná, to put clear blue water between the Church and the government. On the ground, Bergoglio was aware of how corrupting the relationship could be. Millions of pesos (at that time equivalent to the US dollar) were being used to fund church projects in exchange for loyalty, and much of it was being siphoned off along the way.

At this time two government officials "who claimed to be very Catholic" came to see Bergoglio at the Flores vicariate, offering him public money for church projects in the shantytowns. Bergoglio was suspicious and got them to admit that of the 400,000 pesos they wanted him to sign as having received, they would give half and keep the rest. Rather than refuse point-blank, Bergoglio told them that any deposits had to be made into the diocesan curia's central bank account and receipts signed for, at which point the men disappeared. But the fact they had come to him with that scheme meant, he later said, that "someone in the Church had previously been open to such an operation."[8]

It was all too easy for a bishop to accept a little largesse, and to prefer the company, and by degrees also the interests, of the wealthy; and thence to slip into spiritual worldliness. Bergoglio dealt with the threat using Saint Ignatius's technique of *agere contra*. Faced with a temptation, said the founder of the Jesuits, you should redouble your effort to go in the opposite direction: to combat greed, for example, you should fast; to combat a loss of interest in prayer, double your prayer time. In Bergoglio's case it meant spending even more time with the young and the poor and turning down all dinner invitations and freebies, preferring to say Mass for prostitutes in San Ignacio church and spending Saturdays in the slums. As Pope Francis would later say in *Evangelii Gaudium*, the option for the poor was a constant, clear imperative of Scripture and the early Church that created "a prophetic, countercultural resistance to the self-centered hedonism of paganism."

He stood by the poor politically, too, backing his team of slum priests when they went on a hunger strike in January 1996. The protest was over the resumption of the building of a major new freeway that went over Villa 31, and specifically an exit road off it that required destroying several blocks of the slum. Elections were close, and the city's mayor, Jorge Domínguez, was campaigning for reelection on the promise of "100 public works in 100 days," one of which was the so-called Arturo Illia freeway. Having failed to reach agreement with the residents over the compensation they were due, Domínguez—a firm Menem ally—ordered in the police and the bulldozers, but they found the entire team of slum priests in their way, along with a pack of reporters jostling among them with cameras and microphones.

For fourteen dramatic days the ten priests ingested only fluids as they lay in a tent in the choking humid heat of the Buenos Aires summer. The coverage was intense: journalists turned up daily, ready to capture the first moments of a priest being taken away in an ambulance. Furious, Menem raged against the priests as *tercermundistas* ("Third-Worldists"), in reference to the pro-socialist clerical group of the early 1970s.

The insult showed that the president was out of touch. These were different times, and the slum priests had changed: no longer socialists who placed the "Church of the poor" against the hierarchy, the young priests saw themselves as politically nonaligned, holding the state to account on behalf of the poor. Bergoglio assisted in this transition. From the start of the dispute, he had stayed closely in touch with them, appearing regularly in the *villa* to check on their health and to see what they needed. Crucially, he persuaded Quarracino, by then unwell, to come with him in a public show of support for the priests, causing the government—whose strategy was to frame them as dissident clergy—to back down. In a deal stitched together by Bergoglio behind the scenes, the priests called off the strike once the authorities agreed on television to put the exit road elsewhere.

The symbolism of this was even greater because Villa 31, close to Retiro station, had been Father Mugica's base. Mugica, gunned down by the Triple A in 1974, was the Church's Che Guevara, whose picture was everywhere in the slums; his martyr's death and love of the poor made him a potent symbol. The death of Marxism and the guerrillas made it now both safe and right for Bergoglio to honor him. In October 1999, after he became archbishop, Bergoglio agreed to a bid by the team of *curas villeros* to bring Mugica's body from the aristocratic cemetery of La Recoleta to be buried in the chapel of his old parish of Christ the Worker, which was by then under the new freeway. Bergoglio took charge of the paperwork and the Vatican permission, and celebrated the Mass, in which he prayed "for Father Carlos's material assassins as well as those who ideologically justified the murder, and for the silent accomplices of a large part of society and the Church." He then unveiled a plaque to Father Mugica, "who honored with his preaching and action his Christian commitment to the poor."

Predictably, there were some on the left—including former *curas villeros* who had left the priesthood—who saw this as a cynical attempt by the Church to domesticate Mugica. But the *curas villeros* themselves were deeply impressed. Bergoglio's option for the poor was real, and measured not just in words but in actions—not least the dozens of visits he made to the slums to be with the people and to support their priests.

His reputation was now spreading among the clergy of Buenos Aires. Father Carlos Galli, who would later be a theological collaborator, had been recruited to replace Bergoglio as teacher of pastoral theology at the Colegio Máximo in 1991 and, being friends with Yorio and his circle, had heard no shortage of bad Bergoglio stories—especially from some in the Society of Jesus. But he also noticed that the younger Jesuits described him in very different terms—the same as those he was now hearing. It wasn't that Bergoglio had changed: what he was doing in Flores was almost exactly what he had done at the Máximo—an intense pastoral focus on the poor by mobilizing the young. But now that the option for the poor was no longer equated with Marxism, there was greater openness to Bergoglio's option for the poor, with its focus on both the *villas miseria* and the traditional sanctuaries. Galli recalls:

> The stories I heard from people who were not involved in the polemics about him was that he was a fine pastor—a priest and a father to people. And I began to think, could this be the same Bergoglio I had

heard about from some of the Jesuits? I think everyone in Buenos Aires was discovering at that time his immense pastoral charity. I began to hear stories all over the place. A nun's mother dies, and he turns up at the wake, not to lead the service but just to sit there and pray the Rosary. A priest in the *villas* can't get a supply, so he replaces him during the summer. And then there was a cousin of mine who left the priesthood and he helped him to discern that he should leave, and then he helps to speed up the process in Rome, gets him a job in a school and gives him money for three years' worth of rent. There are so many such stories of his immense pastoral charity, but you'll never hear about them from him.

Bergoglio was at this time handing out Mary, Untier of Knots prayer cards and suggesting her intercession to all who came to see him with a problem. One such person was Ana María Betta de Berti, who in the 1990s worked in the administrative department of the Salvador University. She fell in love with the picture and oil-painted a copy, which was hung in the university chapel. *Maria Knotenlöserin* was now an Argentine immigrant, and as immigrants do, had adopted a creole version of her name: *María Desatanudos*. People began arriving at the university asking to see the picture, and took away prayer cards with the image. Stories of favors she had granted—little miracles of healing and reconciliation—began to circulate.

Shortly after he became parish priest, Father Rodolfo Arroyo was asked by three devotees of the image if he would hang the copy in his parish. Father Arroyo had a large blank wall at the back of San José del Talar church in the barrio of Agronomía, and couldn't think of a reason to say no, but he knew nothing about holy pictures and told them he would speak to the archbishop. Quarracino told Arroyo he was a devotee of the Virgin of Luján, Argentina's national shrine, and that "the *Desatanudos* is Bergoglio's thing: ask him." But when Arroyo called Bergoglio, he was told: "Look, don't get me involved. I just brought the prayer card over. But if Quarracino says it's OK, go for it. It's a beautiful image."

Father Arroyo got permission from the cardinal, and did some research into the rites for inaugurating a holy picture. When it came to the official hanging on December 8, 1996, the Feast of the Immaculate Conception, the priest had a shock: 5,000 people came to venerate the picture that day, with long lines forming down what was normally a quiet street in the barrio of Agronomía. It was just the beginning. Father Arroyo found his church swamped by 10,000 people on the eighth of each month, and tens of thousands each December 8, reaching 70,000 in 1998 and 130,000 in 2011. The numbers were easy to track, because every visitor received a prayer card.

In 2012, Cardinal Bergoglio celebrated the December 8 Mass in San José del Talar. The Virgin's grace, he told an immense crowd, was to untie the knots caused by original sin. "Knots in our personal or family lives, knots in our communities and workplaces—all these knots, which are caused by sin, weaken our faith to the point where God's grace cannot flow freely through the silk threads of our lives," he explained. He added: "Mary's kind hands unravel these knots one by one, and the angel shows us that the thread is untied, as if telling us that we can pray with confidence, because we will be heard."[9]

✍

AUXILIARY bishops are usually moved on after some years to take charge of a diocese, but Bergoglio had told the cardinal that if possible he preferred to remain as an assistant bishop in the capital. "I'm a native of the city and I'd be useless outside Buenos Aires," he told Quarracino.

At the time of the priests' hunger strike in early 1996, Quarracino had begun to suffer from cardiovascular problems, presiding over Corpus Christi in July that year in a wheelchair. Because of his ill health, he knew that the following year, when he turned seventy-five, his resignation was likely to be accepted. Quarracino's secret plan was to name Bergoglio as his coadjutor archbishop with right of succession, meaning that when the cardinal died or stood down, Bergoglio would become archbishop of Buenos Aires without any need for a formal nomination from Rome, which could be blocked by the government.

Quarracino faced strong opposition to his plan from a powerful aide to President Menem, Esteban "Cacho" Caselli, known also as "the bishop" because of his close ties to the highest levels of the Vatican. Caselli was the link between the Vatican and Menem, securing Argentine financial and political support for Rome in exchange for political influence. Much to their annoyance, Caselli had persuaded the Vatican in the mid-1990s to soften John Paul II's criticisms of the social situation in Argentina when he addressed its bishops on their visit to Rome.

Caselli had ties above all to two men: the all-powerful secretary of state, Angelo Sodano, sometimes described as the "vice-pope"; and the Argentine diplomat who would be his number two, or *sostituto*, from 2000, Archbishop Leonardo Sandri. Sandri and Caselli were tied by a number of bonds—including membership of a chivalric order, the Knights of Malta—to Héctor Aguer, one of the Buenos Aires auxiliaries. It was Aguer whom they wanted to succeed Quarracino.

Quarracino's bid for Bergoglio to succeed him brought him up against this powerful nexus. When the cardinal flew to Rome to persuade the Vatican's Congregation for Bishops to name Bergoglio as coadjutor, he found himself blocked. It was a major knot. Quarracino however for the second time went over their heads to the pope, who had great affection for him and a dislike of the Church being in bed with political power. In one account, Quarracino wrote out a letter of appointment for the pope to sign and gave it to the Argentine ambassador to the Holy See, Francisco Javier Trusso, to give to John Paul II at a forthcoming scheduled audience. When Trusso gave the pope the letter, he signed it there and then, and gave it back to the ambassador, who sent it on to Quarracino.[10]

Why John Paul II agreed is not clear. But one hypothesis seems reasonable. Quarracino was aware by that time that the Church in Argentina, through him, had become too closely identified with Menem and his entourage, and that revelations of corruption would sooner or later bring the spotlight onto the Church. The austere Bergoglio, he may have argued to John Paul II, was the Church's best chance of moving clear of the muck headed toward them down the tracks.

The nuncio in Argentina, Ubaldo Calabresi, broke the news to Bergoglio in his customarily mischievous way, this time by calling him on the morning of May 17, 1997, and asking him to lunch. When they had reached the coffee course, the waiters suddenly appeared with a cake and sparkling wine. Bergoglio asked if it was the nuncio's birthday. No, said Calabresi, grinning. "What's happening is that you're the new coadjutor archbishop of Buenos Aires."

When his nomination was made public in June it again caused surprise, for the sixty-year-old Bergoglio had almost no public profile: the bishops' conference president, Archbishop Karlic, was the best-known face of the Church, and other bishops familiar to the media had been touted as Quarracino's successor. Bergoglio's elevation, reported *La Nación*, "was in response to a request made directly by Cardenal Quarracino to the pope that he be relieved of his pastoral obligations owing to his health problems."

Much of the journalist's story was taken up with the gap between Bergoglio's invisibility and his attainment of high office. "Archbishop Bergoglio prefers not to speak and zealously protects his lower-ranking image," wrote *La Nación*'s veteran religious affairs commentator, Bartolomé de Vedia, adding: "He will continue to do everything possible to avoid the attention of journalists" and to maintain "the low profile he has cultivated . . . since arriving in the archdiocese." The other theme of the profile was the high esteem he enjoyed among his clergy as a good shepherd, who described him as accessible, ready to listen, intelligent and prayerful, a humble man of few words but great lucidity. "Among the young clergy, he is one of the best-loved auxiliaries," de Vedia wrote.[11] The religious correspondent of the other major daily, *Clarín*, saw the appointment as confirmation of John Paul II's priorities of theological orthodoxy, social concern, and distance from political power. Bergoglio, wrote Sergio Rubín, "is an unpretentious and affable Jesuit, who is very far from the susceptibility to the corridors of power that the *menemistas* were looking for."[12]

Bergoglio's elevation, coming on top of the new cold wind from the bishops' conference under Archbishop Karlic, was a major setback for the Menem/Caselli strategy of co-opting the Church. Having been in the early 1990s the darling of the world's financial markets, Argentina was at that moment having its knuckles rapped over its chronic corruption, uncontrolled spending, and a debt that had soared from $67 billion to an eyewatering $127 billion in a decade. The bishops' conference not only deplored the failure to tackle growing poverty, unemployment, and gross social inequalities but the lack of separation of state and judiciary that underlay the scandalous impunity of Menem's millionaires. Having lost the support of the body of bishops, the government's strategy was to redouble its efforts to keep the Vatican onside. Not long after Bergoglio's nomination was made public, Menem's Vatican fixer, Caselli, replaced Trusso as ambassador to the Holy See.

Although Quarracino remained technically in charge of the diocese, traditionally the coadjutor archbishop increasingly took on the cardinal's duties. In August 1997, Bergoglio led for the first time a massive procession of six hundred thousand to the shrine of San Cayetano ("Saint Cajetan"), patron saint of bread and work, in the barrio of Liniers. The historic numbers reflected soaring unemployment levels and the pain of millions of hard-pressed workers. In his first homily before such a large crowd, Archbishop Bergoglio said work, like food, had to be shared out. "Everyone should have some work," he said. "Work is sacred because when we work we are being formed. Work teaches and educates; work is culture. If God has given us the gift of bread and the gift of life, no one can take from us the gift of earning it through work."[13]

Later that month, he celebrated a huge Mass at the cathedral to welcome the arrival of a statue of the Virgin of Caacupé, who is venerated by Paraguayans. The Virgin had been brought to Buenos Aires by Father Pepe Di Paola, a charismatic young priest whom Bergoglio had helped through a crisis in his vocation. Bergoglio had sent Padre Pepe that year to take charge of one of the poorest and most violent slums in the city, Villa 21, where more than half of the forty-five thousand residents were Paraguayan immigrants and where the grip of the drug mafias was tightening all the time.

Bringing the statue from Paraguay was Padre Pepe's idea. At the end of Mass, thousands turned up at the cathedral to collect the Virgin and take her to the shantytown. "We were walking back with her and we realized that Bergoglio was walking behind us, praying," recalls Padre Pepe. It was a sight the residents of Villa 21 would become familiar with over the next fifteen years. Bergoglio was there so often that at least half of the *villeros*, about twenty-five thousand people, met him and had their picture taken with him in this one *villa* alone, reckons Father Juan Isasmendi, whom Bergoglio sent to Villa 21 in 2008 to support Padre Pepe. Bergoglio, who always came by bus (you need two from the Plaza de Mayo), never missed the big feasts, and did the confirmations himself, which sometimes took the whole day. The *villas*, says Father Isasmendi, were where Bergoglio "filled his lungs with the oxygen he needed to guide the Church."[14]

✧

IN the mid- to late 1990s, Bergoglio grew close to an intellectual mentor he had first met back in the late 1970s: Alberto Methol Ferré, a Uruguayan lay Catholic intellectual who worked in the theology commission of CELAM and had been a major influence on the Puebla document.

Methol Ferré was arguably the most significant and original Latin-American Catholic intellectual of the late twentieth century. A writer, historian, journalist, theologian, and autodidact—he described himself as a "wild Thomist, without either seminary or academy"—he was converted to Catholicism by the writings of G. K. Chesterton while working in the port authority of Montevideo. A follower of Étienne Gilson and Perón, his two passions were the Church and Latin-American continental integration, which came together in his work for CELAM over twenty years, between 1972 and 1992. He and Bergoglio were natural bedfellows: believers in the national and popular tradition of Peronism, fired by Medellín but opposed to the revolutionary Marxism that followed, and deeply committed to continental unity. After Methol Ferré's death in 2009, Bergoglio described him as a "dear friend" and a "great man who did so much good for the conscience of the Church and for Latin America."

Although Bergoglio was familiar with Methol Ferré's writings by then, they didn't meet face-to-face until 1978, when Bergoglio was Jesuit provincial, at a lunch at the Colegio Máximo organized by the USAL rector, Francisco Piñón. The talk over lunch, recalls Piñón, was of the historic moment for the Latin-American Church, and the role of culture that would play such a major part in the Puebla document. Methol Ferré and the Gera group of Catholic intellectuals foresaw the Latin-American Church as the catalyst of a common Latin-American destiny—*la patria grande*—in a global future marked by continent-states. After the failures of both the North Atlantic model of economic growth and Cuban-style socialism, they were convinced that the stage now belonged to the People of God. During the 1980s, Methol Ferré's journal *Nexo* was the wellspring of these ideas, and Bergoglio, an assiduous reader of the journal, drank deeply from its insights.

Looking back through Christian history, Methol Ferré saw that in every era a Church in one part of the world becomes a "source" for the Church elsewhere, which it to a large extent reflects. Thus Alexandria and Syria were the source Church of the first Christian era, as were Spain and Italy at the sixteenth-century Council of Trent, and France and Germany at the Second Vatican Council. The Church in Latin America had been a "reflection" throughout the colonial and early-national period, but had started to move in the direction of becoming a source in the 1950s, when Pius XII encouraged the creation of CELAM, a regional Church body with a vocation to unify and integrate Latin America. CELAM was the first continent-wide collegial structure in the modern Church, one that enabled Latin-American Catholicism both to express its distinctiveness and to decide on its own pastoral policies. Methol Ferré saw the distinctive theology that came out of the CELAM gathering at Medellín in 1968 as characteristic of a source Church. Marxism had deviated it, but the CELAM gathering at Puebla in 1979 had rescued it.

That self-confidence, however, had since evaporated. Partly the decline was due to the demise of liberation theology in the 1980s, but in large part it was due to the centralist papacy of John Paul II. The pope's concern above all was to unite the Church after the debilitating divisions of the 1970s. That meant not just asserting the papacy on the world stage through endless trips, a vast body of teaching, and an authoritarian style of government that sharply increased the power of the Vatican over the Church, but also putting the brakes on the growth of bishops' conferences and other expressions of collegiality. In Latin America this meant promoting to key positions a group of conservative bishops who adhered to his centralist view of the papacy and wanted CELAM taken down a peg. For this he counted on three bishops in particular. Two of them were Colombian: Alfonso López Trujillo, whom John Paul II made a very young cardinal in 1983, and Darío Castrillón Hoyos, CELAM's president after Quarracino; the other was a Chilean, the archbishop of Valparaíso, Jorge Medina Estévez. This conservative triumvirate were the enforcers in Latin America of John Paul II's centralism.

CELAM had become the symbol of collegiality not just because it was the largest and oldest bishops' council, but because it was consciously engaged in theological reflection, even speaking of a "Latin-American magisterium" or teaching authority, which for the centralists was a heretical idea. The tensions came to a head in 1992 over the Vatican's attempt to run CELAM's Fourth General Assembly in Santo Domingo, the capital of the Dominican Republic. Rome rejected CELAM's working document, replacing it with its own text rich in quotes from John Paul II; then, when CELAM appointed twenty *periti* (theologian advisers), eighteen of them were removed by Rome and replaced with Vatican appointees. In a brazen assertion of papal *potestas*, John Paul II did not just open the conference but stayed for three days, before sending his secretary of state, Angelo Sodano, who had served as nuncio under General Pinochet, to steer the conference, aided by Bishop Medina Estévez. The Legionaries of Christ, the conservative Mexican order, ran an office in the conference center with direct lines to Rome, allowing Sodano to keep John Paul II informed. This micromanaging by Rome of the continental gathering of the Latin-American Church flew in the face of everything CELAM stood for.

Toward the end of the gathering, CELAM rebelled. When the Vatican appointed five members to redact the final declaration, CELAM bishops voted on a sixth member, the president of the Brazilian bishops' conference, Luciano Mendes de Almeida. As the conference drew to a close, the CELAM bishops through Archbishop Mendes tried to counter the Rome version but were continually blocked by Sodano. Eventually Mendes, with the CELAM bishops, stayed up all night to redact their alternative version, which was a defense of the approach the Latin-American bishops had taken at Puebla and Medellín. The next day he went straight to the microphone and read it. "Sodano could do nothing," recalls a bishop prominent in CELAM at the time, who is now a key cardinal in the Francis papacy. "He just sat there, powerless, while the whole auditorium broke into applause. It was like the Holy Spirit had won out after all, at the eleventh hour."[15]

That final declaration, rescued by the local Church, contained a call dear to Quarracino, Methol Ferré, and Bergoglio to "encourage and assist efforts in favor of the integration of Latin America as a *patria grande*." But in general, Santo Domingo was a damp squib. The pre-conference tussles and Roman interventions had weakened participation, and the results were meager. Reflecting on it many years later, Methol Ferré pointed out that, just three years after the fall of the Berlin Wall, the conference lacked the needed perspective to reflect on a world that was no longer bipolar and in which "neoliberalism"—as Methol referred to a belief in unfettered free markets—appeared triumphant.[16]

Methol Ferré left CELAM after the conference and moved back to Montevideo, from where he would regularly visit Bergoglio over the River Plate in Buenos Aires. They spent many hours discussing the state of the world, and Latin America's place in it, concerned that the decline of liberation theology and the rise of neoliberalism had undermined the Church's engagement with the poor. Methol Ferré was convinced that the enemies of that engagement were now relativism and consumerism, and that the

Latin-American Church needed to recover its option for the poor, asserting the sacrifices needed for true solidarity.

With Quarracino ailing, Bergoglio was invited as a Latin-American Church delegate to Cuba during John Paul II's historic visit to the island in January 1998. The Holy See and Havana had long danced around each other, with visits being prepared and then canceled. The pope wanted to speak of democracy and freedom, and to encourage the long-suffering Cuban Church; Fidel Castro, still a master of the dark arts of propaganda, saw it as a chance for a little favorable publicity, and to add to the pressure on the United States to lift its forty-year trade embargo, which the Vatican had long opposed. Media fascination over the trip, naturally, was intense: here were two veterans, each a symbol of their respective global creeds, for a few days occupying the same stage.

It was a success for John Paul II, yet without humiliating the socialist regime. The pope offered Cubans the prospect of a new revolution—one that would return Cuba to its Christian and democratic roots—while giving Cubans an experience of freedom they would not again taste. After years of an official discourse of dialectical opposition and confrontation, they heard a new language—of peace, freedom, solidarity, and reconciliation—and long-lost tunes that reminded them of their true selves.[17]

A little-known book Bergoglio wrote about the visit came out later that year, the second half of which contained the speeches by the pope and Castro. As an author, Bergoglio could not have been more self-effacing: nowhere does he even mention that he was present in the Cuban visit, while describing himself as the book's "coordinator." The text was dutifully written, at the request of the Vatican. But the main interest of *Diálogos entre Juan Pablo II y Fidel Castro* (Dialogues Between John Paul II and Fidel Castro) is the way it steers a resolutely independent course, one that rejects both Marxism and neoliberalism as alien to the soul of the Cuban *pueblo*—and by extension that of Latin America as a whole.

The régime comes in for heavy criticism—in terms very similar to those expressed by Cuba's bishops—for the totalitarian state's restrictions on freedoms, both religious and political, as well as for the "anthropological error" of socialism and the destitution that sat alongside the wealth of the dollar (tourist) economy. Bergoglio was particularly devastating about the way communism had destroyed a popular culture that passed values and virtues from one generation to the next, as well as the dismemberment of the family through sky-high rates of abortion and divorce, alcoholism and promiscuity, not to mention emigration and the imprisonment of political prisoners.

Yet the book also strongly objects to neoliberalism. The Church, Bergoglio pointed out, had no difficulty with capital accumulation that increases productivity—what he calls "capitalism as a pure economic system"—but rather "the spirit that has driven capitalism, utilizing capital to oppress and subject people, ignoring the human dignity of workers and the social purpose of the economy, distorting the values of social justice and the common good." Although neoliberalism respected religious values, it did so by relegating them to the private sphere, he went on, adding that "no one can accept the precepts of neoliberalism and consider themselves Christian." The core Christian concept was that of solidarity—knowing how to share what God has abundantly given. The opposite was neoliberalism, which "brings about unemployment, coldly marginalizing those who are superfluous," empties economic growth of human content, is "concerned only for numbers that add up," and "corrupts democratic values, by alienating from these the values of equality and social justice."[18]

SHORTLY after that trip, on January 25, news reached him of the death of Cardinal Eduardo Pironio from the bone cancer he had battled for months. Pironio's remains were brought from Rome to Buenos Aires, where thousands paid their respects before a solemn funeral presided over by an ailing Cardinal Quarracino, along with forty bishops and nearly 150 priests. Pironio was Argentina's most famous churchman, a close collaborator of both Paul VI and John Paul II, and considered *papabile* in the conclave of 1978. But his greatest achievement was the 1968 CELAM conference at Medellín that gave the Latin-American Church its voice. In a poignant symbol of how the Latin-American Church had, since Puebla, lost that voice, among the twenty new cardinals Pope John Paul II created just after Pironio's funeral were just four Latin-Americans, two of whom had led Rome's intervention in Santo Domingo: Medina Estévez and Castrillón Hoyos.

Days later, Argentina lost its other cardinal. After spending time in the hospital on a respirator, fighting for his life following an intestinal blockage, Quarracino died on February 28. His friend President Menem asked Bergoglio to allow the lying-in-state to take place in the Casa Rosada, the presidential palace, rather than the cathedral, so the nation could honor him. Bergoglio said no: the wake was held in the cathedral. To the fury of Caselli, he also refused to allow Menem to give a speech there; Bergoglio was the sole speaker.

Bergoglio spent three days in a silent retreat, preparing for what now lay ahead of him. He emerged to lead a packed funeral attended by Argentina's religious and political elite and a congregation of three thousand. In his tribute, he said that few had seen behind Quarracino's bluff persona to his forgiving heart, but that God's faithful people had known it. He was, said Bergoglio—paying him the highest of his compliments—a true pastor.

Bergoglio was now archbishop of Buenos Aires, but there was little to suggest the fact. He refused a ceremony of installation and reception, and gave no interviews. He didn't even want new clothes. He asked the nuns who cooked in the curia to adjust Quarracino's purple-piped black tunics to his size (the cardinal was a bulky man). His first official function on March 18 was a celebration organized by Menem in the White Room of the presidential palace to mark the fiftieth anniversary of the ordination of the papal nuncio, Ubaldo Calabresi. Bergoglio, in a simple clergy suit, was a ghost amid the bonhomie. Many of the high-ranking dignitaries had no idea who he was.

In taking on the new mission he sought to change as little as possible of his own lifestyle. He turned down the official archbishop's residence—a seigneurial affair fifteen miles from the center in the leafy suburb of Olivos, close to the presidential mansion—as well as the official limousine and chauffeur. Instead he moved into the modern archdiocesan office building known as the curia, next to the cathedral on the north side of the Plaza de Mayo. (The Olivos residence became a hostel for clergy and the driver was found another job.)

Inside the curia he refused the elegant and spacious archbishop's office in order to occupy a small office on the same floor with a desk and three chairs. On his desk he placed images of Saint Joseph, Saint Thérèse of Lisieux, and María Desatanudos. On the third floor he took a small bedroom with a simple wooden bed above which he hung the crucifix that belonged to his grandparents Giovanni and Rosa, and an adjacent room with a cupboard to hang his clothes and some shelves for books and private papers. In his bedroom he had a heater, which he put on in winter after the staff went home and on weekends, when the building's heating shut down.

He had a little kitchen with a stove to boil water for his mate and to rustle up pasta, and close by a chapel with a statue of the Virgin of Luján where he would spend the beginning of each day from 4:30 a.m. contemplating the Scriptures of the day and making decisions by discerning spirits. At 7:00 a.m. he said Mass in the curia chapel (or in his private chapel on the second floor at other times). After breakfast and the papers he would be at his desk by 8:30 a.m., before the first meetings of the day. After a light lunch prepared for him by the nuns in the curia and a forty-five-minute nap, he would be back at work in the afternoon, sometimes spending the early evenings in parishes or on visits. He was usually in bed by 10:00 p.m., the time many *porteños* are having dinner.

Although he would in time have two secretaries to help manage his correspondence and calls, he kept his own diary and usually phoned directly. Unlike most archbishops, Bergoglio did not have a "private" secretary—usually a priest—to shadow him, and he continued to move around the city by public transportation and on foot, turning up alone, usually in a simple priest's suit.

Having power meant a capacity to act, to make things happen. But with it came many temptations—above all the lure of the efficiency god—which were fatal for a pastor, for they distanced him from his sheep and made him foreign to the poor. Jesus showed his disciples how to act against that temptation on the night of the Last Supper before he died, when—as recounted in John's Gospel—he got onto his hands and knees to clean his disciples' feet.

Not long before Easter that first year as archbishop, Bergoglio called the chaplain of the Muñíz Hospital in Buenos Aires—the national center for the treatment of infectious conditions—and asked if he could say the Holy Thursday Mass there. "I'd like to be there. Can I?" he asked. When the archbishop arrived, Father Andrés Tello explained that eight of ten of the patients had AIDS; they had an average age of twenty-eight; many were drug addicts or prostitutes; some were transgender. "I told him that while the Gospel talks about twelve male apostles, here we had men and women as well as transvestites, but he said: 'you choose them, I'll wash their feet,'" recalls the priest.

> The Mass was very emotional. Everyone was in tears. He gave Communion to every one of them. And when he finished, he said: "Now I want to take Communion to those who couldn't attend because they are bed-bound." The patients were totally overwhelmed to have a bishop kissing and hugging them. He always insisted to us that when you're a priest, you're a priest for everyone, and that we should use generous criteria when giving the Sacraments.

Thereafter, every Holy Thursday, Bergoglio always went to a prison, or home of the elderly, or a hospital to wash the feet of the poor.[19]

FOR Bergoglio, haunted by the final pages of the theologian Henri de Lubac's *Meditations sur l'Église*, the worst thing to happen to the Church was spiritual worldliness. "It is what Jesus saw going on among the Pharisees: 'You who glorify yourselves. Who give glory to yourselves, the ones to the others,'" he told his priests in 1999, before quoting de Lubac's description of spiritual worldliness as "something infinitely more disastrous than any worldliness of the purely moral order." It was a form of religious anthropocentrism, using the Church for temporal ends—for political or personal gain—so turning it into an instrument of human maneuvering, and in the process obscuring the face of Christ that the Church exists to reveal.[20]

After Quarracino's death, Bergoglio uncovered an elaborate network of spiritual worldliness stretching from the Church in Buenos Aires to the Vatican via the Casa Rosada.

Quarracino had accepted many government favors—including funds for his foundation—and Bergoglio was expected to do the same. When he flew to Rome in June to receive from John Paul II the pallium, a narrow band of wool with black crosses that symbolizes the link between the pope and the major dioceses, the Casa Rosada sent him a first-class ticket. Bergoglio returned it. ("I don't get Bergoglio," Caselli was said to have remarked. "You try to help him and he just throws it back in your face.") Menem had a similar experience when he sent two of his men to sound out Bergoglio on the president's bid to alter the constitution so that he could run for a third term. They never found out, because the archbishop wasn't willing to discuss it. But the assumption that he would be spoke volumes.

The Caselli-Sandri-Sodano nexus allowed the Menem government to offset the chill of domestic criticism from the Argentine bishops with warmth from the Vatican. The three men were linked by a dense network of entwined interests. Caselli, a Menem strongman with broad business dealings, had found jobs for Sandri's nephews in the Argentine intelligence service and saved Sodano's brother's construction business. Two weeks before the legislative elections of October 1997, Caselli through Sodano arranged for Menem to meet John Paul II; and on May 25, 1998, Argentina's national day, Caselli organized a Mass by the secretary of state at which Sodano spoke of the "permanent and warm relations between Argentines and the pope," remarks that the Menem government ensured were widely reported as papal backing for him. (That was in turn countered by a brief statement from the bishops deploring the attempt to use religion for political ends, and specifically the attempt to suggest that the pope supported the Menem administration.)[21]

Another challenge for Bergoglio lay in the close links that had grown up between the archdiocese and a large and distinguished Catholic family, the Trussos, whom Quarracino knew well from his old diocese of La Plata. The family included Father Alfredo Trusso, a pioneer of post-Vatican Council liturgical reform who produced an Argentine translation of the Bible for popular use; and his brother, Francisco ("Paco") Trusso, whom Quarracino persuaded Menem to appoint as Argentina's ambassador to the Holy See between 1992 and 1997. Paco's sons, Francisco Javier and Pablo, were directors and shareholders of the La Plata–based Banco de Crédito Provincial (BCP). A third brother, Juan Miguel Trusso, was legal adviser to the bank and vice president of the diocesan charity agency Caritas.

The Trussos were prodigious donors to, and fund-raisers for, the Church, channeling donations and gifts, and giving or lending money to fund many diocesan projects. The archdiocese had a number of accounts in the Trussos' bank—as it did in seven other banks.

Quarracino was especially close to the director of the BCP, Francisco Javier Trusso, with whom he had almost a father-son relationship. The cardinal relied not just on his technical advice and help, but on the BCP's line of credit, which allowed, for example, small Catholic organizations to borrow money via the diocese. As the court papers would later reveal, a stream of cash channeled via Trusso also paid for the flights and hotels enjoyed by Quarracino and his two assistants, Monsignor Robert Toledo and Norberto Silva, on their trips abroad. What was also revealed was the way that Quarracino frequently used his authority and contacts to help the Trussos' business.

In 1996, for example, Quarracino helped to secure a major account for the BCP, a large military pension fund called the Sociedad Militar Seguro de Vida (SMSV). At a meeting at the curia at which Francisco Javier and Monsignor Toledo, Quarracino's private secretary, were also present, the cardinal assured the SMSV's president, Captain Eduardo Trejo Lema, that the Trussos were honorable and pious people in whom the Church had complete trust. After Trejo Lema opened an account at the BCP, he was fêted in Rome by the Argentine ambassador, Trusso *père*, who arranged for him to attend Mass said by John Paul II and to meet the pope afterward; and at Cardinal Quarracino's request, Trejo Lema was admitted to the prestigious chivalric order, the Knights of Malta.

Trejo Lema was later approached by Francisco Javier Trusso, the BCP's vice president, who asked him for a six-month $10 million loan to the archdiocese; the BCP, explained Trusso, was unable to provide the capital at that time but would underwrite the loan. The captain agreed, and the funds were transferred at the end of June 1997 to a diocesan account in the BCP. That account, it later transpired, was in the red by close to $9 million as a result of two checks signed on behalf of the archdiocese by Monsignor Toledo, who did not have the proper authorization to do so.

A few weeks later, a TV documentary revealed that the BCP was hugely in debt and had a massive liquidity gap. After the Central Bank refused to bail it out, the bank collapsed, leaving at least twenty thousand furious clients. The SMSV expected the return of its $10 million because the loan had been made to the diocese; but when it approached the cardinal's office, Monsignor Toledo told them that the signatures were not authentic and that there was no money to pay them back. Quarracino, who insisted that he had never signed any papers taking out a loan, was appalled. The stress and publicity triggered his illness and, it was thought, contributed to his death shortly afterward.

A police investigation was launched from La Plata. Francisco Javier Trusso fled to Brazil, where he was later caught and jailed, but escaped. Pablo Trusso spent six months in jail but was released. Juan Miguel Trusso spent three weeks in jail, then was acquitted, without any charges. Monsignor Toledo was jailed for three days.

After he became archbishop in February 1998 Bergoglio hired an international accountancy firm to do a thorough audit of the diocesan finances. It showed that the archdiocese regularly ignored both canon law and the Argentine bishops' own guidelines for monitoring and authorizing payments. As a result of its report, Bergoglio instituted a radical cleanup. He sold the archdiocese's shares in other banks in order to sever inappropriate links, and instituted strict accountability and transparency procedures.

Meanwhile, the SMSV was suing the diocese for the return of its $10 million. In December 1998, the police raided the curia, carrying off boxes of files following a court deposition; the investigating judge had tipped off the press in order to embarrass the diocese. Father Marcó, the young priest Bergoglio had gotten to know soon after being made an auxiliary, received a call from his archbishop. "He was very calm, but said if I had a minute would I mind coming down there because there was a whole pack of journalists at the door." Marcó organized the first press conference on behalf of the new archbishop.

As result of the hearings which followed, the SMSV dropped its case against the diocese and both issued a joint statement saying they had been swindled. The auditor's report commissioned by Bergoglio was so thorough that it left no questions hanging, and the archbishop's reputation was, if anything, enhanced by his handling of the affair.

The scandal, along with other dubious practices Bergoglio discovered after taking over from Quarracino, influenced many of his addresses in his first year, which reflected his determination to purify his clergy of any attempt to use the Church for personal gain. In a 1999 talk to clergy, for example, he challenged his priests to ask themselves if they were mediators or intermediaries. A mediator, he said, was a bridge, who brought others together at his own expense. An intermediary, on the other hand, was one who profited at the expense of others. In both cases, a priest stands between, in the middle; yet there was a world of difference. The mediator is a pastor whose evangelizing fervor is born of an encounter with Christ, who grows in his belonging to God's holy faithful people, whereas an intermediary is a "state cleric," a functionary in whom the fervor has long died and who lives mainly for himself.[22]

In an article he wrote in 1991 but did not publish until much later, Bergoglio used de Lubac's treatise to distinguish between sin and corruption. While sin could always be forgiven, corruption could not be, because in a corrupt soul there was no desire for forgiveness. Corruption grows, infects others, and then justifies itself. When a corrupt person has power, he will always implicate other people, bringing them down to his level and making them accomplices, yet, like the Pharisees, he will be an assiduous adherent of norms and rules. Corruption, Bergoglio said, was intrinsically proselytizing; it generates a culture—a moralizing, self-justifying culture of good manners that looks down on others.[23]

The inquiry into the collapse of the BCP still goes on, but after 17 years has been unable to substantiate the lurid allegations circulating at the time: almost all those involved have been either acquitted or never charged. When Francisco Javier Trusso was arrested after two years on the run, he was hiding in a house in Pinamar that belonged to the sister of the Argentine Vatican official, Archbishop Leonardo Sandri. Trusso was sentenced to eight years but was freed following a personal guarantee by the Buenos Aires auxiliary Héctor Aguer, who in 1998 was made archbishop of La Plata.

In 2000 Sandri became Sodano's *sostituto*, or number two, in the Vatican's Secretariat of State. Caselli, a lavish entertainer who would soon launch a career as an Italian senator, would often lament, with Aguer, the way Bergoglio focused on social, rather than moral, issues.[24]

※

IN October 1998, just before the police raid on the curia, Bergoglio brought the diocese together by celebrating two vast outdoor Masses in one day. The celebrations close to the zoo in Palermo were attended by close to one hundred thousand people. Huge numbers were confirmed: five hundred priests laid their hands on eight thousand children in the morning, twelve thousand young people and adults in the afternoon; Bergoglio himself confirmed dozens of disabled. "The success of evangelization hangs on the witness of unity which the Church gives," he said in his homily. "You who have been confirmed can and must now witness to Jesus."[25]

Assuming he would be in the saddle until the age of seventy-five, Bergoglio was likely to have twelve or thirteen years as archbishop. As he put in place his strategic priorities from 1999 to 2000, he began to emerge—with Father Marcó's help—from the shadows into public life, but he would continue to be known as publicity-shy and aloof. It was a time of deepening economic and political crisis. In October 1999, a new government made up of Radicals and dissident Peronists (known as the Alliance) took power. The new president, the conservative Radical Fernando de la Rúa, offered much the same neoliberal economic policy as Menem's but promised to clean up government and balance the books. That turned out to be a pipe dream: the economy continued to shrink, and de la Rúa had neither the vision nor the political capital to turn it around. When the crisis of December 2001 struck, he would be forced to abandon the Casa Rosada by helicopter to escape the angry crowds.

If Bergoglio's overall priority was combating spiritual worldliness wherever he found it, he had four major areas he wanted to develop: the poor, politics, education, and dialogue with other Churches and faiths.

The option for the poor ran through all his pastoral, educational, or political policies and was key to his own choices and witness. But it was also a priority in itself. It meant focusing resources and efforts in deprived areas. He would increase from eight to twenty-six the number of slum priests and spend at least an afternoon a week in the *villas*. But as the crisis affected the lower middle class, above all, especially after 2001, he would mobilize Catholics to deliver material help through food kitchens and material assistance. While the state shrank, the Church in Buenos Aires hugely expanded its activity, building schools, clinics, and drug rehab centers. The option for the poor also meant lending his authority to helping unprotected or vulnerable groups—garbage collectors, prostitutes, trafficked workers, undocumented migrants—to organize, as well as using his authority and access to the media to influence public policy: in 2000, for example, he called for a pathway to citizenship for undocumented migrants. The annual San Cayetano Mass became the locus of his messages to workers and the jobless; the Plaza de la Constitución Mass was when he spoke to and about trafficked workers and prostitutes; while the annual Mass of the Lord's Supper became a chance to focus on other vulnerable groups: prisoners, the elderly, the disabled, the addicted, the sick.

The second priority was a critique of power and the renewal of public life. In keeping with the bishops' conference new policy, Bergoglio put clear blue water between the Church and government, turning the traditional Te Deum—a traditional Catholic prayer of thanksgiving—on Argentina's national day, May 25, into a chance to challenge and teach political leaders on behalf of the *pueblo*. He also placed the Church at the service of political renewal. In 2000 he began to organize meetings of public leaders across the political spectrum to rebuild trust, strengthen institutions, and get politicians to focus on the common good, a set of aims that came under the umbrella of the culture of encounter. He drew on Catholic social teaching, the four principles he had developed to assist him in his own leadership, as well as his deep thinking about Guardini's concept of contrasts, to help his country build a new political culture, one based on pluralism and dialogue and concern for the common good. In the wake of the 2001 meltdown, the Church became, in effect, the host space for the national recovery.

The third priority was improving and increasing access to the education offered by the Church through its schools, including the teaching of Catholic faith, known as catechesis. In 1998 Bergoglio created a Vicariate for Education to coordinate the expansion. In less than a decade, the diocese's schools went from forty-four to sixty-six, and student numbers grew by 80 percent to nearly forty thousand—four times more than private or state schools in the same period. Bergoglio made the inspiration and education of teachers and catechists a major priority, and his carefully crafted annual addresses were an opportunity to develop the culture of the People of God.

If those three priorities can be seen as developments of his previous concerns or passions as provincial and rector in the Society of Jesus, the fourth was wholly new but would become one of the most outstanding achievements of his time as archbishop. From an initial, modest gathering of members of other churches and faiths in 2000, when they planted an olive tree in the Plaza de Mayo, an impressive network of relationships with Jews and Muslims and evangelical Christians came into being that went far beyond what ordinarily passes for interreligious or ecumenical dialogue.

As the BCP scandal had shown, Bergoglio needed a way of liaising with the media: avoiding Quarracino's media *débacles* was not enough. He agreed to a proposal by Father Marcó and a young communications expert, Roberto da Busti, for a professional press office. It was a strategic operation that focused on building relationships of trust with media proprietors, meeting the demand for stories while at the same time helping to shape them. Bergoglio supported the strategy but wanted to remain in the dark. "He wanted to communicate, but he didn't want it to be him," says Da Busti. "We called him *el gato* ["the cat"] because he was always slipping away." Bergoglio would speak, and leave Marcó to answer the questions. Marcó's job, joked José María Poirier, editor of the Catholic monthly *Criterio*, was to interpret his boss's long silences.[26]

The strategy the archbishop agreed with Marcó meant that—in addition to his homilies and public pronouncements—Bergoglio would speak primarily through his actions and gestures, gradually increasing his exposure. Although he resisted at first, Bergoglio allowed Marcó to bring in photographers to capture the annual feet-washing ceremonies, which generated front-page pictures. The press also began covering San Cayetano and Bergoglio's pastoral visits to prisons and hospitals. "We did something unheard of before then," Marcó recalls. "We actually interested the media in religious stories."

Marcó organized annual Christmas drinks for journalists at the curia, where they could meet Bergoglio informally. The first of these, on December 23, 1999, was given extra interest by reports circulating the previous day of the archbishop's death. The story—based on a misfiled obituary—had reached a number of radio stations before being scotched. "Someone really wants this and obviously couldn't wait," Bergoglio jested to the journalists.[27]

Marcó also introduced key correspondents to his boss one by one, developing relationships that could later be called upon. One of them was Horacio Verbitsky, the guerrilla turned journalist who that year interviewed Yorio. In April 1999 he described Bergoglio as "the most overwhelming and conflictive church personality in decades, loved by some and hated by others"—citing as evidence for the hated part the same left-wing Jesuit sources. But he made no new allegations. Marcó brought Verbitsky to meet Bergoglio, who gave the journalist access to the curial archives and an interview in which he explained the efforts he made to free the Jesuits. Verbitsky for a time conceded that there were positives in the archbishop's favor, but did not retract the allegations. "I've asked them to ignore it, not to get involved," Bergoglio told Clelia Podestá when she asked him why his clergy and spokespeople didn't set the record straight. "These things die on their own." For a time they did, until Verbitsky returned to the attack in 2005.[28]

In 1967 Clelia Luro—then a separated woman with six children—had been at the center of a major church scandal when her affair with a progressive bishop was exposed. Jerónimo Podestá, the bishop of Avellaneda, resigned, and later left the priesthood and married her. Both Clelia and Jerónimo became well-known campaigners for (among other liberal causes) a married priesthood. Although there is no doctrinal obstacle to it—there are married Catholic priests among former Anglicans and in the Eastern churches—John Paul II strongly objected, and would bang the table whenever the subject was mentioned. When Podestá, who hadn't entered the cathedral for over twenty years, came to see Bergoglio in 2000, they spoke for two hours, and when he was dying a few months later, the archbishop came to give him the last rites. Bergoglio and Clelia remained in touch thereafter (she died in 2013): she wrote to him almost weekly, and he would always reply by ringing her up. "When Podestá was dying, Bergoglio was the only Catholic cleric who went to visit him in hospital, and, when he died, the only one who showed public recognition of his great contribution to the Argentine church," recalls Margaret Hebblethwaite, who knew Luro.[29]

The media could see that despite his allergy to the limelight, the new archbishop was carving out new territory for the Church in public life, a posture that was not deferential to government yet far from disengaged. Just how "political" the new archbishop could be had become clear at the Te Deum on May 25, 1999. The traditional thanksgiving had always been a ceremony of consensus, when the institutions of Church and state came together in solemn prayers for Argentina: the archbishop's job was not to speak but to bless the government of the day on behalf of the nation. But Bergoglio turned that on its head: the Te Deum became a challenge by the Church to the government on behalf of the people. With God's blessing came accountability.

Standing only feet from the current (Menem) and future (de la Rúa) presidents and the cream of Argentina's political class, Bergoglio delivered a lengthy and biting address that combined Old Testament prophecy with the soaring rhetoric of a US presidential inauguration. Warning of a coming social disintegration while "diverse interests maneuver, alien to the needs of all," he reminded the nation of Argentina's genius and creativity, but also of its tendency to fratricide. "The silent voices of so many dead clamor from heaven begging us not to repeat the errors," he said, referring to the dirty war, and "only if we hear them will their tragic destiny have meaning." Deploying John Paul II's critique of free-market idolatry—the neoliberal myth that market forces alone could deliver prosperity for all—he challenged the politicians to see the social emergency building around them, and to open the state to civil society. To be a citizen, he said, was to be called to a good, to a purpose, and to turn up. Yet unless "all have a place at the table, not just a few," the social divisions would widen and, rather than take part in the building of a nation, people would turn on each other. It was time, he said, to take notice of the eruption of community and neighborly initiatives—"a whirlwind of participation seldom seen in our country"—that pointed to a people in solidarity, determined to rise again.

In words almost identical to those he had used in addressing the Jesuits in 1974, he went on to speak of his *pueblo fiel* idea: "our people has soul," he said, "and because we can speak of a soul, we can speak of a hermeneutic, of a way of seeing, of an awareness." Just as he had urged the Jesuits to abandon ideology and take on the values of the *pueblo fiel*, so he now called on politicians to spurn "those who claim to distill reality into ideas, the talentless intellectuals, the unkind ethicists" and to drink from the cultural reserves of the wisdom of ordinary people. This, he said, was the "true revolution": to recover the values that made Argentines great: their love of life but acceptance of death, their solidarity in the face of pain and poverty, the way they celebrate and pray. Turning specifically to the politicians, he called on them to renounce their individual and partisan interests and hear the call of the people for greater participation in civic life. "We are all invited to this encounter," he concluded, "to realize and share this ferment that while new is also the revivified memory of our greatest history of sacrificial solidarity, of social integration and struggle for freedom." The speech ended with the reiteration of his four principles.[30]

It was high altitude rhetoric of a kind no longer heard from Argentine statesmen, let alone bishops. The criticism was not long in coming—that Bergoglio was interfering in the temporal, arrogating what belonged to Caesar. Yet anyone familiar, as was Bergoglio, with the seventeenth-century Jesuit theologian Francisco Suárez, whose ideas underpinned Argentine nationhood and democracy, would see it differently. Here was the Church assuming its proper role as the moral conscience of the community, which had delegated (and could withdraw) its consent to the government to rule on the community's behalf. It was not to the institution of the Church that Bergoglio was demanding that the state defer, but to the ordinary people in a culture imbued by the Gospel, of whose values the Church was guardian and protector.

At the following year's Te Deum, in the Jubilee year, he was briefer, issuing a rallying cry for Argentina in the new millennium to recover "the adventure of a new nation" and "to be reborn in the promise of the pioneers who began our fatherland." That meant, he said, restoring social bonds and solidarity, and reaching out to the young, the jobless, the migrants and the elderly. He again pointed to the growth in community organizations as a sign of hope, and called on the politicians to "make the community the protagonist." But he presented the grim image—prophetic, as it turned out—of a people profoundly disillusioned with their self-referential politicians, incapable of generating the solidarity needed for a functioning democracy.

> We need to recognize, with humility, that the system has fallen into a broad umbral cone, into the shadow lands of distrust, in which many of the promises and statements sound like a funeral cortège. Everyone consoles the bereaved, but nobody resurrects the corpse. Get up! This is the call of Jesus in the Jubilee. *Arise, Argentina!* as the Holy Father said to us on his last visit, and as our pioneers and founders dreamed. But until we face up to the duplicity of our motives there will be neither trust nor peace. Until we are converted, we will not know happiness and joy. Because unchecked ambition, whether for power, money, or popularity, expresses only a great interior emptiness. And those who are empty do not generate peace, joy, and hope, only suspicion. They do not create bonds.[31]

The task of helping to create those bonds was given to Father Accaputo's social-pastoral office which helped build the public relationships that the archbishop would draw on in the coming years. The broader purpose was to rebuild public life, inspired by a 1999 document of the French bishops that he much admired.[32] The aim was to build bonds of friendship and trust, forged by people focused on the horizon of the common good rather than as rivals for access to public resources. At least a year before the collapse of the Argentine state, Bergoglio's culture of encounter showed politicians how to rebuild a nation.

The first such gathering was held in December 2000: a meeting of 150 public officials in the city government of Buenos Aires—including legislators and leading civil servants—to reflect on the political vocation and the challenges ahead. It became news because the head of the Buenos Aires city government, Aníbal Ibarra, was a self-declared agnostic, yet enjoyed a close relationship with the archbishop via Accaputo. Bergoglio's presence and speech that day made an impact on those present. "Bergoglio is different," one of the legislators told a journalist. "He understands politics. He understands the logic of power. You can really talk to him."[33]

It was a very Bergoglio paradox. The austere, incorruptible mystic at war with spiritual worldliness—the pastoral bishop who smelled of sheep—was the most astutely political Argentine since Perón.

SEVEN

GAUCHO CARDINAL

(2001–2007)

THE BUENOS AIRES evangelical pastors with whom he used to pray each month got to see their old friend Jorge Bergoglio in the Vatican about ten weeks after he was elected pope. It happened that Pastor Carlos Mraida of the Central Baptist Church, Pastor Norberto Saracco of the Pentecostal Evangelical Church, Pastor Angel Negro from the Christian Community, and Pastor Omar Cabrera of the Future Vision Church were all due to be in Europe at about the same time, and God clearly wanted Jorge Himitian of the Christian Community to join them, because the pastor managed to find the funds for the flight just in time.

The pastors greeted Pope Francis outside the Santa Marta with Argentine-style embraces and kisses. Francis laughed at Pastor Himitian's greeting: "So you've managed to bring us to the Vatican after all!" Inside, they told him how amazing it had been in Argentina since his election: they had to pay to put Jesus Christ on the airwaves, but here was Francis putting Him out for free on all the big shows. They told him how there was a new openness now in the Argentine media, how journalists who had long said they were atheists and agnostics were all talking about what it meant to be Catholics and Christians; how suddenly it was OK to talk about Christian values.

Francis was the same old Jorge, says Himitian, yet he wasn't. "What everybody had been talking about, the way he had become so effusive, so joyful—we had seen that side of Jorge for ourselves in our retreats, when he preached, but outside of those times he was a very serious man. But now, as pope, he was *exultante* ('elated') all the time, just as he had been with us."

Inside the Santa Marta at the end of May, they prayed together, just as they used to in Buenos Aires. According to Himitian, Pastor Saracco said to Francis: "Jorge, let me share something with you. Last night I was praying about this meeting and I said, 'Lord, if you have a *word* for Jorge, give it to me.'" In the evangelical and charismatic tradition, to ask in prayer for a *word* means to ask the Holy Spirit to inspire a person to turn to a particular chapter or verse in Scripture that has particular meaning for them at this time.

Saracco brought out his iPad and read from the prophet Jeremiah, chapter 1: *Before I formed you in the womb, I knew you, and before you were born I consecrated you; I appointed you a prophet to the nations. . . . See, today I appoint you over nations and over kingdoms, to pluck up and to pull down, to destroy and overthrow, to build and to plant.*

When Saracco—who had come to Rome from Buenos Aires via the United States—started reading the Jeremiah passage, Mraida and Himitian elbowed each other. Amazingly, Himitian had told Mraida he received the same *word* before setting off from Buenos Aires and even had exactly those verses printed out on a sheet of paper. When Saracco finished, Himitian handed the pope the sheet. "Jorge, I didn't know about him and he didn't know about us, but I brought you the same *word!*"

The pope laughed. "Let me tell you now what happened to me."

Two days before Bergoglio left Buenos Aires to join the cardinals in Rome for the conclave, a man who worked in the archdiocesan curia came to see him. Mario Medina was an evangelical, who regularly prayed with the archbishop. "Father, excuse me," he said, "but yesterday I was praying for you, and God gave me a *word*: Jeremiah, Chapter One."

"We were amazed by how God had confirmed this," says Himitian. "For if there was a prophetic voice during those years in Buenos Aires, it was his."

THE story of how Jorge Mario Bergoglio came to be a contender in the conclave of 2005 and to be elected pope in 2013 begins a long way from Argentina, in a pretty, snow-clad town in northeastern Switzerland. With its location in the precise center of Europe and its multilingual population of seventy-five thousand, St. Gallen is well placed to headquarter the Council of the Bishops' Conferences of Europe. The CCEE, which includes as members thirty-three bishops' conferences in forty-five nations, was formed in the years after the Second Vatican Council, at a time when Pope Paul VI— inspired by Latin America's CELAM—was encouraging similar continent-wide collaboration in order to restore strength and identity to the local Church. Hence the CCEE's intimidating mission statement: "the exercise of collegiality in hierarchical communion *cum et sub romano pontefice.*"

With and under the pope. It is a phrase that harks back to the early days of the Church, when local synods and councils were the norm, when the Church in different places had a strong identity, regulated by its own laws and customs, yet always with the Church of Rome as the focus of unity, "presiding in charity" over the other Churches, as the second-century formula has it. The understanding of the Catholic Church in its first centuries was that it was many yet one; plural yet united; local *and* universal. The Church as a whole was more than the sum of its parts—it was a universal body, anchored in Rome—yet the local diocese was not merely a department or province of a world Church, but wholly the Church in that place, under a bishop.

This was not just good theology—or, to be more exact, ecclesiology—but had implications for the way the Church was governed. Often throughout the Middle Ages popes sought to assert control over local dioceses, to gain freedom from meddling princes, or to push through reform; yet they faced pushback if they tried to use that control in ordinary times. There was always a healthy tension between primacy, which emphasized papal authority, and episcopacy, which called for that authority to be exercised in collaboration with the bishops. But the balance shifted decisively in the eighteenth and nineteenth centuries, in response to absolutist regimes— whether kings or parliaments—that sought to nationalize the Church; now the papacy asserted in fact what it had sometimes claimed on paper. The First Vatican Council (1869–1870) took a view very different from that of the early centuries of the Church in asserting boldly that all sovereignty in the Church derived from the primacy of the pope. This idea was enshrined in the 1917 Code of Canon Law, which said the pope has full, supreme, and universal power in the Church.

This didn't go unchallenged. In the first half of the twentieth century, while totalitarian dictatorships in Europe fought each other, theologians rediscovered the eucharistic notion of the Church as a hierarchical communion. The papacy had come to look like an absolutist monarchy, complete with all the trappings, but the Second Vatican Council in the 1960s reimagined it in early-church terms. The Church, said one of its most important documents, *Lumen Gentium* ("Light of the Nations"), is governed by its bishops *cum et sub Petro*—with and under the pope—who together form an apostolic college, *collegium*, which governs the universal Church. From "college" comes the name of the doctrine that expresses this idea: "collegiality." The idea was rescued and developed by Yves Congar in the 1950s, who argued that Christ instituted two "successions": while the pope succeeds the apostle Peter, the bishops succeed the College of the Apostles.

After the council fathers had finished their work on *Lumen Gentium* in November 1964, they submitted it to the pope for his consent. In the document, the bishops had restated the doctrine that the pope has full, supreme, and universal power over the Church but had added the collegial doctrine that the College of Bishops also exercises such power. The prudent Paul VI sensed danger: these two statements could lead to future misunderstandings, even rival claims. So with the help of theologians he drafted a "Previous Interpretative Note," which stated that the pope, as the vicar of Christ, was entitled to rule as a monarch, but he is also head of the episcopal college and therefore may turn to collegial government. Whether to implement collegiality, in short, was in the gift of the pope.[1]

Paul VI brought in two key collegial reforms in the teeth of opposition by some in the Vatican old guard. One was the synod of bishops that since 1967 has been held in Rome every two or three years, in which around 250 delegates of local Churches deliberate for three weeks on questions facing a particular region or matters affecting the universal Church. The other innovation was the creation of collegial bodies of bishops, both nationwide (thus, for example, the United States Conference of Catholic Bishops, or USCCB) and continent-wide. CELAM in Latin America was the pioneer of the second kind, which since the 1970s has inspired similar councils in Europe (CCEE), Africa (Symposium of Episcopal Conferences of Africa and Madagascar, or SECAM), and Asia (The Federation of Asian Bishops' Conferences, or FABC). Yet of these, only CELAM has had a strong identity, because its two great meetings at Medellín (1968) and Puebla (1979) took place before John Paul II's recentralizing drive of the 1980s and 1990s.

John Paul II chose to govern monarchically. During his twenty-seven-year pontificate, collegiality was reinterpreted by the Vatican to refer to bonds of trust and fellowship between bishops and the See of Peter, rather than the local Church sharing in the governance of the universal Church. "Affective" collegiality came to replace "effective" collegiality. Synods became three-week talking shops rather than instruments of governance, their agendas and their conclusions carefully managed by the Roman Curia. At the same time, the new continent-wide bishops' councils such as CELAM were warned not to improvise their own theology: there was only one "Magisterium," or teaching authority, in the Church. In 1992, the same year that the CELAM gathering in Santo Domingo was steamrollered by the Vatican, the pope's doctrinal watchdog took a position that looked to some critics as if it were harking back to the days before the Second Vatican Council. The prefect of the Congregation for the Doctrine of the Faith (CDF), Joseph Ratzinger, claimed that the universal Church was "ontologically prior" to the local Church.[2] This wasn't merely a theological assertion. In the 1990s, bishops who visited Rome increasingly felt talked down to by the Vatican, as if they were mere delegates of the Curia.

It was this growing concern that provoked the meetings at St. Gallen. Its bishop, Ivo Fürer, began in the late 1990s to host in his residence annual private meetings of concerned European cardinals and archbishops, which in themselves were expressions of collegiality. The dominant figure was the Jesuit Cardinal Carlo Maria Martini, who until 2002 was the archbishop of Milan. Another senior cardinal, the archbishop of Brussels, Godfried Danneels, was also a significant voice in these meetings. There would normally be six or seven others around the table at the two-night meetings, drawn from across central and northern Europe. In 2001, the group was joined by three archbishops who were made cardinals in February 2001 alongside Bergoglio. One was Walter Kasper, the bishop of Rottenburg-Stuttgart, who in 1999 was put in charge of the Vatican's department for relations with Christians and Jews. The other two were the presidents of the bishops' conferences of Germany and England and Wales: Karl Lehmann, the bishop of Mainz in Germany, and Cormac

Murphy-O'Connor of Westminster, England. Others came and went, from France and central Europe, but these names formed the core of the St. Gallen group.

Martini and Danneels, often dubbed by journalists as liberals or progressives, were more accurately described as reformers (*riformisti*) as opposed to the conservatives (*rigoristi*) who dominated John Paul II's Curia. There were two different emphases involved: where the *rigoristi* wished Church teaching above all to be clear and unambiguous, the *riformisti* wished it to be credible in a pluralist society. Behind these two tendencies lurked two different ecclesiologies. The *rigoristi* wanted to tighten Vatican control over questions of doctrine and discipline, where the *riformisti* wanted greater freedom of action in applying church norms to local situations. The *rigoristi* liked to close down debate, making clear that norms were clear and unchanging; the *riformisti* preferred to keep some things open, believing that, in matters of ecclesiastical discipline, rather than unchanging doctrines of faith and morals, the local Church should help the universal Church discern the need for changes in pastoral practices.

As senior churchmen and theologians who headed major metropolitan dioceses on the front lines of Europe's increasingly secular, pluralistic societies, the *riformisti* were aware of the growing gap between the norms of the Church and the realities of people's lives. For the St. Gallen group, the lack of collegiality was not just a theological question; it made it harder for the Church to evangelize. Another factor for the group—which included a number of senior churchmen on the front line of dialogue with other Churches—was that the lack of collegiality made the search for Christian unity much harder. For leaders of churches in the reformed or orthodox traditions, the assertion of papal power in the centuries after the Reformation was cited as a major stumbling block on the road to Christian unity. John Paul II had made an offer in 1995 to other Churches to help him find new ways of exercising his primacy. But it was hard to take the offer seriously at a time of increasing papal centralism, and little happened.[3]

The St. Gallen group began meeting in the late 1990s, as John Paul II's health began its sharp decline. Its figurehead, Cardinal Martini, told the 1999 synod on the topic of Europe that another gathering of the world's bishops would be needed in order to implement collegiality, which the Second Vatican Council had called for but which had been frustrated by

John Paul II's Curia. Without, apparently, any sense of irony, the curial body that ran the synod suppressed the publication of the speech, which journalists only learned of from leaks.

In addition to Martini, there were two major voices arguing for the restoration or implementation of collegiality at the time. One was the archbishop of San Francisco, John R. Quinn, whose best-selling book *The Reform of the Papacy* came out in 1999. The other was a member of the St. Gallen group: the German bishop theologian, Walter Kasper, who famously went head-to-head in a friendly theological dispute with Cardinal Ratzinger over the question of the primacy of the universal and local Church. In a widely published article in December 2000, which disputed Cardinal Ratzinger's 1992 document, Kasper said that Cardinal Ratzinger's argument became "really problematic when the one universal Church is identified with the Roman Church, and de facto with the Pope and the Roman Curia," describing it as "an attempt to restore Roman centralism." He went on to argue that collegiality was vital to resolve pastoral questions such as the admission of divorced and remarried persons to Communion, as well as making credible the Catholic invitation to unity with other Christians. Progress on unity depended, he argued, on this recognition of the value of the local Church. "The ultimate aim is not a uniform united Church, but one Church in reconciled diversity." The phrase "reconciled diversity" was one Bergoglio adopted in Buenos Aires when discussing relations with other Christians and other faiths.[4]

In their meetings during the winter years of John Paul II's papacy (1999–2005), the St. Gallen group was concerned by the deterioration in the Vatican that an enfeebled pope was powerless to prevent. Under the secretary of state, Cardinal Sodano, the Curia had grown haughty and unaccountable, as well as intransigent. Sometimes its failures were linked to actual corruption, most notoriously in the case of Father Marcial Maciel, head of the conservative Mexican priests' order, the Legionaries of Christ. There was mounting evidence that Maciel was a serial pedophile and drug addict. His regular donations to the Church via Sodano coincided with nine former members of the order going public with their accusations against Maciel, writing to the pope to complain of Vatican inaction, which continued for years. Ever since his days as nuncio in Latin America, Sodano had been Maciel's supporter, and Sodano's nephew Andrea had business dealings with him.[5]

More often it was ineptitude, or sclerosis. But at times—as when cardinals publicly disagreed with one another over the ethics of condoms in the context of AIDS, say—it showed that the John Paul II model of central governance, built for clarity, was unable to tackle new challenges. Even *rigoristi* criticized the synod as unwieldy and unproductive. As was clear from the Vatican's response to the emerging clerical sex abuse crisis, there was a tone deafness, an insularity and defensiveness, which the St. Gallen group saw as fruit of an excessive centralism, symptoms of a Vatican turned in on itself, cut off from the realities and needs of the local Church.

The problem was acute in the last years of John Paul II. He had been a compelling evangelizer, but a poor governor even when fit, an outsider to the Curia who had never been much interested in its inner workings. Now that he was no longer robust—his Parkinson's diagnosis was made official in 2000—he remained the Church's evangelizer in chief, giving a powerful witness through his public displays of weakness and vulnerability. But the Curia increasingly did its own thing, undermining that witness. Now, with the pope's infirmity, the chances of reforming the Curia were increasingly remote.

The St. Gallen group believed that what was needed was a thorough reform of governance, a restoration of the balance between the local and universal Churches, toward an authentic collegiality. They were not the only senior church leaders who agreed with this diagnosis and cure. Their view found a particular echo among Latin-American archbishops, not least because of CELAM's long experience of exercising collegiality and its experience of Vatican centralism at Santo Domingo. A whole new generation of Latin-American pastoral leaders were about to be made cardinals. Among them was the archbishop of Buenos Aires, who was not only influenced by Martini, but had many of his own reasons for identifying with the St. Gallen group's concerns.

❧

EMERGING resolutely into a sunstruck St. Peter's Square in flashing gold vestments, John Paul II's disabilities seemed the last thing on his mind: he was eighty, struggled to walk and speak, was deaf in one ear, and had a face frozen by Parkinson's, yet he was as commanding as ever, like a biblical patriarch. After his homily, in which he declared this to be a "great feast for the universal Church," he created forty-four new cardinals, bringing to 135 the number of electors—that is, those under eighty years of age—who would vote for his successor. To each he handed a scarlet biretta and a scroll with the *Titulus*, placing them nominally in charge of a church in the diocese of Rome. No doubt because he was a Jesuit, Bergoglio was given the church of St. Robert Bellarmine, named after a famous seventeenth-century Jesuit cardinal.

Among those who also stepped forward at that consistory in February 2001 was a diminutive seventy-two-year-old Vietnamese bishop who would die the following year. After Paul VI in 1975 named François Xavier Vân Thuân coadjutor archbishop of Saigon, the communists had sent him into the jungle, where he spent nine years in solitary confinement. It was a poignant reminder that the streams of scarlet in the square on the day of that consistory stood for the blood of martyrs. *Five Loaves and Two Fish*, Cardinal Vân Thuân's meditations secretly penned on tiny scraps of paper, was among Bergoglio's favorite spiritual reading. (Pope Francis would later put the cardinal on the path to sainthood.)

The cardinals knew that their most solemn responsibility would be, at some point soon, to name John Paul II's successor. This was the most global college of cardinals in history. The sixty-five Europeans—including twenty-four Italians—were still the largest continental grouping, but they were outnumbered for the first time by non-Europeans. Latin America now had twenty-seven cardinals, while North America, Africa, and Asia had thirteen each, and Oceania four.

Among the other new cardinals that day was an Argentine, Jorge Mejía, head of the Vatican library, whom Bergoglio would become close to in his visits to Rome, and ten archbishops who ran dioceses in Latin America. Among these were four future close Bergoglio collaborators: Oscar Rodríguez Maradiaga of Tegucicalpa in Honduras, recently stepped down as CELAM president, who had led the anti-Sodano rebellion in Santo Domingo in 1992; his successor as president of CELAM, the archbishop of Santiago in Chile, Francisco Errázuriz; and two Brazilians: the archbishop of São Paulo, Claudio Hummes, and Geraldo Majella Agnelo of Bahia.[6]

From the boisterous crowd in St. Peter's Square it seemed as if Latin America's hour had already come. Yet there were few Argentines among them, because Bergoglio had stopped a campaign to raise funds for pilgrims to travel to Rome, telling its organizers to distribute what they had raised to the poor. During the consistory he opted for austerity and a low profile. Where others were put up in their colleges or hosted by relatives in large hotels, he stayed, as he always did in Rome, in a simple priests' guesthouse at no. 70 Via della Scrofa, not far from the Piazza Navona, where he prayed at 4:30 a.m. before saying Mass in the chapel. Where others were driven to the Vatican by priest secretaries, he walked alone each morning over the Tiber; where others had ordered their scarlet vestments from Gamarelli, Rome's ecclesiastical tailor, Bergoglio's wore Quarracino's hand-me-downs, taken in by the nuns; and where others— not least the energetic, communicative Cardinal Rodríguez Maradiaga, a pilot and piano player—held press conferences and parties, Bergoglio put on his customary cloak of invisibility.

He did, however, give a rare interview to *La Nación*, saying two red hats were an honor for Argentina, and that he shared his people's pride. "I'm living this religiously," he told Elisabetta Piqué, who later recalled his mixture of shyness and astuteness. "I pray about it, speak to the Lord about it, I plea on behalf of the diocese." He didn't feel promoted, he told her. "In Gospel terms, every elevation implies a descent; you have to abase yourself in order to serve better." Asked if he agreed with being classified as a conservative in doctrine but progressive in social matters, he said such definitions always reduced people. "I try not be conservative, but faithful to the Church, yet always open to dialogue."[7]

John Paul II called the cardinals back to Rome in late May for a three-day, closed-door meeting known as an extraordinary consistory. The theme was how to increase *communio* in the Church, a theological term that referred to the bonds of unity. For the St. Gallen cardinals, communion needed to be both forged and expressed through greater effective collegiality, a case they made through the press: Lehmann said national bishops' conferences should play a role in the Church's decision making, while Danneels told journalists that "the theme of collegiality will be without doubt one of the major challenges for the third millennium." Rodríguez Maradiaga echoed the call on behalf of the Latin-Americans: "All of us are convinced it is necessary to increase collegiality," he told a press conference. But while, according to press leaks, Cardinals Martini, Danneels, Lehmann, and Murphy-O'Connor made similar calls inside the consistory, the issue was barely discussed. The secretariat of state had crowded the agenda with twenty-one points taken from the pope's recent apostolic letter. The Curia was pushing back.[8]

Bergoglio used this time to listen and bond with brother cardinals. He reconnected with Cardinal Martini, whom he had known since they were both delegates at the Jesuits' General Congregation in 1974 and whose books he often quoted. Martini in turn introduced him to the St. Gallen group, initiating relationships that would develop on Bergoglio's fleeting visits to Rome in the next years.

In October Bergoglio was back in Rome for the third time that year as vice-chair of the bishops' synod. His role was to assist the rapporteur (*relator*), Cardinal Edward Egan of New York, who arrived in Rome from a city devastated by the horror of 9/11. The topic, ironically, was the role of the bishop, which naturally raised the issue of the relationship of the episcopate to the Vatican. Yet collegiality was mentioned only twice in the forty-thousand-word working document. In June, the curial official in charge of the synod, Belgian cardinal Jan Schotte, insisted that there was no true collegiality outside an ecumenical council such as Vatican II, only "expressions" of it; this was the standard curial defense of the status quo.

The point was not lost on those attending: here was a bishops' synod being held on the topic of the bishop that excluded the topic of collegiality. Only half of the bishops' conferences had sent in comments on the lofty, abstract working document sent out by the Curia, the lowest response rate in the synod's history. When the meeting opened, John Paul II—exhausted from a recent visit to Azerbaijan—sat slumped in his chair, either dozing or reading. In the press hall, journalists joked that he was poring over the synod's conclusions.

Bergoglio's own speech—brief, as ever—was a lyrical meditation on the distinction between, on the one hand, a bishop who oversees (*supervisa*) and watches over (*vigila*) his people, and on the other, one who keeps watch (*vela*) for them.

> *Overseeing* refers more to a concern for doctrine and habits, whereas *keeping watch* is more about making sure that there be salt and light in people's hearts. *Watching over* speaks of being alert to imminent danger; *keeping watch*, on the other hand, speaks of patiently bearing the processes through which the Lord carries out the salvation of

his people. To *watch over* it is enough to be awake, sharp, quick. To *keep watch* you need also to be meek, patient, and constant in proven charity. *Overseeing* and *watching over* suggest a certain degree of necessary control. *Keeping watch*, on the other hand, suggests hope, the hope of the merciful Father who keeps watch over the processes in the hearts of his children.[9]

After the first week of speeches, when Cardinal Egan had to return unexpectedly to New York to lead a service of remembrance for the victims of 9/11, Bergoglio was appointed *relator*, responsible for distilling the 247 bishops' speeches into a report, or *relatio*, that would shape the group discussions and conclusions. What he produced was concise and elegant and won plaudits all around. It captured the key themes as well as Bergoglio's own idea of a bishop, one who has an option for the poor and a missionary approach, who "sets free values tainted by false ideologies," and who is called to be "a prophet of justice," in whom the marginalized, disappointed by their leaders, place their trust. Inside the hall, Bergoglio received high praise for the way he reflected bishops' concerns without causing disunity. "What people admired him for was how he rescued the best of the synod debate despite the limitations of the structure and method," recalls Bergoglio's long-standing friend in Rome, Professor Guzmán Carriquiry.

Around one in five of the delegates had directly or indirectly touched on the issue of Vatican centralism, but Cardinal Schotte wanted that discussion excised from the *relatio*. Sitting next to Schotte at his first Vatican press conference, Bergoglio was shy, speaking softly in Spanish in order, he said, to be better understood, although his Italian was clearly fluent. Asked about collegiality, he said that "an in-depth discussion on this theme exceeds the specific limits of this synod" and needed to be tackled "elsewhere and with adequate preparation." It was a deft reply that made clear that the issue needed to be dealt with but not in a Curia-controlled synod. He impressed journalists with his clarity and conciseness, although he gave no indication to them that he was a reformer, and they regarded him as a safe pair of hands.[10]

In retrospect, it is clear that the synod launched Bergoglio in the universal Church, winning him many admirers: Cardinal Timothy Dolan, who was made archbishop of New York after Egan retired in 2009, recalled how his predecessor "had often spoken glowingly of this archbishop of Buenos Aires."[11]

But Bergoglio couldn't get back to Argentina fast enough. It wasn't just that his country was entering a state of emergency. As cardinal, he had been named to various Vatican *dicasteries* (departments) dealing with liturgy, clergy, consecrated life, the family, and Latin America, but he missed many meetings. "He did not like to come to Rome, and even less with everything that was happening—the way the Curia was being run," recalls Carriquiry. "He came to Rome much less than he was supposed to." When he could, he tried to come only once a year, in February—his staff jested that it was his Lenten penance—when he spent no longer than was absolutely necessary: when he later said, as pope, that he hardly knew Rome, he was not exaggerating. His press officer from 2007, Federico Wals, says that Rome for Bergoglio represented "the heart of everything that he believed the Church should not be: luxury, ostentation, hypocrisy, bureaucracy—everything that was 'self-referential.' He hated going."

Yet he was not forgotten by those looking beyond John Paul II. In 2002 a leading Vatican commentator wrote of Bergoglio that since the synod,

> the thought of having him return to Rome as the successor of Peter has begun to spread with growing intensity. The Latin-American cardinals are increasingly focused upon him, as is Cardinal Joseph Ratzinger. The only key figure among the Curia who hesitates when he hears his name is Secretary of State Cardinal Angelo Sodano—the very man known for supporting the idea of a Latin-American pope.[12]

BERGOGLIO came back at the end of 2001 to a country sliding into an abyss. The Argentine economy was contracting, the banks were close to collapse, and because the state had run out of money, public employees were being paid in worthless tokens. After the International Monetary Fund (IMF) withheld a loan tranche, there was a rush on the banks, leading President Fernando de la Rúa in early December to freeze bank accounts, limiting withdrawals to $250 a week. The so-called *corralito* suddenly sucked cash from the economy, and businesses across the country went to the wall. In every city, lines at parish soup kitchens trebled.

Together with the UN Development Program (UNDP) the bishops organized a meeting of national leaders on December 19 at the headquarters of the church agency Caritas, close to the Plaza de Mayo. There Cardinal Bergoglio and the head of the bishops' conference, Archbishop Estanislao Karlic, spelled out the gravity of the situation: unless an emergency package of social assistance were put in place, the country would self-destruct. President De la Rúa, who had to be persuaded to attend, dismissed the warnings as exaggerated, but as he was leaving he was pelted with eggs and stones. The angry crowd forming in the square was the start of a massive popular protest. In what became known as the casserole revolt, or *cacerolazo*, hundreds of thousands over the next days took to the streets banging pots and pans to demand the resignation of the government. De la Rúa declared a state of siege.

Bergoglio, incensed by the scenes of police brutality in the Plaza de Mayo he could see from his third-floor window, called the Interior Ministry to demand that they allow peaceful protest. In a communiqué, the cardinal praised the fact that this was a genuine people's uprising—most demonstrations in Argentina are orchestrated—and said that behind it was a simple demand for an end to corruption.

The next day, reports came in of the deaths across the nation of dozens of protesters—including seven in the Plaza de Mayo—and hundreds of wounded. As crowds surged against the barriers around the Casa Rosada, de la Rúa fled in a helicopter, formally resigning the next day. In the following two weeks there were four presidents and the largest sovereign loan default in world history. Argentina's $95 billion foreign debt was staggering for a population of thirty-seven million, and an indictment of a decade of public profligacy and corruption.

On Christmas Eve, as the economy and the state lay in ruins, Cardinal Bergoglio invited people at Midnight Mass to peer through the enveloping darkness to the light of the crib in Bethlehem. "Tonight there are many things we can't explain, and we don't know what's going to happen," he said softly. "Let's take charge of hope. That's all I want to say to you tonight. Simply that."

In the New Year, following an agreement between the parties, the Peronist Eduardo Duhalde agreed to serve out the remainder of De la Rúa's term, until September 2003, and not to seek election. The convertibility law—which had long been undermined by reckless spending and lack of dollar reserves—was finally abandoned, and the peso lost 40 percent of its value. The wealthy, who kept dollars abroad, became far richer, while the salaried middle classes and the poor endured the worst peacetime crisis since Weimar Germany.

For the next two years, the economy continued to shrink; businesses and factories collapsed, or moved to Brazil and Chile; and unemployment came close to 50 percent of the working population. Some eighteen million people entered the ranks of the poor, while nine million became destitute, living on less than a dollar a day. The new desperation was symbolized by the *cartoneros*, people who scoured the city's rubbish in search of paper and cardboard that could be sold for a few pesos. In a country that once fed the world, children were dying of malnourishment. In a nation born of immigrant dreams, hundreds of thousands of young people queued for passports outside the Spanish and Italian consulates, hoping to reverse their grandparents' journeys.

Among those forming lines outside parish soup kitchens were educated people who had lost their homes after the collapse of their businesses, and often their marriages. The crisis was in many ways more devastating for what was once Latin America's largest middle class. For an older generation, it was a fast route into depression and despair. Without social security to depend on, and lacking the resilience of the long-term poor, for hundreds of thousands of destitute Argentines the diocesan charity network was, literally, a lifeline.

Because every parish in the country had a Caritas office, the infrastructure was already in place to mount a major relief operation. The Church became a battlefield hospital. In Buenos Aires, Cardinal Bergoglio mobilized the city's 186 parishes, eight hundred priests, and fifteen hundred members of religious orders, and close to a million practicing Catholics, urging them to go out into the streets to find people in need. It became normal for Mass-goers to bring any little extra food that could be distributed. Churches were opened at night to shelter rising numbers of homeless. Ovens using gas cylinders were set up to make bread under bridges, and nursing stations appeared, offering medicines. Caritas also expanded its citywide projects as donations poured in from abroad, above all building shelters for the homeless and creating job-training programs for thousands in search of work.

For Bergoglio, this was the time of watching over his people, helping to feed and shelter them until the crisis passed. Bergoglio told Caritas staff and volunteers not to get hung up on protocols and legal niceties, but to set up projects that could deliver quickly and directly to those in need. But being effective must never mean losing sight of the person; people's dignity, he told them, required time and attention. Inaugurating a new project in a former razor blade factory in March 2002, Daniel Gassman, Caritas director in Buenos Aires, recalls him telling them how their assistance must be "artisanal, not industrial." For Bergoglio there were no numbers, only persons, and when Caritas staff asked for donations, they were not for beds but for those who slept in them. Theirs must be a Samaritan giving, he told them, which looked in the eye, touched wounds, and embraced.

The Church's credibility at this time was as high as that of politicians was low. Back in 1983, the Church was seen as a power broker complicit with dictators, more interested in itself than in ordinary people. Now a Gallup poll put the Church first of institutions that Argentines most trusted, with politicians and judiciary at the bottom. Bucking the continent's trend, Argentines self-identifying as Catholics had actually gone up in the previous ten years, from 83 to 89 percent. The Karlic-Bergoglio policy of critical distance from the government, and the bishops' consistent denunciation of the neoliberal, borrow-and-spend policies that had brought on the crisis, were part of the reason for the Church's popularity. Another was the impressive capacity it demonstrated for assisting people. But mostly it was because what the Church did and said were congruent. The Church lived for the people, not itself. Cardinal Bergoglio, in particular, symbolized power as service. Even those who saw him as aloof admired his dignity and austerity, which threw into even sharper relief the rapacity of their political leaders.

PRESIDENT Eduardo Duhalde was an exception. A practicing Catholic whose outlook wasn't far from the bishops', he sought to carry Argentina through the crisis without personal gain, and to put in place—with the few resources at the state's disposal—emergency relief for the poor. Cardinal Bergoglio and Archbishop Karlic went to see him at the Casa Rosada three days after his inauguration in early January 2002. They agreed to formalize what had begun that day in December: the Church would host the meetings, which Duhalde would commit the government to, while the UN supplied technical support. Thus was born the *Diálogo Argentino* (Argentine Dialogue), a seven-month process of intense civic engagement that not only kept society from total breakdown but created the potential for a new kind of politics. Duhalde would later write that Bergoglio was one of the "giants" of that time, people who behind the scenes worked to save Argentina from disaster by shoring up civil society.[13]

The *Diálogo*'s great strength was that it gave voice to the expansion of civil society in those years, in which the Church was the main but by no means the only player. People banded together to organize transport, food, child care, health care, and other basics, and exchanged goods and service by bartering. The networks and neighborhood groups began uniting and demanding a say, occupying the vacancy left by a bankrupt state. In all, some two thousand organizations found their voice through the *Diálogo*, which dealt with both immediate and long-term challenges, creating consensus for short-term initiatives while crafting ideas for long-term reforms to institutions. "Everyone came to talk. It was a way of channeling people's anxieties," recalls Bishop Jorge Casaretto, who coordinated the Dialogue on behalf of the Church. "People came to ask for things, to make demands. But this was very important, because it helped define a national strategy."[14]

Bergoglio was adamant that it was Duhalde, not the Church, who convened and led the Dialogue. "The Church offers the space for dialogue, like one who offers his house for his brothers to meet and be reconciled," he told an Italian journalist, Gianni Valente. "But it is not a sector or lobby, a party taking part in the Dialogue alongside interest or pressure groups." Equally, their involvement did not compromise the bishops' independence from government, which they continued to critique on behalf of civil society. "We bishops are sick of systems that produce poor people for the Church to look after," Bergoglio said in a document handed to the president a month after his inauguration. "Just 40 percent of state assistance reaches those who need it, while the rest vanishes along the way because of corruption." Bergoglio blamed the way the deification of the state by left-wing ideologies had been followed by the evisceration of the state by neoliberalism. The only way out of the crisis was to rebuild from below. "I believe in miracles," he told Valente, before going on to quote a character in Manzoni's *The Betrothed*: "'I have never found that the Lord has begun a miracle before ending it well.'"[15]

Bergoglio spelled out the miracle at the May 25 Te Deum attended by President Duhalde that year. Using the story of Zacchaeus in Luke's Gospel, he said Argentina was like the corrupt, short publican who climbs a tree to see Jesus, who notices him and invites him to come down and join him, leading to Zacchaeus promising to give back what he stole. Argentina could again rise to its correct height, said the cardinal, but first it needed to accept the invitation to come down, for "no project based on great plans can be realized unless it is built and sustained from below, through the renunciation of our own interests, and lowering ourselves to the patient daily work that conquers all arrogance." The publican was not asked to be what he wasn't but to be like everyone else—an ordinary, law-abiding citizen. It was an invitation to be part of the *pueblo* and serve it.

> Let us contemplate the end of the story. A Zacchaeus who has come to terms with the law, who lives without pretensions or disguises alongside his brothers and sisters, who is seated next to the Lord, confidently and with perseverance allowing his initiatives to develop, capable of listening and dialoguing, and above all able to give way and share joyfully. History tells us that many peoples have been raised up, like Zacchaeus, from ruin and abandoned their meanness. We must give space to time, and to creative organizing efforts; we should rely less on sterile demands, on illusions and promises, but dedicate ourselves instead to firm, persevering action. This way we allow hope to flower, this hope that will not disappoint because it is God's gift to the heart of our people.[16]

Bergoglio's hope was that from his nation's purgation a new democratic politics and economy could be born, one that was rooted in, and served, the people, and in which vigorous civil-society institutions could hold the state accountable. In this Te Deum and in others, he kept urging Argentines to take advantage of the moment, to be patient, and to build; it was as if—as he had described the bishop's role at the synod—he was keeping watch over his people, to give God time and space to act. Yet there were many pressures and temptations to take shortcuts out of the process. His reference to "sterile demands" was a likely critique of the *piqueteros*, a new form of social protester who in traditional Argentine fashion made angry claims on the state.

The cardinal feared that a state-focused populist could capitalize on this anger, using it to polarize Argentine society. His fears turned out to be well founded. Néstor Kirchner, the governor of the oil-rich Patagonian state of Santa Cruz, was a little-known figure nationally with a reputation locally for an efficient, high-spending administration. He and his glamorous senator wife, Cristina Fernández, had been active in the Peronist revolutionary left in the early 1970s, close to, if not active in, the montoneros. After the coup they had gone south to build a successful law firm specializing in mortgage foreclosures before entering politics—Néstor as mayor of Rio Gallegos, then governor of Santa Cruz, Cristina as a member of the provincial assembly and later the national Congress.

Unable to persuade his preferred candidates to run, yet anxious to stop Menem's third bid for the presidency, Duhalde reluctantly gave his backing to Kirchner. The election came down to a run-off between two candidates, Kirchner and Menem, the first of whom was unknown, the second discredited. After Menem withdrew at the last minute, Kirchner won unopposed, but with a mere 22 percent of the votes, most of which came from Duhalde's backing. His first task after his inauguration on May 25, 2003, was to build a political base, just as the economy began growing again. At the Te Deum that day, Bergoglio warned against returning to the "resentment of sterile internal arguments, of endless confrontations," insisting that "only healing reconciliation will bring us back to life."[17]

Kirchner wasn't listening. Rather than look to the Argentine Dialogue to build his base from civil-society organizations, using its copious recommendations as the basis of his program, Kirchner opted instead for a 1970s rhetoric based on a friend-enemy logic and a traditional carrot-and-stick use of state largesse. When he was offered two thick files of proposals from civil society, the fruit of seven months' work by the *Diálogo*, the president wasn't interested. "We offered him what we had," recalls Bishop Casaretto, "but they said no, we're going to govern with a different plan."

The plan was to resurrect the old binary politics, pitting "people" against the "corporations"—the armed forces, the agro-export sector, the big industries—who were blamed for colluding at the time of the dictatorship to suppress "the people." Kirchner, who described himself as "a son of the Mothers of the Plaza de Mayo," began at once to give political posts to human-rights groups, and—to their delight—derogated the amnesty laws passed by Alfonsín and Menem to allow retrials of military officers. The official line of the government was that there was only one reprehensible violence in the 1970s, that of the army (the guerrillas were fighting for "the people") egged on by their right-wing allies, the Church and the oligarchy. Any attempt to claim otherwise was tarred as a discredited "two-devils" theory.

Buoyed by high economic growth rates linked to favorable world trade conditions, Kirchner reproduced the model of governance he had used in Santa Cruz and began channeling income from exports to reward loyalty from cash-starved public administrations. In a short time he had his own substantial political base, gaining more than 40 percent in the 2005 midterm election. Yet rather than tone down the rhetoric and adopt a politics of inclusion, he sharpened the polarization: no longer dependent on Duhalde or even the Justicialist (Peronist) party, he reduced his cabinet to Kirchner intimates who shared his sectarian worldviews. Over the next years, with the help of loyally pro-government journalists like Horacio Verbitsky, Kirchner mobilized supporters by making repeated attacks on the regime's clearly defined enemies at home and abroad—the generals, the bishops, the bankers, and the exporters, all in league with foreign interests in the United States, the United Kingdom, and the World Bank.

Shortly after taking power, Kirchner's secretary called the cardinal to invite him to the Casa Rosada for a meeting with the president. Bergoglio, sensitive to the choreography of Church-state relations, said no, but would be delighted to receive him across the square in his offices in the Curia. "If the president wants to see me, he comes to my office. If I want to see him, I go to his," he explained to his staff. President and cardinal eventually met in August 2003, when Bergoglio went to the Casa Rosada with the new president of the bishops' conference, Archbishop Eduardo Mirás of Rosario, for a meeting the bishops had asked for. But it soon became clear that Kirchner—whom his fellow Peronist Julio Bárbaro describes as having zero religious sensibility—had no interest in listening to a Church he could not control.

After sending a courtesy copy of his May 25, 2004, address to the Casa Rosada, Bergoglio received through a government intermediary a haughty reminder that the purpose of the Te Deum was to pray for the nation in thanksgiving for the Revolution of May 1810.[18] Undeterred, the cardinal's fifth address on Argentina's national day was his most powerful and passionate yet, and strikingly similar even in some of its phrases to his Jesuit talks and articles in the 1970s. He was back in battle with ideological elites on behalf of the *pueblo fiel.*

The Gospel was Luke's account of Jesus returning to his hometown of Nazareth and reading from the prophet Isaiah in the synagogue, provoking astonishment that turns to anger and an expulsion. The title of his address was a line from the same Gospel: "A prophet is without honor in his own country." Bergoglio suggested that those who were scandalized by Jesus were self-sufficient, self-justifying elites disconnected from the wisdom of their people. In seeking to stone Jesus, he said, their "weak way of thinking" and mediocrity were exposed. The cardinal went on to reframe the idea of social exclusion, which was caused, he said, not solely by unjust structures, but by attitudes of sectarianism and intolerance that claim to divide society into those who belong and enemies. Yet "the soul of our people" was not taken in by deceitful and mediocre stratagems or partisan squabbles, but was focused on "the great challenges" that face any society. He ended with an image of Christ among his people proclaiming a message that was intolerable to the enlightened elites, who sought to stone him and run him out of town. Bergoglio invited his listeners, in Ignatian fashion, to choose with whom they wanted to identify.[19]

Kirchner, who had a fever that day, told journalists he thought the address had referred to some of the country's realities in a clear way. Argentina, he said, was rediscovering its identity and that "recovering social inclusion is a fundamental task."[20]

In early 2004 Bergoglio began to be treated by a practitioner of Chinese medicine, a Taoist monk who had been recommended to him by a priest. When Liu Ming sat opposite the cardinal at their first meeting in his third-floor office, Bergoglio stayed silent, looking at him. "At that moment I had the feeling he was transmitting his thoughts to me," remembers the monk, who had arrived from Jiangsu in China only a year earlier. "Then he told me about his health problems."

In addition to diabetes and a creaky gallbladder, the cardinal, then in his late sixties, was suffering heart pains for which his doctors had prescribed a battery of pills. Bergoglio had lived with a phenomenal workload throughout his country's crisis and was paying for the constant stress in blocked arteries. The monk said he wanted to use regular acupuncture and massages to get the blood flowing and to shift the blockages; in the meantime he should forget the pills. The cardinal agreed.

When Bergoglio took off his clothes for the first acupuncture session, Liu Ming was shocked. "His clothes had holes, they were very old and worn. I thought, 'How can such an important man be so humble?'"

For the next three years Liu Ming saw him twice a week, until Bergoglio felt better; thereafter, when he was cured, once a month. The cardinal called him his Chinese torturer, tried to persuade him to support San Lorenzo, suggested a name for his daughter (as a result she is called María Guadalupe), and gave him books: the *I Ching* in Spanish, the Bible, and a book called *Reasons to Believe*. Liu Ming chatted to him about how the body contains within itself its own capacity to heal itself, how Western medicine considers only the outside, not the inside, how with Chinese medicine you can live 140 years ("you think I'll live that long?" Bergoglio asked him, laughing), and about Tao and God; the cardinal always listened attentively. Liu Ming was amazed at his pulse, which was stronger than any he had encountered. And he was impressed by his spirituality, his lack of ego: Bergoglio "was not concerned with what was outside but what was within," the monk-doctor later said.[21]

It was a lesson Pope John Paul II was, at that time, giving every day. In the past three years his deterioration had been steady; by July 2004, when he went to the French shrine of Lourdes at the foot of the Pyrenees for his last apostolic visit, he had become an icon of human suffering. Drooling, slumped, trembling, no longer in control of his body, John Paul II taught from his wheelchair some of the most important lessons of his papacy. There was a moment in Lourdes that summed it all up. At the conclusion of the recital of the Rosary at the famous grotto, a young handicapped man, also slouched and with his body twisted to one side, was brought forward to receive a blessing. The two men gazed at each other wordlessly from their wheelchairs, equal in their shared vulnerability, for a prayer-pregnant eternity.[22]

Bergoglio had first encountered John Paul II in 1979, the year after Cardinal Wojtyla's election, when the Jesuit provincial joined a group reciting the Rosary led by the pope in Rome. While there he had a profound experience that he later recorded, after the pope's death in 2005, as part of the evidence being gathered for the cause of his canonization.

One afternoon I went to pray the Holy Rosary that the Holy Father was leading. He was in front of us, on his knees. It was a very large group. With the Holy Father's back to me, I entered into prayer. I was not alone, but praying in the middle of the People of God to which I and all those who were there belonged, led by our Pastor.

In the middle of the prayer I became distracted looking at the pope. . . . And time began to fade away. I began to imagine the young priest, the seminarian, the poet, the worker, the child from Wadowice, in exactly the posture he was now, praying Hail Mary after Hail Mary. His witness struck me. I felt that this man, chosen to guide the Church, was the summation of a path trod together with his Mother in heaven, a path that began in his childhood. And I suddenly realized the weight of the words spoken by the Mother of Guadalupe to Saint Juan Diego: *Do not be afraid. Am I not your Mother?* I grasped the presence of Mary in the pope's life.

His witness did not get lost in a memory. From that time onward I have prayed the fifteen mysteries of the Rosary every day.[23]

In the same evidence, he recorded how after he was made archbishop in 1998 he had had a number of "private personal meetings" with John Paul II, in which he had been deeply impressed by the pope's "almost infinite memory: he remembered places, people, and situations he had encountered on his journeys, proof that he was paying total attention at all times." Bergoglio remembered how the pope had put him at ease. "Because I was a bit shy and reserved, at least on one occasion when I had finished speaking to him about the topics we were covering at the audience, I made to leave so as not to waste his time. He grabbed me by the arm, invited me to sit down again, and said, 'No! No! No! Don't leave,' so we could keep speaking." Bergoglio had no doubt, he told the tribunal, that John Paul II "lived all the virtues in a heroic way."[24]

When the pope entered the last stage of his life in February 2005, Cardinal Bergoglio was dealing with the aftermath of a Buenos Aires nightclub fire weeks before that had led to almost two hundred deaths and close to fifteen hundred injured. He was one of the first on the scene at the República de Cromañón club in Once, accompanying the relatives, anointing the bodies, praying with the bereft, standing quietly and supportively amid the shock and pain. He put one of his auxiliaries, Jorge Lozano, in charge of a team giving pastoral support to the wounded and the grieving, and ordered Mass to be celebrated on the thirtieth of each month to remember the date of the tragedy.

His firm but gentle presence from dawn until late at night in the hospital and at the morgue won the hearts of the city. It also showed up the politicians, who seemed absent and unsure. As the causes of the tragedy unraveled—a sad litany of safety measures bypassed for the sake of the bottom line—it was clear why: behind it lay a putrid nexus of corruption, cover-up, and connivance involving high-ranking city officials and police.

"What was revealed were networks of corruption that caused people to look the other way," recalls Bishop Lozano. "The emergency exit doors were shut up with chains and padlocks to stop people getting in without paying, and there were many more people inside than were allowed. What Bergoglio pointed to out of this was how society in Buenos Aires organized spaces for young people without caring for them, putting profit first, and how those who should be controlling were being paid not to control." The cardinal, furious at the immolation of the young on the altar of greed, gave voice to the feelings of his people. "We are neither powerful nor rich nor important," he said at the cathedral on January 30, 2005, "but we suffer . . . a pain that cannot be expressed in words, a pain that has overtaken whole households." And he prayed for justice, "that this humble people not be mocked."

At an anniversary Mass later that year, in one of his best-remembered homilies, in a cathedral packed with hundreds of grieving relatives, he led an extraordinary outpouring of emotion. Speaking softly, his voice cracking, he created the image of a city that was both a grieving mother and a distracted, self-obsessed place that was trying to bury its pain.

Today we are here to enter into the heart of that mother who went to the temple full of hope and who returned with the certainty that those hopes would be shattered, cut short. Entering into this heart let us remember the children of the city, of this city that is also a mother, that they be recognized by her, that she realize that these, like the children of Abraham in the First Reading, are the children of her inheritance; and the inheritance that those children who are no longer with us give us, is a very clear one: *harden not your hearts!* Their photos here, their names, their lives symbolized in these candles, are shouting at us not to let our hearts harden. This is the inheritance they have left us. They are the children of an inheritance that tells us: "cry!"

Distracted city, spread-out city, selfish city: cry! You need to be purified by tears. Those of us here praying, we give this message to these our brothers and sisters of Buenos Aires: let us together cry—we so need to cry in Buenos Aires. . . . Let us cry here. Let us cry outside, too. And let us ask the Lord to touch each of our hearts, and the hearts of our brothers and sisters of this city, that they, too, may cry; and that with our tears we might purify this, our superficial, flighty city.[25]

In February, John Paul II was rushed to the hospital with severe respiratory difficulties. It was serious, but many assumed he would rally as he had done so often before. But by the end of March, after a tracheotomy, there were signs that the end was near. John Paul II tried to deliver an Easter Sunday blessing from his apartment in the Apostolic Palace but no words came out. He looked defeated. An aide made to steer him from the window, but the pope pushed him away; he wanted to stay a moment, to communicate with his people, just as he had on the day of his election in October 1978, when he had spoken to the people in the square to tell them that the cardinals had gone to "a far country" to seek the bishop of Rome and asking them to correct his Italian. Now, raising his hands to his throat as if to explain why he could no longer speak to them, he made a sign of the Cross in the air; then he just stayed, looking. At that moment, the realization spread through the crowd: he was saying good-bye. Thousands stood in the square and openly wept.

At Mass at the cathedral on April 4 Bergoglio paid warm tribute to a man of total integrity, who never deceived, lied, or tricked, who "communicated with his people, with the coherence of a man of God, with the coherence of one who every morning spent long hours in adoration, and who, because he adored, let himself be shaped by God's strength." John

Paul II was a "coherent man," said the cardinal in a startling phrase, "because he let himself be chiseled by God's will."

> This coherent man who . . . saved us from a fratricidal massacre; this coherent man who loved to take children in his arms because he believed in tenderness; this coherent man who more than once had homeless people brought from the Piazza Risorgimento to speak to them and give them a new start; this coherent man who when he had recovered asked permission to visit the prison to speak with the man who had tried to kill him. He is a witness. I end with his words: "What this century needs is not teachers but witnesses." In the Incarnation of the Word, Christ is the faithful witness. Today we see in John Paul an imitation of this faithful witness. And we give thanks that he has ended his life in this way, coherently, that he might have finished his life being simply this: a faithful witness.[26]

THEN he left for Rome, which for the next few weeks became the turning point of the globe. Some four million people were arriving in those days, forming a great flood of humanity from the Tiber to St. Peter's, singing, praying, waiting—and queuing, sometimes all day and night, to pay their respects. As they arrived from the five continents, the cardinals and visiting dignitaries were brought into the basilica through the aptly named Porta della Morte, emerging out of a narrow marble and stone corridor into an astonishing scene that assaulted the senses.

Kneeling on a prie-dieu before the shrunken, waxen body laid out on a red velvet bier—the pope's head was raised on three red pillows, his feet shod in his trademark oxblood shoes—the cardinals saw, sliding behind the catafalque, a gentle torrent of grieving, praying humanity. Here, as had never been seen in modern times, was an eruption of God's holy faithful people, bussing out of small towns across central Europe or flying in on budget airlines, drawn to the inert remains of their pope by some ancient magnet that the world's media struggled to explain.

Awestruck by this outpouring, and conscious that they had been handed a precious legacy to preserve, the cardinals joined their confrères for daily meetings in the synod hall. Except for the dean of the college, Joseph Ratzinger, and US cardinal William Baum—the only electors to have been given their red hats by Paul VI—this was a wholly new experience for the cardinals: no pope had died, and none had been elected, since far-off 1978.

Yet while the media outside endlessly drew up profiles of the ideal next pope, there was little chance for the cardinals to do the same in their meetings, known as the General Congregations. During the *sede vacante*—the time between the death of a pope and the election of his successor—cardinals govern the Holy See, and must debate and vote on a series of often tedious matters. The first week of the General Congregations was mostly taken up with a careful line-by-line examination of the canon law of the *sede vacante*, followed by long discussions of the funeral on April 8, which would be the most-watched event in the history of television. Only after the funeral, during the so-called *novemdiales*, or nine-day mourning period prior to the conclave, were the cardinals able to get down to discussing the needs of the Church and its future direction.

After a 2003 consistory had added twenty-three more cardinals, there were now 115 electors from dozens of nations, plus some 50 who were too old to vote. A few cardinals had newspaper cutouts with profiles of each, so they knew who was speaking. Their task was to elect one among them, yet they hardly knew each other.

Cardinal Ratzinger chaired these sessions superbly. He had been at the head of the Vatican's doctrinal watchdog, the Congregation for the Doctrine of the Faith (CDF), for twenty-four years, greeting bishops on their Vatican visits, and had a phenomenal memory. He was a paradox: the theologian who justified Roman centralism was also the most collegial of the curial cardinals, praised by visiting bishops for his courtesy and attentiveness to them. Now, at the general congregations, these qualities proved vital. The cardinals knew him, and he them; he could name them and usually speak their language. Over that fortnight before the conclave, he pastored and united a body that was fragmented and disoriented.

The general congregations themselves were a poor forum for discerning John Paul II's successor. The addresses were long-winded and vague—cardinals who were over eighty, unable to vote, were keen to share their wisdom at the first conclave in nearly thirty years—and often went over the seven-minute limit, leading some to grumble wryly that it was all too much like a bishops' synod. Perhaps half of those present did not speak

Italian, and the translation facilities were poor; nor could they learn much about each other through the media, because the cardinals had self-imposed a ban on interviews after the funeral.

The real discussions, in fact, went on in the evenings, when cardinals hosted discreet dinners at their national colleges or—in the case of the *curiali*—in their Roman apartments. Here the discussion could be more intimate and forthright, and might turn to specific candidates. Cardinal Murphy-O'Connor of Westminster, for example, hosted a dinner for the St. Gallen group and their guests at the English College after the funeral. Yet most cardinals, and especially those from Asia and Africa, were ignorant of these gatherings and depended on the general congregations for their discernment.

The *riformisti* had no obvious candidate: Cardinal Martini was eighty and had Parkinson's disease; he walked with a stick, and in any case, had excluded himself. The reformers were relying—fatefully, it turned out—on the pre-conclave process for a candidate to emerge. In contrast, the curial bloc of cardinals had for some time been putting forward Cardinal Ratzinger. Even though few remembered the last one, the *curiali* knew how a conclave worked—that what counted in a conclave was early momentum, how the votes traveled to whomever had a strong showing fresh off the starting block—and they worked hard in the days before the conclave so that Ratzinger could count on a good share of the first vote.

Promoting the Ratzinger candidacy among the English- and German-speaking cardinals was Christoph Schönborn of Vienna, while the two Latin-American curial cardinals, Alfonso López Trujillo and Jorge Medina Estévez, buttonholed Spanish and Portuguese speakers as they arrived in Rome. A Brazilian cardinal who spoke anonymously to *O Globo* later that year described how not long after putting down their suitcases, the two Latin-American *curiali* had invited them to meetings and dinners. "In those conversations they made it clear that they had consulted Ratzinger and he had given a green light for the campaign." The *rigoristi* argued persuasively that Ratzinger was a towering theologian, the only one capable of carrying forward John Paul II's legacy, and whose experience in the Curia meant he could take on the problems there, too.[27]

In the run-up to the conclave, the Italian newspapers were claiming that Ratzinger could count on perhaps forty votes. There was a long list of other potential *papabili*, but the main speculation was that the next pope would be a Latin-American. Bergoglio was included in the lists, but mostly reporters pointed to the mediagenic Oscar Rodríguez Maradiaga of Tegucigalpa, Honduras, or the Franciscan, Claudio Hummes of São Paolo, Brazil, who had higher profiles. But the speculation was just that. Apart from López Trujillo and Medina Estévez on behalf of Ratzinger, the Latin-American cardinals were neither organizing nor being organized, Bergoglio least of all. He refused all dinner invitations, gave no interviews, and stayed over quietly, as ever, at the Via della Scrofa, dining with friends rather than other cardinals.

Bergoglio had with him Father Marcó to refuse interviews on his behalf and to deal with any stories arising out of events in Buenos Aires. One of those stories was aimed at Bergoglio in Rome. Three days before the conclave, a human-rights lawyer filed a complaint in a Buenos Aires court claiming that Bergoglio had been complicit in the kidnapping of Yorio and Jalics. The lawsuit—which Marcó told the press was an "old calumny"—went nowhere legally, but it created a news story, as was surely intended, and the impression, on the eve of the voting, that Bergoglio had a past that would be raked over if he became pope.

The lawsuit was based on the claims in *El Silencio*, a book published in February that year by Horacio Verbitsky, the former montonero who had become a close ally of Kirchner's. The book, which was about the alleged complicity of the Church in the dirty war, claimed in one chapter to have new evidence to support the old Emilio Mignone claim about Bergoglio's actions over Yorio and Jalics.

Verbitsky in the book said he had kept an open mind about Bergoglio, conscious that the founders of his human-rights organization CELS, Mignone and Alicia Oliveira, had been at odds over the archbishop's dirty war record; and that in interviewing Bergoglio in 1999 he had found his version of events to have merit. But since then, Verbitsky wrote, he had stumbled on new evidence that led him to doubt the cardinal's testimony. Before getting there, however, Verbitsky reviewed the old allegations, including that of the unnamed Jesuit accusing Bergoglio of wanting Yorio and Jalics out of the slum "and when they refused let the military know that they were no longer under his protection, and with that nudge and a wink had them arrested." (Verbitsky did not identify the anonymous Jesuit as Juan Luis Moyano, nor mention that Moyano was in Peru at the time of the events he claimed to know about.)

When he finally pulled it out, Verbitsky's smoking gun turned out to be a 1979 memorandum written by an immigration officer who had spoken to Bergoglio in connection with a passport application on behalf of Francisco Jalics, who had wanted to return to Argentina. According to the memo, Bergoglio told the officer that Jalics had been arrested for alleged guerrilla contacts, which led the officer to refuse Jalics a passport. This showed, Verbitsky triumphantly declared, that Bergoglio was Janus-faced, claiming to help someone while behind their backs undermining them—the same behavior he was accused of over Yorio and Jalics; the repetition of which, ipso facto, demonstrated the truth of Mignone's account. Yet Verbitsky omitted to mention that it was Bergoglio himself who applied on Jalics's behalf for the passport; that in Bergoglio's application he had said nothing of Jalics's arrest, but that the officer to whom he delivered the letter had asked him why Jalics had left the country in such a hurry. Bergoglio had had to give him the reason, but added emphatically that it wasn't true, that Jalics had had absolutely nothing to with the guerrillas. The officer had, however, omitted from his memo that part of what Bergoglio told him.[28]

The Verbitsky claims were summarized in anonymous envelopes delivered to Spanish-speaking cardinals in Rome in the days before the conclave.

Two elements of this dirty-tricks campaign remain unclear. The first was who was behind it. The Argentine press cited Vatican sources in Rome following Francis's election, claiming that it had been a Kirchner government sting, organized by Argentina's ambassador to the Holy See, Juan Pablo Cafiero, with the collaboration of a friendly cardinal. (Cafiero strongly denied this.) The second question is what impact it had. Cardinals loathe outsiders—especially those with political interests—trying to influence the conclave, and the accusations (if the cardinals had time to trawl through them) are likely to have elicited sympathy rather than horror. One senior American cardinal said in 2013 that in 2005, "we all knew about the allegations, and we knew they weren't true."[29]

The cardinals moved into the new Vatican guesthouse, the Casa Santa Marta, on the evening of Sunday April 17, and the next morning concelebrated the *pro eligendo papa* Mass—a special liturgy "for the election of a Roman Pontiff"—in St. Peter's. That afternoon, April 18, the 115 cardinals processed into the Sistine Chapel, which Bergoglio saw for the first time in his life. There they swore the oaths—to obey the procedures, and not to reveal details of the election—before the doors were closed on them and an enormous key turned in the lock: "conclave" comes from *cum chiave*, "with a key." The first round of voting, or scrutiny, was at 5:30 p.m. Twenty-four hours later, on the first scrutiny of the afternoon of the next day, the fourth of the conclave, Joseph Ratzinger was elected Benedict XVI.

DESPITE the oath of confidentiality, a picture of the way the votes went emerged later from a diary kept by one of the cardinals, who felt the tallies should be part of the historical record. The account, which formed the basis of an Italian foreign affairs journal article in September 2005, has not been contradicted, and is accepted by most Vatican commentators as authentic, not least for little scenic details such as the patriarch of Lisbon, Cardinal José da Cruz Policarpo, popping out of the Santa Marta for a cigar.[30]

On the first vote on Monday evening, Ratzinger received forty-seven votes, followed by Bergoglio with ten and Martini with nine. There were a handful of others, including four for Sodano, three for Rodríguez de Maradiaga, and—according to the anonymous Brazilian cardinal—some for Hummes. But the real surprise was Bergoglio, whose support indicated that more than half of the eighteen Latin-American residential cardinals (that is, excluding the Latin-American *curiali*) had voted for him, and most of the rest for Rodríguez and Hummes.

The *riformisti* did the math. If Bergoglio—a Latin-American pastoral archbishop, a Jesuit like Martini, who shared the reformers' concerns for collegiality—added Martini's votes, as well as those for Rodríguez and Hummes, to his own, there could be a two-horse race, and a genuine choice.

Back in the Santa Marta, they got to work. The diarist describes the president of the German bishops' conference, Karl Lehmann, and Godfried Danneels, the archbishop of Brussels, as the leaders of "a significant squad of U.S. and Latin American cardinals, in addition to a couple of curial cardinals." There were animated conversations at the table over supper, and in small groups of two or three meeting in the corridors and suites. The reformers' strategy was to raise Bergoglio's support to at least thirty-nine through an alliance of European and US reformers plus Latin-Americans who agreed on wanting a more collegial, pastoral church governance. That would leave Ratzinger unable to reach the necessary two-thirds majority of seventy-seven. Either his votes would travel to Bergoglio or, if the college stayed divided, another candidate would then emerge, as happened in the second conclave of 1978 that produced John Paul II.

The next morning there were two scrutinies. In the first, Ratzinger's votes increased to sixty-five, and Bergoglio's to thirty-five, with fifteen votes scattered elsewhere (Sodano's four remained, but those for Martini, Rodríguez, and Hummes had gone to Bergoglio). By the second scrutiny, the reformers had done it: Ratzinger had reached seventy-two, five short of the two-thirds needed, but Bergoglio had hit forty, meaning that—assuming the Argentine cardinal's support held—Ratzinger could not be elected. Both teams returned to the Santa Marta in some excitement.

Bergoglio at this point pulled the plug. What happened over lunch is not described by the diarist, but another source says Bergoglio begged the other cardinals "almost in tears" to vote for Ratzinger, whether by speaking to them individually or by making a general announcement is not clear.[31] That afternoon, in the first scrutiny, Bergoglio dropped to twenty-six, and Ratzinger was elected with eighty-four votes.

Why had he been upset? The diarist says he went up to vote with an expression of suffering on his face, gazing up at Michelangelo's *Last Judgment* "as if imploring, 'don't do this to me.'" Yet after the conclave, when a cardinal asked Bergoglio what name he would have taken had he been elected, he didn't hesitate. "I would have taken the name John, after *il papa buono* [the 'good pope,' John XXIII] and I would have been totally inspired by him," Bergoglio told Francesco Marchisano, the archpriest of St. Peter's.[32] To have pondered both name and program does not indicate a man unsure or afraid. Yet he *had* been upset. When he saw Father Marcó, he told him he had never needed prayers as much as that Tuesday morning. And back in Buenos Aires, he told a friend: "You'll never guess what they did to me."

One of his biographers suggests that Bergoglio stepped aside in order to avoid a prolonged conclave that would have indicated a Church divided. But this does not explain why Bergoglio was so perturbed. One commentator believes he was angry at being "used" by the progressive party, who had misread him: Bergoglio "was very much part of the pro-Ratzinger coalition" and "doubtless appalled by the whole exercise on his putative behalf," claims George Weigel.[33] But while this has truth to it—the reformers made a mistake in not seeking Bergoglio's consent—its premise is false: Bergoglio esteemed and liked the future Benedict XVI, and thought he should be pope, but he was not part of any group or coalition, least of all the *rigoristi*. Equally, the reformers knew that Bergoglio wanted reform and collegiality, but he was not "of" that party the way the St. Gallen group was.

Indeed, his problem was that there were parties at all. What upset Bergoglio was that he was the focal point of a fracturing, one destined to polarize, as in the 1970s, into ideological blocs. It upset him at a purely psychological level, in the sense that overcoming this divide had been a major part of his life's work. But what was more likely was that he had discerned the presence of the bad spirit. The conclave should be guided by the Spirit in the direction of unity and consensus; Bergoglio saw the 2005 conclave going in the opposite direction. "The evil spirit always divides, and divides Jesus," as he told the Spanish bishops to whom he gave an Ignatian retreat in January 2006. "Thus it denies unity."[34] That is why he felt able, indeed obliged, to put a stop to what was happening. And it was why he was upset: not for himself, but for the Church. He had glimpsed the serpent's tail in the Sistine Chapel.

He also believed he was not ready: more important, Latin America wasn't. His Uruguayan philosopher friend, Alberto Methol Ferré, explained as much in an interview just days after John Paul II's death. Latin America, as the oldest of the non-European Churches, had been moving from a "reflection Church" to a "source Church" that would in time invigorate the universal Church; but that process had been halted, even reversed, in the 1980s and 1990s. Until the continent's bishops came together through the next CELAM General Conference—it had been thirteen years since the disaster of Santo Domingo—any pope elected from Latin America would represent only his nation's reflection of the European Church.

Methol Ferré had been convinced that what was needed was a transitional European papacy, and that Cardinal Ratzinger "was the most suitable to be pope at this time."[35] On this point "their views coincided," says the Uruguayan at that time in the Council for Laity, Guzmán Carriquiry, who knew both men well. As Pope Francis told journalists on the plane back from Rio: "I was so happy when he was elected pope."

This explains why, when Bergoglio returned to Rome later that year, just after the publication of the cardinal's secret diary, he was so upset by its picture of him as an anti-Ratzinger blocker or stalking horse. "He may have been seen as an alternative by some of those who voted for him, but he never—absolutely never!—wanted to be seen as an alternative to Ratzinger," says Carriquiry, who saw him soon after he arrived. Bergoglio was annoyed enough to tell journalists he was "confused and a bit hurt" by "these indiscretions," which he said had given a false picture. Giving anecdotes and facts about the conclave suggested that it was the men who were doing the deciding, he said, whereas "we were all conscious of being nothing but instruments, to serve divine providence in electing a proper successor for John Paul II. That is what happened."[36]

He had returned to Rome for the October synod on the Eucharist, the first under Benedict XVI. The synod showed welcome signs of greater openness and genuine discussion, not least because of the death earlier that year of its controlling secretary general, Cardinal Schotte. The question of admitting to Communion practicing Catholics across the Western world who had entered second (civil) marriages emerged as a major topic in bishops' speeches. One New Zealand delegate described it as a "eucharistic hunger" that could be compared to physical hunger. But like collegiality, the question of Communion for the remarried was too big an issue for the synod's existing structure, and so the existing practice was simply reaffirmed, leaving many bishops frustrated. According to press leaks, of the 250 bishops, 50 did not vote for Proposition 40, which said that if a couple's marriage could not be annulled, and "objective conditions render their cohabitation irreversible," they could only receive the Eucharist if they were able to transform their relationship into a "loyal friendship." Later, Cardinals Kasper and López Trujillo clashed through the media, the first claiming that the issue could not be considered closed, the second insisting that it was "neither disputed, nor disputable."[37]

Bergoglio did not speak on that neuralgic topic, but meditated on the link between the Eucharist, Mary, and the *pueblo fiel*. Later, as Pope Francis, he would act on the conclusion he reached at that time: that the topic needed a more thorough treatment in a very different kind of synod, one with stronger powers, as part of a far-reaching collegial reform.

Shortly before the synod's conclusion he was elected by the highest number of delegates' votes (eighty) onto its council, to oversee the development of the synod's conclusions. Back in Argentina the following month, he was elected president of the bishops' conference.

The year 2005 had been rich in votes, not all of them welcome.

THE Ignatian retreat Bergoglio gave to Spanish bishops in January 2006 showed that, nearly fifteen years after moving away from the Society of Jesus, he had not lost his touch as a Jesuit spiritual director. The meditations drew on some of his old retreats and writings, supplemented by quotes from Cardinal Martini—a controversial figure to some in the Spanish hierarchy—as well as his favorite Church document, Paul VI's *Evangelii Nuntiandi*. But what made the meditations especially rich was the application of Saint Ignatius's discernment rules to the experience of running a major diocese. The retreat, which tackled a huge range of lights and shadows in the modern Church, displayed Bergoglio's formidable depth of vision.

Addressing fellow bishops in a European nation where the Church felt beleaguered by a hostile state and a sharp drop in religious practice, he warned them against seeing faith in terms of success and failure, of progress and decline, and so missing something deeper. In this mind-set of desolation, he told them, "we take bitter note of the weakening of the faith, declining Mass attendance, and we compare today with the good old days." He went on:

> We forget that the Christian life is a continual battle against the seductive power of idols, against Satan and his effort to lead man to unbelief, to despair, to moral and physical suicide. We forget that the Christian road is measured not only by the distance traveled, but also by the magnitude of the battle, by the difficulties encountered, by the obstacles overcome, and by the ferocity of the assaults that have been repulsed.
>
> That is why arriving at a sober assessment of the faith in our day is so complicated. Sociological statistics are not sufficient. It is not enough to count the number of Christians, the number who practice, etc. One also has to consider the sometimes dramatic battles that Christians must wage every day in order to continue believing and acting according to the Gospel.[38]

Bergoglio in 2006 was increasingly bold, demonstrating more and more of the *parrhesia*, or apostolic courage, of which he spoke regularly in that retreat. Back in Rome for the post-synod meetings after the Spanish retreat, he met Pope Benedict in a bid to free the Argentine Church from the Sodano-Caselli nexus, which since 2003 had been strengthened by Sodano's appointment of a conservative nuncio to Argentina, Adriano Bernardini. According to media reports based on Vatican sources, for some years the views of the Argentine episcopate had been ignored in the selection of new bishops: the conservative appointees were favorites of Caselli and Aguer, not of the Argentine bishops' conference. When he returned to Buenos Aires, Bergoglio was quick to play down the suggestion of any conflict—"the Holy Spirit is not in those who have made a political reading of church affairs," he said—but spoke warmly of the pope, rather than the Holy See. A few months later, the matter was partly resolved when Benedict XVI removed Sodano as secretary of state, although Bergoglio's appointees would continue to be blocked in Rome.

Back in Buenos Aires, Bergoglio and Kirchner continued to dance around each other. The president had avoided John Paul II's funeral (Duhalde and Menem were there) but attended Benedict XVI's installation; when the ambassador to the Holy See tried to bring the cardinal and the president together beforehand, they both said it was unnecessary. But in April there was a brief thaw, on the occasion of a prayer service remembering the 1976 massacre of the Pallottine fathers at the church where they were killed, a religious event that Kirchner could embrace politically.

It was uncertain if the president would come, and he arrived late, but Bergoglio insisted on waiting on the steps of San Patricio parish. When he arrived, they shook hands and went inside together. Kirchner prayed the Our Father. It was a brief moment, says Marco Gallo of the Sant'Egidio Community, who organized the event, "but it suggested that something else was possible." As he left the service, Kirchner told journalists that he had never had a bad relationship with the Church. No one believed him: the fact that he was in the same place as the cardinal qualified as news.[39]

Having refused to attend the May 25 Te Deum at the cathedral the year before amid tension over the president's unilateral sacking of a military chaplain, Kirchner returned to the cathedral for the 2006 national ceremony. The cardinal preached on the Beatitudes in an address that had not been sent beforehand to the Casa Rosada. "Blessed are we when we stand against hatred and permanent confrontation, because we do not want the chaos and disorder which leave us hostages to empires" was one, widely reported dart, aimed at the soft flesh of the Kirchners' anti-imperialist discourse. A more skilled and secure politician would have turned the address to his advantage by engaging with it; but that would have meant acknowledging a spiritual authority outside the state. By taking umbrage—Kirchner would never step inside the cathedral again—he made himself look weak, and Bergoglio paradoxically powerful.[40]

Later that year relations again nosedived after the retiring bishop of Puerto Iguazú ran against the state governor of Misiones, a Kirchner crony, in order to prevent his perpetual reelection. The Spanish-born bishop Joaquín Piña—who won by 60 percent of the vote—saw it as a local matter of justice for the people of Misiones; Kirchner saw it as the Church defying the government. On the grounds that Bergoglio was president of the bishops' conference and both men were Jesuits, Kirchner publicly accused the cardinal of orchestrating the campaign, declaring him to be—in a phrase that would become famous—"the spiritual leader of the political opposition."

The cardinal, as always avoiding direct confrontation, stayed silent, but a week later, giving the homily during a massive pilgrimage to the national shrine at Luján—over two million went that year—he criticized elites distant from the people who foment the division among them. He prayed to the Virgin to be allowed to live as brothers and sisters, free from the devil, "the father of discord." The news media called Marcó insistently, demanding to know if the cardinal was referring to the Kirchners. "Say that I was aiming it at everyone," Bergoglio told him. But the line wasn't convincing, and Marcó allowed himself, on one call, to express the personal opinion that it was not good for presidents to point accusing fingers. In the furor that followed, Kirchner said that if pursuing justice for his people was sowing discord, then he was sowing discord. He added, in the acid language of old-fashioned anticlericalism, that "the devil gets to everyone: those of use who wear trousers and those who wear soutanes."[41]

Kirchner now took a cue from the regimes he admired in Cuba and Venezuela, and began to treat Bergoglio not just as an enemy of the government but of the state (there was little distinction in his mind). A senior Catholic layman who at this time went to see the cardinal was surprised to find a classical radio station playing in his office at a volume higher than background music, yet not so loud to prevent them speaking. When the layman commented on this, Bergoglio took him to the window and pointed down at a white truck with aerials on its roof. He explained that the SIDE—the state intelligence agency—had a highly sensitive microphone trained on his window that could pick up conversations. But it wasn't a problem, he said, because after a pang of conscience the engineer in the truck had come to confess what he was doing. Not wanting the man to lose his job, they had agreed that the eavesdropping should continue, but with the right level of music to prevent Kirchner's men hearing him across the Plaza de Mayo.

THE photo of the cardinal on his knees, eyes closed, with pastors holding their hands over his bowed head, created shock waves when it appeared in *La Nación*, and led some traditionalist Catholics to declare him an apostate. Bergoglio's bold move came at a charismatic prayer gathering of thousands at a Buenos Aires stadium in June 2006. His growing openness, in his late sixties, to charismatic spirituality—involving Spirit-filled praise, praying in tongues, and an early-church expectation of miracles and wonders—represented a significant shift in his interior life.

From his early days as archbishop, building on Quarracino's existing relationships and assisted by Father Marcó, who was involved in interreligious dialogue, Bergoglio had developed strong bonds with leaders of the historic Protestant and Orthodox churches, as well as with Jewish and Muslim leaders. The relationships were forged during various crises between Cardinal Ratzinger's *Dominus Iesus* in 2000—a Vatican document that offended non-Catholic Christians—and Mel Gibson's 2004 movie *The Passion of the Christ*, which was perceived as anti-Semitic. The dialogue bore fruit, above all, in the economic crisis of 2001–2002, which saw a series of meetings, declarations, and pledges to work together to tackle common problems. As a result, by 2005 Buenos Aires—to a unique extent in Latin America and possibly the world—had a flourishing interreligious and interchurch dialogue, at the heart of which was Bergoglio's web of friendships. Marco Gallo, head of the Sant'Egidio community in Buenos Aires, recalls that at an interreligious meeting in 2004 organized by the bishops' conference, "Bergoglio was the one most at ease with the faith leaders. He knew them all really well."

But while relations with the historic Churches were warm, Bergoglio at that stage had few links with evangelicals. Before the Second Vatican Council the Catholic Church considered them heretics, after it, separated brethren; but as Pentecostalism expanded in Latin America in the 1980s and 1990s, they were disparagingly described in Catholic documents as "sects." Bergoglio had no links to them before being made a bishop, and inherited no relationships when he took over from Quarracino. That changed only after he began to get to know Catholic charismatics.

The so-called charismatic renewal began in the Catholic Church in the late 1960s after Catholics were prayed over by Pentecostals, and came to share with them the conviction that the Church was being called to a new baptism in the Spirit. The official estimate for the number of charismatic Catholics is 120 million, perhaps 20–25 percent of the practicing Catholic population in the world.

Charismatics use a spiritual style of worship similar to that of Pentecostal evangelicals, combining it with a fully sacramental and orthodox Catholic belief and practice. As Jesuit provincial, Bergoglio, like other church leaders at the time, had little time for this phenomenon, and in the 1970s criticized charismatics for "claiming to be in possession of the Holy Spirit."[42] Both he and the provincial who succeeded him, Andrés Swinnen, forbade Alberto Ibáñez Padilla—the Jesuit who brought the renewal to Argentina—from being involved. As Francis explained in 2013 on the plane back from Rio de Janeiro, he used to think that charismatics "confused the holy liturgy with a school of samba," but that later he was "converted when I got to know them better and saw the good they do."

The conversion happened in 1999, when he began celebrating an annual Mass for the charismatic Catholics in Buenos Aires. "He saw what was holy and profound in the charismatic renewal," recalls one of its leaders in Buenos Aires who later became a close collaborator of Bergoglio's. "He said, 'When I hear the praise as I'm coming to the altar, I feel my heart fill.' As a man of deep prayer, he recognized that this was the Holy Spirit." They asked him if, when he raised the eucharistic host and chalice, he could allow them fifteen seconds of praying in tongues, and he agreed.

In 2000 Bergoglio began giving talks at the Catholic charismatics' annual school of formation, in which he developed his thinking about the renewal of the Church: how lay people needed to assume their responsibility to evangelize, how the Church had to get out into the street, how he preferred a Church that was bruised and dirty to one that stayed inside. "Everything you hear Francis saying now," says Bergoglio's collaborator, "he said to the charismatic renewal in those talks."

Out of a friendship born in Italy between the Buenos Aires evangelical pastor Jorge Himitian and a Catholic charismatic renewal leader, Matteo Calisi, a unique ecumenical initiative was born in Argentina, started by four evangelical pastors and four lay Catholics.The Communion of Renewed Evangelicals and Catholics in the Holy Spirit (CRECES) began to hold prayer-and-praise type gatherings from 2003, and grew rapidly amid talk of a fresh outpouring of the Holy Spirit. In 2004 and 2005 the cardinal discreetly attended the CRECES gatherings, not getting involved ("I'll just be there like everybody else," he told the organizers), but sat among the Catholics and evangelicals, with his flask and gourd of mate, observing the invocations of the Spirit, the high-octane "praise" music, the initially unsettling practice of singing in tongues, and the way people prayed over each other, confident of the healing power of the Holy Spirit.

In June 2006, when CRECES invited the pope's official preacher, the charismatic friar Raniero Cantalamessa, to preach in Buenos Aires, Bergoglio arranged for the event to be held in the seven-thousand-seat-capacity Luna Park stadium. Amazingly, it was packed that day with an audience made up more of Catholics than evangelicals. An ecumenical gathering on this scale was a first anywhere in the world.

Leading the praise was the Mexican evangelical musician Marcos Witt, and as well as Cantalamessa there were the four CRECES pastors, including Himitian. The cardinal spent the morning, as usual, seated in the rows along with everyone else. At one point, Pastor Witt invited people to take the hand of whoever was beside them and pray for them. Bergoglio was caught by the photographer Enrique Cangas in an intense prayer with a forty-two-year-old evangelical, the cardinal's head resting on the man's shoulder. Edgardo Brezovec later said he had not known who it was, and only realized when the people behind him said the priest was the archbishop of Buenos Aires.

In the afternoon, when Bergoglio was invited to come up and speak, he asked the preachers first to pray for him, and knelt, with his head bowed, as they held their hands over him. The pastor's prayer was long, in the charismatic style, wordy and urgent, thanking the Lord for raising up a prophetic voice in Argentina, and asking for the cardinal to be blessed with gifts of wisdom and leadership. "Lord, as brothers in Christ, without differences or barriers, we bless him, in the name of Jesus of Nazareth, and ask you to cancel out all power of evil over your servant," intoned Pastor Norberto Saracco, who, as the stadium erupted in applause, ended with a crescendo of invocation: "Fill him with your Spirit and power, Lord! In the name of Jesus!"

When Bergoglio took the microphone he spoke of the beauty of a people becoming a "reconciled diversity," in which no one had to give up being who they were, yet who could walk together in a common path. He went on to preach around three themes: the wind, the embrace, and the wound. But what was extraordinary, especially to those who knew him, was the new fervor—the passion, urgency, clarity, and strength—with which he preached. He even shook raised arms and stabbed the air in the best revivalist tradition.

The cardinal was on fire.

"That was a turning point," says Pastor Himitian's daughter, the journalist and Bergoglio biographer Evangelina Himitian. "He began to feel much freer. The key was his openness to the Spirit, his letting himself be guided by a new experience, even at his age." Thereafter Bergoglio would not just attend CRECES meetings but be up onstage, staying for the whole day of prayer and praise. Enrique Cangas, a freelance photographer who followed the cardinal around for twelve years, says: "The best smile I ever got from him—almost the only one in all that time—was at CRECES."

The next surprise came straight after that Luna Park gathering. Bergoglio, who did not know the pastors, told Himitian he would like to pray regularly with them. "So we met once a month, beginning in 2006," the pastor recalls,

> four or sometimes five of us, for an hour and a half. We talked a little about the situation and we prayed together for the country and for society. We didn't speak about Scripture, we mostly just prayed. We prayed spontaneously, the way we evangelicals do, and he did the same, prayed with great directness and simplicity. From the first day he asked us to use [the informal] *vos* rather than [the formal] *usted*,

and to forget "archbishop" and "cardinal"—either we're brothers or we're not, he'd say. We discovered a man who was humble, simple; a man of prayer, close to the people.

The pastors—Himitian, Saracco, Carlos Mraida, Angel Negro, and later Omar Cabrera of the Future Vision Church—took turns hosting the meetings, to which Bergoglio would always arrive by bus and subway. The pastors saw the meetings as a fulfillment of Jesus's words in Matthew, chapter 18, that when two or three gather in His name, He would be among them. In this case, it was two or three churches, traditions, rivals for five hundred years, that were now praying together, united by the same Holy Spirit.

After one of the meetings, in 2009, Himitian told the cardinal that they were concerned that the Catholic Church was talking about a new evangelization, yet 95 percent of its priests had not had a personal experience of the Risen Christ. "Jorge [Bergoglio] said, 'I agree. What do you suggest?'" The pastors proposed a spiritual retreat for clergy in which they would preach on conversion. "We told him: 'We'll get the pastors, you get the priests.' He agreed and pulled out his diary and asked, 'What date?'"

It was held in the bishops' retreat house in 2010, the pastors preaching to around a hundred clergy for a day and a half. It was repeated in 2012, this time with Father Cantalamessa joining the pastors after returning to Luna Park. There were objections from people in both traditions. Some of the Catholic bishops didn't like it, and the pastors were given a hard time by some evangelicals. But the priests liked it. And nobody was trying to convert anybody, except to the one Jesus Christ. For Bergoglio, it was about "reconciled diversity."

The pope's preacher was bowled over. In all his years spent on the spiritual frontier between Catholics and evangelicals, he had never seen anything like it. "The whole Church is watching very carefully what is happening in Buenos Aires," Father Cantalamessa told the thousands on his return to Luna Park in 2012.[43]

BERGOGLIO's boldness in the years after the 2005 conclave was also born of a sense that the Church in Latin America was resuming its historic journey to integration, to becoming *la patria grande*, and a source for the world Church.

Just days after John Paul II's death, Bergoglio finished a prologue to a book by his friend in the Vatican, Guzmán Carriquiry. The book, *Una Apuesta por América Latina* ("Betting on Latin America"), was an essay on the continent's historic destiny and challenges, to which Bergoglio's prologue reads like a State of the (Latin-American) Union address.

"This is the time for educators and builders," the cardinal declared. "In the next two decades Latin America will play a key role in the great battles that are taking shape in the twenty-first century." Above all, he wrote, "it is time to move along the paths to integration, toward the configuration of the South-American Union and the Latin-American *patria grande*." The journey would mean confronting major challenges: new models of sustainable economic development to defeat some of the sharpest social inequalities on the planet, as well as a reform of politics and the state to ensure that these served the common good. Yet none of this could happen without "a vast task of education, mobilization, and participation" of peoples—an "organized community" that drew on "a Catholic and Latin-American self-consciousness."

The door to this bold future was a new evangelization to unleash the energies of solidarity, freedom, and hope. What would close that door would be a return to anachronistic ideologies or the decadent culture of "individualistic ultra-liberalism" and "consumerist hedonism."

Bergoglio saw particular dangers in two kinds of "weak thinking." The first was an imperialistic version of globalization that destroys particular identities (he suggested that the proper image of a "true" globalization was not a sphere but a polyhedron, in which each culture preserved its own identity but united in a common good). The second was what he called an "adolescent progressivism" based on a militant secularism— he had in mind not just *kirchnerismo* in Argentina but *chavismo* in Venezuela—which was merely a new imperialism of state-centered ideologues. Both of these strains threatened to sap evangelizing energies and condemn Latin America to endless destructive cycles.[44]

The task now was to equip the Latin-American Church for that historic task of evangelization. A month after the conclave, Bergoglio was in Lima, Peru, to commemorate the fiftieth anniversary of the founding of CELAM. He said it was time for a continent that included half of the world's Catholics "to lend a service to the universal Church," to share the gifts that the Holy Spirit had showered on its people. "This is the prophetic dimension that Latin America must assume in this Fifth Conference," he told them.[45] When the theologian Father Carlos Galli, on his way to a planning meeting for the Conference, called the cardinal to ask him if there was any point he wished him to emphasize, Bergoglio told him: "Christ and the poor." Galli thought that was a little obvious and asked him two more times if there was anything else. "Three times he gave me the same answer: 'Christ and the poor,'" Galli recalls.

The path to that new continent-wide gathering, the first since 1992, had encountered endless knots in the last years of John Paul II, but one by one they began to be untied. John Paul II's secretary of state, Cardinal Sodano, and the Latin-American *curiali* who had with him streamrollered CELAM at Santo Domingo, had opposed the idea of another General Conference, arguing instead for a special synod in Rome—part of their strategy to reduce CELAM to a secretariat rather than the voice of the local Church. But Benedict XVI did not indulge their view. After his election, the pope held a meeting with four Latin-American cardinals: the new CELAM president, Francisco Errázuriz of Santiago, Chile; Pedro Rubiano Sáenz, archbishop of Bogotá, Colombia, where CELAM was based; the Brazilian Claudio Hummes, recently appointed to head a Vatican department; and Bergoglio of Buenos Aires. At that meeting it was agreed that the Fifth General Conference would be held in Latin America, at the shrine of Aparecida, Brazil, in May 2007.

Alberto Methol Ferré, the visionary whose conviction that Latin America was becoming a source Church had so influenced Bergoglio, was too ill to attend Aparecida, and he died two years later. But like Moses on Mount Nebo glimpsing the Promised Land at the end of his life, the Uruguayan prophet lived to see it happen. In his intellectual testament, *Latin America in the Twenty-First Century*, which Bergoglio would distribute to many friends when it came out, Methol Ferré had predicted that Benedict XVI's engagement with the Latin-American Church in the 1980s would bring about a new spring of Latin-American Catholic thinking loyal to the Magisterium.[46] That, essentially, is the story of Aparecida.

It now seems clear that Benedict XVI shared Methol Ferré's view that Latin America was becoming a source for the universal Church. According to Carriquiry, on the flight from São Paulo to Aparecida to open the CELAM assembly, Benedict XVI said: "I am convinced that from here will be decided—at least in part, but a fundamental part—the future of the Catholic Church. For me this has always been clear."[47]

This also explains the apparent paradox that Benedict XVI, who as Cardinal Ratzinger had provided the theological justification for Vatican centralism in the 1980s and 1990s, now allowed CELAM to prepare for the Fifth Conference in complete freedom, without interference from Rome, yet with his support and blessing—just as had happened in Medellín (1968) at the time of Paul VI. The Peruvian theologian Gustavo Gutiérrez, pioneer of liberation theology, would later say that "Aparecida mostly happened thanks to Ratzinger."[48]

Cardinal Bergoglio, who redacted the magnificent final document that came out of that gathering, described it as "an act of the magisterium of the Latin-American Church" which Benedict XVI had green-lighted: "the pope gave general indications on the problems of Latin America, and then left it open: over to you, over to you!," he recalled later that year.[49] Benedict fully recognized this magisterium—the authority to teach—of the Latin-American Church because it was carried out in dialogue with the pope; it was *cum et sub Petro*. CELAM's president, Cardinal Errázuriz, recalls that "we took the conclusions to Pope Benedict XVI for him to look at and approve, but he said he wasn't going to approve them in order not to confuse the episcopal with the pontifical magisterium." The pope would later pay his own compliment to the document by quoting often from it. Aparecida, recalls Cardinal Errázuriz, was "a beautiful experience of communion with the pope."

The three-week meeting of two hundred Latin-American bishops in the great Marian shrine one hundred miles northeast of São Paolo was held next to the world's largest basilica. Smaller than St. Peter's, yet holding many more (forty-five thousand), and drawing twelve million visitors a year, the basilica houses the little blackened wooden statue of the Virgin which is the source of all the fuss. In 1717 the statue turned up in the nets of three fishermen from nearby Guaratinguetá who had prayed to her for a good catch. The miracles attributed to her raised the dignity of the fishermen and slaves, and it is above all the poor who continue to flock to her shrine.

The constant backdrop of God's holy faithful people was a reminder of what Benedict XVI in his opening address called "the rich and profound popular religiosity" of the Latin-American peoples that was the

Catholic Church's "precious treasure." Bergoglio would later say that the document "was born of the interplay between the labors of the bishops and the simple faith of the pilgrims, under Mary's maternal protection." The theme of popular religiosity became, as a result of the Argentine contingent at the conference, a key theme in the document.

The Aparecida gathering offered a glimpse of what the synod of bishops in Rome could be. Rather than working from a predetermined document, it began with a diagnosis of contemporary culture and trends from each country, then worked them into concrete issues that could be discussed. It was bottom-up, not, as in the synods, top-down. Key to its success were warm relationships between the different national bishops' conferences, and a close friendship between the conference's two principals, the CELAM president, Cardinal Errázuriz, and the chair of the drafting commission, Cardinal Bergoglio. Father Mariano Fazio, an Argentine priest of Opus Dei sent out from Rome as one of the eleven theological experts, was struck by the collegiality of the meeting. "There were disagreements, as is right and normal, because there are different points of view, but there was a basic unity. Those who had been in Santo Domingo told me they couldn't believe the contrast with Aparecida." The Vatican representatives were warmly received, and spoke with complete freedom. But it was CELAM's show.

Speaking first as president of the Argentine bishops' conference, Bergoglio said that those who earlier had been spoken of as marginalized or oppressed could now be called *sobrantes*, the left-over people, because they are superfluous to a market economy that does not need them. He linked that idea to what he called the *cultura del descarte*, the throwaway culture: the poor, the elderly, the children, the unborn, the migrants—these were now dispensed with like out-of-date gadgets. In his homily at a huge Mass in the shrine after the departure of Benedict XVI, Bergoglio used another striking metaphor when he spoke for the first time (at least in a major public arena) of *las periferias existenciales*, the existential margins. Almost every bishop at Aparecida lived in a city whose peripheries were being constantly swelled by the arrival of migrants, and the phrase struck many chords. It suggested not just the slums, but a world of vulnerability and fragility, a place of suffering and longing and poverty, yet also joy and hope—the place where Christ had chosen to reveal Himself in contemporary Latin America.

It was this genius for identifying trends and giving them a new, startling language that led the delegates to vote overwhelmingly for Bergoglio to take charge of writing the concluding document. It was an epic task of synthesis that required distilling and converging proposals emerging from a host of subcommissions, then securing approval for modifications as the document developed. "It was amazing to watch him move in Aparecida," recalls Father Víctor Manuel Fernández, then vice-dean of the Catholic University in Buenos Aires, "to see his ability to knit together a consensus, to create the right atmosphere, to instill trust."[50] Fazio recalls that "he acted with a super-low profile and real efficiency. He spoke with everyone, was always available, forged agreements between people of different views, never lost his cool, and worked hard late into the night, always smiling." It was a brilliant performance that brought people clapping to their feet at the end of the conference. Bergoglio left Aparecida a leader of the Latin-American Church.

Yet throughout he had been almost invisible to the outside world, glimpsed usually deep in conversation while walking with other bishops and staying well clear of the media. "A tall, thin, serious-looking man, he has always refused to give interviews to the press," complained one correspondent, who resorted to asking a Central-American participant who had met him for the first time to describe the Argentine cardinal. "He is very silent, and offers an opinion only when he is asked," said the delegate. "He is very humble. But also very intelligent. He is a holy man."[51]

Together with another Argentine theologian, Father Carlos Galli, Fernández assisted Bergoglio in the final task of drafting. Both were thoroughly imbued in the Argentine *teología del pueblo*; Galli was a disciple of its pioneer, Lucio Gera. Bergoglio was keen that the final document boost the importance of popular religiosity, and asked the theologians to draft those sections, which are among the document's most beautiful and striking.

The Argentines were aware that, even though the document was the fruit of consensus—each paragraph had to be voted on by delegates—the Argentines' emphasis on popular religiosity took the document in a different direction from what had been planned. "In a complicated moment, Bergoglio said to Fernández, 'If the document turns out badly, they're going to blame us, because here we are, three Argentines working on it,'" recalls Galli. But they pulled it off. Cardinal Errázuriz says this part of the document was very much an Argentine contribution—"we were struck by how much Argentina valued popular religiosity"—but says the delegates were grateful. "The text is easily the best thing there is on popular religiosity. We applauded the Argentines for how they reflected it."

Bergoglio's other achievement at Aparecida was less visible, yet also far reaching.

Early in the drafting, many delegates wanted the document to begin with an analysis of contemporary realities using the traditional see-judge-act method. Bergoglio had no problem with the method but wanted it preceded by an introductory chapter on *how* to see, namely, as missionary disciples moved primarily by "the love received from the Father, through Jesus Christ, by the anointing of the Holy Spirit" (no. 14). After debate and some tension, Bergoglio's view carried.[52] When, as Pope Francis, he returned to Brazil in July 2013, he spoke to the CELAM leaders of "a temptation that has been present in the Church from the beginning: the attempt to interpret the Gospel apart from the Gospel itself and apart from the Church." He gave the example of the Aparecida meeting, "which, at one particular moment, felt this temptation . . . to opt for a way of 'seeing' that was completely 'antiseptic,' detached, and disengaged, which is impossible. The way we 'see' is always affected by the way we direct our gaze. . . . The question was, 'How are we going to look at reality in order to see it?' Aparecida replied: 'With the eyes of discipleship.'"

That had been his argument with the progressive Jesuits in the 1970s. In claiming to be using scientific analysis to view society's problems, they were discarding the eyes of faith. That left them open to ideology, which turned faith into an instrument—the error of Marxist liberation theology.

The Aparecida document was the fruit of the Argentine Church carrying the flame of Latin-American theology over twenty years, safeguarding the insights of liberation theology from the pitfalls of liberal and Marxist thinking. It had done so by sticking close to the poor and their culture—the *pueblo fiel* hermeneutic—which Bergoglio's Argentine team ensured took pride of place in the document. As a result, Aparecida could safely unleash, to a greater extent even than Medellín in 1968, the riches of the Latin-American Church, and give flesh to its great insight, the option for the poor, which appears dozens of times.

Aparecida was the expression of a new maturity, of a local Church come of age—Methol Ferré's source Church. In its vision and vigor, its fierce advocacy of the poor and its missionary spirituality, its bold proclamation of the birth of a new springtime of faith, Aparecida was now the program, the key to a major new effort of evangelization in Latin America. Nowhere else in the world was there anything to compare with it. That made it, just as obviously, the program for the universal Church.

All that was needed now was a Latin-American pope to bring the flame out from the periphery, into Catholicism's increasingly tired and desolate center.

EIGHT

MAN FOR OTHERS

(2008–2012)

To FIND CRITICS of Cardinal Bergoglio it helps to go north from Avenida Rivadavia to the Barrio Norte, which is not one but many barrios bordering the banks of the River Plate. In the neighborhoods of La Recoleta, Palermo, Belgrano, and Olivos, great avenues—Libertador, Santa Fe, Córdoba—fan out from Retiro station like spokes from a hub, past the Jockey Club and the Aeroparque and the Hippodrome, the museums and the art galleries and the embassies. The streets here are lined with marble-fronted apartment blocks that look out on craft markets and organic pasta stalls. There are awesome mansions and high-rises, but mostly these streets glimpse Argentina's frustrated destiny as a middle-class crossroads of European urbanity and New World ambition. This is the Buenos Aires people hope to live in and try hard not to leave.

For Catholics in the Barrio Norte, Francis has been a revelation, for they hardly knew Cardinal Bergoglio. But for the launch of some book whose prologue he had written, he was seldom present at gatherings or functions, and people complain that he hardly ever came to parish functions or dinners, and when he did he couldn't get away fast enough, saying his brain didn't work well after 9:00 p.m. "I don't know if he didn't feel comfortable there, but he didn't see it as a priority," says the recently retired bishop of San Isidro, Jorge Casaretto. It wasn't just geographical. A senior priest who has spent many years working to connect the business world with the Church's social teaching says Bergoglio "showed no interest at all in the middle-class world of Catholics—not the world of business, or banking, or the arts or university."

This was not a pastoral neglect. Barrio Norte had a bishop, and no shortage of clergy to minister there. Nor was this an inverse social prejudice: Cardinal Bergoglio had relationships with people of all backgrounds, including the wealthy, the powerful, and academics. But he only had so much time away from his desk and the cathedral, and he chose to spend it in the poorer parts of the city. This choice, exercised consistently over thirteen years, gave the cardinal an elder son problem. In the Gospel parable of the Prodigal Son, a dissolute younger brother returns to the loving embrace of his forgiving, indulgent father, while his upright elder sibling—who had worked the fields all the time his feckless brother drank away the family inheritance—seethes with resentment. The father focuses on his younger son not because he loves him more but because the prodigal son needs him more, and has a heart cracked open by repentance to receiving his father's love. The parable is the iconic gospel tale of God's reckless mercy. But it might also be about what happens in a diocese whose bishop takes seriously the preferential option for the poor.

A distinguished group of Barrio Norte liberal Catholics complains—just as the Jesuit intellectuals in the Argentine province did in the 1980s—about Bergoglio's embrace of popular devotions. Their assumption is that the poor need to be weaned off their premodern religiosity, not indulged by their archbishop. The María Desatanudos fervor drives one priest in this group to distraction: "What sense can it have, in a city stuffed with devotions, to introduce another?" Under Bergoglio, he complains, "popular devotion has become the paradigmatic piety." Listening to them develop this topic—calls to improve catechesis and the understanding of the sacraments—it's hard not to hear something of the elder sibling: on the one hand are the faithful Catholics who turn up to Mass weekly and worship according to the rules and the rubrics; and on the other there are those people who don't seem to go to Mass much at all, yet who turn out in great numbers on pilgrimage to the national shrine of Luján, often arriving drunk.

Other groups in the Barrio Norte raise different objections. The anti-Peronists object that the cardinal's style of government was personalist rather than republican, and that his idea of *pueblo* risked confusing a political with a theological category. Left-wing intellectuals suspect him because of Yorio and Jalics, right-wing intellectuals say he gave too much time to social commentary rather than morality. Liturgical traditionalists claim he made it hard for Catholics to celebrate the old Mass, progressives that he didn't oppose the Vatican. In the Barrio Norte, in short, there are many critics, and they are happy to share their views, before adding what a wonderful pope Francis is—and asking not to be identified.

Barrio Norte Catholics took the same image from TV as everyone else, and saw Bergoglio as aloof and dour. Their refrain is one of metamorphosis: unable to reconcile the unsmiling cardinal in Argentina with the joyful and charismatic pope in Rome, they say it's a miracle how he's changed. Juan Martín Ezratty, a documentary maker who lives in the Barrio Norte, used to have this view, too. But scrolling through archive footage of Bergoglio in the slums or at shrine festivals like San Cayetano to make a film about Francis's pre-papal existence, he was shocked to find a different man from the one he thought he knew, one whose face was lit up like the pope's.

Father Lorenzo "Toto" de Vedia, who runs a team of three priests in Villa 21, says Bergoglio preferred the southern zone because "he is a son of Medellín: that was the Church that nurtured him, a poor Church, for the poor." Viewed from Father Toto's Virgin of Caacupé parish, Buenos Aires looks very different. Here, forty-five thousand people are jammed into 175 acres, in brick and corrugated iron houses squeezed up against each other on narrow dusty streets zigzagged by feral kids and stray dogs. While men in overalls drill and hammer, teenagers with tattoos and nose rings drape street corners, and somewhere, above the banging and barking dogs, there is shouting and crying and the *thud-thud* of a ghetto blaster. The people here are smaller and darker, and, being mostly Paraguayan, many speak Guaraní, while their Spanish lacks the Italianate *porteño* lilt of Buenos Aires speech. They are eager to share Padre Jorge stories.

In Villa 21, as in other slums and working-class parishes across the southern part of town, the story is precisely the reverse of the refrain in the Barrio Norte. Here people say that Bergoglio and Francis are the same, that how he is now on Wednesdays in St. Peter's Square is how he was in the *villas*. They say Padre Jorge came around all the time, at least once a month, to give talks or retreats, to hear their confessions, or sometimes just to *callejear*, to walk down those streets and chat, maybe go inside somebody's house to share a mate, ask about the kids. Almost everyone in the little choked streets around Caacupé parish can prove this with photos on their phones. They say Padre Jorge always stayed for the big festivals, including the last one, the Virgin of Caacupé in December 2012, just before he left for Rome and never came back. At the festival, they remember, he had taken his turn serving the *choclo*, the chewy blanched sweet corn, and the cheesy-doughy balls called *chipás*.

Bergoglio made the decision, from the start, to focus on these peripheries, choosing to spend some time every weekend in the new barrios. Despite the Kirchners' angry antiestablishment rhetoric, their policies consistently benefitted the urban middle classes, not the poor. Numbers living in slum housing rose from 10 percent in 2004, when the economy had picked up again, to 17 percent in 2010, when the bishops estimated that 11 percent of children there went hungry. But the peripheries also meant the suffering and the vulnerable: hospital patients and prisoners, the addicted and the afflicted. Bergoglio would spend entire nights hearing confessions at the shrines of saints on their the feast days—the Virgin of Luján, San Cayetano, San Pantaleón, the Miraculous Medal—and when he wasn't in the confessional, he would spend two or three hours in the crowds, hearing stories and exchanging hugs. Where he went, his priests followed: some of his youngest and most able clergy were sent to work in the *villas* or in the hospitals and prisons, or to minister to the crowds at the sanctuaries.

Bergoglio evangelized the city from its margins. "The idea is that the Church is first among the poor and from there reaches out to everyone," says Father Gustavo Carrara, whom Bergoglio put as the head of his slum priests' vicariate. "It's the opposite of what in economics is called the trickle-down effect—only it never does trickle down. It's not about the poor and only the poor. It's *from* them, to the rest." The vicariate, created in August 2009, was a way to incorporate the pastoral slum outreach into the official structure of the diocese. Its first coordinator, Father Pepe Di Paola, says that for Bergoglio "the center of Buenos Aires is not the Plaza de Mayo, where the power resides, but *las periferias*, the outskirts of the city."[1]

In Latin America the majority poor live their faith differently from the minority middle class. Religious expression isn't a moment in the week but throughout the week; the sacred is part of life. That gives rise, says Carrara, to a culture organized around transcendent values rather than wealth and power. Hence the conviction of the twenty-two slum priests he works with, that in the *villas* they receive more than they give. Hence, too, the respect the priests give to forms of popular religiosity— the devotions and the processions, the shrine festivals and the offerings, the novenas and the rosaries—which are described so powerfully in the Aparecida document as the place where the poor encounter God, make vital decisions, and are converted. Carrara, a smart and thoughtful priest, a Bergoglio disciple, accepts that everyone's faith needs purifying, but he is cautious about judging, say, people who might not go every week to Sunday Mass but who go daily during festivals. "In the end, the only one who can measure faith is God."

Carrara thinks Bergoglio went to slum *fiestas* but not Barrio Norte cocktail parties because in the fiestas the poor celebrate Christ, not themselves. "A fiesta has a different dimension: with Mass, food, dances in honor of the Virgin, Christ. The fiestas are happening because they are feasts of Christ and the Virgin. They're linked to the religious, yet with a deep human dimension." Father Toto agrees. "Here in the *villas* they live values that have been lost elsewhere: the people know each other, and the neighbor is very important. To have the basics, to survive, you have to depend on others. And that produces a strong sense of community, for good and ill. The guy you were in a knife fight with yesterday you stay up all night with, because his mother is ill. It's an intense existence."

Bergoglio wanted the city to learn from this solidarity. He told a Caritas retreat in 2010 that the slums could teach the people in the tall apartment buildings how to create fraternal bonds. At the end of 2012, in an interview with Father Juan Isasmendi on the Villa 21 community radio, he said that he had always been struck by two things in the barrios:

First is a great sense of solidarity. You can be pretty pissed at someone, or whatever, but there's a need and immediately solidarity makes itself felt. It does me good to see solidarity. There's less egotism than in other parts, there's more solidarity. The second thing is the faith that is here, faith in the Virgin, faith in the saints, faith in Jesus. I'm really struck by how, not just this one, but all the [shantytowns] are barrios of faith. It's true, Jesus always made clear that where there was humility it was easier for faith to enter. He said: "If you don't become like a little child, you won't enter the Kingdom." And "if you're not pure in heart, if you're not poor in your heart, it's difficult to enter the Kingdom." When you have a humble life, and you live from your work, which is what gives us our dignity, then faith takes root even more. These two things have always struck me: solidarity and faith. Put them together, and what do you get? The ability to celebrate. It's great how in these barrios people celebrate, make fiesta—they're joyful. So you have those two things, faith and solidarity, and when you put them together you get joy.

WHAT convinced Bergoglio to create the new slum priests' vicariate in August 2009 was the drug dealers a few months earlier announcing their intention to kill Padre Pepe.

The dealers didn't like a declaration by the slum priests in March that year in response to a congress debate on the decriminalization of drugs. The priests said that drugs were already de facto legal in the *villas*, where they were bought and sold with impunity, and wreaked havoc in the lives of fragile people. The priests also objected to the media assumption that drug-linked violence and crime was a problem that came out of the *villas* and affected the city; in fact, they pointed out, the drugs and all that went with them came from outside, peddled by dealers working for men in suits and fast cars who lived in the Barrio Norte. The priests went on to document the effect of crack cocaine (*paco*) and the diabolic way in which adolescent craving for love and acceptance was exploited and perverted into addiction and enslavement to criminal gangs. Finally, they made a number of practical suggestions for attacking the problem at its root.[2]

The document was headline news, and provoked media discussion over many days. Padre Toto's predecessor in Villa 21 was Padre Pepe. The bearded young priest who with Bergoglio's support had brought the Virgin of Caacupé to the slum in 1997 was the architect of a thirteen-year parish operation that had given birth to fifteen chapels, a high school, a trade school, a home for the elderly, various soup kitchens, drug prevention programs, a recovery center, two farms where recovering addicts live and work, a day care center for kids, and a community newspaper and radio. As the leader of the slum priests, and with Jesus-like bearded good looks, Padre Pepe inevitably led the media interviews on the drugs document.

The first warning came when he was bicycling back to the parish one night in April, when a man in a suit came out of the shadows and told him to get out. "Once this comes off the news, you're toast," he told Padre Pepe. "They've got you marked."

The next day, after a priests' meeting during which further threats turned up on his cell phone (there were text messages as well as letters), Padre Pepe took Bergoglio aside and told him, "Look Boss, they've threatened to kill me, and I think it could be serious." The cardinal fell silent for a time. "First of all, we have to be calm, because we are acting in accordance with the Gospel," he said, before adding: "If someone has to die, it should be me. I will ask God to take me, and not you."

They agreed that, because the mafia clung to the shadows, the spotlight of public attention would afford the greatest protection. The following day, when the cardinal was celebrating an annual Mass for the start of the academic year, the media were on hand to record him telling two thousand teachers and five thousand students that one of his priests had been threatened by what he called "the merchants of darkness." His homily gave details: "The priests in Villa 21, down by the Riachuelo, recently opened three homes to help young addicts. The drug dealers did not like this. Some have got nervous and threatened to kill a priest." He added: "We don't know how this will end."

The story led that night's news. The next day 356 Buenos Aires priests signed a declaration backing the *curas villeros* and condemning the threat. Padre Pepe went on to a press conference where he gave countless interviews, before returning to the *villa* to find a rally in his support. As he walked with the crowd, people came out of their houses to join in, which led to more first-class TV footage. The following day Bergoglio went as usual to Villa 21 to spend hours walking the streets with Padre Pepe and greeting people, sharing a gourd of mate here, some biscuits there. The message was clear: the shepherds were one with their flock, and ready to die for them. The story was still running the next day, when the streets around Virgin of Caacupé parish were packed with thousands of people chanting for Padre Pepe to stay. The story by this time had been picked up across the world. Over the next months, Bergoglio created the vicariate for slum priests and named Padre Pepe to head it. The vicariate became an interlocutor with the public authorities, negotiating for improvements. The publicity had exposed how little presence the state had in the slums.[3]

The Church, deeply embedded in the lives of the *villeros*, now became their public advocates. When, the following year, Argentina began a series of bicentenary anniversary celebrations of its six-year process of independence from Spain (which began with the town-hall declaration of May 25, 1810, and concluded with the declaration of independence in Tucumán on July 9, 1816), the slum priests' vicariate called for the city to recognize its shanty dwellers not just as objects but as subjects of history. Just as the so-called lower orders (*bajo pueblo*) were the agents of change at the nation's birth yet never got streets named after them, they argued, so history will regard the *villas* of Buenos Aires.

The document argued against both private-property fanatics who claimed the *villeros* were illegal occupants of unowned land, as well as the government bureaucrats who saw the *villas* as a problem to be "solved" from on high. They proposed that the *villeros* should be seen as a distinctive group within the city, with its own customs and mores, to be listened to and dialogued with. During the six-year celebrations of independence, the priests argued, the *villas* should be integrated with the city via a new social agreement that allowed the slum dwellers to be heard as citizens. In the *villas* were youth, energy, a high birthrate, and immigrants ambitious for their children. It was where the Argentine dream began, they said, and in embracing its shantytowns the nation would be owning its future.[4]

FIRED up by Aparecida's call to work for a new order of justice, Bergoglio saw the bicentenary as an opportunity to push for a new *proyecto de país* ("country project") that would give the nation a new birth. If there could be agreement on core values around which Argentines could come together, a series of fundamentals that would survive changes in government, it could transform public life. At the heart of this agreement would be a commitment to eradicate poverty and include the marginalized, promoted by a politics and economics based on the common good. The idea was proposed by the Argentine bishops under Bergoglio's presidency in an extraordinarily ambitious document issued in December 2008 called Toward a Bicentenary in Justice and Solidarity.[5]

The deep thinking behind the document can be found in a prologue Bergoglio wrote to another book by Guzmán Carriquiry. There, Bergoglio noted the price Latin America continued to pay for its elites' utopian, disincarnate ideas of liberty, detached from both the lived reality and the core values of the *pueblo*. This was not a new idea: he had written much the same in the 1970s. But the times had changed: what held the *pueblo* back was no longer messianic Marxist ideology but what he called a "theist gnosticism," a new, disembodied thinking that in Church terms could be expressed as "God without Church, a Church without Christ, Christ without a people." Against this elite "airspray theism," Bergoglio set what he called *lo concreto católico*, the "concrete Catholic thing," which was at the heart of the history and culture of the Latin-American people. The implication was clear: no Latin-American "country project" could be effective without being rooted in the concrete Catholic thing.

He went on to draw a distinction between country, nation, and *patria* ("fatherland"). The first was a geographical area, the second the institutional scaffolding, the third the inheritance of the past that each generation hands on to the next. A country's borders can change, and a nation can be transformed, but the *patria* "either preserves its foundational being or it dies. . . . We can expand it, but not adulterate it."[6] This is the key notion behind the Argentine bishops' bicentenary document: that the Christian values set deep in the national DNA—the foundational being (*ser fundante*) that predated the Argentine nation-state—are the basis on which to construct a new national project.

The bicentenary document was a bold attempt to translate the vision of Aparecida into a new kind of politics. It called for Argentina to "ratify and empower the option of the preferential love for the poor, which flows from our faith in Jesus Christ" and quoted Aparecida's call that "new structures must likewise be created to promote a genuine human coexistence, prevent arrogant domination by some, and facilitate constructive dialogue for the necessary social consensus." By forging new bonds of fraternity and solidarity and an agreement to enshrine the option for the poor in state policy, Bergoglio believed that Argentina could resist the negative impacts of globalization; the dissolution of community and social bonds could be reversed by a strengthening of family and civil society.

The document identified core Argentine structural failings: stubbornly high unemployment despite economic growth, deep-seated public corruption, political clientelism, an explosion of drugs and gambling, a lack of respect for life and family, and, of course, a growing population of *los descartables*, "throwaway people." The new country project was an invitation to learn from the dialogue and solidarity that emerged in the crisis of 2002, and to tackle together Argentina's failures, mobilizing the energies of civil society and renewing public life. Helpfully, the document went on to list suggestions for strengthening the country's institutions and its democracy.

The Casa Rosada, as usual, was not interested. Cristina Kirchner—elected president in December 2007 after Néstor stood aside—was, like her husband, ideologically impervious to the possibility that the Church could have anything to teach politicians. She consented to regular meetings with the bishops to hear their concerns, and generally relations were less tense than with Néstor, yet the policies and politics remained the same, together with the with-us-or-against-us polarized rhetoric, and the official snarling every time the Church offered an X-ray of social ills: whenever the bishops raised their voice over poverty, they were lectured on their "complicity" in the dirty war. But there were glimpses of other possibilities, as when, in 2008, Bergoglio successfully mediated in a dispute between the agricultural sector and the government, which threatened to escalate disastrously; or when, later that year, Cristina accepted an invitation from the cardinal to attend a Mass at the shrine of Luján. Yet the Kirchners were too busy trying to preserve the state from the Church—which they saw through ideological filters as a retrograde corporation—to contemplate working with the bishops to repair the nation's fabric.

Bergoglio kept up the pressure, angry that the Church needed to expand its charitable provision to care for the growing numbers of poor at a time of economic growth. But he was careful not just to blame the government. At the annual San Cayetano Mass in August 2009, for example, Bergoglio deplored the "scandalous" way Argentina failed to take responsibility for its poor, thundering that "in our city every day we see people who have no place, who don't fit, who are surplus, and who are discarded, as if thrown away in existential dump trucks." But he made clear he was criticizing everyone—"we all carry the blame"—and held up frivolous consumerism as an example of how money was diverted from where it was needed. Rewriting the words in Matthew, chapter 25, Bergoglio said Jesus would tell people at the Last Judgment: "Go away from me because I was hungry, and you gave me nothing to eat, for you were busy blaming the government."[7]

※

THERE was one issue over which a direct confrontation with the government was inevitable. Although Cristina was president, it was Néstor Kirchner—then a national deputy—who drove the government's out-of-the-blue same-sex marriage bill in 2010, inspired by the Spanish socialist measure five years earlier. Although he had never shown the least interest in gay rights or gay people, the policy was perfect tinder for Kirchner's polarizing strategy. By positing same-sex marriage as a minority civil rights issue, he could frame the defenders of the traditional understanding of marriage as opponents of equality and the Church as seeking to impose its morality on the law. It was the kind of fight he relished: one that would galvanize the Kirchner political base while throwing his opponents into confusion.

Bergoglio knew many gay people and had spiritually accompanied a number of them. He knew their stories of rejection by their families and what it was like to live in fear of being singled out and beaten up. He told a Catholic gay activist, a former theology professor named Marcelo Márquez, that he favored gay rights as well as legal recognition for civil unions, which gay couples could also access.[8] But he was utterly opposed to any attempt to redefine marriage in law. "He wanted to defend marriage but without wounding anybody's dignity or reinforcing their exclusion," says a close collaborator of the cardinal's. "He favored the greatest possible legal inclusion of gay people and their human rights expressed in law, but would never compromise the uniqueness of marriage as being between a man and a woman for the good of children."

Bergoglio had not raised strong objections to a 2002 civil unions law that applied only to Buenos Aires and that granted rights to any two people cohabiting for more than two years, independent of their gender or sexual orientation. He regarded it as a purely civic, legal arrangement that left marriage unaffected; it granted some privileges but not the right to adopt or any automatic right to inheritance. Yet Bergoglio was criticized from Rome for failing to oppose it when, the following year, the Vatican issued a document binding bishops and politicians to give "clear and emphatic opposition" to any legal recognition of homosexual unions.[9]

At the same time, Bergoglio was quick to react to any attempt to undermine the law's conjugal understanding of marriage. In 2009 he wrote an emphatic letter to the head of the Buenos Aires city government, Mauricio Macri, when he did not immediately strike down an attempt by a judge to authorize—contrary to the law—the "marriage" of a same-sex couple. It was the first time in his eighteen years as a bishop that he openly criticized a public official by name.[10]

Federico Wals, who had been Bergoglio's head of press since 2007, explained in early April 2010 that the cardinal's position was resolutely in favor of the existing law upholding marriage as a union of a man and a woman, and that a same-sex "marriage" was an impossibility. But this did not prevent, he said, revising and extending the concept of civil unions, as long as this left marriage intact. At the plenary meeting of the hundred Argentine bishops a few weeks later, this was the position that Bergoglio, as their president, urged them to adopt as both right and strategically intelligent, warning them that if they opted simply to oppose the bill (without proposing an alternative that advanced civil rights for gay people), they would play into Kirchner's hands and make a same-sex marriage law more likely.

That is precisely what happened.

It was the only occasion during his six-year presidency of the Argentine bishops' conference that Bergoglio lost a vote, albeit narrowly (60 to 40). The *rigoristi*, led by Archbishop Héctor Aguer of La Plata, urged simple opposition on the grounds that the 2003 Vatican document prohibited legal recognition of same-sex unions in any form. Whether the document referred to civil union laws that gave rights to all cohabiting couples, not just same-sex ones, was not clear; but because the document had been signed by the man who was now Benedict XVI, it was easy for Aguer to claim that any endorsement of civil unions was against the pope's wishes and amounted to formal cooperation in what the document called "gravely unjust laws." The Vatican document was a classic example of what the St. Gallen group of cardinals had long criticized as Roman overreach: the document's detailed prescriptiveness tied the hands of local bishops, depriving them of the room to maneuver in any battle to preserve a greater good.

The agreed bishops' declaration, which made no mention of civil unions, was a vigorous defense of marriage as rooted in the complementary sexuality of man and woman, vital to society and to children, whose essential properties were key to their upbringing. The bishops rejected the idea that such a concept was discriminatory, while arguing that a same-sex marriage law would reduce the legal understanding of marriage to a mere partnership, thereby weakening it in the eyes of future generations.[11]

The bill was narrowly passed (126 to 110) by the lower house, the Chamber of Deputies, on May 5, redefining marriage as a partnership between any two people, with full rights to adopt children. The bill then went for endorsement from the upper chamber, where there was strong opposition from most of the seventy-two senators, especially those representing interior provinces. In the run-up to the Senate debate in mid-July, Bergoglio mobilized the diocese, urging Catholics to make their views known and asking for the bishops' statement to be read out in all of the churches on July 8.

But that day another, private letter that Bergoglio had sent a fortnight earlier to the four Carmelite monasteries of Buenos Aires was leaked—how and why is not known. Its dramatic language ensured that it dominated the headlines and eclipsed the public statement. The letter to the nuns has been described as a "dangerous tactic" that backfired.[12] But it wasn't a tactic at all. It formed no part of any political or internal church strategy, and was never intended to be made public. Bergoglio had an intense devotion to the Carmelite saint Thérèse of Lisieux and was close to the Carmelite nuns in Buenos Aires. He had great confidence in their power of prayer, and had often over the years sent the nuns letters asking for their prayers for this or that intention, especially when he was under pressure. This was no exception. "It was a letter in which he was sharing what was in his heart with his intimates, intercessors, in the language of spiritual people," says Bergoglio's close collaborator.

The cardinal told the Carmelites what he discerned at stake in the same-sex marriage legislation: a serious threat to the family that would lead to children being deprived of a father and a mother. It was "a frontal attack on God's law": not simply a political battle but "a bid by the father of lies seeking to confuse and deceive the children of God." He went on to ask for the nuns' prayers for the assistance of the Holy Spirit "to protect us from the spell of so much sophistry of those who favor this law, which has confused and deceived even those of goodwill." He had spotted the serpent's tail, with all its usual telltale signs: hysteria, division, confusion, envy. This was "God's war," as he put it later in his letter.

To anyone who knows his spiritual writings, this was vintage Bergoglio. It was the language he had used with the Jesuits, language that is common among contemplatives, on retreats, or in spiritual direction. He saw behind the political battle another, spiritual contest, in which the devil, driven by and provoking a sense of rivalry (gay people suddenly discovering a resentment at being disqualified from marriage), appeared, as usual, *sub angelo lucis*, in the guise of light (equality, justice, and civil rights—all good things), and thereby deceiving people of goodwill.

At the heart of the bill was a lie: same-sex marriage claimed to add to conjugal marriage or to exist alongside it, while in reality dismantling it. Allowing gay people to marry required that the ancient, natural, God-given institution of matrimony be stripped of the very thing that made it a reflection of the divine plan: the bonding of man and woman, and the begetting and raising of children by their natural parents in a relationship of permanence and sexual exclusivity. As Bergoglio put it in his official, public letter, a law that recognized marriage as male-female did not discriminate but appropriately differentiated—appropriately, because a man-woman bond, like a child's need of a father and a mother, were core human realities. To try to make marriage something else was "a real and serious anthropological step backward."[13]

Taken out of its context of spiritual discernment, and without this accompanying explanation, the letter was a firebomb. It sparked outrage from the *kirchneristas* and considerable discomfort in the Church, where many lamented its language. Because the bishops had vetoed Bergoglio's bid to advance the social inclusion of gay people, Kirchner had been handed a huge target. As he triumphantly declared that it was time for Argentina "definitively to leave behind these obscurantist and discriminatory views," the government-funded Mothers of the Plaza de Mayo dutifully declared that the Church's complicity with dictatorship meant it "lacked the moral authority" to argue on the issue. From China, Cristina Kirchner adopted a presidential pose of regret at the tone of the opposition to the bill. It was a shame, she said, that "equal marriage" was being seen as a question of "religious morality" when "all we're doing is looking at reality as it is."

All eyes were now on the Senate. As Catholics and evangelicals demonstrated outside on July 15, the senators divided into three groupings: those favoring the government bill redefining marriage as gender-neutral, those opposing, and those proposing a French-type *pacte civil* (but which also included the right to adopt). With Bergoglio's backing, the Federal Peronist (anti-Kirchner) senator of San Luis, Liliana Negre de Alonso, brokered an agreement between the second two groups to reject the government bill in favor of an expanded civil unions bill but without the right to adopt children. "The fact that Bergoglio understood the need for an alternative proposal and supported us was a huge comfort," recalls Negre, a member of the Catholic organization Opus Dei. "With great effort we managed to get agreement for a civil union bill that offered practical benefits [to gay people] but left marriage law intact. I sought the advice of many people at that time, among them the cardinal. He called me at home and said, 'You're on the right track.'"

Heading into the debate, the Negre proposal had the support of a clear majority of the senate. But over the next twenty hours, the *kirchnerista* senators used the cardinal's leaked letter to mount a ferocious, scornful attack in the tradition of fanatical anticlericalism. "The things I heard about the cardinal during those twenty-four hours we were in session are unrepeatable," Negre recalls. She was herself reduced to tears with accusations that she was a Nazi who wanted to do to gay people what Hitler did to the Jews. At the end of the debate, the Senate president, under pressure from the leader of the pro-government bloc, arbitrarily nullified the compromise solution, forcing senators to vote yes or no on the government bill. In the midst of confusion and angry scenes, during which a number of senators walked out in protest at the government's steamrollering, the bill passed by just six votes. "We beat Bergoglio!" Negre remembers the head of the *kirchnerista* bloc crowing, "as if the whole debate had been between them and him."[14]

❧

THREE months later, Néstor Kirchner was dead at the age of sixty. His cardiac problems had twice that year led to him being hospitalized—

Bergoglio had sent a priest to offer the sacrament of extreme unction, who had been turned away by Cristina—but the heart attack at his Patagonian home in Santa Cruz was a huge shock. A wake was held at the Casa Rosada, followed by a funeral back in the South. Bergoglio said a requiem Mass at the cathedral the same day the news broke. Given all Kirchner had thrown at the Church and at him in particular, his homily was a model of graciousness. "We are here to pray for a man named Néstor," the cardinal said, "who was received by God's hands and who in his time was anointed by his people."

Kirchner's discourse had exemplified what Bergoglio called adolescent progressivism. It was based on vengeance for the dictatorship and a vindication, politically and morally, of the guerrillas, in which "the people"—in reality, young urban progressives—were pitted against cardboard-cutout enemies: Church, army, establishment newspapers like *Clarín* and *La Nación,* foreign banks, agro-exporters, the United States, and Britain (the list was long).

The government's key allies for the previous seven years had been the human-rights organizations, bound by ties of blood and sympathy to the previous generation's guerrillas. The government had channeled huge sums to many of these groups to fund inquiries and hearings into the dirty war that were then used to bring prosecutions. By 2010 there had been close to one thousand charges, and hundreds were serving sentences in prison. Bergoglio had always cooperated with any requests for information, giving access to church archives, and speaking out on the need for relatives of the disappeared to get at the truth. He told Rabbi Skorka that many people still did not know what happened to their relatives: "They lost the flesh of their flesh and have nowhere to cry over them." But healing and reconciliation had to follow. "Hatred will solve nothing," he said.[15]

The efforts of the vast, state-funded human rights industry had led to little new information about disappearances—the final toll of *desaparecidos* was actually less than the Sábato commission had estimated in the 1980s—while in many ways making it harder for Argentines to come to terms with the 1970s. Any attempt to bring the role of the guerrillas into the equation was met with blasts of official scorn, there being, in the official view, only one devil—the armed forces and the death squads. This simplistic dualism fueled a punitive attitude. Convinced that those responsible had not yet paid the price of their iniquity—the Alfonsín and Menem amnesties were continually excoriated—the human-rights groups used witnesses' evidence in fact-finding hearings to bring more and more prosecutions. This was what lay behind the summons to the cardinal to give evidence in November 2010 on the Yorio and Jalics case, as part of an epic long-term inquiry into the naval torture center ESMA.

Two months earlier a catechist who had been present in the Bajo Flores shantytown at the time of the Jesuits' abduction claimed it had happened because Bergoglio had withdrawn their license to minister, thereby leaving them exposed, and had done so because he had objected to them working with the poor. This sounded suspiciously similar to the mythical Verbitsky narrative, but the attorney driving the inquiry, Luis Zamora, a Trotskyite politician and a long-standing colleague of Verbitsky's in the human rights organization CELS, was not about to question it. His starting assumption, as he told a TV program, was the "undisputed fact that the Church was complicit in the dictatorship and formed part of its repressive apparatus."[16] Seizing on the testimony to arraign the cardinal, Zamora was determined to prove the Verbitsky accusations over two days of questioning and extract something from the cardinal that would allow a prosecution against him.

Argentine law allows senior public figures to be questioned in a place of their choosing. Conscious that Zamora was trying to stage the hearing as if the cardinal were being accused of a crime, Bergoglio chose for the hearing to take place in the archdiocesan curia rather than in the courts. ("They wanted to make him part of a show," says Wals. "He wasn't going to let them do that.") Bergoglio was tense beforehand, but told his staff to carry on as normal, telling them: "They're coming for me, not you." *El Jesuita*, Bergoglio's book-long interview with journalists Sergio Rubín and Francesca Ambrogetti, had come out earlier that year. There he had spoken for the first time in public about the dirty war, referring vaguely to those whom he had helped escape. Wals wanted to contact them, so they could tell journalists their stories, but the cardinal said no: only they could choose to reveal themselves if they wanted to. "Relax, Federico," he said, "the time will come."

After the hearing, Zamora tried to claim that Bergoglio was evasive and had something to hide. "It was a very reticent testimony," he told a

TV reporter. "He knew after three days where the priests were being held, but when I asked him how he knew, he was vague, refused to give names. When he did give a name, it was someone who was dead and so couldn't be called."[17] Both video and transcript tell a different story. Under at times aggressive questioning—the judge repeatedly had to remind Zamora that the cardinal was not on trial—Bergoglio volunteered detailed information about both events and their background over four hours, which was more than sufficient to destroy the Verbitsky version. He did hold back names of Jesuits, in order to protect them from the government's inquisitorial machine, and he avoided making any criticism of Yorio and Jalics or anyone else. He never tried to justify himself, but stuck to facts, supplying full contextual information to help the inquiry understand what happened. It was a tour de force, which left Zamora fuming.

The cardinal gave further evidence the following year over a woman who had turned to him for help in 1977 and whom he had referred on to a bishop. The Grandmothers of the Plaza de Mayo and Verbitsky would afterward claim that he had lied in his testimony when he said that he had only found out in the 1980s about the systematic taking of babies born to mothers in detention. Verbitsky said he "must have" known. But this was one of the dirty war's dirtiest secrets, and while there were rumors at the time, it would be surprising if he had known anything concrete.[18]

Although their standing abroad was intact, in Argentina the credibility of the iconic human-rights group, the Mothers of the Plaza de Mayo, had been severely damaged over the years. In addition to its financial scandals and endless internal disputes, the Madres leader, Hebe de Bonafini, had harshly pro-abortion and anticlerical views, and her expressions of sympathy for terrorists—she applauded the attacks on the Twin Towers as well as the atrocities committed by the Spanish and Colombian militants, ETA and FARC—frequently left even *kirchneristas* spluttering. It was not easy for Bergoglio to have relationships with groups that hurled accusations at him that he was a "betrayer" (*entregador*) and complicit in torture—representative of what they called a "right-wing Church" rather than what they called "the Church of the people." But he never responded to the attacks; and asked by Rubín and Ambrogetti if he agreed that Bonafini's rhetoric was unhelpful, he kept the focus on the Madres' pain. "I imagine these women searching desperately for their children and coming up against the cynicism of the authorities, who humiliated them and sent them from pillar to post. How can we not understand what they're feeling?"

Away from the political gallery, the cardinal had plenty of behind-the-scenes meetings with human-rights activists and relatives of the *desaparecidos*. He would receive any who asked to see him, and they found him unfailingly sympathetic and always helpful in their pursuit of information. They could meet on shared ground, for Bergoglio, too, had lost people dear to him in the dirty war.

The wave of sympathy for the president, Cristina Kirchner, in the wake of Néstor's death, ensured her a second term at the end of 2011. Her government remained hermetically sealed within its own narrative and became increasingly authoritarian. Outside the narrow world of government, however, Father Accaputo's Social Pastoral office had over many years built a formidable web of relationships among politicians and business and union leaders across the divides. Like the Dialogue of 2002, its purpose was the rebuilding of Argentine public life, fostering a new generation of leaders committed to Bergoglio's big themes: politics as service, the preferential option for the poor, the culture of encounter, solidarity, and the common good.

The Jornada de Pastoral Social ("Social Pastoral Day"), which Bergoglio and Accaputo built up over a decade, is an extraordinary phenomenon: an annual Church-hosted gathering of the nation's leaders from all parties and major interest groups who come together on panels to discuss national challenges and priorities. The object is to develop an understanding of how the interests that each represented could be seen as part of a whole, and to see those who represented other interests as sharing a common humanity. "At the moment you discover that behind a politician or business leader there is a person like you, a person who suffers, has problems, existential doubts, then you discover the person and not the personality," Father Accaputo explains. "When you can get to that, you can generate a relationship in which people can encounter each other."

The *jornadas* were (and remain) a practical attempt by Bergoglio to overcome the besetting sin of Argentine political life, personalized factionalism, and to build a political culture whose fruits may not be reaped until the post-Kirchner era.[19]

CARDINAL Bergoglio was a master builder of cross-frontier relationships, many of which developed into deep friendships. Jean-Louis Tauran, the French cardinal who heads the Vatican's council for relations with other faiths, refers to the "Argentine model of interreligious dialogue, unique in the world." What made it special, says Father Guillermo Marcó, who with Bergoglio's backing set up an interfaith dialogue institute in 2005, is that it relies on friendship rather than on reaching theological agreement. The dialogue takes place not among institutions or representatives of religions, but through the friendship among leaders of different faiths or denominations, who take on also each other's concerns without ever compromising their identity. The "Argentine model" partly reflects the way it came into being, as a result of the 2001–2002 crisis, when the lack of trust in state institutions caused people to look to religious leaders, who needed to get together to respond practically to the needs of the moment.

Among many remarkable relationships, three in particular stand out: with a Muslim, a Jew, and an Anglican evangelical.

The million-odd Argentine Arabs of Syrian and Lebanese extraction who arrived in the 1920s are mostly (like former president Menem) Christians. But Omar Abboud, whose Argentine grandfather, a sheikh, was the first Muslim to translate the Qu'ran into Spanish, puts the Muslim population (Sunni, Shiite, and Alawite) somewhere around three hundred thousand: it is hard to know, exactly, because Argentine censuses do not give a breakdown of non-Christian affiliations.[20] But practicing Muslims are relatively few; Buenos Aires has just three mosques. It was a quiet, integrated population until the September 11 attacks in New York shone a spotlight on them, and Abboud—by then working in the Islamic Center of the Argentine Republic—found himself in the media explaining the difference between terrorists radicalized by Islamist ideology and ordinary faithful Muslims.

Following contacts with Father Marcó, the cardinal in May 2004 paid the first visit to the Islamic Center, which since its foundation in 1931 had never been visited by a bishop, let alone the Argentine primate. "I give thanks to God, the Merciful," Bergoglio wrote in the visitors' book, "for the fraternal hospitality, for the spirit of Argentine patriotism I found here, and for the witness of commitment to the historic values of our fatherland." Until his death a year later, the president of the Islamic Center at the time, Adel Made, began to meet regularly with the cardinal, who returned to the Center in August 2005 to pray at the sheikh's wake. By that time, the interreligious institute had been set up, with an agreement not to allow tensions from abroad to affect the relationships in Argentina: this meant, for example, that Benedict XVI's Regensburg speech in September the following year, which caused anger across the Muslim world after a sentence was quoted out of context, caused little Muslim-Catholic friction in Argentina. (It did, on the other hand, lead to Marcó standing down as the cardinal's spokesman, after comments lamenting the pope's speech he made in a personal capacity were reported as the cardinal's.)

"Bergoglio was the one who showed us and taught us about dialogue," recalls Abboud, who took over from Made as the Center's director. "He brought minorities to the table, to create an unprecedented civic space." Bergoglio gave Abboud and other religious leaders the place of honor at the annual Te Deum, for example, and arranged common declarations and pledges so that there was a joint religious voice on social issues.

Abboud, an articulate forty-seven-year-old descendant of Syrians, became close to Bergoglio, whom he used to visit regularly at the curia, where they drank coffee and ate *alfajores*, and spoke of soccer and politics, as well as literature, music, and opera ("I learned through him to appreciate Wagner's *Parsifal*"). Abboud explained to him about Islam, but found the cardinal already well informed. Bergoglio lent him books that would allow him to see parallels between Christianity and Islam, and taught him the importance of his four civic principles—the whole is greater than the part, unity is superior to conflict, reality is superior to the idea, time prevails over space—which Abboud translated into Islamic concepts and uses all the time.

"How can a Muslim learn from a Catholic priest?" Abboud shakes his head in amazement. "I learned the dynamic of Islamic mercy through his words." Their discussions roved over the divine attributes—the Muslim insistence on divine oneness, versus the Catholics' understanding of God as a plurality of three persons in one—as well as what Abboud calls "the vision of an Islamic Jesus that is also miraculous." But the richest discussions took place on the common ground of mercy, the quality of the divine. "From Bergoglio it was a whole lesson in the exercise of mercy, in improving your view of the other by putting yourself in their shoes," recalls

Abboud, who admired Bergoglio's extraordinary spiritual depth—the product, he said, of a lifetime's rigor and prayer—and his "zero attachment" to material things. "The fact is," says Abboud, "I love him a lot."

Another who loves Bergoglio is Rabbi Abraham Skorka.

Bergoglio's father, Mario, used to tell his son how the Jews had been persecuted over the centuries, including by the Church, and that he should know that Jesus was a Jew. Growing up, Bergoglio knew a number of *rusos* in Flores. It's a term of affection: most Argentine Jews are Eastern European Ashkenazi, who came off boats after the 1880s (Buenos Aires was mostly their second choice, when New York's quotas had filled): Skorka's Polish grandparents came in the 1920s, and he spoke Yiddish at home.

The Argentine Jewish population of around two hundred thousand is smaller than it was—emigration to Israel increased after the 2001–2002 Argentine economic crash—yet it remains the largest and most important Jewish diaspora in Latin America, with over a dozen synagogues in Buenos Aires and a number of significant institutions. Despite the anti-Semitism of nationalist Catholic intellectuals in the 1930s and 1940s, which reappeared in the higher echelons of the military junta during the dictatorship of the 1970s, Jews are on the whole safe and integrated in Argentina. But in the early 1990s the Middle East conflict came to Buenos Aires, when foreign Islamic radicals car-bombed the Argentine-Israeli Mutual Association (AMIA), killing eighty-five, just two years after an attack on the Israeli embassy in which twenty-nine died. The attacks left their mark: there are bars in the windows and round-the-clock security guards at Skorka's synagogue, Benei Tikva, tucked away in a silent street in Belgrano. But the rabbi always believed that real security meant not letting locked doors hem you in, and in the mid-1990s he began building relationships with priests and local Muslim leaders. He was also a regular writer on Jewish matters for the newspaper Bergoglio read, *La Nación*.

Bergoglio inherited the Jewish community's strong relations with Cardinal Quarracino, who had taken the unprecedented step of installing in the cathedral a glass mural that contained documents rescued from the Holocaust. Shortly after he became archbishop, Bergoglio had the mural expanded to include a commemoration of the 1992 and 1994 attacks, and held a service at the cathedral to commemorate victims of the Shoa. Over the next years, he took Jewish-Catholic relations in Buenos Aires to a whole new level. He regularly took part in the yearly commemoration of the Nazi persecution of Jews, the Kristallnacht, and hosted it more than once in the cathedral, asking forgiveness on behalf of those who in the 1930s stood by and let the Holocaust happen. He made sure the Shoa was taught in diocesan schools and seminaries, and in 2012 he sent three trainee priests to Yad Vashem, the Holocaust museum in Jerusalem. He asked his auxiliary bishops to represent the Church at the Jewish community's yearly commemoration of the AMIA victims, and in July 2010 he himself attended, praying in front of the mural and telling journalists that the attack was "another link in the chain of sorrow and persecution that the chosen people of God has suffered in its history."[21]

Bergoglio also built strong relationships with Jewish leaders. Among them were Rabbi Daniel Goldman, who was part of the Interreligious Institute with Father Marcó and Omar Abboud, and Sergio Bergman, rabbi of Argentina's primary synagogue, who is also a center-right politician. Bergman and Bergoglio for many years worked on developing common civic virtues to rehabilitate politics: the cardinal wrote the prologue to Bergman's 2008 essay on citizenship, while Bergman describes Bergoglio as his "rabbi" and the spiritual leader of all Argentines, not just Catholics, the creator of a civic space in which all can take part and contribute without sacrificing their identity.[22] Claudio Epelman, executive director of the Latin-American Jewish Congress, and Alberto Zimerman, of the Delegation of Argentine-Israeli Associations (DAIA), were also friends, whom Bergoglio invited to dine with him on Christmas Eve, bringing in kosher food.

Skorka, the sixty-three-year-old rector of the Latin-American Rabbinical Seminary in Buenos Aires, had been a chemistry student, like his friend Jorge. They became close after the rabbi invited him in September 2004 to join his community for the penitential service of Selichot, where they prayed and broke bread together. Thereafter, Skorka was a regular visitor to the cardinal's office, where they ribbed each other about which of their soccer teams (Skorka supports River) was on the wane, and began working together on many projects. Bergoglio prologued a book of Skorka's, and later asked the rabbi if he would do the same for the cardinal's book-long interview with Sergio Rubín and Francesca Ambrogetti, *El Jesuita*, which came out in 2010—a gesture that deeply touched Skorka ("'What is this?' I thought. 'You're asking me, a rabbi, a Jew?'").

In 2010 Skorka and Bergoglio met every month for a year in the company of a journalist who transcribed and edited their discussions on mostly moral and ethical topics, such as euthanasia, divorce, abortion, globalization, poverty, marriage, as well as the Holocaust. The discussions were turned into a book published in 2011 as *On Heaven and Earth*. "Dialogue, in its most profound sense, is to draw the soul of one close to the soul of another, with the result revealing and illuminating one's interior," Skorka writes in his introduction. All three—the rabbi, the cardinal, and the journalist—dealt that year with the loss of a loved one: the cardinal's brother Alberto died in June and the rabbi lost his mother-in-law. When Skorka accompanied the cardinal to his brother's wake—"We were speaking about deep things; what else do you talk about at a wake?"—he asked Bergoglio why he had asked him to write the prologue to his book. "He said, without thinking, 'It came out of my heart.' I was overwhelmed."

In October 2010, Bergoglio and Skorka began taking part in an unusual three-way dialogue broadcast on the archdiocese's TV channel, Canal 21. The chair was Marcelo Figueroa, a Protestant theologian who coordinated what turned out to be thirty-one hour-long monthly programs. Each took a social theme—such as solidarity, sexuality, authority, happiness—and centered the discussion on the Bible, the book that all three traditions shared and all three men knew deeply.[23] Two years later, on the fiftieth anniversary of the Vatican II document *Nostra Aetate*, which transformed Catholic-Jewish relations, Bergoglio awarded Skorka an honorary doctorate from the Catholic University in Buenos Aires—an event without precedent in Argentina.

There is a deep affection between them. Bergoglio, says Skorka, is *un amigo campechano*—a real pal, a straight-down-the-line friend. Yet there is a seriousness to their relationship, signaled by the use of the formal Spanish *usted* form, rather than the familiar *tú*. "It marks a framework of absolute respect, with an enormous affection," says Skorka. These linguistic nuances are hard for outsiders to understand, but it's like this, says the rabbi: we don't take each other for granted; we defer to each other's tradition. Beneath the joshing and the affection lies a serious purpose. "Whenever we got together, we always asked ourselves, 'What are we doing so that there is a little bit more spirituality in the world?' We would always ask each other, 'What is our next project? What is our next mission?'" They wanted to develop a deeper understanding of what Jewishness means to Christianity and vice versa; if Jews were the Christians' "elder brothers" in the faith—the modern Catholic formula—what could or should that brotherhood look like? Bergoglio's focus on Jesus's identification with the poor and the marginalized recalls the prophets of Israel and the Torah, says Skorka, and allowed the two Argentines to meet constantly on shared ground. "He feels us to be at the root of his belief."

In the best Jesuit tradition, Bergoglio remained, as cardinal, a man of the frontier, called to live in the tension of conflicting identities and to support others who trod similar tightropes. One of them was Tony Palmer, a British-born South African Anglican evangelical bishop. Tony met and married his Italian wife, Emiliana, in Cape Town, where they were both living and working. At that stage, they were both evangelicals, Tony a preacher. They left South Africa in 2004 to live in Italy, where Tony began to work with Matteo Calisi, the Italian Catholic charismatic leader whose friendship with the Argentine pastor Jorge Himitian led to the Luna Park gatherings in Buenos Aires. Palmer and Calisi formed a fraternity promoting unity with Christians of other denominations (two Anglicans and an Orthodox) united by a shared conviction: that the Holy Spirit was drawing together the Christian traditions toward a future oneness.

Through the charismatic movement, Emiliana was reconciled with the Catholic Church, while Tony was accepted by the Communion of Evangelical Episcopal Churches (CEEC), a body set up in the 1990s by Protestant and Anglican leaders who also see themselves as part of the convergence movement. (To add to the complexity, the CEEC is Anglican but is not part of the Anglican Communion, whose figurehead is the archbishop of Canterbury.) Through the CEEC, he was ordained a priest in 2005 and, in 2010, a bishop.

A year after his ordination as a priest, Palmer was in Buenos Aires with Calisi and the fraternity on a mission to bring together Catholics and evangelicals. Five of them met Cardinal Bergoglio, who asked to hear their stories. He was especially interested in Palmer's because of his ecumenical marriage. Palmer said that while it worked very well—they were complementary in their diversity—there was a problem. "I told him that since I led my family back to the Catholic Church, I am not allowed to take Communion. I have to stay in the benches on Sunday morning. So my kids come back after taking Communion and say, 'Dad, why would you join us to a church that separates a family?'" At this, recalls Palmer, Bergoglio's "heart broke—his eyes filled with tears." As they were walking out, Bergoglio took Palmer aside and asked if he was willing to start a relationship with him, perhaps to study together the sacrament of marriage. Palmer agreed, and each time he was in Buenos Aires over the next few years to work with young people, they met, staying in touch in between visits by e-mail and telephone. (They always spoke in Italian; Palmer called him "Padre Mario.")

They had deep conversations about the issue Palmer had first raised—the Church's rules preventing non-Catholic Christians from receiving the Eucharist at Mass. Palmer passionately argued that the Eucharist was not a sign of institutional unity but unity in Christ, and that the Catholic Church's rules meant it was claiming that the altar was Rome's, not Christ's—a form of blasphemy. "I wasn't giving him Protestant theology but straight-down-the-line Catholic sacramental understanding," Palmer insists. The cardinal, he says, did not try to defend the Church's rules, but affirmed Palmer's sacramental theology, empathizing deeply, and seeking only to persuade Palmer to be patient. "He wanted to calm me down, to make me a reformer, not a rebel."

In 2009, when Pope Benedict XVI created a new legal church structure for Anglicans to join the Catholic Church known as the ordinariate, Bergoglio called the Buenos Aires–based Anglican primate of the Southern Cone (in communion with Canterbury), Bishop Gregory Venables. Over breakfast, "he told me very clearly that the ordinariate was quite unnecessary and that the Church needs us as Anglicans."[24] This was also Bergoglio's message to Palmer, who was looking at the ordinariate and wondering if it was for him. "He told me that we need to have bridge builders. He counseled me not to take the step because it looked like I was choosing a side and I would cease to be a bridge builder." Palmer says Bergoglio believed he should remain an Anglican "for the sake of the mission, this mission of unity," and that he was "divesting" himself of being a Catholic "for this mission, this mission of unity." Palmer says whenever he went to see the cardinal, it was "not as an Anglican but as his spiritual son."

Palmer, who had at the time little sense of Bergoglio's rising importance within the universal Church, was in awe of the centrality of Christ in the cardinal's life. "He has enfleshed the Gospel," says Palmer. "He is living a sacramental life at the deepest level: he has allowed the Gospel to become him." Bergoglio's humility and simplicity are deceptive, says Palmer. "If you don't listen to him properly you don't hear the depth of what he's saying. He doesn't use emotions to do it; he is quite stoic in that way—he might be emphasizing a point but you're not aware of it. That's why you have to listen: to be calm and to listen."

IN addition to building up the Church among, and evangelizing from, the shantytowns, and forging deep bonds across boundaries of religion and politics, there was a third dimension to Bergoglio's mission in his final years as cardinal archbishop. It involved a challenge to the mafias who ruled the seamy Buenos Aires world of gambling, people trafficking, prostitution, and sweatshop labor. The bishops' bicentenary document had drawn attention to the explosion of gambling and drugs, and the addictions and violence that followed them, while also spotlighting corruption and the exploitation of vulnerable workers, particularly undocumented migrants. All had metastasized after the collapse of the state in 2002–2003, corrupting police, judges, and public officials, and not a few high-ranking members of both city and federal government.

The growth of legal gambling was a symptom of the collusion of state and market. As private companies were given more and more concessions in exchange for party donations and kickbacks, gambling went from floating casinos, lotteries, and bingo halls to game parlors on virtually every street corner, especially in poor areas, producing an epidemic of addiction and family breakups. One company in particular, headed by business allies of Néstor Kirchner and the head of Buenos Aires city government, Mauricio Macri, dominated all the others, generating not just massive profits for the company but millions of dollars in revenue to both federal and city governments.

From 2008, Bergoglio began challenging the nexus. That year there was a strike of workers at the floating casino in Puerto Madero, whose attempt to improve their tawdry working conditions (including sexual exploitation) led the company to fire them. The sacked workers camped out in the Plaza de Mayo in protest, backed by the cardinal both in writing and publicly, which led to the press raising questions about both the gambling concessions and the links to government. Through a combination of this exposure, vigorous statements by the Church, and lobbying by politicians close to Bergoglio, the cardinal scored a major victory in December when Macri vetoed a new series of concessions for bingo and slot machines.

The Church had persuaded the state, at least in this instance, to put the common good above its financial interests. Bergoglio kept up the pressure. In a December 2010 document, he and the bishops pointed out that gambling was closely linked to money laundering by traffickers of drugs, weapons, and people, describing it as "a business that moves great sums of money for the benefit of a few to the detriment of many, especially the poorest." After listing the many serious consequences for poor families of gambling addiction, they called for the state to control and regulate the industry, and led a national awareness campaign in the run-up to Easter 2011.[25]

The appearance of the *cartoneros*—men, often boys, naked from the waist up, who at night scour the garbage of Buenos Aires for recyclable materials to sell—was one of the pitiful images of the post-2001 crisis. The city's three-thousand-odd *cartoneros* had formed a Movement of Excluded Workers (MTE) with the help of Juan Grabois, a lawyer, the son of an old Guardia colleague of Bergoglio's in the 1970s. The cardinal supported the work of the MTE from the beginning, turning up at their base in Plaza Houssay to help them strategize and plan. Whenever Grabois was arrested or attacked, Bergoglio would call to find out how he could help. He became chaplain and friend to the *cartoneros*, supporting them, marrying them, and baptizing their children. One of their leaders, Sergio Sánchez, says Bergoglio was "the only person who was at our side when our struggle was hardest."

The MTE worked closely with a textile workers' cooperative turned anti-trafficking campaign called La Alameda, which offered new lives and protection to workers fleeing the city's sweatshops and brothels. The clandestine textile factories had come to light in 2006, when a fire in one in Caballito caused the death of six trafficked Bolivians, four of them children locked in a room upstairs in order not to distract their mothers from working. A report that year estimated at least two thousand such factories in which undocumented female migrants worked in slave-like conditions, for a dollar an hour, eighteen hours a day, sleeping and eating on the floor next to the sewing machines, their identity papers taken from them by their overlords. Police were paid to turn a blind eye. Without money or papers, the women had nowhere to turn during the few hours their bosses allowed them out each week.[26]

As word spread about La Alameda, the women began turning up

there, asking for help. Their stories enabled its president, an engaging former teacher named Gustavo Vera, to piece together a picture of a mafia operation that involved many of the same people and interests as in drugs and gambling. The network stretched high into the ranks of the federal police and city government. As he took the women in and reported their evidence, Vera began to receive threats from the gang masters. Unable to look to the police, who were in their pay, he agreed to Grabois's suggestion to meet the cardinal. Vera was a Che Guevara leftist and atheist but was impressed by what he had read of Bergoglio's denunciations of the way feral capitalism turned people into commodities. At the end of August 2008 Vera left a letter in the curia to ask for the cardinal's help, and got a call an hour later from his secretary asking him to come in. When they met, Vera was amazed by how quickly Bergoglio grasped what he was telling him.

A week later, the cardinal celebrated a Mass in the sanctuary of Our Lady of Emigrants in the port area of La Boca attended by a congregation of *cartoneros*, trafficked seamstresses, and former prostitutes mobilized by La Alameda and the MTE. He told them he had realized that what he had been taught at school, that the Constitution of 1813 had abolished slavery in Argentina, was a lie, and that there were more slaves in Buenos Aires now than then. He said he had seen, a few nights earlier, a cart full of flattened cardboard boxes being pulled along the street, and had looked for a horse, only to find it was being pulled by two children less than twelve years old. City laws had long banned animal-drawn transport, he added, but what was this? Was a child worth less than a horse?[27]

The Mass became an annual July event in the Plaza de la Constitución, gathering tens of thousands of *cartoneros*, exploited and trafficked workers, prostitutes, and migrant workers. Over five years Bergoglio used the event to bring to the surface a hidden population. The Mass served a twin function: to bolster the courage and hope of the victims of trafficking by showing that the Church was their ally, working for their liberation, and to challenge those who benefitted from, or closed their eyes to, this pernicious industry.

Bergoglio often took the subway on Saturdays to La Alameda's base in Parque Avellaneda, to drink mate and chat with the eclectic mix of staff, volunteers, and survivors, atheists and agnostics, leftists and Catholics. They called him Jorge and he was always available to them, one time baptizing the three daughters of a seamstress who had been rescued from one of the textile sweatshops, with an atheist and a Jew standing in as godparents. He helped Vera and the other directors make strategic decisions about how and when to go public with accusations, and encouraged the women struggling to make new lives. In his five years supporting them, La Alameda brought eighty-five successful court cases against the clandestine factories for breaking labor laws and safety regulations, and freed over three thousand workers.[28]

Many of the trafficked women were sold into prostitution. As they struggled to get free, they and anyone helping them would find themselves in the crosshairs of pimps and rotten cops. Just as he did for Padre Pepe, Bergoglio would publicly back the women involved, providing a shield of publicity, while placing them in convents or retreat houses until it was safe. In this way the cardinal met dozens of prostitutes and helped them find shelter and new lives, just as Saint Ignatius of Loyola and his first companions had done in Rome.[29] Bergoglio became their public advocate, telling their stories. In his Plaza Constitución homily of July 2010, for example, he said:

> The night before last a poor girl was taken out of a brothel where she had been forced to work, and rushed to the hospital. To break her will they had got her drunk and injected her with drugs and she had gone into a coma. This is what the mafias do, the elegant gentlemen whose money is drenched in blood. They are the slave traders of our time, who run organizations whose purpose is to corrupt young people, break their wills, destroy them with drugs, and exploit them. They are important, influential gentlemen who do this, who never show their faces and never face the music because of that great Buenos Aires solution known as *la coima*, the bribe. . . . Let us not cross over in order to avoid the poor person beaten by the side of the road. Let us instead stand up and point out the focal points of slavery and corruption, the clandestine factories, brothels, and cabarets, the places where they sell drugs, these grinders of blood, these modern altars where our brothers and sisters are offered in sacrifice.

Vera reckons that the cardinal had more than eighty meetings with trafficked women. Each time Bergoglio would ask Vera what help the women had, whether they had work and somewhere to live. He never took notes, but would just say *bueno*, "fine." Vera didn't know what that meant at first, but two or three days later he would be called by union leaders, businessmen, or nuns, friends of the cardinal, with offers of jobs and shelter for them. Jorge always remembered each case, each name, each story, and he wanted Vera to let him know how they were doing.

The women came out from their meetings with the cardinal, said Vera, "in a state of total peace," saying no one had ever listened to them so deeply nor looked at them with so much love. When the cardinal came out, his eyes were always red with tears. He told Vera one time: "I see in them the wounds of Christ."

José María Poirier, editor of the Catholic weekly *Criterio*, recalls that the cardinal's office was "excessively modest, because it was uncomfortable. You had to open the door, move a chair in order to close it, and then move the chair back into its place."[30] Compared with 1998, when Bergoglio was starting as archbishop, much was the same: the priorities for the diocese, his option for the poor, his austerity and humility. One thing above all remained constant: he still rose not long after 4:00 a.m. to pray, and this was the time—with mind alert and heart open—when he made the most important decisions.

He genuinely governed, say those who worked with him, by seeing everything in the light of God's will. His dawn discernments made him decisive, yet experiences in prayer also led him to reconsider. He was instinctively hostile to the idea of deacons, for example, seeing them as clericalized laity, but told three of them who had trained for the role: "I really don't like deacons. But the Virgin came to me last night and asked for three deacons for Buenos Aires."[31]

His fellow bishops were amazed by his capacity for work. "Outside the time he was praying and seeing people, he was always working," says Bishop Jorge Casaretto. He gave up watching television in the 1990s after making a promise to the Virgin, and never went to the movies or the theater. When Archbishop Jose María Arancedo of Santa Fe asked him what he did during the January vacation, he was told he stayed in the curia and relaxed by praying and rereading the classics. Yet Federico Wals, his head of press, says the cardinal's downtime was mainly in the slums and the sanctuaries on weekends, just being a pastor. "It's where I saw him relax. It nourished him, being with ordinary people."

He spent a lot of time writing. For letters he used an Olivetti electronic typewriter with a one-line memory he had bought in a sale in Germany in 1986, but otherwise wrote everything in longhand. "Bergoglio writes well, he likes writing, and he has a good style," says Father Carlos Galli, who worked with him on the Aparecida document. "He likes to correct, and polish, until it's right." Claretian Publications in 2005 and 2006 had published a number of collections of his carefully crafted homilies and addresses, and brought out more in 2011 and 2012. There were also many articles in journals as well as book prologues.

Archbishop Arancedo believes Bergoglio's familiarity with the classics helps explain "his superb Spanish style and the beauty of his prose." As all good writers try to do, Bergoglio avoided stale phrases. If it had been said before, he preferred not to say it or would find new language. This meant that, unusually for a Catholic bishop, he made the Church's constant teaching sound like news. Part of that ability came from his directness; he intuited what mattered to people, and spoke to it. It was also the result of his simplicity, a use of language that was both lyrical and accessible. This did not come naturally; he had a complex, multilayered mind and needed to work on his texts to make them accessible, streamlining the messages and invigorating them with startling metaphors.[32]

Bergoglio remained reticent with the press, giving few interviews, and was happy for other bishops to be the interface with the media. But he spoke off the record to journalists he knew and trusted—as well as *Clarín*'s Sergio Rubín, there was Francesca Ambrogetti and Silvina Premat, plus Carlos Pagni and Mariano de Vedia of *La Nación*, and in Rome Gianni Valente and Elisabetta Piqué—to brief them on this or that story, sometimes suggesting that they attribute his view to "sources close to the cardinal." Although he no longer watched television, he was behind the creation of a diocesan TV channel, Canal 21; and while he had no idea himself how to use social media—he used neither computer nor cell phone—he sent Wals to take a course to get acquainted with the new technologies, seeing them as a way of reaching people far from the Church: in 2012 in Rome he told the journalist Andrea Tornielli that "we try to reach people who are far away by means of digital media, the Web, and short messages."[33] Afterward, whenever Wals was putting one of the cardinal's homilies on the Web, Bergoglio would tell him: "Remember to put it up on that 140-character thing."

He had become a firmly collegial, collaborative leader, meeting his six auxiliary bishops—all his nominees—every fortnight collectively to manage their vast diocese. Bishop Jorge Lozano recalls that

> he listened to us, he respected each of us in our area of responsibility, but he was always the archbishop. When we had to consider changes in the priests, for example, we functioned as a diocese: we all sat down together and spoke about which parish needed a priest, which needed to change; but if there was a sensitive issue, he would speak directly to the bishop concerned first. Everyone around the table expressed their view, and then he would say fine, I'm now going to think about it and I'll let you know. A couple of days later the bishop closest to the situation would get a call before he made the final decision, to check with him if he agreed, and if he did, he would call all of us with the decision he had made. Between the auxiliary bishops and him there was a very positive relationship of collegiality and communion.

There are many stories of the astute way he went about forging consensus. Another of his auxiliary bishops recalls a daylong planning meeting at a retreat house that got gridlocked in the morning discussions. At lunchtime, the cardinal told the bishop: "I'm going to do some lobbying and we'll get this fixed." He disappeared with an apple to his room to take his usual forty-five-minute siesta and to meditate. The others meanwhile had lunch, with wine, and were chatting sleepily away when the cardinal reappeared, fresh as morning grass. One by one he took them aside to chat about the problem. By the time the group had blearily reassembled, the solution was obvious, and everyone was behind it.[34]

Many describe him, as the Jesuits had, as inscrutable. Bishop Casaretto says Bergoglio's personality was "rather hermetic." Despite his warmth and love of people, he was an introvert whose instinct was to slink away unobserved. His real forte was his one-on-one relationships. "He created a network of face-to-face relationships that was simply unbeatable," says Sergio Rubín. "When he creates a personal relationship, he's fantastic."

Bishop Casaretto, who was not a friend of Bergoglio's but got on well with him, describes him as "extraordinarily wise, one of those people who sees below the surface" and who was extremely well-informed, with considered opinions on just about everything. He disconcerted people with his knowledge. "You couldn't just feed him a line of crap because he'd see right through it," recalls Father Juan Isasmendi in Villa 21. "You couldn't just say, 'Everything's fine, the parish is going great,' because before long he'd ask a pointed question that made it crystal clear he knew perfectly well what was going on. You couldn't get anything past him, and if you tried, he didn't buy it." Poirier, the editor of *Criterio*, in late 2005 wrote a profile of Bergoglio for an English newspaper that began: "What does Cardinal Bergoglio think? Nobody knows." At a book launch some time later, Bergoglio approached Poirier, and said, laughing: "So no one knows what I think?"[35]

Poirier had written in that article that Bergoglio "can move pieces along with the best chess-player." It is a metaphor that many use of him. Father Mariano Fazio, Opus Dei's vicar in Argentina who had been with the cardinal in Aparecida, says, "At times you could feel like a chess piece on a board—he had the whole game in his head." The same analogy is used by Father Marcó. "He's a silent chess player, moving the pieces and seeing many moves ahead. He knows when to stop and when to make his move. You'll never know his rules, because he never shares them." Bergoglio, adds Poirier, "conveys the confidence of someone who knows where he stands, knows what he wants to do, where he is headed, even though he won't tell you explicitly."

In this respect—playing his cards close to his chest—he was the same leader as in the 1970s, and in another respect, too. "He listened to everyone, dialogued with everyone, and then went off to discern the decision," says Wals. "But when the decision was made, that was it—everyone was expected to fall in behind it." Those who worked with him testify to his core of steel: once he had decided on a course of action, he couldn't be influenced, pressured, or distracted: he had deeply absorbed Saint Ignatius's injunction—*age quod agis*—to stay focused. Rabbi Skorka says he was a bulldozer. "When he decides something, he puts everything behind it: he opens up a path and *baam!* he just plows ahead, throwing aside the rocks in his way."

This focus and tenacity coexisted in a person of unusual thoughtfulness and sensitivity. Many people's favorite anecdotes about Cardinal

Bergoglio relate to these qualities: the little handwritten note of appreciation, the surprise phone call (introducing himself as "Padre Bergoglio") on a person's birthday, the gracious expressions of consideration and empathy. He continued to see the big horizon in the smallest of gestures. As the world later learned, Bergoglio at the end of each month used to cross the Plaza de Mayo to return to the newspaper kiosk owner, Daniel del Regno, the rubber bands he had used to deliver his daily copy of *La Nación*. "It's part of your work," the cardinal told him, when Daniel objected that it wasn't necessary.[36]

Francesca Ambrogetti, who with Sergio Rubín wrote the interview-profile *El Jesuita*, says that if she had to highlight a single quality, it would be this "attentiveness to the other person, his listening, being sensitive to what the other person needs." Almost everyone cites his prodigious memory—helped by his notebook and diary—which allowed him to remember what mattered to others. Jorge Rouillón, religious columnist in *La Nación*, once asked Bergoglio to pray for him because he had some medical tests coming up. Rouillón's tests showed up nothing, and he quickly forgot about it. Three months later, when he ran into the cardinal, Bergoglio asked him: "Can I stop praying for you now?"[37]

BERGOGLIO lived in an impossible tension, which all bishops face: being an effective leader of a major civil-society institution while remaining an attentive pastor to every individual seeking his help. If Bergoglio came closer than most to succeeding, it was because he had struggled so much with the temptation to "play Tarzan," as he put it in *El Jesuita*—to act the omnicompetent executive who was too busy managing his demanding role to see Christ in others.

At a retreat for the church agency Caritas in 2010, he gave an example of a failure in this regard that had long haunted him. At home as a child a woman called Concepción María Minuto had come two mornings a week to help his mother. She was Sicilian, a widow with children, a hard worker, and was much loved by the family. Later, when the children left home, she got work elsewhere, and Bergoglio heard no more about her. Decades later, around 1980, when he was rector of the Colegio Máximo, he was told that she was at the door to see him. Bergoglio was extremely busy and gave the message for her to come back the next day. She never did.

A few weeks later, he began to feel intense remorse, and to pray for her. For over twenty-five years the guilt never went away, until a chance meeting of one of his priests with the woman's son, a taxi driver, allowed him to track her down. In 2006 Concepción, then in her nineties, came with her daughter to see the cardinal. "That day was the happiest of my life," recalled Bergoglio. He learned from her that she had come to the Máximo that day to say good-bye, because she was going back to Italy, but it hadn't worked out and she had returned. "Listen, Jorgito," she told him. "I'm going to die soon and I wanted to give you this." She handed him a holy medal necklace that he wears to this day. Thereafter they met and spoke often, until she died. "I felt so blessed," the cardinal told Caritas. "It's amazing how you do things without realizing, and then the Lord gets you to realize. I had the chance, eventually, after so many years of prayer, to put that right. She gave me so much."[38]

In *El Jesuita* Bergoglio tells of another time when, as an auxiliary bishop, he was leaving the cathedral to catch a train on his way to give a retreat to nuns, when a young man asked to confess. He told him to wait until the duty priest arrived that afternoon, but as he began to walk away, he felt deep shame and turned back to hear the man's confession. As it turned out, he still caught the train and made it on time. After the retreat he went to make his own confession, thinking that if he didn't he would be unable to say Mass the following day. What he confessed, thinks Ambrogetti, was that for a fleeting moment he forgot his mission.[39]

That mission was to be—as the former Jesuit general, Father Arrupe, famously put it—a "man for others." In his last years as cardinal, he became the icon of that notion, the embodiment of a life lived in *caritas*. The stories of his personal availability and generosity are legion, although most only became known after his election as pope.

Poirier recalls one remarkable yet not untypical example. The cardinal got to know one of the communist protesters who camped out in the Plaza de Mayo, and learned that he was unable to pay rent on the house where he lived with his wife and children. Says Poirier: "Bergoglio took an interest in the case and told him, 'I can help you. I can pay your rent for three years, but during those three years you have to promise that you will finish high school, get a job, and send your children to school. That is the deal.' Apparently he phoned him every weekend to see how his children were doing in school, how he was doing, and if he was fulfilling his side of the bargain. The man eventually graduated, got a job, and was able to pay the rent."

Bergoglio at seventy-five was a man of many spiritualities. He remained Ignatian to the core: the *Exercises*, and his contemplative reading of Scripture—imagining himself in the different characters—fed his homilies, retreats, and of course his daily prayer, including the *examen*. But he was also imbued with the spirituality of the diocesan clergy, based on the Divine Office—psalms and readings that all clergy must pray—and the daily Eucharist. He prayed the Angelus each day, said fifteen decades of the Rosary, and sat in the chapel for an hour before the Eucharist (Catholics call this Adoration) at the end of the day. At the same time he was inspired and nourished by the so-called new ecclesial movements in the twentieth-century Church, a diverse group of mostly lay-led associations of Catholics focused on a central charism or mission. They were often regarded with suspicion by both religious orders and diocesan bishops, yet Bergoglio praised them as "miracles of new life within the Church."[40]

As well as the Charismatic Renewal, he was especially close to three movements originating in Italy with a presence in Argentina: the Sant'Egidio community, with whom he shared a vision of a Church for the poor, interreligious dialogue, and justice; Focolare, whose call to unity had much in common with the "culture of encounter"; and the Communion and Liberation movement, the works of whose founder, Luigi Giussani, he said had done him good. He prayed to the founder of another important Catholic organization that emerged in the twentieth century, Opus Dei, spending more than thirty minutes in July 2003 in front of Saint Josemaría Escrivá's tomb in Rome to give thanks for a favor answered.[41]

But for heavenly help Bergoglio mostly turned to a trusted threesome. He had a statue of the Virgin of Luján in the chapel, a statue of a sleeping Saint Joseph in his room, and a picture of Saint Thérèse of Lisieux on his bookshelf. He looked especially to Santa Teresita, as she is known in Spanish, when he was under pressure and worried, confident that this French Carmelite nun was as active from above as she had promised to be in *The Story of a Soul*. (She died in 1897 at just twenty-four but became world-famous through her posthumous spiritual autobiography.) In Rome, he would always stop at a little Franciscan church close to the Vatican known as La Nunziatina to pray before the statue of Saint Thérèse there.

"When I have a problem," Bergoglio told Rubín and Ambrogetti, "I ask the saint, not to solve it, but to take it in her hands and help me accept it. And as a sign, I almost always receive a white rose." Stefania Falasca recalls Bergoglio telling her in Rome that "one time, when he had to make an important decision about a complex matter, he left it in her hands. Sometime later, an unknown woman placed three white roses at the door-step of the sacristy."[42] His collaborators in Buenos Aires say this happened often. Bergoglio often found a white rose on his desk—left at the door for him by a stranger—and would say: "So Santa Teresita's been in, I see." The anonymous rose-givers tracked him down even when he was away from the curia. Bergoglio's close collaborator remembers one time being at a meeting with the cardinal at a church on the outskirts of Buenos Aires, when a woman appeared at the church door with a huge bunch of stun-ning white roses. "Are they for the Virgin?" she asked her. "For the cardi-nal," the woman said and, leaving them, vanished.

Federico Wals's white rose story is even more dramatic. The cardinal's head of press used to accompany him to the San Cayetano shrine festival every August 7, a physically grueling day that included a huge outdoor Mass, a major homily on work and unemployment, followed by a ten-block walk down a long line for a three-hour meet-and-greet with God's holy faithful people. Bergoglio looked forward to it, but when the cardinal came in a car driven by a friend to collect Wals on the icy wet morning of August 7, 2010, he looked awful. He told Wals he hadn't slept all night from a terrible pain in his leg and none of the analgesics he had swal-lowed had taken effect. But he had prayed to Santa Teresita, he said, and if God willed, he would make it.

After the Mass, however, the pain was worse, and the cardinal was limping badly. As he began to walk the ten blocks down the line of thou-sands of people, shaking hands and exchanging words, his face was wreathed in pain, and Wals was sure he couldn't go on. At the start of the second block, he sent Wals to ask the car to wait at the next corner. Wals gave the driver the message and returned to keep the cardinal company.

> When we got to the second corner, this big burly guy appears. He must have been about forty; he really was tall—the cardinal is tall, but had to look up. The guy stepped out in front of him, with his arm inside his raincoat, like Napoleon, and in a very rapid movement, he took out a white rose and gave it to him. The cardinal took the rose,

looked at him, blessed him, and didn't say anything. The guy just stood there. So I made to guide the cardinal to the car, and he said to me, "No, no, you don't get it. This is the message I've been waiting for. It will be okay now." He gave me the rose, and at that moment I looked up at the guy and he had gone. The cardinal said: "This is the presence of Santa Teresita. Tell our car to wait for us at the Vélez soccer pitch. We're going to make it." The cardinal carried on, and he was fine, walked the whole ten blocks, feeling no more pain in his leg that day.

IN September 2011, Bergoglio stood down at the conclusion of his six-year term as president of the bishops' conference, handing the mantle to an ally, Archbishop Arancedo of Santa Fe. Two months later, when he turned seventy-five, he submitted his offer of resignation to the pope, as church law requires bishops to do. The letters are offered *nunc pro tunc* ("now for later"), for the pope to act on at some point in the future, unless health or some other imperative requires an immediate acceptance. But he could expect his successor to be announced perhaps late in 2012 and installed in early 2013. He knew there was pressure in Rome from the usual quarters to install Héctor Aguer of La Plata as the next primate of Argentina, and that part of the same plan was to get Bergoglio out of the way by naming him head of a Vatican department. This was a fate he dreaded (he joked to Wals about "being taken prisoner in the Vatican"), and he planned to resist. As rumors began to fly, Wals teased him that he had already been named and he was keeping it from them. "Are you crazy?" Bergoglio told him. "They'll never drag me to Rome. You know I'm going to die in Buenos Aires." He had a ground-floor room booked in the clergy retirement home on Condarco Street in Flores. Asked what he planned to do there, he said he would "finish the doctoral thesis I never completed, share the home with the other priests, work in Flores. Of course," he added presciently, "you never know what role God is preparing for you."[43]

In late 2011 he contacted the director of the Claretian publishing house in Buenos Aires that had earlier brought out the anthologies of his homilies and addresses. He told Father Gustavo Larrazábal that he was sorting through his writings in preparation for his retirement, and wanted him to assess which were worth publishing. Over the next year,

Claretian brought out a series of collections, culminating in his favorite, a series of forty-eight meditations—many of them from his Jesuit days—published as *Mente Abierta, Corazón Creyente* (Open Mind, Faithful Heart), a compendium of a lifetime's wisdom and insight. The mature Bergoglio was still an acute discerner of spirits, an exposer of deceit and false directions, a master retreat-giver who could fire up and send out. But there was now a lyrical gentleness that had been lacking in the younger Bergoglio. Writing, for example, of the exile from Eden of Adam, whom he likened in one meditation to the Prodigal Son, he reached for something close to poetry:

> Even when wandering far from home, the son felt in his bones the unsettling memory of the Father's house. Although a drifter, the son was gifted with a sense of direction, and, in obedience to that gift, he sought a re-encounter with his truer self. He found space for questioning and sought to correct the direction in which he was heading. He realized the significance of that guiding star within his heart, though he knew not whence it came nor where it led. That is, he prayed—and he prayed for his return. All flesh follows its own paths, and it is precisely in prayer that the meaning of its existence falls into place. It is only in prayer that our heart comes to see clearly where it's coming "from," what it's moving "toward," and where it presently stands.[44]

The final meditations, which concern the triumph of divine power through human failure, bring out more clearly than ever why Bergoglio saw the need to be close to the poor. "Our Catholic elites," he writes, "miss the point of the Beatitudes, which Jesus proclaimed precisely for those times when we experience failure. . . . Jesus was speaking mostly about the failures that humble folk experience, since it was to them that he addressed this message, but when our privileged elites hear the same message, they turn up their nose at the thought of failure and are scandalized."[45]

He was seventy-five, and still worked more intensely than most men half his age; but in 2012, as he waited on his fate, people noticed in him a new tiredness. You had to lean in, sometimes, to hear him; and in the cathedral, where the acoustics were anyway a challenge, it was sometimes a strain to make out what he was saying. What weighed on him was a repeat of what he had undergone in the 1980s, when he had been forced powerlessly to watch the undoing of God's work. The reform of the arch-diocese in line with the vision of Aparecida was under way and would need at least another generation to be implemented. But it could all easily be reversed. Wals thinks he was tired by a sense of what might not, now, be achieved. "He had a clear program for the Church from Aparecida but couldn't implement it without reforming the universal Church."

Bergoglio's theologian assistant at Aparecida, the rector of the Pon-tifical Catholic University of Argentina (UCA), Archbishop Víctor Man-uel Fernández, recalls meetings at this time in which, looking ahead to Bergoglio retiring, some Argentine bishops together with "some repre-sentative of the Holy See" (not, he made clear, the nuncio) felt free now to excoriate Bergoglio. "They criticized him for not being more demanding with the faithful, for not being clearer about priestly identity, for not preaching enough on matters of sexual morality, etc." Fernández was struck by their confidence that the succession would go their way.

Bergoglio's friendship with the then archbishop of Quebec, Cardinal Marc Ouellet, led him to accept Ouellet's invitation to speak at the 2008 International Eucharistic Congress, the only time, apart from Rome and Aparecida, he was away from Buenos Aires in those years. After Ouellet was made head of the Congregation of Bishops in 2010, Bergoglio could finally have his bishop nominees accepted. A 2012 Argentine press report carried the names of a *terna* of three archbishops being put forward by Bergoglio and the bishops' conference; Aguer was not one of them.[46]

But the conservative, anti-Bergoglio faction in Rome remained strong, and they continually backed Argentine *rigoristi*. It had taken the cardinal eighteen months to get Fernández officially sworn in as rector of the UCA, for example, because some conservative groups in Argentina had raised question marks over the rector's orthodoxy. Yet when Bergoglio arranged for Fernández to respond to the claims in Rome, the rector was continually rebuffed: after having appointments rescheduled, Fernández would turn up in Rome to be told that they had no record of the appoint-ment, and subsequent attempts to book an appointment were met with silence. Bergoglio urged Fernández to be patient, but the cardinal himself was furious: this arrogance was symptomatic of a Curia that stifled, rather than served, the local Church.[47]

The Vatican was at that time imploding. As Bergoglio traveled to

Rome for the February 2012 consistory to create twenty-two new cardinals (most of whom were *curiali*), the headlines were full of what became known as the Vatileaks scandal. It had begun in January with the airing of an Italian TV documentary, and would reach new depths in May with the publication of documents copied from the pope's desk by Benedict XVI's butler, Paolo Gabriele. The sensational fact of the leaks themselves—not to mention the image they conjured of an ineffectual pope sitting powerlessly atop a Vatican riven by Borgia-style factionalism and rivalry—eclipsed the reporting of their content. What the letters showed was that many believed Benedict XVI's attempts to reform the Curia (especially the scandal-dogged Vatican Bank) and clean up corruption were being endlessly blocked by powerful factions within the Vatican, as well as by his secretary of state, Tarcisio Bertone. The letters also revealed mounting frustration at the way Benedict XVI, an increasingly remote and inaccessible governor, was being kept in the dark about what was going on under his nose. Gabriele had acted out of frustration: his purpose had not been to harm the pope but to sound the alarm, to show the world what was happening and so force action. The frustration behind Gabriele's desperate action was widely shared.[48]

There was a sense in Rome of an era coming to an end. Diplomats accredited to the Holy See compared themselves to the final ambassadors to the Republic of Venice just before its collapse in 1797. Yet if Bergoglio saw this, he was giving nothing away. In an interview with the *vaticanista* Andrea Tornielli, Bergoglio said that the Church was his mother, and that he should look at its faults as he would look at his own mother's, preferring to remember the good and beautiful things she had done for him rather than her failings. He took the same line when asked about the Vatican Curia, acknowledging that it had its faults but that most people who worked in it were good and holy. Although he spoke against spiritual worldliness and vanity, nothing in his reply suggested that he believed the Vatican needed reform, or what that might look like. If anything, he went overboard the other way, blaming the media for focusing only on scandal and dirt, which made him sound like a member of the Vatican old guard whose reaction to any exposure of impropriety was to blame the messenger.[49]

In Benedict XVI's speech to the cardinals in February 2012 there was little to suggest that resignation was on his mind. He asked for their prayers "that I may continually offer to the People of God the witness of sound doctrine and guide the holy Church with a firm and humble hand." But the following month, at the end of a fleeting trip to Mexico and Cuba, he realized that he could not go on. He had stumbled on the steps of the cathedral of León in the Mexican state of Guanajuato, and that night he hit his head on the sink as he fumbled his way to the bathroom in his hotel in the city. The cut was not deep, and few knew because his skullcap covered it, but, as often happens to old people after such falls, it brought a sudden cognizance of his frailty.[50]

It was this, not Vatileaks—traumatic though it was for him—that led Benedict XVI to design a plan to stand down. Guarding the secret from all but a few of his very closest advisers—which, given the porosity of the Curia at the time, was no small feat—he agreed with them to a resignation date less than a year later: February 28, 2013, to be announced two weeks earlier. It would give time to allow a new pope to be installed in time for Easter 2013 and to go on to lead World Youth Day in Rio de Janeiro the following July. Given Benedict XVI's confidence in the Latin-American Church he had showed at Aparecida, there is something poignant about the old German pope, unsteady on his feet in Mexico, thinking ahead to Brazil, and deciding to be the first pope in six hundred years to stand down, possibly even guessing that the Argentine cardinal would be elected as his successor. Looking back, it is hard not to see in that decision an exhausted European Church standing back to allow the vigorous Church of Latin America to step forward.

Tired was precisely the word used of the Church in Europe by that other towering figure of twentieth-century Catholicism, Cardinal Carlo Maria Martini, who died at age eighty-five on August 31. He had given an interview a few weeks earlier to a longtime Jesuit collaborator, with instructions that it be published after his death. When it was, between his death and his funeral, it provoked a slew of headlines. Martini began:

The Church is tired, in the Europe of well-being, and in America. Our culture is aged, our churches are large, our religious houses empty; the Church's bureaucratic apparatus is growing, and our rites and vestments are pompous. Do such things really express what we are today? Well-being weighs us down. We find ourselves like the rich young man who went away sad when Jesus called him to become his disciple. I know that it's not easy to leave everything behind. At least we could find people who are free and closer to their neighbors, as Bishop Romero was, and the Jesuit martyrs of El Salvador. Where, among us, are our heroes to inspire us? . . . How can the embers be freed from the ashes in order to rekindle the flame of love? . . . I advise the pope and the bishops to look for twelve people outside the lines and give them leadership positions, people who are close to the poorest and surrounded by young people and trying out new things. We need that comparison with people who are on fire so that the spirit can spread everywhere.[51]

While the more intellectual Italian cardinals did their best to explain away Martini's message with a fug of elaborate theorizing about what he must have meant, others dismissed his uncomfortable words as the product of dementia. Yet thoughtful Catholics on all sides of the Church saw it as a mature light-and-shadows discernment, fearlessly expressed, which nailed a truth: something had died in the rich Church of the north, while the Church in the poor south exhibited an impressive vigor and prophetic power.[52]

One of the symptoms of the Church's weariness identified by Martini was the way the sacraments had become a bar to inclusion rather than a means of healing. "The sacraments are not a disciplinary instrument, but a help for people at times on their journey, in life's weaknesses," Martini said, adding: "Are we bringing the sacraments to people who are in need of a new strength?"

It seems too much of a coincidence that just two days after that interview was published, Bergoglio issued a searing denunciation of priests who refused to baptize children born out of wedlock, calling their attitude "hypocritical Pharasaism." He painted a picture of a woman who had refused the pressure to abort—"had the courage to bring that child into the world, when she could have thrown it away"—who "went from parish to parish, looking for someone to baptize him." Those who refuse such women, he said, "are the hypocrites of today, those who clericalized the Church, keeping the people of God from salvation." Bergoglio saw baptizing babies, however they came into the world, as part of what it meant to be pro-life.[53]

Borrowing an image from the Jesuit theologian Karl Rahner, Martini had spoken in his interview of how to kindle the fire of the Holy Spirit: "I see in the Church today so many ashes above the embers that I'm often assailed by a sense of powerlessness. How can the embers be freed from the ashes in order to rekindle the flame of love?" A few weeks later, Bergoglio used the same phrase in a retreat to Caritas. The Church, he said, "has to find the embers of faith, the embers of hope, the embers of love." What kept the ashes cold was what he called "the disenchanted Church"—a self-sufficient Church of fear and spiritual worldliness that had Jesus tied up in the sacristy and failed to let him out. This Church, he said, was distant from the "enchantment" that the Holy Spirit brings to God's holy faithful people caring tirelessly for others, "the enchantment that the Holy Spirit gives when it speaks in our hearts and prays for us, with those sighs too deep for words that Saint Paul talks about."[54]

Bergoglio spoke in that retreat of the synod of bishops that had finished a few days earlier in Rome. Its topic was the "new evangelization," a concept first formulated in Latin America and articulated by John Paul II in the 1980s, but which under Benedict XVI had increasingly been used to refer to mean rescuing Europe from secularism. A new pontifical council had been created to develop the concept; the synod was intended to give the council ideas and strategies for implementing it.

Father Carlos Galli, Bergoglio's theological assistant at Aparecida who was teaching in Rome in early 2012, was alarmed by the preparatory document, which suggested that the synod's primary topic was the crisis of faith in Europe. He called Bergoglio, who urged him to make clear to the organizers that the new evangelization was about all five continents, not just Europe. The synod council confirmed that it was, yet comments by leading curial cardinals continued to reflect a Eurocentric assumption: that the European crisis of faith was the only really important question; that what was good or bad for the Church in Europe was good or bad for the universal Church; and that the strategy developed for the new evangelization in Europe would somehow also work for the Churches elsewhere. Both diagnosis (the problem is relativism and secularism) and the perceived cure (creative strategies are needed to engage contemporary Western culture, using the new ecclesial movements as a model) were very far from the Aparecida vision of a missionary Church focused on the margins. Father Galli realized with alarm that this Euroecentric model was what the Curia was projecting for the universal Church post-Benedict.[55]

The Latin-American bishops coordinated their inputs at a CELAM meeting in Bogotá, Colombia, in July 2012, and met again in Rome just after the start of the synod in October, which was attended by forty-nine cardinals, seventy-one archbishops, and 127 bishops from across the world. Almost every Latin-American bishop's speech in those three weeks referred to Aparecida and its missionary, periphery-oriented evangelization. Their language and their outlook—hopeful, energetic, pastoral—struck a chord with other developing-world bishops at the synod, especially the Asians, who spoke of hope and joy, fruits of the Spirit, despite often severe persecutions and challenges. The Europeans and the Americans, in contrast, focused on declining congregations and the threat to the Church and religious freedom posed by an increasingly hostile culture. The cumulative effect of their speeches was depressing: tellingly, Cardinal George Pell of Sydney said they lacked "fire and energy," while a frustrated Cardinal Timothy Dolan of New York told reporters that "instead of whining about [secularism], or running from it, perhaps we should think about ways to better engage it." Yet, as ever, the synod's modus operandi allowed no chance of examining any of the Church's norms that made that engagement harder.[56]

Father Galli, who was part of the Argentine delegation at the synod, said afterward that the most impressive contributions had been from the Church in poor countries: "The wind blew from the south," was how he put it to Vatican Radio.

Down in Buenos Aires, Cardinal Bergoglio saw it, too. The synod had exposed what Alberto Methol Ferré had foreseen: Europe was no longer the source Church. In Ignatian terms, the European Church was in desolation: turned in on itself, excessively focused on the shadows, with an exaggerated fear of perceived threats. Why else was it that an Asian or Middle East bishop whose flocks were deprived of basic liberties, or even being killed and bombed, could be so hopeful and joyful, yet bishops in a Church where nobody suffered that real kind of persecution spoke as if Christianity faced annihilation?

Bergoglio saw that the rich-world Church was blaming the culture, rather than itself, for its decline. But the first obstacle was not the culture, but the Church, which was no longer evangelizing. It had allowed the living water to go stale. It had become comfortable, worldly, self-sufficient, "disenchanted." The problem was that "we have Jesus tied up in the Sacristy," he told the Caritas retreatants. Citing a verse from the book of Revelation about Jesus standing at the gate, calling, Bergoglio said he had come to see that it wasn't about Jesus knocking to be let in, but about Jesus being trapped on the inside, asking to be let out.

NINE

CONCLAVE

(2013)

STARING AT THE Vatican's video link in her agency newsroom, Giovanna Chirri knew more than enough Latin to grasp what the pope was uttering in a deadpan voice: *ingravescente aetate non iam aptas esse ad munus Petrinum aeque administrandum.* . . . He had even given the date it would happen: February 28. But could she run the story without official confirmation? The reporter dialed the director of the Vatican press office, Father Federico Lombardi, but after leaving a message decided she couldn't wait: after all, she had heard the pope with her own ears. She dictated the story and called her editor. "The amazing thing is," she began, but then broke off because Father Lombardi was on her cell phone. "You understood correctly," he told her. "The pope is resigning." Chirri's scoop flashed out on the wires, sparking a media tsunami. "I collapsed on my desk," she remembers. "And I cried."[1]

February 11, 2013, was a Vatican holiday, marking the day in 1929 when the fifty-nine-year standoff between Italy and the Holy See over the occupation of the papal states was finally resolved. Benedict XVI had called a minor consistory, involving only the cardinals resident in Rome, officially to make the less-than-shattering announcement of three new saints. One of those in the Consistory Hall that day was a Scottish official in the secretariat of state, Archbishop Leo Cushley, who thought Benedict looked tired but otherwise well, and had no idea what was about to happen.

After Cardinal Angelo Amato read the list of the three *beati*, or "blesseds," to be canonized, Pope Benedict, with his secretary, Archbishop Georg Gänswein close by, began to speak, reading as ever from a prepared text. Cushley's Latin allowed him, too, to understand what the pope was saying—"I have come to the certainty that my strengths, due to an advanced age, are no longer suited to an adequate exercise of the Petrine mystery"—and as it sank in he felt his stomach turn over. Something not seen for six hundred years, the voluntary resignation of a pope, was happening in front of his eyes.

> It seemed to me that, in slow motion before me, an assistant television cameraman put his hand to his mouth in a cartoon-like gesture of astonishment, the monsignor sitting next to me started to sob quietly, Archbishop Gänswein's shoulders seemed to drop. The cardinals leaned forward to make sure they understood precisely what was being said and I found myself checking that my jaw wasn't dropping open. Then there was silence.[2]

In Buenos Aires, Cardinal Bergoglio praised the decision as a "revolutionary act" that had been carefully thought out in the presence of God. He spent the next fortnight making arrangements for a three-week absence before landing in Rome on an overnight flight on February 27, the day before Benedict XVI's resignation took effect. He had been sent a first-class ticket by the Vatican but had changed it for coach class, asking for an emergency exit seat with more leg room because his sciatica troubled him on long journeys. The conclave date could not be fixed until the cardinals began their meetings, but most expected it to be around mid-March, with the new pope's inauguration Mass a few days later. His return ticket was for March 23, to allow time to go over the homilies he had prepared for the Easter liturgies at the end of the month, some of which he had sent out to his evangelical and Jewish friends for comment. He had told the kiosk owner on the other side of the Plaza de Mayo, Daniel del Regno, that he would be back in twenty days and that he should keep delivering his *La Nación* in the meantime.

This time—unlike 2005, when he had Father Marcó with him—Bergoglio traveled alone. At Fiumicino Airport there were limousines scooping up the arriving cardinals, but after collecting his small suitcase from the carousel he took the train as usual to Termini station, then a bus to the Via della Scrofa where, for 85 euros ($110) a night (including meals), he checked into his room in the Domus Internationalis Paulus VI residence for clergy. As he unpacked in the seventeenth-century stone palazzo that was once a Jesuit college, on the other side of the Tiber Benedict XVI was giving his last general audience, telling tens of thousands in St. Peter's Square of the peace of mind his decision had brought him, how there had been times in his eight-year papacy when the water was rough and "the Lord seemed to sleep."

The media in those weird, interim days were looking back over the highs and lows of Benedict's papacy and ahead to who might now take the reins in the Church's hour of need. The consensus among the *vaticanisti*—the dozens of permanently accredited Vatican journalists—was that the field of candidates was wide open, with no obvious front-runner. The lists of *papabili*—cardinals who fitted the unusual job description—ranged from three or four names to more than a dozen. Hardly any included Bergoglio, although the more knowledgeable fingered him as a kingmaker, a respected veteran whose opinions would influence his Latin-American peers. But he was off the *papabile* radar, partly because of his age—most cardinals were saying that the next pope should be in his late sixties or early seventies—and mostly because, Bergoglio hardly ever having been in Rome and invisible when he was, few knew much about him. Almost none of the four thousand journalists pouring in from sixty-five countries could have said much about the archbishop of Buenos Aires beyond his reputation for austerity and not giving interviews. The *vaticanisti* knew that he had been *papabile* in 2005 but believed his moment had passed. No runner-up at a conclave had ever been elected pope in a following one, and who had heard much of him since?

THE poignant drama of Benedict XVI's departure the night of February 28 to the papal residence in Castel Gandolfo was told through the lens of the Vatican Television Center, whose recently appointed director was a Milanese former professor of cinema, Monsignor Dario Viganò. He arranged a stunningly elegaic mise-en-scène. After the white helicopter rose—*ascended* was the better word—above the Vatican, it twice encir-cled the dome of St. Peter's before moving across the sky above Rome, throwing a shadow that slid over the city's sun-kissed monuments. The images paid homage to the famous opening scene of Federico Fellini's *La Dolce Vita*, when a statue of Jesus suspended from a helicopter transporting it to the Vatican seemed to bless the city's houses with its shadow. Viganò, too, wanted to make this "a journey of blessing of the pope."[3]

The Church was now *in sede vacante*, governed, in the absence of a pope, by the college of cardinals. They began meeting on March 4 for their daily general congregations in the synod hall, while workmen installed a false floor and jamming devices in the Sistine Chapel in preparation for the conclave. Most cardinals turned up in limousines to escape the media throng, but Bergoglio walked each day to the Vatican in his black raincoat, unrecognized.

There were 151 cardinals once the last had arrived. Of these, 115 were under eighty and eligible to vote, the same number as in 2005. But this conclave differed from that one in vital respects. There were no funeral arrangements to soak up the discussion time, and the bigwigs in the college—the dean, Cardinal Angelo Sodano, and the chamberlain, Cardinal Tarcisio Bertone—were too associated with Vatican scandals to be *papabili*. This time, too, the cardinals knew each other much better, for Benedict XVI had brought them together five times in his eight-year papacy, and had included a daylong meeting before each consistory.

The general congregations took place behind closed doors, but between Father Lombardi's daily briefings, the US cardinals' press conferences up at the Pontifical North American College (known as the NAC), as well as leaks by translators in the pay of Italian newspapers, it was broadly known that Vatican corruption and dysfunction were a common thread in the speeches. Three cardinals appointed months before by Pope Benedict to probe the rot were on hand to brief their *confrères* on their three-hundred-page confidential report, which would be on the next pope's desk.

The American cardinals were especially keen to discuss the dysfunction, for they had had the benefit over the previous months of an insider briefing. Archbishop Carlo Maria Viganò (no relation to the Vatican TV director), the Holy See's ambassador to Washington, DC, had warned Benedict XVI that the secretariat of state had named him to the post in October 2011 to get him out of Rome, after he had uncovered corruption in the awarding of contracts that cost the Holy See millions of euros.

Deeply shocked by what they had learned from Viganò, the US cardinals—the American Church, together with the German, is a key Vatican funder—were determined that the next pope would bring with him a big broom. As the archbishop of New York, Cardinal Timothy Dolan, puts it in his conclave memoir: "We knew that the world awaited the election of a pontiff who might usher in some significant reforms that begged for implementation within the Church."[4]

Curial dysfunction was more than financial corruption. It was also about petty factionalism, the way different patronage networks—the Italians use the English word *lobby*—led to some being promoted beyond their abilities and others with the right qualifications being frozen out. The so-called gay lobby was one of these: a group of lay people, and some priests, who used blackmail and preferment to protect and advance its interests. The four thousand lay people and one thousand priests in the Curia were mostly competent and good, and many were exceptionally dedicated, but they battled with a culture of entitlement in which middle-level bureaucrats expected jobs for life, and competence was less important than who you knew. What was needed was wholesale culture change—a new ethos of service to the pope's mission.

There was much talk of reform of governance—the need for a pope who was accessible, informed, and free to act—and for fluid contact between Rome and the local Church. Collegiality had been "a constant theme in these discussions," Father Lombardi told journalists on March 9. "We were all pretty certain that there would be dramatic changes and a new way of looking at the Curia, with more collegiality," recalls the archbishop of Boston, Cardinal Seán O'Malley.[5] The diagnosis of the St. Gallen group in the early 2000s was now the *plat du jour*. All could agree that Vatican dysfunction was a serious impediment to evangelization, and that Roman centralism and lack of accountability were major causes of the dysfunction. Some spoke of reforming the synod of bishops so it could manage real change; others wanted to discuss the Institute for the Works of Religion (IOR), the so-called Vatican Bank, and the mysterious firing of its reforming president, Ettore Gotti Tedeschi. All agreed on the need for the Curia to live less for itself and to better serve the local Church. At least one cardinal suggested that the task of governing the universal Church was simply too great for one man and that the next pope needed a council of cardinal advisers from outside Rome to assist him.

Among the most eloquent on this topic was Cardinal Francesco Coccopalmerio, a Vatican canon lawyer who had been an auxiliary bishop under Cardinal Martini in Milan. He spoke of the need for restructuring the Curia, ensuring contact between heads of the departments and the pope, and between local dioceses and Rome. The implosion of the Vatican had turned even *rigoristi* into reformists. The energetically conservative Cardinal George Pell of Sydney, for example, was shocked to discover curial appointments of people without proper technical knowledge and the constant leaking of confidential information to the media. In the general congregations, he was among the most vigorous advocates of curial reform and the need for the pope to consult outside Rome. The only defenders of the status quo, in fact, were curial cardinals convinced that they alone were qualified to treat the Vatican's malaise.[6]

Normally, with the assistance of the Italian diocesan cardinals, the *curiali* stitched up the conclave in advance, but this time needle and thread had slipped from their hands. The *curiali* were divided between pro-Bertone and pro-Sodano factions, although both wanted to stop Cardinal Angelo Scola, the brilliant but sulfurous archbishop of Milan, who was seen by many outside Italy as the natural successor to Benedict XVI, but opposed by heads of major Italian dioceses. An attempt at organizing an alternative to Scola came from the curial faction around the powerful former secretary of state and now dean of the college of cardinals, Angelo Sodano, who was too old to vote but remained the Curia's kingmaker. His group's plan was to promote the cardinal archbishop of São Paolo, Brazil, Odilo Scherer, a former Vatican official they saw as pliant. The idea was that, as pope, Scherer would appoint the Argentine curial official Leonardo Sandri, Sodano's former number two, as secretary of state, thus securing the status quo ante. By bringing in an outsider to govern, they believed they could restore the insiders to power. But the plan was neutered by being exposed in the press even before the congregations began, contributing to the generalized anti-Italian feeling in the college, which had spread even to the Italians.[7]

Spotting their moment, the initiative was now seized by the European reformists who in 2005 had pushed for Bergoglio. Some of them, like Cardinal Cormac Murphy-O'Connor, were too old to vote in the conclave; others—including Walter Kasper (who was just under eighty when the papal see fell vacant), Godfried Danneels, and Karl Lehmann—were electors. In keeping with conclave rules, they did not ask him if he would be willing to be a candidate. But they believed that this time the crisis in the Church would make it hard for Bergoglio to refuse if elected. (On the eve of the conclave, Murphy-O'Connor jokingly warned him to "be careful," that it was his turn now, and was told: *capisco*, "I understand.") Then they got to work, touring the cardinals' dinners to promote their man, arguing that his age—seventy-six—should no longer be considered an obstacle, given that popes could resign. Having understood, from 2005, the dynamics of a conclave, they knew that votes traveled to those who made a strong showing out of the gate. Their objective was to secure at least twenty-five votes for Bergoglio on the first ballot. An ancient Italian cardinal kept the tally of how many votes they could rely on before the conclave started.

Team Bergoglio could count on the bulk of the nineteen-strong Latin-American cardinals, who since Aparecida regarded the Argentine cardinal as their leader. But they needed a solid number of Europeans, who made up more than half of the electors. As well as reformists like themselves—a number of the Germans, French, and Central Europeans came into this category—they could count on some of the Spanish cardinals who fondly remembered Bergoglio's 2006 retreat. The Spanish cardinal Santos Abril y Castelló, archpriest of St. Mary Major in Rome and a former nuncio in Latin America, was vigorous in canvassing on Bergoglio's behalf among the Iberian bloc. European support was also helped by Cardinal Christoph Schönborn of Vienna, one of Ratzinger's main backers in 2005, and by Cardinal André Vingt-Trois of Paris, both of whom were pro-Bergoglio going into the conclave, if not before.

There were eleven African and ten Asian cardinals. For the ones from historically English-speaking nations, the British cardinal, Murphy-O'Connor, was a reference point, and key to bringing them onside. Bergoglio was at one stage approached by the African cardinals' kingmaker, Cardinal Laurent Monsengwo Pasinya of Kinshasa, Congo, who inquired about his lung. Bergoglio told him he had been operated on in the 1950s and that it had functioned pretty well ever since.[8]

The North Americans—eleven cardinals from the United States and three from Canada—were the largest group outside Europe and Latin America, and crucial to win over. They began to consider Bergoglio only after March 5, at the end of the second day of the congregations, when a major dinner was held in the Red Room of the Pontifical North American

College (NAC), with Murphy-O'Connor of Westminster and Pell of Sydney among the guests.

"The American cardinals were quite divided about where to go," recalls Murphy-O'Connor. Their kingmaker was the archbishop of Chicago, Francis George, who was trying to choose between Scola and the other high-caliber *papabile*, the Canadian head of the bishops' congregation, Cardinal Marc Ouellet. Murphy-O'Connor threw Bergoglio's name into the ring, but it didn't catch fire that night. Cardinal O'Malley of Boston (to whom Bergoglio had given a CD of the Argentine Mass, the *Misa Criolla*, when they spent time together in Buenos Aires in 2012) was in the "pro" camp. But for the other Americans he was an unknown quantity. Cardinal George in particular was worried about Bergoglio's age. "The question is, 'Does he still have vigor?'" he wondered.[9]

The following day, Wednesday, March 6, O'Malley of Boston and Daniel DiNardo of Galveston-Houston told journalists at the NAC press briefing that the cardinals were not ready to set a conclave date and needed more time to discern what and whom the Church needed. That turned out to be their last briefing until after the conclave: at the congregations that afternoon it was agreed that the US cardinals should cease their daily press conferences, to enable a more private discussion. They were furious. They had been scrupulous in respecting the confidentiality of the discussions and saw the global media spotlight as a heaven-sent opportunity to speak not just to Catholics back home but to evangelize wider American society. A number of the cardinals, especially Dolan of New York, felt they were being scapegoated by the *curiali* for the indiscretions of the Italian cardinals (or translators).

The result of the ban was that the leaks—paid and partial—from the general congregations to the Italian *vaticanisti* came to dominate the preconclave media discussion, producing an echo chamber that exaggerated the significance of intra-curial and intra-Italian tensions. Dependent now on the Italian press for their pre-conclave insights, the world's media reported that it was shaping up to be a Byzantine contest between different Italian and Vatican factions. For this reason, and because those urging his election stayed carefully below the radar, the Bergoglio bandwagon that began to roll during the week of the congregations went undetected by the media, and to this day most *vaticanisti* believe there was no organized pre-conclave effort to get Bergoglio elected. Not for the first time, the Argentine would appear to come out of nowhere, like a gaucho galloping in from the pampa at first light.[10]

☙

BERGOGLIO was a once-in-a-generation combination of two qualities seldom found together: he had the political genius of a charismatic leader and the prophetic holiness of a desert saint. When he rose to speak at the general congregations on the morning of March 7, both were in play. In a pithy but powerful address, he managed to freeze-frame the moment the Church was in and offer both diagnosis and cure.

He spoke for barely three and a half minutes, just about the only time in that week of speeches that a cardinal used less than his allotted five minutes. Not much longer than the Gettysburg address—363 words in Spanish, compared to Lincoln's 271 in English—and comparable in its simplicity and lyrical quality, his remarks reminded his listeners what they were there for, and, in a larger sense, who they were. His speech created a new narrative, or rescued one that had gotten buried. In the fog of endless interventions that week theorizing and analyzing, Bergoglio's call to action rang out clear and strong, like the summons of a monastery bell across a field.

There would have been no record of this papal Gettysburg had Cardinal Jaime Ortega of Havana not afterward asked Bergoglio for a copy. The Argentine had no speech to copy—he had spoken in Italian from notes—but later wrote it out in Spanish with a fountain pen, handing it to Ortega the next morning. After Francis was elected, Ortega had a PDF scan of it uploaded onto the Havana diocesan website, which is how the world found out about it.

Se hizo referencia a la evangelización . . . "Reference has been made to evangelization," Bergoglio began. "This is the Church's reason for being: Pope Paul VI speaks of 'the sweet and comforting joy of evangelizing.' It is Jesus Christ himself who, from within, impels us." Evangelizing, he said,

implies in the Church the *parrhesia* [apostolic courage] to come out from itself. The Church is called to come out from itself and to go to the peripheries, not just the geographical but also the existential peripheries: those of the mystery of sin, of suffering, of injustice, of ignorance and lack of religion, those of thought and those of every kind of misery.

When the Church did not do this, he warned, "it becomes self-referential and gets sick: the bent-over woman in the Gospel (Luke 13:11) comes to mind." Now he added his diagnosis of what had gone wrong in the Church, deploying an insight he had shared only a couple of months earlier in the Caritas retreat in Buenos Aires:

The evils that, over time, appear in Church institutions have their root in self-referentiality, a kind of theological narcissism. In the book of Revelation, Jesus says that he is at the door and calling, and evidently the text refers to him standing outside the door and knocking to be let in. But I sometimes think that Jesus is knocking from the inside, for us to let him out. The self-referential Church presumes to keep Jesus Christ for itself and not to let him out.

Without being aware of it, he went on, the Church becomes self-referential when it comes to believe it has its own light, and ceases to be the *mysterium lunae*, the "mystery of the moon." The phrase was used by the early-church fathers to describe how, just as the moon is lackluster, lacking light of its own, but at night shines brightly as it reflects that of the sun, so the Church has no other purpose but to reflect Christ. When it ceases to do so, and tries to live from its own light, Bergoglio went on, it falls into "spiritual worldliness," which, according to the theologian Henri de Lubac, he said, "is the worst evil that can befall the Church."

He went on to distill the choice that the Church faced: on the one hand, an evangelizing Church that comes out from itself, devoutly listening to and faithfully proclaiming the Word of God, or "the worldly Church that lives in itself, of itself, for itself." This, he said, "should give rise to the possible changes and reforms that have to be carried out for the salvation of souls." He concluded:

Thinking of the next pope: he should be a man who, through the contemplation of Jesus Christ, from the adoration of Jesus Christ, helps the Church to go out from itself toward the existential peripheries, and helps her to be the fruitful mother who lives from "the sweet and comforting joy of evangelizing."

It was not the accepted practice to clap, but the stillness that followed was louder than applause. "I looked at the faces around me," recalled Cardinal Murphy-O'Connor. "Many were moved by what he said." Cardinal Schönborn turned to a neighbor and said, "That's what we need." Cardinal Ortega described it as "magisterial, illuminating, committed, and true." Cardinal George told Murphy-O'Connor that he got it now—he understood what they had meant about him. Bergoglio had given the cardinals a way forward: a reform that ran deeper than just ridding the Curia of corruption or improving governance, one that would recall the Church to its purpose and the source of its life. That afternoon, the cardinals voted to enter the conclave the following Tuesday, March 12. Leaving the synod hall, Cardinal George's beaming expression said it all. "We're ready!" he told journalists.[11]

Over the weekend, Bergoglio put on his invisibility cloak. While the frontrunner *papabili*—Scola, Scherer, and Ouellet—celebrated Sunday Mass at their media-mobbed titular churches, Bergoglio stayed away from St. Robert Bellarmine, preferring to lunch quietly with the ninety-two-year-old sister of his old friend, the former nuncio in Argentina, Archbishop Ubaldo Calabresi, who had died in 2004.

He knew by this time he was *molto papabile* and felt the weight of it. When he bumped into the Canadian priest and TV producer Father Tom Rosica in the Piazza Navona, Bergoglio grasped his hands and asked him to pray for him. "Are you nervous?" Rosica asked. "A little bit," he answered. But when Gianni Valente and Stefania Falasca, Catholic journalists who were old friends, came by the Domus that evening, they found him serene and relaxed. "I'm sleeping like a baby," he told them.[12]

The next morning, Tuesday, March 12, the cardinals moved into the 120-room Vatican guesthouse, the Casa Santa Marta, in readiness for the opening of the conclave that afternoon. The cardinals were relieved of their cell phones and laptops, and had their bags X-rayed. The windows were shuttered and mobile signals jammed.

Across the hall from Bergoglio's room, no. 207, was Cardinal Kasper's. The German theologian had recently received copies of a Spanish translation of his latest theological work, *Barmherzigkeit*, on the subject of mercy. He had a couple with him and gave one to Bergoglio. "Ah, mercy," said Bergoglio when he saw the title, *La Misericordia*. "This is the name of our God."

In his room, Bergoglio found on his bed a white rose.[13]

AFTER the *pro eligendo pontifice* Mass the next day in St. Peter's, the 115 cardinals returned to the Casa Santa Marta for lunch and a rest before entering the Sistine Chapel that afternoon to take their solemn oaths. Then the doors were closed, and they proceeded to the first ballot, sealed off from the waiting world.

Despite the tension, a conclave is silent and solemn, like a retreat; the cardinals are in choir dress, as if attending a liturgy. The scrutinies, as the ballots are called, are ponderous. Nobody dawdles, but it isn't fast. The conclavists move from their table—there are four long rows of tables, two on each side of the chapel, facing each other—one by one, in order of precedence, to vote. Kneeling before the altar, looking up at Michelangelo's *Last Judgment*, each cardinal declares that, as Christ is his witness and judge, his vote is given to the man who, in the sight of God, he believes should be elected. Rising, he places his folded ballot paper—inscribed with the preamble *Eligo in Summum Pontificem*, "I choose as Supreme Pontiff . . ." and the name he has written next to it—onto a silver plate, or paten, on the altar, then tips it into an enormous silver chalice and returns to his seat, and so on, 115 times, until the three scrutineers, chosen by lot from among the electors, take the chalice and make the count, calling out each name. The acoustics are poor: at this conclave the scrutineers enlisted a strong-voiced Mexican cardinal to repeat the names of each cardinal voted for.

The negotiating and discussion necessary to bring a candidate to the two-thirds majority take place back at the Santa Marta. Unlike 2005, no cardinal has stepped forward with a "secret diary" with an account of the voting tallies, forcing the *vaticanisti* to piece together tidbits from the electors' post-conclave remarks. There are significant variants among the accounts. Bergoglio's backers' start-gate target of twenty-five was comfortably met, but whether it put him ahead on the first ballot is unclear. Scola, Scherer, and Ouellet also took votes, as the Italian media had forecast. But what all agree is that the next day the Argentine moved ahead of the field, reaching more than fifty votes on the second vote of the morning, the third ballot of the conclave.

At this point, apart from Bergoglio, only Scola remained as a possibility. Lunch in the Santa Marta was tense. Cardinal O'Malley sat next to Bergoglio and found him somber, barely eating. "He seemed very weighed down by what was happening," O'Malley later said. Whatever took place that lunchtime—in some accounts, Scola asked his supporters to back Bergoglio in an echo of the Argentine's gesture in 2005—it was nearly over on the first ballot of Wednesday afternoon, the fourth vote of the conclave, when Bergoglio came close to the seventy-seven needed. That afternoon, said Cardinal Dolan, "there was a remarkable calmness and tranquility about Cardinal Bergoglio. . . . He obviously sensed that this was the will of God."[14]

Then came a surprise. The second ballot of the afternoon, the fifth of the conclave, was annulled after the scrutineers found one more ballot paper than there were cardinals. The offending item was a blank voting sheet that had stuck by mistake to one bearing a name. Although it could not have affected the outcome, the rules were clear, and the cardinals had to vote all over again. Because the papers are not burned until the end of the morning or afternoon's voting, all that was known outside was that two ballots must have taken place by then, that black or white smoke should have appeared at around 6:00 p.m., and that the delay implied some problem: a medical emergency perhaps, or a smoke machine malfunction.[15]

In the corner of the Sistine Chapel, close to the entrance, stood the only means of the cardinals communicating the results of each ballot to the world: two enormous bronze-colored stoves, like Daleks from an underfunded sci-fi movie.

The one on the right, used for burning the ballot papers at the end of the scrutinies, was first used in 1939 and in the five conclaves that followed. To indicate that no pope had been elected, the attendants used to add damp straw to the burning ballots to blacken the smoke, but it was a risky business. There was the conclave in 1958 that elected John XXIII, when the first *sfumata* wrongly came out white (the straw had dried; until they managed a second *sfumata*, the news spread that a pope had been chosen after just two ballots). Special powders were later added, so as to make the white white and the black black, but at the 1978 conclaves, which elected John Paul I and II, there was no end of problems: more than once the crowd had been convinced the smoke was white, and left the square annoyed. And at one of the conclaves that year, a downdraft had sent fumes back into the chapel, causing cardinals to come out wheezing and hacking.

In 2005, the stove hadn't been big enough to incinerate 230 ballots from the scrutinies plus all the other papers, so there were two black smokes on the morning of April 19. It wasn't an issue in the afternoon, because Benedict XVI was elected after just one scrutiny, and so all the papers fit; but even then for a time no one was quite sure if the gray smoke was meant to be white or black. (The world was told to wait for the bells of St. Peter's to confirm the election, but there were no bells for more than ten minutes because of a Baroque confusion over telephones and lines of authority.)[16]

In 2013 they were taking no chances. An auxiliary stove was installed whose sole purpose was to generate smoke. To its side were boxes of cartridges marked *fumo nero* (black smoke) and just one box marked *fumo bianco* (white smoke). On Tuesday evening and Wednesday lunchtime the black smoke from the exploding cartridges was sucked from the auxiliary stove into the narrow heated tube bolted to the chapel wall, up through the vaulted ceiling, before belching out of the little steel stovepipe on the tiled roof that half the globe was watching. There was a lot of it, the smoke, and it lasted for a full seven minutes, billowing with such fierceness that any second you expected to hear the wail of a fire engine.

With the eyes of the global media locked on that chimney, the tension of the uncertainty on Wednesday evening made for great TV. Up on the platforms overlooking the square the commentators tried to come up with explanations for the delay while the presenters slowed their voices, introducing little history-is-being-made pauses to heighten the anticipation. It was a medieval system, the conclave, but it could have been designed for the age of twenty-four-hour news. What other global organization would announce its new leader this way, by means of smoke signals, the news reaching everyone, prince and pauper, at precisely the same moment?

Inside, as he prepared for what he would later describe as his "change of diocese," Bergoglio was at peace. "I'm the kind who worries, who gets anxious," he later told members of Latin-American religious orders. "But I was at peace. That confirmed to me that this was of God."[17]

When the scrutineers said *Eminentissimo Bergoglio* for the seventy-seventh time there was a collective gasp—a release of tension, like the rush of air from a deflating ball. The cardinals stood and applauded. "I don't think there was a dry eye in the house," Cardinal Dolan recalled. It was then that the Brazilian cardinal Claudio Hummes, a member of the order founded by Saint Francis of Assisi, hugged Bergoglio, kissed him, and told him: "Don't forget the poor."

The cardinals sat down again. Not until all 115 votes were called out would he be asked whether he accepted. He had some minutes. *Don't forget the poor.* The word *poveri* turned in his mind, like a mantra used to meditate, until the name leaped into his heart: Francis of Assisi, the man of poverty, the man of peace, the man who loves and cares for creation.

The count was over: he had more than ninety-five votes. Now Cardinal Giovanni Battista Re came over to him with the Question: did he accept his canonical election as Supreme Pontiff? It was 7:05 p.m. when Jorge Bergoglio said *accepto* in his good Latin, adding: *even though I am a great sinner.*

Flawed yet called. He had heard once again the invitation of the Good King, and made a choice as Saint Ignatius in the *Exercises* describes it, *when God our Lord so moves and attracts the will that without doubting or being able to doubt, the faithful soul follows what is shown, just as Saint Paul and Saint Matthew did when they followed Christ our Lord.* His first "yes" had been over half a century earlier, on Saint Matthew's feast, in a wooden confessional box in the Basilica of St. Joseph in Flores. From that "yes" until now his life's journey had been tied together by a thread, its knots unraveled by a great and gentle power.

Quo nomine vis vicari? "What name will you take?" asked Cardinal Re. *Vocabur Franciscus.* "I choose the name Francis," Bergoglio said firmly, "in honor of Saint Francis of Assisi." The cardinals, stunned, again broke into applause.

Francis was taken into the adjacent Room of Tears to be fitted with his white cassock and sash, choosing to keep his old black shoes and silver pectoral cross. The chapel was opened to let in the attendants, who put the ballots in the stove and loaded the *fumo bianco* cartridge. As white smoke gushed from the Sistine stovepipe into the wet black night, a roar rose from the square. Soon the great bells of the basilica began rocking, mixing a joyous *gong-gong* with the cheers of the crowd.

When Francis came back into the chapel in his white cassock, the cardinals applauded again. An ornate chair was brought out for him to sit to receive them, but he stayed standing as one by one the cardinals came up to embrace him. Then, conscious of the wet waiting crowd outside, he began to make his way toward the balcony. On the way he experienced a disturbance of spirits. "I was seized by a great anxiety," he later recalled. Flanked by Cardinal Hummes and Cardinal Agostino Vallini, the vicar for Rome, Francis entered the Pauline Chapel, as Benedict's reformed papal election rules required, and knelt in the back pew. Fear of the mission, he once told a group on retreat, can be "a sign from the good spirit."

> When we realize we are chosen, we feel that the weight on us is too great, and we experience fear—in some cases, even panic. That is the beginning of the Cross. At the same time, we feel deeply drawn by the Lord who by his very summons seduces us to follow him with a fire burning in our heart.[18]

As the world held its breath, inside the Pauline Chapel Francis drew himself into stillness. Here, in the antechamber of his new existence, he took a moment to be fueled by a strength not his own. Eventually the disturbance lifted, and he was flooded with joy and peace. "I was filled with a great light," he later recalled. "It lasted a moment, but to me it seemed very long."

Only God our Lord can give consolation to the soul without preceding cause, wrote Saint Ignatius in his Second Week discernment rules. *For it is the Creator's prerogative to enter the soul and leave her, and to arouse movements that draw her entirely into love of his Divine Majesty.*

Monsignor Dario Viganò, director of Vatican TV, whose cameraman was filming all this for posterity in high-resolution 4K, described what he saw as the images were fed back to his TV truck.

> The Pope is crossing the Sistine Chapel looking down, accompanied by Cardinal Vallini and Cardinal Tauran [sic]. He is looking down; he doesn't greet the cardinals, as if he was carrying an enormous burden. Entering the Pauline Chapel, they had prepared a throne, but he does not sit on the throne. He forcefully takes the cardinals to sit on either side of him in the last pew. He prays in silence. At a certain moment, the Pope rises. He turns around, exits into the Sala

Regia and at that moment he is a different person. It's a person who is smiling. It's as if he had entrusted the burden of this choice, as if God had said to him personally, "Don't worry. I'm here with you." It's a person who is no longer downcast. His face is no longer tilted downward. It's a man who looks and asks himself what he needs to do.

To many people Francis has since confirmed this account, telling one cardinal that he felt "a great sense of inner peace and freedom come over me, which has never left me." To another he said: "I believe the Holy Spirit has changed me."[19]

THE Francis era began with a *buona sera* ("good evening"). On the loggia balcony of St. Peter's at 8:22 p.m., flanked by Cardinals Hummes and Vallini, he stood before two hundred thousand rain-soaked people below and millions more on television. Down in the square, the phones and tablets flashed in the dark, like twinkling stars. Francis spoke shyly but firmly into the microphone in his fluent Italian.

Joking that "my brother cardinals have gone to the ends of the earth" in order to "give Rome a bishop," he asked for prayers for "our Bishop Emeritus Benedict XVI" and led the world in reciting an Our Father, a Hail Mary, and a Glory Be. Then he said: "And now let us begin this journey. Bishops and people. This journey of the Church of Rome that presides in charity over all the Churches. A journey of brotherhood, of love, of trust between us." Few recognized the famous ancient formula— "presides in charity"—that described the relationship of universal and local Church, or understood its implications: Francis was signaling that his would be a papacy bent on implementing collegiality. The Great Reform had been announced.

Yet what most people remember from that night was what came next: Francis asking for "the blessing of a people over its bishop—your prayer over me." The pope bowed his head low in a gesture of great humility, and a swollen silence followed. In this touching gesture of mutuality a lasting bond was formed. The new pope was seeking the blessing of God's holy faithful people before imparting his own blessing *urbi et orbi*, to the city of Rome and to the world, and to "all people of goodwill."

He returned with the electors to the Santa Marta, spurning the papal limousine to ride back with them on the bus. Over dinner he told them: "May God forgive you for what you have done," which Cardinal Dolan said "brought the house down." The next day, the first of his pontificate, Francis crossed Rome in a Vatican police car to the Basilica of St. Mary Major, arriving shortly after 8:00 a.m. The basilica houses the Marian image of *Salus Populi Romani*, protector of the Roman people, held to have been painted by Saint Luke. Francis left a bouquet of flowers there, before spending time in a chapel where Saint Ignatius of Loyola celebrated his first Mass in 1538. Then he went to pray at the tomb of Saint Pius V, the sixteenth-century pope whose Dominican habit established the tradition of popes wearing white cassocks. On the way back to the Vatican he stopped at the Via dell Scrofa to collect his suitcase—he went up to his room and packed his belongings himself—and to the astonishment of the staff, paid his bill, telling them that as pope he should set an example.

That afternoon he celebrated Mass with the cardinal electors, surprising them by coming to vest with them in the Hall of Blessings, as they had done throughout the conclave. The masters of ceremonies crowded around him with instructions on what to do and when at his first Mass as pope, but he batted them away, saying, "That's all right, you don't have to worry about me. I've been saying Mass for fifty years. But stay close, in case I need you."

During the Mass he preached standing at the pulpit as a parish priest does, rather than sitting in a chair, as popes do; and rather than read a prepared text, he spoke spontaneously in impeccable Italian, preaching, as he always had done, for seven or eight minutes, around three key points: the importance of walking, building, and confessing. "We can walk as much as we want, we can build many things, but if we do not confess Jesus Christ, things go wrong," he told them. "We may become a charitable NGO [a nongovernmental, or philanthropic, organization] but not the Church, the Bride of the Lord." He also quoted the radical French convert León Bloy, whom he had read with his friends in the Guardia de Hierro in the 1970s: "Anyone who does not pray to the Lord prays to the Devil."

That evening he entered the papal apartments—sealed since Benedict's departure—with Archbishop Georg Gänswein, prefect of the papal household. As Gänswein fumbled with the light switch, Francis found himself peering into a gilded cage: cavernous, marble-floored rooms with heavy furniture, each leading into the next, that seemed to go on forever.

Recognizing a feeling of desolation, he saw only loneliness and isolation, and decided at that moment to remain living in the Santa Marta, using the apartments for meetings.

He made calls: to his dentist in Buenos Aires to cancel his appointment, to Daniel del Regno, his paper deliverer ("Seriously, it's Jorge Bergoglio, I'm calling you from Rome") to thank him for his years of service, and to his sole surviving sibling, María Elena.

"He told me, 'Look, it happened, and I accepted,'" she recalls. "But I said, 'but how are you, how do you feel?' He was dying of laughter, and said, 'I'm fine, relax.' I said, 'You looked really good on television, you had a radiant expression. I wish I could give you a hug.' He said, 'We are hugging, we are together, I have you very close to my heart.' It's not easy to explain what it is to talk to your brother, and your brother is the pope," recalls María Elena, between laughter and tears. "*Es* muy *complicado*—it's *really* complicated."

A few months later, in July, the English and Welsh bishops had an audience with Francis. When he saw Cardinal Murphy-O'Connor, he broke into a broad smile. "It's your fault!" he laughed. "What have you done to me?"[20]

EPILOGUE: THE GREAT REFORM

A T THE END of the morning's second scrutiny on the day of Francis's election, the archbishops of Havana and Buenos Aires sat together in the minibus that whisked the cardinals back from the Sistine Chapel to lunch at the Santa Marta. It was cold and wet outside. Cardinal Ortega turned to Cardinal Bergoglio. "Jorge, I need to talk to you about Latin America, because this afternoon you're going to be pope."

"Well, unless the omelet gets flipped, yes," agreed Bergoglio. "When do you want to talk?"

"Right now," said Ortega. "We have forty minutes before lunch."

Unlike Bergoglio's tiny room on the fifth floor, Ortega had lucked out with a downstairs suite. There they discussed the big shifts in Latin America since they were young priests in the 1960s, and the new openings that lay ahead. Back then Church documents spoke of the vast social inequalities and the continent's cultural and political dependence on the United States. The inequalities remained, but Latin America had come of age. Yet politics in the continent continued to be dominated by what Bergoglio called "adolescent progressivism." What polarized the politics of the region was the U.S.-Cuba standoff. Latin Americans were constantly presented with an unappetizing choice between suffocating state socialism or sink-or-swim individualism. What was needed was a new leadership, imbued with social Christian humanism.

"The Church can never be a mere spectator," said Bergoglio. "The Church has to accompany these processes in dialogue."[1]

Paul VI, whom Francis would later describe as his "great light," called dialogue "love's new name." Dialogue was about creating new spaces for the Holy Spirit to act; it was the means Christ had given the Church to change the world.

Dialogue meant speaking directly, humanly, and humbly. It meant reaching out, not lecturing. It meant connecting with the seekers and the critics, not just affirming the dwellers. It meant a significant shift in the culture of the Church like that of the Second Vatican Council, when the pastors smelling of sheep flew in from the four corners of the earth, blowing past the sentinels of orthodoxy in their tinted-glass cars.

✌

AT the moment Francis appeared on the balcony in white, Liliana Negre de Alonso—the politician hounded in 2010 for defending him over same-sex marriage—was fumbling furiously with her phone, which was vibrating furiously in the middle of her senate address. An aide showed her a beaming Francis on an iPad. The senator for San Luis broke from her speech, her voice trembling. "My heart swells with pride," Negre eventually managed, "because an Argentine brother has become the successor of St. Peter."[2]

Bergoglio's friend Alicia Oliveira, the human rights judge who had always stood by him against Verbitsky, was in a café when she saw it on the TV, and at once burst into tears. "Señora, what's the matter?" a man at a nearby table asked her. "Is he such a bad man, this Bergoglio?"

"No, no," she explained between sobs. "It's just that he's my friend and I'll never see him again."

In fact, Oliveira saw him just days later when she became the instrument of a rapprochement between the Argentine government and the new pope.

Like the grim Polish generals following the election of John Paul II, President Cristina Kirchner's initial response had been a cold, formal message of congratulations. When the Ecuadorian president, Rafael Correa, called to congratulate her, she told him that Bergoglio was a *facho*—nasty right-wing—enemy of her government. But as stunned and screaming headlines caught the wave of euphoria and amazement breaking that day over Argentina, she came to her political senses, and reached for the reverse gear. Oliveira was asked to call Francis to broker an invitation, and accompanied the president to Rome. Verbitsky—and his accusations—would soon disappear.[3]

When Francis invited Cristina Kirchner to lunch the day before his inauguration on March 19, she presented him with the iconic Argentine expat package of yerba mate, together with gourd and metal straw, bicentennial vacuum flask, and even a packet of sugar. *Lo tomo amargo,* he told her, smiling: "I take mine without sugar."

She told journalists afterward that it was the first time she had been kissed by a pope. She would not be the last. Francis has abandoned the tradition that popes never kiss or receive kisses.

In the very early hours the next morning, a crowd at a vigil outside the cathedral in the Plaza de Mayo in Buenos Aires suddenly received a call from him, relayed through loudspeakers. In language of great immediacy and tenderness, as if to his own family, he asked them to care for each other, for the old and the young, for the world around them. *No le saquen el cuero a nadie,* he told them, using an old gaucho expression: "Don't flay each other." The pope spoke to them not just in their own language, but using their idioms and inflection; he was now other, yet still the same—a *porteño* Pontifex Maximus.

"WE'RE going to have to get used to a new way of doing things," Father Lombardi warned journalists in Rome who were trying to adjust to the new pope's freedom. After celebrating his first Mass as pope at the little Vatican church of Sant'Anna in a surplice so simple that it sent shivers down the spines of the lace police, Francis greeted the congregation one by one as they came out, leading the media to dub him "the world's parish priest." Some thought that this undignified self-demotion would dismantle the monarchic papacy. The abbot Enzo Bianchi was one of them, but he approved. Francis, he wrote in the daily *La Stampa,* is "the Pontiff become man."[4]

Francis used both the Mass and the Sunday Angelus that followed to announce a *kairos* of mercy—an appointed time in the purpose of God. "Mercy is the Lord's greatest message," he told crowds in the square below from the balcony of the Apostolic Palace. He had a clear, joyful message he gave over and over: that God never tired of forgiving. Mixing humor and anecdotes, he commended Cardinal Kasper's book *Mercy,* which he had read during the conclave, while laughing that he wasn't just trying to increase the German's book sales.

The inauguration Mass, held on the Solemnity of Saint Joseph, was attended by the delegates of 132 states, dozens of religious leaders, and a crowd of two hundred thousand. The religious leaders included, for the first time at a papal inauguration since the Great Schism of the eleventh century, the Orthodox patriarch of Constantinople, Bartholomew, drawn by Francis's reference to himself as bishop of Rome presiding in charity. Just as in 2001, when he became cardinal, Francis sent a message home (this time via the nuncio) that he did not want people wasting money on flights to attend the Mass, and to give the money instead to the poor. But among his own invited guests was the *cartonero* leader, Sergio Sánchez.

Francis's theme was Saint Joseph's protective, tender leadership:

> Let us never forget that authentic power is service, and that the pope, too, when exercising power, must enter ever more fully into that service which has its radiant culmination on the Cross. He must be inspired by the lowly, concrete, and faithful service that marked Saint Joseph and, like him, he must open his arms to protect all of God's people and embrace with tender affection the whole of humanity, especially the poorest, the weakest, the least important, those whom Matthew lists in the final judgment on love: the hungry, the thirsty, the stranger, the naked, the sick, and those in prison (cf. Mt 25:31–46). Only those who serve with love are able to protect!

Cardinal Christoph Schönborn of Vienna, who had known Jorge Bergoglio since he was an auxiliary bishop of Buenos Aires, was in tears throughout the homily. "Tim, he speaks like Jesus," he whispered at one point to Cardinal Timothy Dolan. "Chris," the Archbishop of New York answered, "I think that's his job description."[5]

After Mass, Francis went among the crowd in the square in an open-air white SUV, giving an unpapal thumbs-up as he rode past banners that quoted God's words to Saint Francis of Assisi RIPARA LA MA CHIESA ("Repair my Church"). For the first time, the Latin American flags outnumbered the European ones. The new source Church had arrived.

Francis spent a very long time among the people, kissing and embracing and shaking hands, stopping occasionally to sip from a proffered gourd of mate, which would become a tradition in his Wednesday audiences. He also began another habit: stepping outside the vehicle to embrace, with deep tenderness, a severely disabled man. The weekly time in the square, with its focus on the sick and the disabled and his banter with the crowds, was key to the Great Reform, a time to heal the wounds of clericalism, which at its most vicious had permitted or covered up sexual abuse.

At the end of the audience with the media a few days earlier, Francis had not given the usual apostolic blessing, because many of them were not Catholics or even believers. "I cordially give this blessing silently, to each of you, respecting the conscience of each, but in the knowledge that each of you is a child of God," he told them.

The reporters had been struck by the graciousness of that gesture, and now, as they packed up after the inauguration Mass and made for home, some of them—and especially those who had arrived in Rome shaking their heads at the stories of Vatican dysfunction—confessed their amazement at what had taken place there over the past fortnight: how a ship run aground was now plowing through the waves again, lifted by a fresh strong wind that seemed to come out of nowhere.

They had seen the wonder of it: that this could happen at just the moment when the long night of institutional failure seemed at its darkest. As Jorge Bergoglio had written twenty years earlier, in the sadness of his Córdoba days: "It is a corpse, and divinity is hidden in it, and will be resurrected. . . . God's reforms happen right there, where there is no other solution but to hope against all hope."[6]

&

"WHEN Cardinal Martini talked about focusing on the councils and synods, he knew how long and difficult it would be to go in that direction," Francis said in October 2013, adding that he was determined to proceed "gently, but firmly and tenaciously" towards the synodal Church of which Martini had dreamed.[7]

Evangelii Gaudium has made clear Francis's intention to give bishops' conferences (including supranational bishops' bodies such as CELAM and CCEE) "genuine doctrinal authority," opening the door to the restoration of the early-church balance of the universal and local Church.

These reforms should mean that the Vatican's steamrolling of CELAM in 1992 can never be repeated, while future Aparecidas will flower in other continents.

When former San Francisco archbishop John R. Quinn, author of a famous work on collegiality, met Bergoglio in Rome in April 2012, the cardinal told him that he was praying that what he described in his book would be implemented. Now he is pope it is possible to imagine, as Quinn does, future self-governing regional patriarchates that appoint their own bishops and decide on pastoral and liturgical questions, leading to the "healthy decentralization" of which Francis speaks in *Evangelii Gaudium*.[8]

Less than a month after his election, Francis created a council of eight (later nine) cardinals from across the world to reform the Roman Curia, one of the most significant acts in Church governance in hundreds of years. With just one Italian among them, acting as secretary, the cardinals, who meet in Rome every two months, are from India, Germany, the Congo, the United States, Australia, and Honduras; many are also heads or former heads of the supranational bishops' bodies, thus making Rome accountable to the local Church. Francis referred to the C9 in his Spadaro interview as "an advisory group of *outsiders*," using a phrase similar to Cardinal Martini's 2012 spiritual testament, when the Jesuit former archbishop of Milan called for "twelve people outside the lines" to be given real responsibility in the Church. Francis sees the C9 as key to his governance reform, "the beginning of a Church with an organization that is not just top-down but also horizontal."[9]

Meanwhile, the college of cardinals itself is assuming a role in governance of the universal Church similar to that of a senate, as in the pre-Reformation era. Over two-day meetings in February 2014 and February 2015, known as consistories, Francis has asked the cardinals to deliberate on major questions: admission to the sacraments for the remarried in the first, and the structural reform of the Curia in the second. In 2015, the cardinals were treated to something they had never expected to hear in Rome—a detailed breakdown of Vatican finances.

Francis's creation of new cardinals in both consistories reveals the future direction he wants for the college: to correct the Eurocentric imbalance by reducing the number of curial cardinals and amplifying the presence of poor countries. Among the new red hats in 2015 were a number from poor, far-flung places such as Tonga and Myanmar, so fulfilling

Congar's dictum that in all true reform the "periphery shapes the center." Francis has been using the consistories to teach the Church lessons about service and humility: in 2014 he invited the cardinals to cease thinking of themselves as princes of the Church, to shun a "worldly mentality" of "rivalry, jealousy, and factions," as well as "intrigue, gossip, cliques, favoritism, and preferences." Being a cardinal, he told them in 2015, "is certainly an honor, but it is not honorific."

The third instrument of collegiality is the most far-reaching of all—a new model of synod. Francis is converting the synod from a predictable Vatican-controlled gathering into a powerful instrument of universal church governance, such that the pastoral realities of the local Church can be brought to bear on questions of doctrine and discipline. Cardinal Lorenzo Baldisseri, whom Francis named to take charge of the reforms, said in June 2013 that the pope was looking for "a dynamic, permanent synod, not as a structured organism, but as an *action,* like an osmosis between center and periphery." In an April 1, 2014, letter to Baldisseri, Francis's ambition for his reformed synod was transparent: it is to have real deliberative power as in the councils of the early centuries of Christianity, a body outside and above the Curia, accountable not just to the pope but also to the bishops.[10]

✎

In early October 2013, after Francis turned up with his briefcase and lunch box for a two-day meeting with Baldisseri's council, it was announced that the synod would tackle a broad gamut of thorny pastoral issues related to marriage and family, including the question that dogged the 2005 synod, of access to sacraments for the divorced and remarried. The new synod would use a wholly different method, beginning with a consultation of the local Church, a consistory of cardinals in February 2014 to shake open the discussion, followed by two assemblies of hundreds of bishop delegates and invited lay experts. A year separated the two synods: the first, in October 2014, to define the questions and the second, in October 2015, to vote on concrete proposals.

Francis's aim with the synod has not been to alter the Church's longstanding doctrine on either the sacraments or the indissolubility of marriage, but to find ways of reinstating those alienated from the life of the Church because of often tragic personal situations. He has told a number of people—among them his old school friend Oscar Crespo—that the reintegration of divorcées in the life of the Church was the number one priority of his papacy. But rather than impose a solution, says Walter Kasper, "he wants to listen to what the Spirit is saying to the Churches."[11]

The big picture behind the synod is the sharp loss of the meaning of marriage in Western culture. The Church, tragically, has for too long relied on that culture to teach couples the meaning of marriage, and its own preparation for couples has been inadequate to compensate. The consequence has been a sharp decline in Church marriages. In Francis's Argentina, the proportion of those entering sacramental marriages has dropped from over 80 percent to under 50 percent in just two decades; while in the U.S., numbers entering Catholic marriages have fallen by over 60 percent since the 1970s, and recently declined from 242,000 in 2003 to 164,000 in 2013, despite Catholic numbers growing by three million in that time. The evidence was also clear from rising levels of divorce among Catholics, currently averaging around a third across the Western world. Catholic countries such as Belgium, Portugal, and Spain have some of the highest divorce rates in the world.

Because Catholics had for decades entered marriage without properly grasping its meaning, many, if not most, marriages are likely to be invalid in the Church's understanding: Francis himself suggested on the papal plane from Rio de Janeiro in July 2013 that "as many as half" could be null. Yet the Church's tribunals are mostly inadequate to the task of examining specific cases: processes are seen as lengthy, cumbersome, and expensive. Even in countries such as the United States where the annulment system is effective and accessible, the numbers of Catholics seeking annulments have dropped markedly, despite the rise in numbers divorcing: in the U.S., applications fell from over 70,000 in 2003 to 25,000 in 2013, while in Argentina they hover between 150 and 200 a year—a miniscule percentage of the tens of thousands of Catholics (nominal or practicing) who divorce each year.

In Francis's view the Church's response to this drama cannot only be to improve its preparation and support for marriage, but that it has to take responsibility for those now alienated from the Church. This means looking at it from the point of view of those who most need the Church's healing support—those who have suffered marital breakdown. There are "two ways of thinking and of having faith," he told the cardinals in February 2015. "We can fear to lose the saved and we can want to save the lost."

In phone calls and personal responses to letters, Francis has urged people in difficult situations not to allow themselves to be turned away—even giving permission directly, in some instances, to people to receive Communion and confession. Because these are private communications, the Vatican cannot confirm them, but Francis knows the stories give a clear message: that changes are coming, and that in the meantime, people should assume they belong in the fold.

In elaborating this new synod, Francis drew on the experience of CELAM, the oldest and most highly developed transnational collegial body in the Church. The synod began not with a document but with a grassroots reality check, called for total freedom in discussion, and allowed consensus to emerge over time. If the synod eventually produced few concrete outcomes and major novelties, Archbishop Víctor Fernández, Bergoglio's theologian assistant at Aparecida, told journalists, it wouldn't worry the pope, "because he has always believed that time is greater than space, that the important things come about slowly, and that the important thing is to initiate processes rather than force decisions. And that these, at the right time, will produce good fruit."

Francis was here drawing on many years of deep study (via Guardini and Möhler) of how the Holy Spirit acts within the Christian body—the subject of the doctorate he began but never finished in the 1980s. Back then, during the turbulence in his Jesuit province, he had set out to understand how differing views in the church, freely expressed and properly channeled, opened spaces for the Holy Spirit to bring about new creative solutions, just as it had in the early-church councils; yet also what destroys that path to convergence—the temptations that turn disagreements into contradictions, when views fall out of the unity of the whole, and develop in opposition to the body, generating rivalry, conflict, and schism.

Referring to the fierce disagreements yet great fruits of the early-church councils, Francis prayed the night before the synod opened on October 5, 2014, for "the gift of listening: listening to God, until we breathe the will to which God calls us," urging participants to "lend an ear to the debates of this time and smell the 'odor' of the people of today, to the point of being impregnated with their joys and hopes, their sadness and anguishes."

The next day, after briefly telling the synod participants to speak boldly and listen humbly, he stayed quiet but was present throughout, arriving early each day to welcome the delegates, and chatting with them over coffee. There was tension and disagreement over matters of procedure, as well as specific issues, and a group of conservative cardinals used the media to publicly express their dismay. Yet the document that finally emerged from the small-group discussions—which would in turn shape the discussion at the concluding synod of October 2015—reflected a broad consensus. Three paragraphs on homosexuality and the question of access to sacraments for the remarried failed to reach the usual two-thirds majority but Francis, unfazed, ordered it published, complete with the vote tallies. "We've set out on a path of openness," he told them. "I want everybody to know what we're up to."

Then the master Jesuit retreat–giver identified the lights and the shadows and movements of the spirit of the previous two weeks, warning against "temptations" to flee the tension, whether through doctrinal rigidity or a desire to be acceptable to the world. He told them not to worry, that those who saw only a "disputatious Church" needed to realize that they were gathered *sub et cum Petro,* with and under the pope, who was the "guarantor of the adhesion of the Church to the will of God, to the Gospel of Christ, and to the Tradition of the Church."

Expressing satisfaction with the process, he told *La Nación* in December 2014 that what had been created at the synod was "a covered, protected space that allows the Spirit to work."[12] However intense the disagreements, he saw a process of genuine ecclesial discernment at stake—a true reform in Congar's sense: pastoral, rooted in core church doctrines, and aimed at lifting the burdens from God's holy faithful people.

Unlike the last four popes, who were all present at the Second Vatican Council, Francis was a theology student when it ended. "Francis doesn't want to waste time interpreting the Council," says Fr. Carlos Galli, the Argentine theologian who remains close to the Pope. "He sees his task as implementing it."[13]

Francis's reformed synod seeks to embed permanently the dynamic of the Second Vatican Council: bringing to bear the pastoral on to the doctrinal. The synod is a mechanism of permanent reform. Reform means to recover the *forma Christi*, the Church that makes Christ more present. Permanent reform, for Francis, means ensuring that Christ, not the Church, remains the focus. And that means, in turn, putting God's mercy front and center of the Catholic offer.

※

THE people of Buenos Aires recall how at Christmas, Cardinal Bergoglio used to take the baby Jesus from the crib to show to the congregation, saying: "This is God. God is tenderness."

Francis is giving the Church and the world that lesson. The word for merciful in Latin, *misericors,* contains *cor,* meaning heart, and *miseri,* meaning the poor—the suffering, the sinners, those who yearn. The notion that God, the all-powerful Creator, is concerned with the distress of individuals, binding their wounds and time and again forgiving their sins "exceeds normal human experience and expectation," notes Cardinal Kasper in *Mercy,* and "transcends human imagination and thought."

Francis has told those close to him that the Church only properly began to recover mercy as the primary attribute of God in recent decades, following centuries in which (after the sixteenth-century Reformation) God's justice was overemphasized. Convinced, like Kasper, that "the proclamation of a God who is insensitive to suffering is a reason that God has become alien and finally irrelevant to many human beings," Francis is making the restoration of mercy through what he calls the "Samaritan Church" the key to evangelization.[14]

Hence his endless calls to the Church to offer that mercy. To experience God as *misericordia* is to enter into the life of God, and to grasp the revelation of Jesus. The word "mercy" appears thirty-two times in *Evangelii Gaudium,* which calls for Church parishes and communities to become, as he put it in his Lenten message 2015, "islands of mercy in the midst of the sea of indifference."

Christopher and Regina Catrambone, a wealthy Catholic couple based in Malta, took that call literally after they saw a winter coat floating in the water while sailing to Lampedusa in 2012 in a chartered yacht. Shocked by the reality hidden by their Mediterranean of luxury ports, and inspired by Francis's visit to Lampedusa shortly after his election, they bought a 140-foot former trawler, the *Phoenix*, along with dinghies and state-of-the art drones to detect the boats of migrants, and fitted it with rescue vessels and a clinic. They spend weeks at sea, rescuing hundreds of north African migrants from the cold sea, washing, treating, and clothing them, saving their lives before handing them over to the Italian navy. Their project, Migrant Offshore Aid Station (MOAS), could stand as a symbol of Francis's call to conversion: it not only saves lives but models a new attitude to the migrant tragedy, one that begins in compassion.

It is in many ways a counterintuitive call. In a society marked by relativism and religious indifference, surely what the world needs is more, not less, judgment? But Francis sees that response as a temptation. The Church's task is to open up paths of return, not to raise the barriers. "If people are hurt, what does Jesus do?" Pope Francis asked in a March 17 homily. "Scold them because they are hurt? No, He comes and He carries them on His shoulders. And this is called mercy. And when God rebukes his people—'I desire mercy, not sacrifice!'—He's talking about this."

Francis's proclamation of a *kairos* of mercy stems from his conviction that a world being rapidly changed by technology and wealth is prone, above all, to the illusion that human beings, not God, are sovereign. Mercy is the great antidote to the Western obsession with autonomy, for it grounds its hope in God and others, rather than in our own resources. That is why the poor are quicker to grasp Francis than the rich and the educated—and why the opposition to Francis has come from elite groups invested in particular narratives.

Francis has declared 2016 a special Holy Year dedicated to the theme of mercy, entrusting it to the Pontifical Council for the New Evangelization created by Benedict XVI. Mercy, in other words, is Francis's answer to the question posed by the 2012 synod, of how to re-present the Gospel message to secularized societies. Mercy, he told the Council, is the response to "the crisis of modern man."

He has developed this idea in his April 2015 10,000-word teaching document, *Vultus Misericordiae* ("The Face of Mercy"). The document takes up the argument he had with the Society of Jesus and progressive Catholics in the 1970s in warning of "the temptation . . . to focus exclusively on justice." Justice was "the first, albeit necessary and indispensable step," he writes in *Vultus Misericordiae,* but the Church had to go beyond, "to announce the mercy of God, the beating heart of the Gospel, which in its own way must penetrate the heart and mind of every person." In urgent, emphatic language he describes how the Church's very credibility—a word he uses three times in the document—is bound up in the extent to which she shows merciful and compassionate love, not just in words, but above all in gestures and actions.

This is why, on his trips, Francis always asks to visit "places of pain"—prisons, drug addiction centers, elderly homes, homes for the disabled—where he can demonstrate God's focus on those in need. It is why, when visiting parishes, he takes detours into the shantytowns. And it is why he spends so much time in St Peter's Square among the crowds at the Wednesday general audiences, such that the traditional fifteen-minute papal address has become a part of a much broader catechesis of actions and gestures.

"The people charge my batteries," Francis told his old friend and former pupil in La Inmaculada, Jorge Milia, during a meeting in May 2014. "When I get off the popemobile and embrace some guy who is so wrecked you wonder how they ever got here, he's happy, because you've reached him. But I never forget the fact that there are all these cameras around me, and that this hug is being multiplied and watched by an infinite number of people in the same situation, who see it on TV and feel as if they're being hugged too." He knows it makes him vulnerable to attacks—"I hope when they get me, it's one clear shot," he told Milia—but he also knows that it is the heart of the message his papacy exists to restore.[15]

THE recovery of mercy as the true face of God is key to Francis's vision of a missionary, outward-oriented Church, one that focuses on primary proclamation that God is love. Because the Vatican—at times haughty, self-referential, and moralistic—has sometimes given the opposite message, modernizing its antiquated structure, built to house a fortress rather than a lighthouse, has been a priority. Describing the Vatican as "Europe's last remaining court," Francis told the Mexican television station Televisa in March 2015 that it must change to become a "working group, at the service of the Church, at the service of bishops."

When the story comes to be told of how some of the greatest names in management consultancy—McKinsey, KPMG, Ernst & Young, Promontory—have helped to overhaul the world's oldest global organization, it is likely to begin with a meeting shortly after his election between Francis and seven financiers at the Casa Santa Marta. They included Jean-Baptiste de Franssu, former chief of the asset management giant Invesco; George Yeo, the former foreign minister of Singapore; and Jochen Messemer, a top executive at a leading German insurer, ERGO.

Francis told them that for the Church's spiritual message to be credible, the Vatican's finances must be, too. He said it was time for strict rules and protocols, complete transparency, and sound financial management, and to cut costs to free up more money for aiding the poor. "When the administration is fat, it's unhealthy," he told them, adding: "You are the experts and I trust you. I want solutions to these problems, and as soon as possible."[16]

The group, known as the Organization for the Economic-Administrative Structure of the Holy See (COSEA) was led by Joseph F. X. Zahra, a senior Maltese banker. Charging nothing for their services, the senior executives met regularly over ten months to put together reforms to the financial management of the Vatican governed by three core principles: that the Vatican should adopt contemporary international financial standards, that its policies and procedures should be transparent, with annual financial statements reviewed by one of the Big Four audit firms, and that there should be multiple sources of authority, each with senior expert international lay leadership exercising control.

A veteran commentator who flew into Rome in February 2014 described "a virtual gridlock of commissions, councils, and consistories," with international consultants and accountancy firms flitting in and out of Vatican offices. That month, the Vatican announced a new Secretariat for the Economy to oversee finances, led by the Australian cardinal, George Pell, who is in turn accountable to a new Council for the Economy made up of professional lay experts, the most senior of whom is Zahra.[17]

In July 2014, the straight-talking Pell announced a series of reforms to the so-called Vatican Bank, stripping out its investment portfolio and reducing it to a savings and loan exclusively for religious congregations. The Institute for the Works of Religion (IOR) had already shrunk its balance sheet, after closing roughly 3,000 accounts that did not meet the new standards. Through these and other measures Francis has put in place a system of financial safeguards unparalleled in Vatican history, cleaning out hidden accounts and rogue budgets, reducing Italian influence over Vatican finances in general, and putting in place lay professionals recruited for what, not who, they know.

Financial reform, which is a largely technical matter, has moved much faster than the redesign of the Vatican bureaucracy entrusted to the C9, which involves much more debatable issues of ecclesiology and theology.

The C9's task is to simplify and streamline the bloated, complex, and frequently overlapping jurisdictions of the Vatican's nine congregations (which are powerful legislative bodies), twelve pontifical councils and seven pontifical commissions (both largely advisory), and three tribunals. Francis wants to increase collaboration and prevent duplication, to make it easier for him to have regular meetings with the department heads as a body. But the aim is also to improve the quality of Vatican staff and the number of lay people, and especially women, working in the Curia. Two new congregations are on the cards: one for Laity and the other for Justice and Charity, which will absorb the existing pontifical councils. Other congregations will be closed or merged. The new congregations send powerful signals: that God's holy faithful people are as important as bishops and clergy, and that justice and charity are at the heart of the mission of the pope.

It is slow work. A new constitution is likely to take until 2017 and there is a long way to go in deciding which departments will be merged or closed. Changing Vatican culture is an even more long-term task. Most curial posts remain unconfirmed; Francis has scrapped bonuses and the title of monsignor for priests under sixty-five; and from February 2014, Vatican department heads were told to end new hires, wage increases, and overtime in an urgent effort to cut costs and offset budget shortfalls. At the same time, Francis has introduced compulsory retreats for all who work in the Curia, and is looking for other ways of nourishing and supporting the four thousand or so staff. But he is determined to change its ethos, combating careerism and nepotism so that the Vatican models the missionary culture that Francis wants to see in the whole Church.

Francis has become the most accessible of modern popes, almost always to be found at lunchtime in the Santa Marta restaurant, where he has his own table set aside, but leaves visitors openmouthed when he queues with his tray like everyone else for the buffet. He comes out of the Santa Marta to greet visitors personally, and shocks people by getting into the elevator with them ("I don't bite," he reassures them). Reaching the pope no longer involves negotiating Byzantine courts-within-courts; his two secretaries can be called or e-mailed, and messages are usually relayed swiftly. Those secretaries, the Argentine Father Fabián Pedacchio and the Egyptian Copt Yoannis Lahzi Gaid, are not powerful intermediaries as under previous popes, but discreet facilitators. Francis will not allow another court to grow up around him, and keeps his own diary.

As a result, in other ways the pope is these days less accessible. Papal audiences are no longer traded by Vatican power brokers, and archbishops express frustration that they no longer know how to arrange for a wealthy donor to meet the pope. Francis has arrogated to a close circle around him what used to be dealt with by Vatican institutions, and the circumventing of the old channels causes great resentment. Francis's extraordinary popularity beyond the borders of the Church is in striking contrast to the view of him in the Vatican, where there is considerable grumbling. The old guard has lost control: once-powerful officials feel out of the loop, and express resistance by continuing to do business as usual, insisting that they will still be there after Francis is long gone.

The Great Reform is barely two years old, and faces opposition from vested interests hurt by Francis's reforms as well as institutional resistance to change. As Machiavelli once observed, nothing is harder than "to initiate a new order of things" for "the reformer has enemies in all those who profit by the old order, and only lukewarm defenders in all those who would profit by the new order." Some in Rome refer to Francis as the "Jesuit experiment" and are quick to recall that while popes come and go, the Curia is immortal. Knowing he cannot afford to alienate his staff, Francis is moving slowly, making strategic appointments which reassure his opponents while at the same time moving key people into position.

Beyond Rome, opposition reflects deep-seated rigorist fears. Francis's emphasis on mercy "provokes in some Catholics a panic, the fear of a lack of certainty that stuns me," says Antonio Spadaro, S.J., editor of the journal *Civiltà Cattolica*.[18] And then there is the apathy of the Church worldwide, which has yet to offer convincing proof that, despite Francis's efforts, it has become missionary in its focus. A sense of where Francis sees the real opposition is revealed in *Evangelii Gaudium*'s critique of "pastoral acedia" and a "tomb psychology" that "transforms Christians into mummies in a museum." Just as Bergoglio used to deploy the image of the laboratory to warn against abstract ideology, now Francis uses the image of the museum as warning to a Church that resists the life of the Holy Spirit, calling in his homily of April 28, 2015, for "the apostolic courage to bring life and not make of our Christian life a museum of memories."

❧

IT is a Bergoglio paradox: the collegial pope, close to the people, exercises his sovereign authority in ways that can seem high-handed. His is a highly personalistic government, which bypasses systems, depends on close relationships, works through people rather than documents, and keeps a tight control. In this the demagogic Jesuit provincial can still be glimpsed, whose leadership struck many as divisive and monolithic.

Yet he long ago learned the lessons of that time. His governance is collegial because it aims to broaden consultation, to include different points of view, and above all to open up the center to the periphery. He encourages, in a way no pope has done before, lively and honest disagreement, saying that the only place Christians do not disagree is the cemetery. But this does not mean that he shares decision making. In many ways Francis is the most centralized pope since Pius the Ninth.

There are glimpses of the old Jesuit Bergoglio in the way he will keep his cards close to his chest while he mulls, before suddenly springing his decision on the world when it is least expected. He understands power, and he has often used it to bypass existing channels or advisers, as well as tradition and protocol. And having executed an order, he will carry the weight of it, even if it costs him dear.

The decision to reassign Bishop Juan Barros from the armed forces to the small southern Chilean diocese of Osorno left even his most loyal supporters bewildered. Barros has been very publicly linked by victims to Fr. Fernando Karadima, a notorious abuser sentenced in 2011 by Rome to a life of prayer and penitence. Barros, who as a young priest was part of Karadima's circle, has been accused of witnessing the abuse and later, as secretary to the then cardinal archbishop, covering up for it.

Barros denies the claims, but because the appointment was destined to rub salt into still-raw wounds, it wasn't only Karadima's victims who opposed it: Chile's senior bishops, along with priests and laity in Osorno itself, strenuously objected to the nomination. After being told during the synod of October 2014 that it was going ahead, the cardinal archbishop of

Santiago, Ricardo Ezzati, met Francis to warn him against the appointment, spelling out to him in detail the consequences for the Chilean Church. Further meetings with bishops followed, and letters of protest to Rome were sent from dozens of clergy and more than a thousand lay people from the diocese. Yet the installation Mass went ahead in March 2015 with only twelve of Chile's fifty bishops in attendance. There were appalling scenes at the cathedral of Osorno, where hundreds of black-clad protestors jostled and heckled Barros as he sought to enter and take possession of his cathedral. In the end the Mass had to be cut short because of the constant disruption.

The decision to proceed with the nomination bewildered the Chilean Church and seemed to contradict two priorities of Francis's pontificate: to give voice to the victims, and to respect the wishes of the local Church. Chileans were reluctant to accept that Francis was behind the decision, accusing the bishops and the nuncio of concealing information from the pope. But the truth was very different: Francis was wholly informed, and regarded it as a matter of justice; Barros was already a bishop when the Karadima allegations came to light, but was innocent in both civil and canon law.

The Barros nomination was a reminder that, for all his winning ways, Francis is not a politician weighing a decision in terms of the impact to his standing, but the pope, whose task is to discern God's will and implement it, whatever the cost to his own popularity and credibility—even with the abuse victims on his commission to protect minors.[19]

In the Barros case, Francis backed a decision taken by the Vatican's Congregation for Bishops. In other instances, however, he bypasses or ignores Vatican gatekeepers, taking a personal initiative that leaves officials scrambling to catch up. An example is his reaching out to U.S. evangelical leaders through his old friend Bishop Tony Palmer, the evangelical Pentecostal whom he had first met in Buenos Aires.

When Palmer met Francis in the Casa Santa Marta in January 2014, he told his old friend, whom he called "Padre Mario," that he would be addressing hundreds of mega-church pastors and evangelical leaders the following week in Texas. Francis suggested Palmer record a message on his iPhone. In the grainy film, Francis, seated in a green felt chair with a poinsettia plant in the background, spoke of his yearning for the separation of Christians to end, and of the "miracle of unity" that had begun.

When the video went viral after Palmer showed the message in Fort Worth, the bishop was inundated with messages from evangelical leaders across the world asking how could they be part of it.

In June 2014, Palmer took a number of senior evangelical leaders—together, they represented possibly 800 million Christians—to meet Francis, the first of a number of convivial gatherings involving joint prayer, shared meals, and plenty of laughter. Francis tells them that their shared baptism, and openness to the Holy Spirit, are enough; that a new era is opening up of relations between Catholics and evangelicals; and that they shouldn't wait for theologians to agree before acting and witnessing together. ("I'm not interested in converting evangelicals to Catholicism," one of them later reported the pope telling him. "I want people to find Jesus in their own community.") The Vatican's Council for Christian Unity is kept informed of these meetings but has no part in them. This is expressly not theological, or institutional, dialogue of the sort that has dominated ecumenism since the 1960s, but Francis typically operating through personal friendships.

In July 2014, after Tony was tragically killed in a road accident, Pope Francis asked that he be buried with the funeral rite of a Catholic bishop at his local parish in Bath, England. Tony's widow Emiliana read out Francis's message to her in which he said he and his dear friend had "prayed often in the same Spirit," that Palmer had given his life, in love, to the cause of Christian unity, and that his work had opened up new possibilities.

Emiliana is now building the support for a proposed future "joint declaration of faith in unity for mission" to be signed by the pope and evangelical leaders. The declaration will open a new era for Christians, encouraging them to act and pray together across the world, in spite of their differences.

In a highly unusual move, Francis has agreed to be patron of the Palmers' Ark Community. He remains close to Emiliana and her children, regularly meeting them and supporting them through their loss, convinced that Tony's death is part of something larger being born.

❧

FRANCIS has shown even greater unilateralism in granting dozens of candid sit-down TV and newspaper interviews, which the Vatican Press

Office is usually the last to learn about. The interviews have generated no shortage of misunderstandings and misreportings. They have also revolutionized papal communication, captivating reporters and dominating headlines with his startling metaphors, earthy asides, and unpapal directness.

The interviews are part of a wider "revolution of normalcy." Rather than reading from scripts seated on thrones—which suggests the stasis of a distant, unchanging institution—Francis's free communication, unfettered by minders, conveys the dynamism of a Church led by the Holy Spirit, one capable of speaking heart to heart through dialogue, in the language of ordinary human beings.

Francis's charismatic and kerygmatic style—focusing on the "primary" proclamation of God's love—sounds to his critics like a great cave-in to the secular culture they have spent so long combating. "The emphasis on truth provoked by the hostility of relativism has led to the reaffirmation of identity as the only road to salvation," writes Argentine professor Roberto Bosca of the growing opposition to Francis. "Now that Pope Francis is restoring the universal truth of love, many believe he is putting in danger the truths of the faith."[20]

This suspicion leads conservatives to take at face value media reports of Francis's words in a way they would never have done with Benedict XVI. There was horror in conservative circles at Francis's widely reported remarks on the plane back from Manila that "to be good Catholics, we don't have to breed like rabbits," which were put together with a claim that he had recommended having three children.

Francis was speaking about Blessed Paul VI's encyclical against the use of contraception in marriage, *Humanae Vitae*, which he portrayed as a prophetic defense of families in poor countries against the "ideological colonization" by the North. Having reaffirmed the ban on contraception as a resistance to neo-Malthusian and eugenic assumptions that the "problem" of development is that there are too many poor people in the world, he then invoked the other part of church teaching that calls for parents responsibly to decide—using natural birth control methods, and seeking guidance—to have the children appropriate to their circumstances, pointing out that fewer than three would lead to depopulation, as in Spain and Italy. But the mythical idea that the Pope disapproved of large families was too good for the newsroom to resist.

Rather than recite well-worn abstract phrases, Francis was communicating the doctrine vividly and accessibly, as good teachers do. Francis "is, in fact, teaching a basically very traditional, old-fashioned Catholicism," notes Paddy Agnew, Rome correspondent of the *Irish Times*; "innovating within the bounds of tradition," as Ross Douthat puts in the *New York Times*. But media projections onto Francis, attempting to portray him as a kind of doctrinal modernizer, are reinforced by conservatives who take these portrayals at face value. "Even though nothing this pope has said or done suggests that he is about to change one dot of doctrine, they imagine the worst," writes Elizabeth Scalia at *Patheos*. Some Catholics, notes John Allen, "are never more comfortable than when a pope is under attack, and never more alarmed than when the world applauds."[21]

Yet far from eroding the teaching authority of the pope, Francis has placed it at the center again of the world stage. The price is misinterpretation: once headlines appear, a narrative takes wing that subsequent clarifications can barely dislodge. Yet on the whole the messages get through. In the Philippines in January 2015, Francis succeeded in doing something until recently considered impossible: to open a discussion on sexuality and family in the Western media. Not only did he powerfully reaffirm Church teaching—opposing the attempt to redefine marriage, and speaking up for the right of a child to a father and mother—but he did so in a compelling way that intrigued, as well as challenged, Western narratives. The attempt to redefine marriage, he said, came from "powerful forces which threaten to disfigure God's plan for creation," and he lodged a protest, on behalf of the poor of the world, against the "ideological colonization" posed by gender ideology, wealth disparity, and consumerism.

Francis has moved papal communication from thinking to doing. In a word-glutted world, where actions speak loudest—or, as St. Ignatius of Loyola put it, "love is known more in deeds than in words"—Francis's directness and spontaneity are certificates of authenticity, turning almost every papal pronouncement and gesture into media gold. In a world of gray, calculated language and of ruthless message discipline, Francis paints in vivid colors, wholly free of political correctness. For Francis, it is more important to speak the truth than to avoid offense; in this, as ever, Jesus is his model.

Despite giving more interviews in two years than all previous popes throughout history combined ("I could kill him," laughs Federico Wals,

Cardinal Bergoglio's former press officer), Francis is not garrulous by nature. The once inscrutable Jesuit provincial and taciturn cardinal has become the most talkative of modern popes because he knows that contemporary culture only regards as credible those who are willing to dialogue. The icon of that dialogue is the sit-down interview, when the journalist is free to ask whatever they wish. That means making himself accountable. At the end of June 2014, a reporter with the Rome daily *Il Messaggero* asked if she could make a criticism. "Of course," said Francis. She took him to task for talking about women only as wives and mothers, rather than rulers of states or big businesses, reflecting a perception that Francis is tone-deaf on women. He did not try to defend himself, said he understood the point, and said they were working on a new theology of women.

Vatican journalists are busy now. Gone are the days when they could prepare a story using carefully crafted phrases from embargoed homilies and statements: every event is made tense by what Francis might do or say when he departs from his script in order to hammer home some point that has come to him in prayer that morning.

The courage and prophetic directness that grew in him following his opening to charismatic spirituality in 2005–6 is what he called for in his famous brief remarks to the cardinals in March 2013 that persuaded many to elect him; it is what he asked of the synod fathers when they gathered in October; and it is what he urges on his cardinals when they gather in Rome for the extraordinary consistories. *Parrhesia* is why Pope Francis doesn't stop talking—and why he will continue to give offense and be misinterpreted: because he believes the Holy Spirit demands nothing less.

Francis has become the most popular figure of the age, a global icon of moral credibility and compassion, uniquely capable of reaching out beyond the choir and into the contemporary street. By the end of his first year Francis had been canonized on the covers of *Rolling Stone, Esquire, Vanity Fair,* and *Fortune,* among many others, including—remarkably— the gay magazine *The Advocate.* In 2014, *Time* declared him Person of the Year, an accolade not accorded to the immensely popular John Paul II until sixteen years into his pontificate. The *Economist* said Harvard Business School should study Francis alongside IBM's Lou Gerstner and Apple's Steve Jobs as an example of "turnaround CEOs" who breathe new life into dying organizations, describing him as "the man who has rebranded RC Global in barely a year."[22]

By the end of his second year, despite grumbling in Rome and the emergence of outspoken opponents from both left and right, he remained immensely popular among rank-and-file American Catholics, with close to 90 percent approval among Republicans and Democrats alike, considerably higher than the 76 percent thumbs-up for Benedict XVI at the close of his pontificate. And despite the accolades from the so-called liberal media, among self-described "conservatives" he was more popular (94 percent) than among "moderates/liberals" (87 percent).[23]

Even among non-Catholics, Francis was riding high: Sixty-two percent of Americans approve of him, compared with less than half who approved of Benedict. In April 2015, the Pope's Twitter accounts in nine languages reached twenty million followers, and a study of world leaders concluded that, as the one with by far the most retweets (on average, 9,929 for every tweet he sends on his Spanish account) Francis was by a long shot the most influential world leader on Twitter—a remarkable achievement for a seventy-eight-year-old man who does not use a computer or smartphone.[24]

Without altering a single core Church doctrine—which a pope is not at liberty to do—Francis had achieved what had seemed impossible before his election: to speak to the heart of contemporary Western culture. The *Time* article struggled with this apparent contradiction, eventually concluding that he must be a master PR operator.

Yet what draws the world to Francis is precisely the opposite: as the *Financial Times* noted, Francis "has a sincerity and authenticity that no world leader can match."[25] What captivates the world—though few dared to put it as plainly as Cardinal Schönborn at the inauguration Mass—is that Francis's actions, words, and gestures have awoken in Western culture a dim, often unconscious, yet powerful memory of someone once loved but since lost. As the headline over a column by Elizabeth Tenety of the *Washington Post* wittily expressed it: "Like Francis? You'll Love Jesus."[26]

❧

A JOURNALIST from the Barcelona newspaper *La Vanguardia* put it to Francis in June 2014 that he was a revolutionary. The pope did not reject the idea, but said the greatest revolution of all was "to go to the roots," and that real change was about strengthening identity, not replacing it. One who goes to the roots is a radical (from the Latin *radicalis* for "forming the root"). Francis's radicalism is born of his extraordinary identification with Jesus after a lifetime of total immersion in the Gospel and mystical prayer. That identification leads him to want to simplify and focus, to recover the *forma Christi*.

Perhaps his greatest achievement is to have grasped, and acted on, the central dilemma for Churches in contemporary society. In an age of secularism and hostility to institutions, the tendency of Christians is to hunker down defensively, raising the drawbridges, and only accept others who believe as they do. Seeing this temptation, Francis has gone the other way—St. Ignatius called this *agere contra*—by opening the Church up to those outside it, reaching out with open hands and heart to those who yearn for truth and to belong but are hostile to institutions.

He grasps that baptized Christians alienated by clericalism and institutional arrogance are not hostile to the Church but want it to change, and that a pope must represent their interests, not just those of the institution, by candidly acknowledging the narcissism or corruption of many in positions in leadership in the Church. By embodying reform rather than institutional defensiveness, he has cut across the gulf separating the Church from contemporary society.

His bold, excoriating, 40,000-word June 2015 encyclical letter on the environment, *Laudato Si'—On the Care of Our Common Home*—may be Francis's greatest legacy. In linking the damage to the planet and the plight of the poor, in calling on the wealthy to drastically alter their lives to avoid impending disaster, he made climate change a primary moral issue. It was a very *bergogliano* mix of the spiritual and the political, wading fearlessly into the science, critiquing a model of economic growth underpinned by frenetic consumption, and challenging environmentalists to care about abortion as well as deforestation. Rich in quotes from Guardini and Sufi poets, bracing in its call for an "integral ecology" capable of restoring man's lost connectedness with God and the earth, the document's radicality, poetic beauty, and theological depth took the Church and the world by surprise. *Laudato Si'* was a landmark in Catholic social teaching, arguably the greatest since Leo XIII's *Rerum Novarum* in 1891.

Francis has become a significant voice against human trafficking, the arms trade, the death penalty, nuclear weapons, and environmental damage. He has excoriated the mafia, declaring them excommunicated, and labeled the massacre of Armenian Christians by Turkey a genocide. And he is the *de facto* leader of a worldwide movement for the recognition of the rights of those at the bottom of the heap in the global economy: the waste-collectors, seamstresses, fruit-pickers, and other workers in the informal sector. Addressing a world meeting of these "popular movements" to call for their rights to be recognized in October 2014, Francis told them that "every worker, within the formal system of salaried employment or outside it, should have the right to decent remuneration, to social security, and to a pension. . . . Today I want to join my voice to yours and support you in your struggle."

He believes that workers have value and generate value, and that the present system denies them recognition as creators and partners in the market, treating them as factors in production. Whenever he visits an Italian town he is followed by people who make presentations of their working lives—their fireman's helmet, or their wooden spoon—and his warm, intimate, and immediate connectedness with ordinary people is of a kind few politicians can dream of. To watch Francis in the midst of migrants or the homeless or working people—to see them swarm around him, naturally at home with him—is to recall the Jesuit college rector among the ordinary folk of San Miguel, or the cardinal in the shantytowns of Buenos Aires.

Francis is constructing a new Catholic populism, one that fiercely advocates on behalf of the excluded.

From Argentina he knows the failure of communism and corporatism, and the way politicians plunder the state for their own benefit. But he is suspicious of the rich resisting interference in the market, as Maurice Glasman, a British Labor peer, discovered when invited to a Vatican conference in early 2015 to speak on Catholic social thought. When he spoke of regional banks, a vocational economy, incentives to virtue, and the representation of the workforce in corporate governance, Lord Glasman encountered considerable hostility from some Americans in the conference, who accused him of being communist. "It all felt a bit uncomfortable," recalls Glasman. "But Pope Francis interjected with a question. He asked my interrogators—for there was more than one—'What is your idea? That the banks should fail and that is the end of the world, but the workers starve and that is the price you have to pay?' Things went much better for me from that point."[27]

* * *

Francis has returned the Church to the center of the world stage. Ambassadors sent to Rome for a quiet end-of-career posting find themselves at the center of a new age of diplomatic audacity for the Holy See.

Francis always starts from the primacy of faith, believing that only an openness to the transcendent will bring about a new world order. After fifty years discerning spirits, he sees the devil not as a myth or theological proposition but as a daily reality in the world, tempting through riches, power, and pride and unleashing furious hatred on the innocent. "More than once we have been on the verge of peace, but the evil one, employing a variety of means, has succeeded in blocking it," he told Israeli president Shimon Peres and Palestinian president Mahmoud Abbas when they came to the Vatican to pray for peace on June 8, 2014.

Just as the devil blocks peace, Francis believes prayer unlocks new possibilities, releasing even the most firmly tied knots. Thus, on September 8, 2013, Francis knelt before an icon of Our Lady in St. Peter's Square while leading a three-hour peace prayer vigil for Syria, accompanied by tens of thousands of people in the square who begged God to bring to an end the barbaric, heartrending carnage in that country. Among the prayers that night were many to Saint Thérèse of Lisieux. The next day, Sunday, while strolling in the Vatican Gardens, a gardener handed Francis a white rose. The day after, the Russian president's plan to destroy Syria's chemical stockpile forestalled a proposed U.S. bombing.

In May 2014 Francis took with him to the Middle East his close Jewish and Muslim friends from Buenos Aires, Rabbi Abraham Skorka and Omar Abboud. When the three hugged in front of the Western Wall in Jerusalem, their tears flowed freely; it was the fulfillment of a longstanding ambition at the conclusion of a trip of extraordinary intensity, taking in three countries, fifteen addresses, and countless meetings.

While in Bethlehem, Francis surprised the world by pausing for five minutes' silent prayer at the twenty-six-foot-high Israeli security wall that corralls Palestinians and consolidates the annexation of their land. At the end of the Mass in Manger Square, he suddenly invited the Israeli and Palestinian presidents to meet at the Vatican for prayer and dialogue. Within an hour, both had accepted, despite months of failed international efforts to bring both sides together. The prayer summit had no immediate obvious impact, but Francis later said that it had opened a door which the smoke and bombs had obscured.

Francis's "artisanal" diplomacy—peace, he told an audience in St. Peter's Square, was not industrial but the fruit of the patience of craftsmen—paid off spectacularly with the astonishing news, shortly before Christmas

2014, of the restoration of U.S.-Cuba relations. As details emerged of the year-long backstory to the ending of one of the world's most intractable standoffs, it was clear that Francis and his diplomats had played a vital role.[28]

A vision of a post-communist Cuba that reflects the island's deep-seated Christian humanist culture was described in the then Archbishop-elect Bergoglio's 1998 book following John Paul II's visit to the island. A Church-brokered transition in Cuba is key to that future, to a new age for Latin America once dreamed of by the *patria grande* intellectuals around Bergoglio three decades earlier. What John Paul II did for eastern Europe, Francis may yet achieve for Latin America, beginning with his three-day visit to Cuba in September 2015.

YET Francis has an intuition that his papacy will not be long: perhaps just two or three years more, he told journalists on the plane from South Korea in August 2014. "I feel that the Lord has placed me here for a short time, and nothing more," Francis repeated to Valentina Alazraki of Televisa in March 2015.

He is operating on the assumption of a five-year papacy, until 2018, when he hopes to have achieved what is in his heart to complete. Then he will consider resigning ("I will do what the Lord asks me to do," he told *La Vanguardia*), unless he is dead by then, whether from an assassin's bullet or sheer exhaustion. If he does resign, some who are close to him in Buenos Aires believe that, improbable as it may seem, Francis would return to his beloved city, to the clergy retirement house in Flores as he had always planned, not to live as a pope emeritus but a simple pastor. Why else would he have renewed his Argentine passport?

He enjoys being pope, but misses being able to pop out for a pizza. His sciatica is often bad, and he has put on a lot of weight, because he is no longer able to walk the streets as he used to in Buenos Aires. His doctors tell him to cut down on pasta, and take more strolls in the Vatican gardens. He often misses his afternoon nap, is frequently sick with colds and chest infections, and tiredness gives him severe headaches. Yet these are hardly surprising consequences of the demands on him, at his age. What is more surprising is how joyfully energetic he remains.

Those close to him say that he cannot resign until Benedict XVI dies—the first time one pope will have buried another. Benedict, a reassuring father figure to Catholic conservatives, is the great enabler of the Francis papacy, the one who discerned the end of an era and nurtured a new one into being. They get on well. The pope emeritus sometimes takes a break from his reading and piano playing to send Francis notes and comments, offering advice but anxious not to interfere. Francis refers to him as *el viejo*, "the old man," as Argentines affectionately do, and tells journalists it is like having his grandfather close by.

He left Buenos Aires with a little case, promising to return. He never did, but Argentines have come to know him far better now as pope than they ever did when he was their cardinal. In Rome, there is a constant stream of Argentines waiting to see him, while in his native city he is everywhere, smiling out beatifically from posters in the slums. He is a national treasure, and the subject of a three-hour "papal tour" organized by the city government of Buenos Aires, who are promoting the city as a pilgrim destination.

The bus starts at the basilica in whose confession he first heard the call around which he has built his life, then takes in the modern little house built over his parents' *casa chorizo* in Flores, the convent where he was taught mercy, the secondary school where he studied chemistry, the clergy retirement house on calle Condarco, the seminary where he had part of his lung removed, and so on, finally to the curia and cathedral on the Plaza de Mayo, where you are shown the kiosk which delivered his newspaper and the barber who cut his hair. On the way, the coach stops in the working-class parish of San José del Talar, where people trickle in all day to touch the María Desatanudos picture and hang their heads in prayer, sharing their anxieties and giving thanks for unexpected gifts. A member of the parish has painted a picture which hangs opposite, which shows a grinning Francis flanked by two knot-untying Virgins. It is called *Las Protectoras de Francisco*—"Francis's protectors."

He will return, for a visit in 2016, and has promised to open the Vatican archives on Argentina's dirty war. But his focus is now elsewhere: the mission is the globe. Yet some things stay the same. He rises at dawn each day, as he has done all his life, before the seven a.m. Mass in the chapel of the Santa Marta. Each day brings novelty, and that's how it should be when the Holy Spirit is given space to act.

It can be trying for those around him. "What is a little difficult is a certain unpredictability in his actions," admits the German prefect of the papal household, George Gänswein, "the last-minute surprises which are never lacking."

"If the Church is alive, it must always surprise," Francis told thousands in St. Peter's Square on Pentecost Sunday 2014, before grinning mischievously. "A Church that doesn't have the capacity to surprise is a weak, sickened, and dying Church. It should be taken to the recovery room at once."

NOTES

ONE   FAR AWAY AND LONG AGO (1936–1957)

1   The term *bergoglismo* was created by Bergoglio's friend and former pupil, the journalist Jorge Milia, on the website Terre d'America. See, for example, "La Jerga de Francisco/8: 'Misericordiando.' Diálogo con el Papa sobre un Gerundio Curioso," www.terredamerica.com (November 20, 2013).

2   John Lynch, *Massacre in the Pampas, 1872: Britain and Argentina in the Age of Migration* (Norman: University of Oklahoma Press, 1998), p. 108. See also Austen Ivereigh, "The Shape of the State: Liberals and Catholics in the Dispute over Law 1420 of 1884 in Argentina," in Austen Ivereigh (ed.), *The Politics of Religion in an Age of Revival* (London: Institute of Latin American Studies, 2000).

TWO   THE MISSION (1958–1966)

1   Viktor Frankl, *Man's Search for Meaning* (Boston: Beacon Press, 1959).

2   The best overview of all things Jesuit is James Martin, SJ, *The Jesuit Guide to (Almost) Everything: A Spirituality for Real Life* (New York: HarperCollins, 2010).

3   Jorge Bergoglio (Pope Francis), *Open Mind, Faithful Heart: Reflections on Following Jesus*, trans. Joseph V. Owen (New York: Crossroad, 2013), p. 113, originally in *Meditaciones para Religiosos* (Buenos Aires: Ediciones Diego de Torres, 1982).

4   Philip Caraman, SJ, *Ignatius Loyola* (San Francisco: Harper & Row, 1990), ch. 17.

5   For the history of the Jesuits in the colonial River Plate, see Guillermo Fúrlong Cardiff, SJ, notably *Los Jesuitas y la Cultura Rioplatense* (Buenos Aires: Editorial Huarpes, 1946), as well as Roberto di Stefano, *Historia de la Iglesia Argentina* (Buenos Aires: Sudamericana, 2009), Jean Lacoutoure, *Jesuits: A Multibiography* (Berkeley, CA: Counterpoint, 1995), and various sources cited in my own *Catholicism and Politics in Argentina, 1810–1960* (Basingstoke, UK: Macmillan; New York: St. Martin's Press, 1993).

6   Father Diego's letter contains the term *la periferia*. "I am convinced," Francis told members of religious orders in November 2013, "that great changes in history came about when things were seen not from the center but rather from the periphery."

7   William Bangert, *A History of the Society of Jesus* (St. Louis, MO: Institute of Jesuit Sources, 1986).

8   Jorge Mario Bergoglio, "¿Qué Son los Jesuitas? Origen, Espiritualidad, Características Propias," in *Reflexiones en Esperanza* (Buenos Aires: Ediciones Universidad del Salvador, 1992).

9   Jorge Mario Bergoglio, "Historia y Presencia de la Compañía de Jesús en Nuestra Tierra," in *Reflexiones Espirituales sobre la Vida Apostólica* (Buenos Aires: Ediciones Diego de Torres, 1987).

10 After the votes went Bergoglio's way in the conclave of 2013, a cardinal wittily suggested he might avenge that notorious decision by taking the name Clement XV. For essays on the expulsion, see Magnus Mörner (ed.), *The Expulsion of the Jesuits from Latin America* (New York: Knopf, 1965).

11 Jorge Mario Bergoglio, "Proyección Cultural y Evangelizadora de los Mártires Rioplatenses," Speech at Colegio del Salvador, May 27, 1988, in *Reflexiones en Esperanza*.

12 Jorge Mario Bergoglio, "The Faith That Frees Us," in *Open Mind, Faithful Heart*, p. 28.

13 Pope Francis, Meeting with the Coordinating Committee of CELAM, July 28, 2013.

14 Jorge Mario Bergoglio, "Principios," Universidad del Salvador, August 27, 1974, at www.usal.edu.ar/principios.

15 Jorge González Manent, *Jesuitas Éramos Los de Antes: Impresiones de un Novicio de Los Años '50* (Buenos Aires: Ed. Dunken, 2012).

16 Literally, "little father," an affectionate term used by Latin-Americans of their priests. Although juniors like Jorge were not ordained, local people didn't make that distinction.

17 Reproduced in Mariano de Vedia, *Francisco, el Papa del Pueblo* (Buenos Aires: Planeta, 2013). My translation.

18 Armando Rubén Puente, *La Vida Oculta de Bergoglio* (Madrid: Libros Libres, 2014), p. 145.

19 In Alejandro Bermúdez (ed., trans.), *Pope Francis: Our Brother, Our Friend* (San Francisco: Ignatius Press, 2013).

20 Morris West, *Eminence* (Boston: Houghton Mifflin Harcourt, 1998).

21 If it still exists, the magnetic tape would contain the first radio interview of the man who became Pope Francis.

22 Pfirter brothers quoted in Elisabetta Piqué, *Francisco: Vida y Revolución* (Buenos Aires: El Ateneo, 2013) pp. 70–71. Carranza quoted in Bermúdez (ed., trans.), *Pope Francis: Our Brother, Our Friend*.

23 The story is told in Chris Lowney, *Pope Francis: Why He Leads the Way He Leads* (Chicago: Loyola Press, 2013), p. 42.

24 J. Milia, *De la Edad Feliz* (Salta: Ed. Maktub, 2006), updated in an Italian edition, *Maestro Francesco: Gli Allievi del Papa Ricordano il Loro Profesore* (Milan: Mondadori, 2014).

THREE STORM PILOT (1967–1974)

1   John Allen, "On Pope Francis's First Year," Radio Boston, March 25, 2014.

2   G. K. Chesterton, *St. Francis of Assisi* (New York: George H. Doran, 1924).

3   Transcript of 2010 judicial inquiry, "Bergoglio Declara ante el TOF," at www.abuelas.org.ar.

4   Carlos Mugica, *Peronismo y Cristianismo* (Buenos Aires: Editorial Merlin, 1973).

5   "Documento de Carlos Paz," July 1971, in MSTM archive at Catholic University of Córdoba and online.

6   Gustavo Morello, *Cristianismo y Revolución: Los Orígenes Intelectuales de la Guerrilla Argentina* (Córdoba: EDUCC, 2003); Richard Gillespie, *Soldiers of Perón—Argentina's Montoneros* (Oxford, UK: Clarendon Press; New York: Oxford University Press, 1982); María José Moyano, *Argentina's Lost Patrol: Armed Struggle, 1969–1979* (New Haven, CT: Yale University Press, 1995).

7   Quoted in Sergio Rubín and Francesca Ambrogetti, *El Jesuita* (Barcelona: Vergara, Grupo Zeta, 2010).

8   "Credo de Jorge Mario Bergoglio, Papa Francisco," www.revistaecclesia.com, September 18, 2013.

9   Orlando Yorio, Letter to Father Moura, November 24, 1977.

10 Quoted in Lowney, *Pope Francis: Why He Leads the Way He Leads*, p. 120.

11 I am indebted to the writer Paul Elie for pointing out to me that the two Jesuits are likely to have coincided at this time.

12 Jorge Mario Bergoglio, "Una Institución que Vive su Carisma: Apertura de la Congregación provincial XV (August 2, 1978)," in *Meditaciones para Religiosos*.

13 Lucio Gera, "Cultura y dependencia, a la luz de la reflexión teológica," *Stromata*, Año XXX (January–June 1974), no. 1/2.

14 Juan Carlos Scannone, "Theology, Popular Culture and Discernment," in Rosino Gibellini (ed.), *Frontiers of Theology in Latin America*, trans. John Drury (Maryknoll, NY: Orbis Books, 1979), and "Aportaciones a la teología latinoamericana," *Vida Nueva* (Cono Sur edition), Part I, Año 2, no. 21 (November 3–16, 2013) and Part II, Año 2, no. 22 (November 17–23, 2013).

15 Ernesto López Rosas, "Valores Cristianos del Peronismo," *Revista CIAS*, no. 234 (August 1975): 7–30.

16 On Damasco and the Modelo Nacional, see Puente, *La Vida Oculta de Bergoglio*.

17 Orlando Yorio, "Reflexión crítica desde la teología," *Stromata*, Año XXIX (January–June 1973), no. 1/2, pp. 131–39.

18 No doubt because it is the date Cardinal Bergoglio mistakenly gave in his judicial testimony in 2010, biographers (e.g., Paul Vallely and Elisabetta Piqué) have put Arrupe's visit in August 1974, a year later. Bergoglio's 2006 homily on the anniversary of Angelleli's death has the correct date, August 1973, which has been confirmed by the Jesuit curia in Rome.

19 Jorge Mario Bergoglio, "Apertura de la Congregación Provincial XIV (18/2/74)," in *Meditaciones para Religiosos*.

20 Quoted in Lowney, *Pope Francis: Why He Leads the Way He Leads*, p. 114.

21 Vocation statistics supplied by Jesuit provincial curia in Buenos Aires. Bergoglio gave details about his efforts to secure vocations of coadjutor brothers in his letter to Father Cayetano Bruno, May 18, 1986.

22 Bergoglio, "¿Qué Son los Jesuitas?" in *Reflexiones Espirituales sobre la Vida Apostólica*.

23 "Discorso del Santo Padre Paolo VI in ocasione della XXXII Congregazione Generale della Compagnia di Gesù," December 3, 1974, at www.vatican.va.

24 Bergoglio, "Una Institución que Vive su Carisma," in *Meditaciones para Religiosos*.

25 Guzmán Carriquiry, *En Camino Hacia la V Conferencia de la Iglesia Latinoamericana* (Buenos Aires: Ed. Claretiana, 2006).

26 Interview with Radio María (Argentina) following a national meeting of clergy in Villa Cura Brochero, September 9–11, 2008.

FOUR CRUCIBLE (1975–1979)

1 John Heilprin and Nicole Winfield, "Vatican has defrocked 848 priests for abuse charges since 2004," Associated Press, May 6, 2014.

2 Austen Ivereigh, "The UN and the Vatican: Understanding What Went Wrong," CV Comment, February 8, 2014.

3 Inés San Martín, "Pope Francis Meets Sex Abuse Victims, Vows Zero Tolerance," *Boston Globe,* July 7, 2014, and Michael Kelly, "Irish Abuse Victim Who Met with Pope Calls It a 'Huge Vindication,'" Catholic News Service, July 7, 2014. Peter Saunders quotes are from interview with the author. See also his interview with Inés San Martín, "Abuse Victim Calls Meeting Pope Francis a Life-changing Experience," *Boston Globe,* July 7, 2014.

4 Horacio Verbitsky, "El Ersatz," *Página* 12 (March 14, 2013). The article reprinted by the *Guardian* was by Hugh O'Shaughnessy, "The Sins of the Argentinean Church," *Guardian* Comment Is Free website (January 4, 2011).

5 This is the thesis of Paul Vallely, *Pope Francis: Untying the Knots* (London; New York: Bloomsbury, 2013).

6 These are government figures from the end of 2013. The original CONADEP official inquiry found in 1984 that there were 8,961 disappeared, but many of the names were subsequently shown to have fled abroad. Under the government of Néstor Kirchner (2003–2007) the inquiry was reopened, this time adding to the total victims of summary executions, leading to the figures quoted here. The figure of "30,000 disappeared" is a media myth based on wild speculations by human-rights groups in the late 1970s. In the period 1969–1983, incidentally, the guerrillas killed 800 and kidnapped 1,748. The CONADEP report (*Nunca Más*) is at www.desaparecidos.org. For updated figures: Ceferino Reato, "Hablan de 30.000 Desaparecidos y Saben que Es Falso," *La Nación,* September 20, 2013.

7 Jorge Rouillón, "Histórico Pedido de Perdón de la Iglesia Argentina," *La Nación,* September 9, 2000.

8 "Bergoglio Declara ante el TOF," transcript of 2010 judicial inquiry, at www.abuelas .org.ar.

9 "Argentina Military Officers Convicted of Bishop's Murder," BBC News, July 5, 2014.

10 See Nello Scavo, *La Lista de Bergoglio: Los Salvados por Francisco durante la Dictadura* (Madrid: Editorial Claretiana, 2013).

11 Bergoglio, "El reino de Cristo," in *Meditaciones para Religiosos.*

12 Bergoglio, "El espíritu del mundo," in *Meditaciones para Religiosos.*

13 Bergoglio, "Una institución que vive su carisma," contains three of the principles in his first (1974) talk; but there are four in "Formación permanente y reconciliación" (1980), both in *Meditaciones para Religiosos.*

14 Bergoglio, "Formación permanente y reconciliación," in *Meditaciones para Religiosos.*

15 Scavo, *La Lista de Bergoglio,* pp. 103–112.

16 Scavo, *La Lista de Bergoglio,* pp. 47–53, and Puente, *La Vida Oculta de Bergoglio,* pp. 173–74.

17 Olga Wornat, *Nuestra Santa Madre: Historia Pública y Privada de la Iglesia Católica Argentina* (Barcelona: Ediciones B, 2002).

18 Ana Delicado, "Mi Hermano Fue un Canje entre la Iglesia y la Dictadura," *El Público,* March 19, 2013.

19 Emilio Mignone, *Iglesia y Dictadura* (Buenos Aires: Ediciones del Pensamiento Nacional, 1986). Also Mario del Carril, *La Vida de Emilio Mignone* (Buenos Aires: Emecé, 2011).

20 Vallely, *Pope Francis: Untying the Knots*, p. 73, claims Bergoglio "told the four priests to give up their work in the slum."

FIVE THE LEADER EXPELLED (1980–1992)

1 "Visita a Papa Francesco il 17 Marzo 2013," *Servizio Digitale d'Informazione SJ*, vol. 17, no. 7 (March 20, 2013).

2 Adolfo Nicolás, SJ, "With Pope Francis at the Beginning of His Pontificate," Letter "To the Whole Society" (March 24, 2013).

3 Adolfo Nicolás, SJ, "A Toda la Compañía" (July 31, 2013). Francis replied on March 16 to Nicolás's letter of March 14.

4 Spadaro writes about the interview in its extended book version, published in English as *My Door Is Always Open: A Conversation on Faith, Hope and the Church in a Time of Change* (New York: HarperOne, 2013).

5 The similarity is suggested by Francis J. Manion, "Echoes from the Pages of a Book: Reading Francis Through Manzoni," *New Oxford Review* 81, no. 2 (March 2014). Father Martin's comment in the 2014 Salt & Light TV documentary, *The Francis Effect*.

6 "Francis: The Gospel Is Not Proclaimed with Inquisitorial Beatings but Gently," *Vatican Insider* (January 3, 2014).

7 I saw this for myself when interviewing Jesuits in Argentina in October–November 2013. Some proudly showed the letters to me, with "F., Casa Santa Marta, Città del Vaticano" penned on the back of the envelopes. One of his severest critics, living in the Jesuit care home within the Colegio Máximo, showed me his with tears in his eyes; others told me how moved they had been to receive them.

8 "Juan Carlos Parodi: El Papa Me Dijo que le Salvé la Vida," *La Nación*, May 21, 2014.

9 On April 16, 2010, Cardinal Bergoglio wrote to Brigadier General Jorge Chevalier with documents from the South Atlantic Theater of Operations (TOAS) group, saying he saw no reason why they should not receive full recognition. The TOAS veterans, who in 2008 began a tent protest in the Plaza de Mayo that was still continuing in 2013, gave me a copy of Bergoglio's letter. Two of the three homilies cited here were at anniversary Masses for the veterans and their families, on April 2, 2008, and April 4, 2012. The homily at the Mass for relatives on their way to the islands was on October 2, 2009.

10 Patricio Downes, "Recordaron a Bergoglio en la Parroquia que Él Fundó y Dirigió en los 80," *Clarín*, March 23, 2014.

11 Hernán Paredes quoted in Lowney, *Pope Francis: Why He Leads the Way He Leads*, p. 57.

12 Bergoglio, "El Reino de Cristo," in *Meditaciones para Religiosos*.

13 According to Spadaro in *My Door Is Always Open*, the Latin phrase *non coerceri a maximo, contineri tamen a minimo, divinum est* "is part of a long literary epitaph composed by an anonymous Jesuit in honor of St. Ignatius of Loyola." The maxim is quoted by Bergoglio in an early essay, "Conducir en lo Grande y lo Pequeño," in *Meditaciones para Religiosos*.

14 Bergoglio, "Magnanimidad y Mezquindad," in *Reflexiones Espirituales sobre la Vida Apostólica*. Antico quoted in Hugo Alconada Mon, "Soy Bergoglio, Cura," *La Nación*, March 17, 2013.

15 Gauffin quoted in Lowney, *Pope Francis: Why He Leads the Way He Leads*, p. 63.

16 Sister María Soledad Albisú, CJ, "He Taught Me That Love Shows Itself . . . ," *The Tablet*, March 23, 2013.

17 Bergoglio, "Examen," in *Reflexiones Espirituales*.

18 Father Renzo De Luca, SJ, interview with *Osservatore Romano*, October 26, 2013.

19 Bergoglio, "El Magis y el Movimiento de Espíritus," in *Reflexiones Espirituales*.

20 Albistur quoted in Bermúdez (ed., trans.), *Pope Francis: Our Brother, Our Friend*.

21 Bergoglio, "La Encarnación y el Nacimiento," in *Meditaciones para Religiosos*.

22 Virginia Carreño, "Los Milagros del Padre Bergoglio," *El Litoral*, December 19, 1985.

23 *Habríaqueísmo* ("we-shouldism") is another Bergoglio neologism. English-speaking Jesuits have been known to speak of "a hardening of the ought-eries."

24 Bergoglio, "Criterios de Acción Apostólica," *Boletín de Espiritualidad*, no. 64 (January 1980), and in *Reflexiones Espirituales*.

25 Bergoglio, 2002 interview with Gianni Valente, "El Imperialismo Internacional del Dinero," in Gianni Valente, *Francesco: Un Papa dalla Fine del Mondo* (Bologna: EMI, 2013).

26 The first document, "Instruction on Certain Aspects of the Theology of Liberation," was issued in August 1984, and the second, "Instruction on Christian Freedom and Liberation," in March 1986. Both at www.vatican.va.

27 The proceedings of the congress (September 2–6, 1985) were published in *Stromata* 41 (July–December 1985).

28 The story was told to Evangelina Himitian, *Francisco: El Papa de la Gente* (Buenos Aires: Aguilar, 2013). The recipe should not be attempted as part of a low-carb diet.

29 Lowney, *Pope Francis: Why He Leads the Way He Leads*.

30 "Reunión de los Provinciales Jesuitas de América Latina con el P. General, Pedro Arrupe, Río de Janeiro, Casa da Gávea" (May 6–14, 1968).

31 Campbell-Johnston makes the remarks in Vallely, *Pope Francis: Untying the Knots*.

32 Jimmy Burns, *The Land That Lost Its Heroes: The Falklands, the Post-war, and Alfonsín* (London: Bloomsbury, 1987), p. 99: "By leaving the newspaper operational, the junta took a calculated gamble." The circulation was small and its Anglo-Argentine readership loyal to the dictatorship.

33 José María Poirier, "El Caso del Jesuita Risueño," *La Nación*, May 24, 2013.

34 Pope Francis spoke about the letter in a meeting with religious leaders. Antonio Spadaro, "Wake Up the World: Conversation with Pope Francis on the Religious Life," November 2013, at www.laciviltacattolica.it.

35 Jeffrey L. Klaiber, *The Jesuits in Latin America, 1549–2000* (St. Louis, MO: Institute of Jesuit Sources, 2009).

36 See the biography by Mignone's son-in-law Mario del Carril, *La Vida de Emilio Mignone* (Buenos Aires: Emecé, 2011). I am also grateful for an illuminating conversation with his son, Father Fernando Mignone, in Vancouver, Canada, in June 2014.

37 Bergoglio recalls waving at the planes in Rubín and Ambrogetti, *El Jesuita*, ch. 12.

38 Bergoglio, "Proyección Cultural y Evangelizadora de los Mártires Rioplatenses," in *Reflexiones en Esperanza*.

39 This was one of several memories of John Paul II that Bergoglio shared with the Rome diocesan tribunal preparing the pope's canonization cause in 2005. Stefania Falasca, "Bergoglio: 'Io, Testimone di Virtù Eroiche di Wojtyla,'" *Avvenire*, April 17, 2014.

40 Jorge Mario Bergoglio, "Necesidad de una Antropología Política: Un Problema Pastoral," in *Reflexiones en Esperanza*.

41 Bergoglio, "Proyección Cultural y Evangelizadora de los Mártires Rioplatenses," in *Reflexiones en Esperanza*.

42 Between 1990 and 2000, 64 joined and 92 left. By comparison, between 1975 and 1989, 333 joined and 67 left. Statistics supplied to the author by the Argentine provincial curia.

43 "Entrevista al P. Alvaro Restrepo S.J. sobre el Papa Francisco," Religión Digital, March 18, 2013.

44 Puente, *La Vida Oculta de Bergoglio*, p. 228; and Wornat, *Nuestra Santa Madre*, p. 301. Carranza quoted in Bermúdez (ed., trans.), *Pope Francis: Our Brother, Our Friend.*

45 Saint Ignatius, *The Spiritual Exercises*, Rules for Discernment 317–322.

46 Quoted in Piqué, *Francisco: Vida y Revolución*, p. 135.

47 Saint Ignatius, *The Spiritual Exercises*, Third Week, no. 195.

48 Bergoglio, "Silencio y Palabra," in *Reflexiones en Esperanza*.

49 Klaiber, *The Jesuits in Latin America*. After Moyano's death in 2006, Verbitsky identified him as the "anonymous Jesuit" he had earlier quoted, and in 2014 described him as a "key source" (*fuente privilegiada*) in his research on Bergoglio.

50 Bergoglio, "En Él Solo Poner la Esperanza," in *Reflexiones en Esperanza*.

Six A Bishop Who Smelled of Sheep (1993–2000)

1 Tim Worstall, "In Which a Good Catholic Boy Starts Shouting at the Pope," *Forbes* website (November 26, 2013).

2 *Evangelii Gaudium*, paragraph 97.

3 Bergoglio, "Nuestra Carne en Oración," in *Reflexiones en Esperanza*.

4 Rubin and Ambrogetti, *El Jesuita*, ch. 12.

5 This account is in Marcelo Larraquy, *Recen por Él* (Buenos Aires: Sudamericana, 2013), pp. 167–68, and confirmed to the author by Father García-Mata.

6 Quoted in Piqué, *Francisco: Vida y Revolución*, pp. 115–16.

7 In the interview with Father Spadaro, Bergoglio recalls an exchange he had while a bishop. Asked provocatively if he approved of homosexuality, he replied: "Tell me: when God looks at a gay person, does he affectionately approve of this person's existence, or does he reject the person with condemnation?"

8 He recalls this in his 2011 dialogue with Rabbi Skorka in Jorge Bergoglio and Abraham Skorka, *Sobre el Cielo y la Tierra* (Buenos Aires: Editorial Sudamericana, 2010), ch. 9.

9 The Desatanudos story is well told by Carmelo López-Arias, "La Devoción Personal del Papa," *Religión en Libertad* website (June 23, 2013); Himitian, *Francisco: El Papa de la Gente*, ch. 6; and Puente, *La Vida Oculta de Bergoglio*, pp. 122–23.

10 Vallely, *Pope Francis: Untying the Knots*, p. 102.

11 Bartolomé de Vedia, "Bergoglio Será el Sucesor de Quarracino," *La Nación*, June 4, 1997.

12 Sergio Rubín, "La Iglesia que Busca Menem," *Clarín*, June 22, 1997.

13 "Una Multitud Oró ante San Cayetano," *La Nación*, August 8, 1997.

14 John Allen, "Pope Francis Gets His Oxygen from the Slums," *National Catholic Reporter*, April 7, 2013.

15 This account is drawn from off-the-record accounts supplied to the author in interviews with CELAM officials in 2003 in Madrid and in Bogotá in 2005.

16 Alberto Methol Ferré and Alver Metalli, *El Papa y el Filósofo* (Buenos Aires: Editorial Biblos, 2013).

17   On the Cuba visit, see George Weigel, *Witness to Hope* (New York: Cliff Street Books, 1999), pp. 790–92.

18   Grupo de Reflexión "Centesimus Annus," *Diálogos entre Juan Pablo II y Fidel Castro* (Buenos Aires: Editorial de Ciencia y Cultura, 1998). Bergoglio is described on the cover as the *coordinador*.

19   Tello quoted in Chilean magazine article, "El Papa Villero," *Qué Pasa*, February 20, 2014.

20   Henri de Lubac, *The Splendor of the Church* (San Francisco: Ignatius Press, 1986).

21   "Obispos Argentinos Piden que no Se Utilice a la Iglesia con Fines Políticos," *Noticias Eclesiales*, August 5, 1998; Carlos Pagni, "De Pronto, Todo Ha Cambiado," *La Nación*, March 18, 2013.

22   Jorge Mario Bergoglio, "Fervor Apostólico," in *Cuadernos de Pastores*, Año 5, no. 15 (September 1999), at www.cuadernospastores.org.ar.

23   Jorge Mario Bergoglio, *Corrupción y Pecado. Algunas Reflexiones en Torno al Tema de la Corrupción* (Buenos Aires: Ed. Claretiana, 2013).

24   On the Trusso-BCP affair, see Wornat, *Nuestra Santa Madre*, pp. 225–73; Larraquy, *Recen por Él*, pp. 175–79; Puente, *La Vida Oculta de Bergoglio*, pp. 267–68, plus other biographies and contemporaneous press reports. The results of the ongoing investigations have been summarized for me by a lawyer close to the events.

25   "Palermo, Escenario de la Fe," *La Nación*, October 13, 1998.

26   José María Poirier, "Quiet Thunder in Argentina," *Catholic Herald*, October 7, 2005.

27   "Bergoglio Rescata la Mirada de los Niños," *La Nación*, December 17, 1999.

28   In Horacio Verbitsky's *El Silencio*, 2nd ed. (Buenos Aires: Sudamericana, 2005), he mentions the Bergoglio interview and quotes from it.

29   Margaret Hebblethwaite, "The Pope Francis I Know," *Guardian* Comment Is Free website, March 14, 2013.

30   "Te Deum, 25 de Mayo de 1999," in Bergoglio, *La Patria es un Don, la Nación una Tarea. Refundar con Esperanza Nuestros Vínculos Sociales* (Buenos Aires: Ed. Claretiana, 2013).

31   "Te Deum, 25 de Mayo de 2000," in ibid.

32   Commission Sociale de l'Episcopat Français, *Réhabiliter la Politique* (February 1999), at www.cef.fr. Father Accaputo says Bergoglio knew the document well. It is footnoted in paragraph 205 in *Evangelii Gaudium* and is described in Pope Francis's interview with *La Vanguardia*, June 12, 2014, as a "beautiful text."

33   "Ibarra, el Agnóstico, Coincidió con Bergoglio, el Arzobispo," *Página 12*, December 2, 2000.

SEVEN GAUCHO CARDINAL (2001–2007)

1   Rembert Weakland, "Images of the Church from 'Perfect Society' to 'God's People on Pilgrimage,'" in Austen Ivereigh (ed.), *Unfinished Journey: The Church 40 Years After Vatican II* (New York: Continuum, 2003), pp. 78–90; Ladislas Orsy, SJ, "The Church of the Third Millennium: An Exercise in Theological and Canonical Imagination: In Praise of Communio," *Studia Canonica* 38 (2004): 5–36; John R. Quinn, *The Reform of the Papacy: The Costly Call to Christian Unity* (New York: Crossroad, 1999).

2   Congregation for the Doctrine of the Faith, "Letter to the Bishops of the Catholic Church on Some Aspects of the Church Understood as Communion" (May 28, 1992) at www.vatican.va.

3   In his encyclical letter *Ut Unum Sint* (1995), Pope John Paul II asked for help in finding "a way of exercising the primacy which, while in no way renouncing what is essential to its mission, is nonetheless open to a new situation."

4   Quinn, *The Reform of the Papacy*. Kasper's article, originally in *Stimmen der Zeit* 219 (December 2000), was published in English as "The Universal Church and the Local Church: A Friendly Rejoinder" in Walter Kasper, *Leadership in the Church* (New York: Crossroad, 2003). Cardinal Ratzinger responded in the *Frankfurter Allgemeine Zeitung*, December 22, 2000, defending the primacy of the universal over the local.

5   Sodano's financial relationship with Maciel is detailed in Jason Berry's 2010 investigation, "How Fr. Maciel Built His Empire," *National Catholic Reporter*, April 12, 1990. John Cornwell, *The Pontiff in Winter: Triumph and Conflict in the Reign of John Paul II* (New York: Doubleday, 2004), portrays the Vatican in the final John Paul II years.

6   Austen Ivereigh, "Streams of Scarlet as Pope Appoints New Cardinals," *The Tablet*, February 24, 2001.

7   "Bergoglio: El País Debe Apelar a Sus Reservas Morales," *La Nación*, February 18, 2001.

8   See Robert Mickens's reports in *The Tablet*: "Extraordinary Rome Meeting Brings Ordinary Results," May 26, 2001; "Cardinals Press for More Sharing in Church Government," June 2, 2001.

9   October 2, 2001. He spoke in Spanish. My translation.

10 Robert Mickens's synod reports in *The Tablet*: "Synod of Bishops to Meet Without Benefit of Reforms," June 9, 2001; "Bishops in a Think Tank," October 13, 2001. I was at Bergoglio's press conference.

11 In Cardinal Timothy M. Dolan, *Praying in Rome: Reflections on the Conclave and Electing Pope Francis* (New York: Image Books, 2013).

12 Sandro Magister, *L'Espresso*, no. 49 (November 28–December 5, 2002), translation "Jorge Mario Bergoglio, Profession: Servant of the Servants of God" at www.chiesa.espresso.repubblica.it.

13 Eduardo Duhalde, "Aquel Hombre Que Estuvo en las Horas Más Difíciles," *La Nación*, March 18, 2013.

14 Austen Ivereigh, "Argentina's New Riches," *The Tablet*, February 15, 2003. This article followed a period I spent in Buenos Aires at the end of 2002.

15 Gianni Valente, 2002 interview in *30 Giorni*, republished in Valente, *Francesco: Un Papa Dalla Fine del Mondo* (Bologna: EMI, 2013).

16 Te Deum address, May 25, 2002: "La Historia del Publicano Zaqueo," in Bergoglio, *La Patria Es un Don, la Nación una Tarea* (Buenos Aires: Ed Claretiana, 2013), pp. 57–66.

17 Te Deum address, May 25, 2003: "La Narración del Buen Samaritano," in Bergoglio, *La Patria Es un Don*, pp. 69–79.

18 The intermediary was interviewed by Larraquy in *Recen por Él*.

19 Te Deum address, May 25, 2004: "Jesús en la Sinagoga de Nazaret: Nadie Es profeta en Su Tierra," in Bergoglio, *La Patria Es un Don*, pp. 81–93.

20 "Bergoglio Tiró Palos, Pero en Gobierno los Esquivaron," *Página 12*, May 26, 2004.

21 "Francisco Va a Vivir Hasta los 140 Años, Dice Su Médico Chino," Revista *Perfil*, October 30, 2013; "El Médico Chino del Papa," Religión Digital website, August 21, 2003.

22 Austen Ivereigh, "Pope in Lourdes Speaks of 'The End of My Pilgrimage,'" *The Tablet*, August 21, 2004.

23 Jorge Mario Bergoglio, "La Presencia de María en la Vida del Papa," *30 Giorni*, special edition dedicated to John Paul II, no. 4 (April 2005).

24 Bergoglio 2005 testimony: Stefania Falasca, "Bergoglio: 'Io, Testimone di Virtù Eroiche di Wojtyla,'" *Avvenire*, April 17, 2014.

25   "Homilía del Arzobispo de Buenos Aires, en Ocasión de la Misa por el Primer Aniversario de la Tragedia de Cromagnon" (December 30, 2005).

26   "Juan Pablo II Fue Simplemente un Coherente," homily (April 4, 2005).

27   Gerson Camarotti, "Cartas Quase Marcadas no Vaticano," *O Globo*, December 25, 2005.

28   Verbitsky, *El Silencio*, pp. 51–61, 101–15. Bergoglio account in Rubín and Ambrogetti, *El Jesuita*, ch. 14.

29   Cardinal Francis George of Chicago told me this at Fiumicino Airport after the conclave of 2013. The allegation was made by Román Lejtman, "Exclusivo: Por Qué Fracasó un Informe Secreto K para Bloquear la Elección de Bergoglio," *El Cronista*, March 28, 2013; denial in Elisabetta Piqué, "Cafiero Negó que Haya Emitido un Dossier Contra Bergoglio," *La Nación*, March 20, 2013.

30   Lucio Brunelli, "Cosi Eleggemmo Papa Ratzinger," *Limes*, September 23, 2005.

31   Marco Tosatti, "Ecco Come Andò Davvero il Conclave del 2005," *Vatican Insider*, October 3, 2013.

32   Marchisano told this to Gianluca Barile, *Diario di un Papista* (Tavagnacco: Ed. Segno, 2013).

33   Piqué, *Francisco: Vida y Revolución*, p. 144; George Weigel, "The First American Pope," *National Review Online*, March 14, 2013.

34   Meditation on the Two Standards, from a translation of the retreat published as *In Him Alone Is Our Hope* (San Francisco: Ignatius Press, 2013), ch. 7.

35   Carmen María Ramos, "No Es Tiempo de un Papa Latinoamericano," interview with Methol Ferré in *La Nación*, April 6, 2005.

36   The remarks in *L'Indipendente* were reported by *Catholic World News*, October 13, 2005: "Argentine Cardinal Refuses to Discuss Conclave Support."

37   Robert Mickens, "Rome Synod: The Inside Story," *The Tablet*, October 29, 2005; and "Curial Cardinals at Odds over Remarried Divorcees," *The Tablet*, November 5, 2005. "Debate la Iglesia la Comunión a los Divorciados Vueltos a Casar," *La Nación*, October 6, 2005.

38   The retreat is published in English as *In Him Alone Is Our Hope* (San Francisco: Ignatius Press, 2013).

39   "Kirchner y Bergoglio, Juntos en una Misa de Homenaje a Sacerdotes Palotinos," *Clarín*, April 11, 2006.

40   "En el Tedéum, Bergoglio Criticó la Manipulación y la Prepotencia," *Clarín*, May 26, 2006. Te Deum address, May 25, 2006: "Las Bienaventuranzas," in Bergoglio, *La Patria es un Don*, pp. 97–108.

41   "Bergoglio y los Kirchner: Seis Años de una Relación Gélida," *La Nación*, November 8, 2011; "Guillermo Marcó ya no Será Vocero del Cardenal Bergoglio," *La Nación*, December 14, 2006.

42   Bergoglio, "Sentido Eclesial," in *Meditaciones para Religiosos*.

43   Raniero Cantalamessa, press conference following October 13, 2012, CRECES meeting, at www.infocreces.com.ar.

44   Bergoglio prologue dated April 4, 2005, to Guzmán Carriquiry, *Una Apuesta Por América Latina* (Buenos Aires: Sudamericana, 2005).

45   In his prologue to Carriquiry, *En Camino Hacia La V Conferencia de la Iglesia Latinoamericana: Memoria de los 50 años del CELAM*.

46   Alberto Methol Ferré, *La América Latina del Siglo XXI* (Buenos Aires: Edhasa, 2006).

47   Guzmán Carriquiry, "La Revolución de la Gracia," *Tierras de América* website, February 18, 2014.

48 Gutiérrez said this at the launch of a book cowritten by Cardinal Gerhard Müller, current CDF head, in Rome. See Joshua McElwee, "With Vatican Doctrinal Czar, Liberation Theology Pioneer Reflects on Troubles," *National Catholic Reporter*, February 28, 2014.

49 Interview with Stefania Falasca, "What I Would Have Said at the Consistory," *30 Days*, no. 11 (November 2007).

50 Interview in *Clarín*, October 27, 2013.

51 *The Tablet*, June 2, 2007.

52 This debate is described by the then bishop of Petrópolis, Filippo Santoro, in Sandro Magister, "When Bergoglio Defeated the Liberation Theologians," *Chiesa* blog, October 1, 2013.

Eight Man for Others (2008–2012)

1 Padre Pepe Di Paola in Bermúdez (ed., trans.), *Pope Francis: Our Brother, Our Friend*.

2 Equipo de Sacerdotes para las Villas de Emergencia, Ciudad Autónoma de Buenos Aires, "La Droga en las Villas: Despenalizada de Hecho," March 25, 2009.

3 These stories are told in Silvina Premat, *Curas Villeros: de Mugica al Padre Pepe* (Buenos Aires: Editorial Sudamericana, 2010), and Premat, *Pepe: El Cura de la Villa* (Buenos Aires: Sudamericana, 2013).

4 Equipo de Sacerdotes para las Villas de Emergencia, Ciudad Autónoma de Buenos Aires, "Celebrar el Bicentenario en la Ciudad de Buenos Aires, 2010–2016," May 11, 2010.

5 Conferencia Episcopal Argentina, "Hacia un Bicentenario en Justicia y Solidaridad, 2010–2016," December 2008.

6 Jorge Mario Bergoglio, Prologue to Guzmán Carriquiry, *El Bicentenario de la Independencia de los Países Latinoamericanos* (Madrid: Encuentro, 2011).

7 "Hace Años que No Se Ocupan de la Gente," *La Nación*, August 8, 2009.

8 "Activista Gay Dice que el Papa Francisco Apoyaba las Uniones Civiles Homosexuales," CNN, March 20, 2013. The headline is misleading. Cardinal Bergoglio supported civil unions whose legal rights and privileges gay people could access rather than civil unions exclusively for gay people.

9 Congregation for the Doctrine of the Faith, "Considerations Regarding Proposals to Give Legal Recognition to Unions Between Homosexual Persons," March 28, 2003. The "objections from Rome" were voiced by Esteban Caselli, who gave a radio interview in August 2003 expressing surprise that Bergoglio had not criticized the Buenos Aires law the year before. But given Caselli's closeness to Cardinals Sodano and Sandri, nobody doubted the origin of the criticism. See Sergio Rubín, "Una Ofensiva Dentro de la Iglesia," *Clarín*, August 10, 2003.

10 See Bergoglio's remarks in Bergoglio and Skorka, *Sobre el Cielo y la Tierra*, ch. 16.

11 Declaración de la Asamblea Plenaria del Episcopado Argentino, "Sobre el Bien Inalterable del Matrimonio y de la Familia," April 20, 2010. Bergoglio's position at the plenary was revealed a few months later by Sergio Rubín in "La Iglesia Puso Todo en Juego," *Clarín* (July 14, 2010), and subsequently confirmed by various sources.

12 Vallely, *Pope Francis: Untying the Knots*. Vallely quotes Father Marcó speculating that this was a "strategy" in which Bergoglio would copy the letter to Rome "to show he was doing what was required." Marcó was not part of Bergoglio's staff or close to him at this time, and his reading is contradicted by those who were.

13 Bergoglio letter to Dr. Justo Carbajales, director of the Argentine Bishops' Conference Department for Laity, July 5, 2010.

14 Senator Negre's account from Bermúdez, *Pope Francis: Our Brother, Our Friend*, and "El Papa Francisco Nunca Impulsó 'Uniones Civiles,'" ACI/EWTN Noticias, April 24, 2013, as well as e-mail correspondence with the author.

15 Bergoglio and Skorka, *Sobre el Cielo y la Tierra*, ch. 25.

16 Luis Zamora appears on the TV show "Palabras Más, Palabras Menos," March 19, 2013, on YouTube.

17 "Luis Zamora Declaración de Bergoglio," Canal de Política Provincia, November 9, 2010, on YouTube.

18 The questions and Bergoglio's written answers are at the website of the Grandmothers of the Plaza de Mayo, www.abuelas.org.uk.

19 I attended the November 2013 Jornada. Among those attending are normally the head of the Association of Industrialists, the leading trade unionists, the head of the Agrarian Federation, as well as the leaders of the non-Kirchner Peronist parties and non-Peronist parties. The fullest expression of the work of the Jornadas was the document produced in September 2007, which is almost a charter for a re-foundation of Argentine political life. Pastoral Social de la Arquidiócesis de Buenos Aires, "Hacia una Cultura de Encuentro: La Política, Mediadora del Bien Común," September 15, 2007.

20 See Fortunato Mallimaci, *Atlas de las Creencias Religiosas en la Argentina* (Buenos Aires: Editorial Biblos, 2013).

21 See Marco Gallo, "El Papa Francisco y la Shoá," in the magazine of the Buenos Aires Shoah Museum, *Nuestra Memoria* 19, no. 37 (May 2013).

22 Sergio Bergman, *Un Evangelio Según Francisco: Maestro, Líder y Estadista* (Buenos Aires: Ediciones B, 2013).

23 Published as *Biblia, Diálogo Vigente* (Buenos Aires: Planeta, 2013).

24 Bishop Venables's comment was published without his consent on the website of the Anglican Communion following Francis's election but he has confirmed its accuracy. The Ordinariate, which was created in response to requests from Anglicans, allows Anglican priests to become Catholics along with their congregations, and to preserve key traditions in liturgy and customs.

25 Comisión Permanente del Episcopado Argentino, "El Juego se Torna Peligroso," December 20, 2010.

26 "Informe sobre Talleres Clandestinos en la Ciudad de Buenos Aires," August 29, 2006, commissioned by the national deputy Elisa Carrió and on her website.

27 Homily, "Misa por las Víctimas de la Trata y Tráfico de Personas," September 23, 2011.

28 Puente, *La Vida Oculta de Bergoglio*, pp. 289–300.

29 Saint Ignatius in the 1540s founded a home in Rome for women escaping prostitution. It was called the Casa Santa Marta, the same name as the Vatican hostel where Pope Francis now lives.

30 In Bermúdez, *Pope Francis: Our Brother, Our Friend*.

31 The story is told by one of them in Piqué, *Francisco: Vida y Revolución*, ch 11. Deacons are clergy who may be celibate or married; can officiate at baptisms, weddings, and funerals; and can assist at Mass by preaching. But they are not priests.

32 Arancedo, preface to Jorge Mario Bergoglio, *Open Mind, Faithful Heart*. Bergoglio describes his typewriter in a 2011 interview with the Argentine Catholic Information Agency (AICA).

33 Andrea Tornielli, "Careerism and Vanity: Sins of the Church," *Vatican Insider*, February 24, 2012.

34 This story was told to me by Maria Lia Zerviño, who worked at the time in the diocese.

35 José María Poirier's article was "Quiet Thunder in Argentina," *Catholic Herald*, October 7, 2005. Isasmendi quoted in Allen, "Pope Francis Gets His Oxygen from the Slums."

36 He tells the story in Juan Martín Ezratty's documentary, *Francis: The People's Pope* (2013).

37 Jorge Rouillón, "Mis Días con Bergoglio," *Diario Los Andes*, May 12, 2013.

38 DVD Caritas Argentina (Buenos Aires), Retiro Anual 2010.

39 Rubín and Ambrogetti, *El Jesuita*, ch. 6. Ambrogetti's speculation is in Juan Martín Ezratty's documentary, *Francis: The People's Pope* (2013).

40 See Bergoglio's essay, "For Man," in Elisa Buzzi (ed.), *A Generative Thought: An Introduction to the Works of Luigi Giussani* (Montreal: McGill–Queen's University Press, 2003).

41 Bergoglio spoke at the launch of two of Giussani's books, praising "the good that this man has done me, in my life as a priest, through the reading of his books and articles." Silvina Premat, "The Attraction of the Cardinal," in *Traces*, July 2001. Bergoglio's prayer at the tomb of Saint Josemaría Escrivà is recalled by the Prelate of Opus Dei, Javier Echevarría, in an interview with José Beltrán, "El Papa Sentirá la Fuerza y la Compañía Espiritual de Benedicto XVI," *La Razón*, March 24, 2013.

42 Rubín and Ambrogetti, *El Jesuita*, ch. 12; Stefania Falasca, "Una Rosa Bianca da Santa Teresa," *Avvenire*, March 24, 2013. Bergoglio told her that the tradition of asking Saint Thérèse for a flower as a sign that a prayer has been heard was started by Father Putigan, a Jesuit, in 1925.

43 "Bergoglio, el Cardenal que Marcó una Época y Será Difícil de Reemplazar," *Perfil*, August 7, 2012.

44 "Homeward Bound" in Bergoglio, *Open Mind, Faithful Heart*.

45 "The Failure of Jesus," in Bergoglio, *Open Mind, Faithful Heart*.

46 "Bergoglio Comenzó a Negociar en el Vaticano el Nombre de Su Sucesor," *Tiempo Argentino*, February 25, 2012.

47 Fernández gives a detailed account of his treatment in "Bergoglio, a Secas," *Vida Pastoral* (June 2013).

48 One of the best summaries of Vatileaks is by Jason Horowitz, "Pope Benedict XVI's Leaked Documents Show Fractured Vatican Full of Rivalries," *Washington Post*, February 16, 2013.

49 See Massimo Franco, *The Crisis in the Vatican Empire* (Milan: Mondadori, 2013), and Tornielli, "Careerism and Vanity: Sins of the Church."

50 The bathroom fall was reported in *La Stampa* after Benedict's resignation was announced. Both the report and the decision to resign following the trip were subsequently confirmed by the Vatican newspaper and spokesman. See Andrea Tornielli, "El Papa Decidió Renunciar Después de una Caída en León, México," *Vatican Insider*, February 14, 2013.

51 "L'Ultima Intervista," *Corriere della Sera*, September 1, 2012. Translation mine.

52 Andrea Tornielli discusses reactions to the interview by Cardinals Gianfranco Ravasi and Angelo Scola in *Carlo Maria Martini: Il Profeta del Dialogo* (Milan: Ed. Piemme, 2012), ch. 18.

53 "Bergoglio les Exigió a los Curas que Bauticen a Hijos de Madres Solteras," *Clarín*, September 4, 2012.

54 Jorge Mario Bergoglio, second reflection at Caritas retreat, on DVD, November 3, 2012.

55 Carlos Galli, "Una Nueva Hora de la Iglesia Latinoamericana, y el Ícono Pastoral de Francisco," *Vida Nueva* (Spanish edition), no. 2864, 2013, pp. 23–30; (Cono Sur edition) no. 24, 2013, pp. 8–13.

56 Austen Ivereigh, "Synod of Bishops Ends with Far-reaching Goals," *Our Sunday Visitor*, October 31, 2012.

NINE CONCLAVE (2013)

1 Interview with Giovanna Chirri of ANSA in various, *Benedict XVI: The Resignation of a Pope* (Turin: Ed La Stampa, 2013).

2 Archbishop Leo Cushley, "A Monsignor Sobbed, Then Silence Fell," *Catholic Herald*, February 7, 2014. Cushley is now Archbishop of Edinburgh and St. Andrews.

3 Monsignor Viganò interview with Father Thomas Rosica, Salt & Light TV, October 4, 2013.

4 Dolan, *Praying in Rome: Reflections on the Conclave and Electing Pope Francis.*

5 Cardinal O'Malley interview with Father Thomas Rosica, Salt & Light TV, October 4, 2013.

6 I was able to speak to Cardinal Pell about these issues while in Sydney, Australia, in May 2013. See also "Cardinal Pell Hopes for a Pope Who Knows How to Govern," *Vatican Insider*, March 4, 2013. On Coccopalmerio, see Andrea Tornielli, "Curia Is in the Firing Line," *Vatican Insider*, March 6, 2013.

7 The curial strategy was revealed by *Vatican Insider* on March 2, 2013: "A Ticket to Vote for the First Latin-American Pope." The Peruvian cardinal, Juan Luis Cipriani, spoke of the anti-Italian feeling in a *Vatican Insider* interview on March 27, 2013: "Papa Francisco: Un Místico con Capacidad de Gobierno."

8 These anecdotes come both from sources in the conclave and from friends of Pope Francis, and were shared on condition of anonymity.

9 Account of this dinner from the staff of the Wall Street Journal, *Pope Francis: From the End of the Earth to Rome* (New York: HarperCollins, 2013), ch. 8. See also Cormac Murphy-O'Connor interview in *The Catholic Herald*, "When Pope Francis First Stepped . . . ," September 13, 2013. On the role of Santos Abril y Castelló: Giacomo Galeazzi, "Operación Santa María Mayor," *Vatican Insider*, March 15, 2013.

10 In his *Francis: Pope of a New World* (San Francisco: Ignatius Press, 2013), ch. 3, the leading Vatican commentator Andrea Tornielli says that there were no "campaigns organized in advance" of the conclave for Bergoglio. There was one.

11 "Cardenal Ortega Revela Palabras del Cardenal Bergoglio," www.palabranueva.net (March 25, 2013). Reaction to the speech in memoirs of Cardinal Dolan, *Praying in Rome,* and Cardinal Murphy-O'Connor, *An English Spring* (London: Bloomsbury, 2015), p. 216.

12 Valente told this to Andrea Tornielli, *Francis: Pope of a New World.*

13 Cardinal Kasper told this story while in New York in May 2014. David Gibson, "Cardinal Kasper Is the Pope's Theologian," *National Catholic Reporter*, June 6–19, 2014. Francis spoke of the rose to an Argentine friend.

14 See Associated Press report, "So What Really Happened Inside the Papal Conclave?" March 14, 2013; and Dolan memoir, *Praying in Rome.*

15 The annulled fifth ballot was revealed by Piqué, *Francisco: Vida y Revolución*, ch. 3. Analysts who gave accounts of the voting in the days after the conclave include Andrea Tornielli (*La Stampa*), Carlo Marroni (*Il Sole*), Andrés Beltramo (*Sacro y Profano*), David Gibson (Religion News Service), and Giacomo Galeazzi (*Vatican Insider*).

16 See Francis Burkle-Young's classic history of conclaves, *Passing the Keys* (Lanham:

Madison Books, 2001). On the smoke dramas at the 2005 conclave see John L. Allen, *The Rise of Benedict XVI* (New York: Doubleday, 2005), and John Thavis, *The Vatican Diaries* (London: Penguin 2013), ch. 1.

17 "Papa Francisco Dialoga como un Hermano más con la CLAR," originally posted on the Chilean website *Reflexión y Liberación* (June 26, 2013) and later removed.

18 "Cross and Mission," in Bergoglio, *Open Mind, Faithful Heart*, ch. 8.

19 Monsignor Viganò's interview was with Fr. Thomas Rosica of Salt & Light TV, October 4, 2013. In fact the cardinals were Vallini and Hummes, not Vallini and Tauran, as Viganò tells Rosica in the interview. In his interview with *La Stampa*, December 14, 2013, Francis recalls how, "before I showed myself, I knelt down to pray for a few minutes together with Cardinal Vallini and Cardinal Hummes in the Pauline Chapel," which Father Rosica has confirmed in an e-mail to me. Francis's recollections about his anxiety and then the "great light" were shared with Eugenio Scalfari of *La Repubblica* in an interview published on October 1, 2013. Because the interview was not recorded, Scalfari reproduced the exchange from memory and many details are questionable. But the experience Francis described is one he has often spoken of. See, e.g., Inés San Martín interview with Cardinal Francisco Errázuriz, "Confidant Calls Pope Francis a Changed Man," *Boston Globe*, July 4, 2014.

20 Murphy-O'Connor, interview in the *Catholic Herald*, September 13, 2013. María Elena Bergoglio and Daniel del Regno in Juan Martín Ezratty's documentary, *Francis: The People's Pope* (2013).

Epilogue The Great Reform

1 Cardinal Ortega recalls the conversation in an interview with Yarelis Rico Hernández, "No hay nada más interesante que ser párroco," in *Palabra Nueva* (Havana), March 30, 2015.

2 Video on YouTube. The senator speaks about that day in Alejandro Bermúdez (ed.), *Pope Francis: Our Brother, Our Friend* (San Francisco: Ignatius Press, 2013).

3 Mariano de Vedia, *En el Nombre del Papa: La Iglesia y el gobierno argentino. Los años en que Jorge Bergoglio fue un enemigo* (Buenos Aires: Planeta, 2015). The Kirchner-Correa conversation is recalled in Laura Di Marco, *Cristina Fernández: La Verdadera Historia* (Buenos Aires: Sudamericana, 2014).

4 Enzo Bianchi, "Il Pontefice che si é Fatto Uomo," *La Stampa*, March 17, 2013; Austen Ivereigh, "Pope Francis Takes Fresh Approach to Papacy," *Our Sunday Visitor Newsweekly*, March 31, 2013; Philip Pullella (Reuters), "By-the-book Vatican Braces for Unscripted Papacy," March 14, 2013.

5 Timothy M. Dolan, *Praying in Rome: Reflections on the Conclave and Electing Pope Francis* (New York: Image Books, 2013).

6 Jorge Mario Bergoglio, "En Él Solo Poner la Esperanza," in *Reflexiones en Esperanza* (Buenos Aires: Ediciones Universidad del Salvador, 1992). I had a number of conversations that day with producers and correspondents from BBC and Sky, among others.

7 Pope Francis, Interview in *La Repubblica*, October 1, 2013.

8 See Archbishop John R. Quinn, *Ever Ancient, Ever New: Structures of Communion in the Church* (New York: Paulist Press, 2013). Quinn recalled Bergoglio telling him this in a speech to priests in St. Louis, Missouri, on June 25, 2014. See Thomas Fox, "Quinn to Priest Group," *National Catholic Reporter*, July 7, 2014. In correspondence with the author, Archbishop Quinn clarified that this conversation took place in 2012 and not, as Fox reported him saying, on the eve of the conclave.

9 Pope Francis, Interview in *La Stampa*, December 14, 2013. In the original Italian of the Spadaro interview, Francis referred to the C9 as "questo gruppo consultivo

outsider." Martini in 2012 spoke of *dodici persone fuori dalle righe per i posti direzionali*, "putting twelve people from outside the lines in positions of responsibility."

10 "Letter of Pope Francis to Card. Lorenzo Baldisseri . . . ," April 1, 2014; Ladislas Orsy, SJ, "Francis's New Order," *The Tablet*, June 19, 2014; Yves Congar, *True and False Reform in the Church*, trans. Paul Philibert OP (Collegeville, MD: Liturgical Press, 2011), p. 262.

11 Walter Kasper, *Pope Francis's Revolution of Tenderness and Love: Theological and Pastoral Perspectives* (Mahwah, NJ: Paulist Press, 2015), chapter 6.

12 "El sínodo sobre la familia: 'Los divorciados vueltos a casar parecen excomulgados,'" Francis interview with Elisabetta Piqué, *La Nación*, December 7, 2014.

13 Talk to Catholic Voices in Argentina, Buenos Aires, April 16, 2015.

14 Walter Kasper, *Mercy: The Essence of the Gospel and the Key to Christian Life* (Mahwah, NJ: Paulist Press, New York, 2013), chapter 1.

15 Interview with the author in Salta, Argentina, April 24, 2015.

16 Detailed account by Shawn Tully, "This Pope Means Business," *Fortune*, August 14, 2014.

17 John Thavis, "Decision time on Vatican reforms?" www.johnthavis.com, February 18, 2014.

18 "Pope Francis and Reform: How far can he go?" *America*, April 21, 2015.

19 I gave a number of interviews on the Barros nomination while in Santiago, Chile, in April 2015: e.g. "Biógrafo del Papa, Austen Ivereigh, desglosa el caso Barros," *La Segunda*, April 17, 2015.

20 Roberto Bosca, "La beligerante resistencia al papa," *La Nación*, November 10, 2014.

21 Paddy Agnew, 'There are Vatican whispers that maybe the pope talks too freely," *Irish Times*, January 21, 2015; Ross Douthat, "Liberal Catholics in the Age of Francis," *New York Times*, December 2, 2013; Elizabeth Scalia, "Amid Storms and Wars, the Daily Outrage that is Pope Francis," *Patheos*, January 28, 2015; John Allen, "Pope Francis and the ambivalence of popularity," *Crux*, March 29, 2015.

22 *Vanity Fair* Italian edition, July 17, 2013; *Economist*, April 19, 2014; *Prospect*, April 23, 2014; *Time*, December 11, 2013; *The New Yorker*, December 23/30, 2013; *The Advocate*, December 2013; *Financial Times*, December 29, 2013; *Guardian*, November 17, 2013.

23 Figures are from Pew Forum, summarized by John Allen, "Here are five Francis forecasts for Año Tres," *Crux*, March 13, 2015.

24 Figures from the annual Twiplomacy survey, "The Twiplomacy Top Twenty Twitterati," www.twiplomacy.com, April 28, 2015.

25 "The Remarkable Figure of Pope Francis," *Financial Times*, December 29, 2013. Tim Stanley, "Time Magazine's Man of the Year Is Pope Francis. Alas, It's Not the Real Pope Francis," *Daily Telegraph*, December 12, 2013.

26 Elizabeth Tenety, "Like Francis? You'll love Jesus," *Washington Post*, December 11, 2013.

27 Maurice Glasman, "Beloved of the people: how the Pope has again become a leader for our times," *New Statesman*, April 2, 2015.

28 James Politi, "How Pope Francis helped melt the US-Cuba freeze," *Financial Times*, December 19, 2014.

Note on Sources

The Great Reformer *is nourished by four main sources: (1) the interviews I conducted in Argentina and Chile in October–November 2013 and subsequently in Rome in February and April 2014; (2) the writings and spoken words of Jorge Mario Bergoglio; (3) the existing books and documentaries on him as well as books on Argentine, Jesuit, and Catholic history; and (4) news media, mainly in Argentina, Italy, France, Spain, the UK and the USA.*

INTERVIEWS

CHAPTERS 1 TO 5

Recollections of Bergoglio as a young man as well as his backstory are taken mainly from interviews and reminiscences in the Argentine media following Francis's election, though nuns of the Mercy Convent in Flores (Buenos Aires) shared their recollections with me.

For his Jesuit period, 1960–1992, the following Jesuit priests (all "Father" with "SJ" after their names) who knew Bergoglio well were invaluable sources of insights and memories. In Argentina: Ignacio Pérez del Viso, Ignacio García-Mata, Juan Carlos Scannone, Enrique Fabbri, Fernando Cervera, Angel Rossi, Alfonso Gómez, Andrés Swinnen, Rafael Velasco, and Leonardo Nardín; in Chile: Juan Valdés and Fernando Montes; and in Rome: Guillermo Ortiz and Miguel Yáñez. The following former Jesuits who were in formation with Bergoglio also shared their memories: (Argentina) Jorge González Mament; (Chile) Raúl Vergara, Juan Eduardo García-Huidobro; (Uruguay) Francisco López.

Father Bill Ryan, SJ, in Canada and Father Juan Ochagavía, SJ, in Chile responded to specific questions by e-mail and phone. I also conducted interviews relating to these chapters with the Peronist politician Julio Bárbaro, Professor Carlos Pauli at La Inmaculada school, Father Miguel de la Civita of Santa Fe Diocese, and with Peter Saunders, founder and chief executive of the British charity the National Association for People Abused in Childhood (NAPAC).

I have indicated in the text where I have also drawn on interviews with Jesuits in Alejandro Bermúdez (ed., trans.), *Pope Francis: Our Brother, Our Friend* (San Francisco: Ignatius Press, 2013), Chris Lowney, *Pope Francis: Why He Leads the Way He Leads* (Chicago: Loyola Press, 2013), and the biographies listed below.

The following Jesuits were also very helpful in clarifying Jesuitica as well as my understanding of complex issues, but cannot be blamed for my conclusions or misunderstandings (again, all "Father" and with "SJ" after their names): in Rome, Michael Czerny; in Canada, Bill Ryan; in the United States, Jack O'Callaghan; and in the UK, James Hanvey.

CHAPTERS 6–9 AND EPILOGUE

The following kindly gave me interviews: *Cardinals*: Francisco Errázuriz (emeritus, Santiago de Chile), Cormac Murphy-O'Connor (emeritus, Westminster). *Argentine bishops*: Jorge Casaretto (emeritus, San Isidro), Jorge Lozano (Gualeguaychú). *Buenos Aires clergy*: Carlos Accaputo, Guillermo Marcó, Carlos Galli, Fernando Giannetti, Gabriel Maronetti, Mariano Fazio, Lorenzo ("Toto") de Vedia, Gustavo Carrara. *Bergoglio lay collaborators*: Federico Wals, Roberto Da Busti, Daniel Gassman, (in Rome) Professor Guzmán Carriquiry. *Journalists*: José María Poirier, Sergio Rubín, Mariano de Vedia, Evangelina Himitian, José Ignacio López, Enrique Cangas. *Academics*: Fortunato Mallimaci, Roberto Bosca. *Ecumenical/interfaith*: Pastor Jorge Himitian, Marco Gallo, Omar Abboud, Rabbi Abraham Skorka, Bishop Tony Palmer, Ricardo Elías. Senator Liliana Negre answered questions via e-mail.

BY BERGOGLIO/FRANCIS

1. WRITINGS

As a Jesuit, Bergoglio wrote mostly in two Argentine Jesuit journals: *Boletín de Espiritualidad* and *Stromata*. His articles, together with his addresses and other meditations, are collected in three books: *Meditaciones para Religiosos* (Buenos Aires: Ediciones Diego de Torres, 1982), *Reflexiones Espirituales sobre la Vida Apostólica* (Buenos Aires: Ediciones Diego de Torres, 1987), and *Reflexiones en Esperanza* (Buenos Aires: Ediciones Universidad del Salvador, 1992).

During his Córdoba exile Bergoglio wrote two long, detailed letters (dated October 20, 1990, and December 20, 1990) full of childhood memories to the Salesian historian, Don Cayetano Bruno. There is also an earlier letter to him (dated May 18, 1986) about vocations. All are available on the Internet.

As coadjutor archbishop (see Chapter 6) he wrote a book about John Paul II's Cuba visit: *Diálogos entre Juan Pablo II y Fidel Castro* (Buenos Aires: Editorial de Ciencia y Cultura, 1998). His 2006 retreat to the Spanish bishops (see Chapter 7) has been published in English as *In Him Alone Is Our Hope* (San Francisco: Ignatius Press, 2013).

From 1998, his writings mainly come in the form of homilies, which are available (from 1999 to 2013) at the Archdiocese of Buenos Aires website, while other documents (letters, addresses, etc.) are at the website of AICA.org.ar. Editorial Claretiana in Buenos Aires has published a large number of anthologies: *Educar: Testimonio de la Verdad* (2013) contains his addresses to teachers between 2006 and 2012; *¡Salgan a Buscar Corazones!* (Buenos Aires: Ed. Claretiana 2013), his messages to catechists and pilgrims; while his Te Deum addresses are collected in *La Patria Es un Don, la Nación una Tarea* (Buenos Aires: Ed. Claretiana 2013). An excellent anthology is Virginia Bonard, *Nuestra Fe es Revolucionaria* (Buenos Aires: Planeta, 2013).

With Rabbi Abraham Skorka he published *Sobre el Cielo y la Tierra* (Buenos Aires: Editorial Sudamericana, 2011), trans. *On Heaven and Earth* (London: Bloomsbury, 2013). With Skorka and Pastor Marcelo Figueroa he published *Biblia, Diálogo Vigente: la Fe en Tiempos Modernos* (Buenos Aires: Planeta, 2013). He also wrote a large number of prologues.

As Pope Francis, a steady stream of anthologies of his homilies and writings has appeared, among the best of which are *Open Mind, Faithful Heart: Reflections on Following Jesus*, trans. Joseph V. Owens (New York: Crossroad, 2013), and *A Church of Mercy* (London: Darton, Longman & Todd, 2014). His main work has been his apostolic exhortation, *Evangelii Gaudium* (November 2013, various editions). His daily Santa Marta homilies transcribed by Vatican Radio have been collected in Papa Francesco, *La Verità è un Incontro* (Rome: Libreria Editrice Vaticana, 2014).

2. INTERVIEWS

BERGOGLIO

The book-length interview (see Chapter 8) by Sergio Rubín and Francesca Ambrogetti, *El Jesuita* (Barcelona: Vergara, Grupo Zeta, 2010), published in English as *Pope Francis: The Authorized Biography* (London: Hodder & Stoughton, 2013), remains the most comprehensive pre-papal source, and contains primary documents he shared with them. He gave no interviews before he became cardinal in 2001, and, apart from one to Radio María in September 2008, before 2010 gave interviews only in Rome: to *La Nación* (February 18, 2001), and various to Gianni Valente in *30 Giorni* collected in *Francesco: Un Papa dalla Fine del Mondo* (Bologna: EMI, 2013). In 2011 he gave an interview to the Agencia Informativa Católica Argentina (AICA); in 2012, he gave three: in February to Andrea Tornielli (*Vatican Insider*, February 24), in November to EWTN Spanish, and in December to the Villa 21 community radio, La 96 Voz de Caacupé.

FRANCIS

As pope, the most significant interview (see Chapter 5) was by Father Antonio Spadaro for *Civiltà Cattolica*, published in the United States by *America* magazine as "A Big Heart Open to God" (September 30, 2013), and as a book by Spadaro (with extra material) as *My Door Is Always Open: A Conversation on Faith, Hope and the Church in a Time of Change* (New York: HarperOne, 2013). Spadaro also recorded an exchange Francis had with religious men and women, available on the *Civiltà Cattolica* website as "Wake Up the World" (November 2013). Other interviews include with Brazilian *TV Globo* (July 28, 2013), *La Stampa* (December 14, 2013), *Corriere della Sera/La Nación* (March 5, 2014), *La Vanguardia* (June 12, 2014), and *Il Messagero* (June 29, 2014). Although not technically interviews, despite his putting words in Francis's mouth, Eugenio Scalfari has twice written about meetings with Pope Francis in *La Repubblica* (October 1, 2013, and July 13, 2014). Francis has also done two long press conferences onboard the papal plane returning from Rio de Janeiro (July 28, 2013), from Tel Aviv (May 27, 2014), and from Seoul (August 18, 2014).

ON BERGOGLIO/FRANCIS

BIOGRAPHIES

There have been five biographies by Argentine journalists. The first two, produced within weeks of Francis's election, were by *La Nación* reporters: Mariano de Vedia, *Francisco: El*

Papa del Pueblo (Buenos Aires: Planeta, 2013), and Evangelina Himitian, *Francisco: El Papa de la Gente* (Buenos Aires: Aguilar, 2013). Later in the year came *Clarín* reporter Marcelo Larraquy's *Recen por Él* (Buenos Aires: Sudamericana, 2013) and *Francisco: Vida y Revolución* (Buenos Aires: El Ateneo, 2013) by *La Nación's* correspondent in Rome, Elisabetta Piqué. In 2014 Armando Rubén Puente published *La Vida Oculta de Bergoglio* (Madrid: Libros Libres, 2014). Among the noteworthy biographical books by non-Argentines are those by Andrea Tornielli, *Francis: Pope of a New World* (San Francisco: Ignatius Press, 2013), The Staff of the Wall Street Journal, *Pope Francis: From the End of the Earth to Rome* (New York: HarperCollins, 2013), Paul Vallely, *Pope Francis: Untying the Knots* (London; New York: Bloomsbury, 2013), and Marcelo López Cambronero and Feliciana Merino Escalera, *Francisco: El Papa Manso* (Buenos Aires: Planeta, 2013).

MEMOIRS

Bergoglio's fellow Jesuit novice/scholastic Jorge González Mament ("Goma") has two memoirs of his Jesuit days: *Jesuitas Éramos Los de Antes: Impresiones de un Novicio de los Años '50* (Buenos Aires: Ed. Dunken, 2012) and his unpublished *Bergoglio y Yo: Vidas Casi Paralelas* (2013). Jorge Milia's schooldays memoir of Bergoglio the teacher, *De la Edad Feliz* (Salta: Ed. Maktub, 2006), with a prologue by Bergoglio, has been published in Italian as *Maestro Francesco: Gli Allievi del Papa Ricordano Il Loro Professore* (Milan: Mondadori, 2014). Cardinal Timothy M. Dolan, *Praying in Rome: Reflections on the Conclave and Electing Pope Francis* (New York: Image Books, 2013) is a very useful conclave memoir.

OTHER

Chris Lowney, *Pope Francis: Why He Leads the Way He Leads* (Chicago: Loyola Press, 2013), links Francis's leadership to his Jesuit formation and spirituality; Robert Moynihan, *Pray for Me: The Life and Spiritual Vision of Pope Francis* (New York: Random House, 2013), is an account of his first days as pope; Andrea Riccardi, *La Sorpresa di Papa Francesco: Crisi e Futuro della Chiesa* (Milan: Mondadori, 2013), is an analysis of Francis's election and its historic significance; and Mariano Fazio, *Pope Francis: Keys to His Thought* (New York: Scepter, 2013), is an introduction to his most important ideas.

Four documentaries contain valuable interviews: Juan Martín Ezratty (dir.), *Francis: The People's Pope* (Rome Reports, 2013); Music Brokers (dir.), *Pope Francis: A Pope for Everyone* (2013); Knights of Columbus, *Francis: The Pope from the New World* (2014); Salt & Light TV, *The Francis Effect* (2014).

BACKGROUND SOURCES

JESUITS

I have used the translation by Michael Ivens, SJ, *The Spiritual Exercises of Saint Ignatius of Loyola* (Leominster, UK: Gracewing, 2004).

The best introduction to the Jesuits is James Martin, SJ, *The Jesuit Guide to (Almost) Everything: A Spirituality for Real Life* (New York: HarperCollins, 2010). I made use of Philip Caraman's biography, *Ignatius Loyola* (New York: Collins, 1990), as well as Jean Lacouture, *Jesuits: A Multibiography* (Washington, DC: Counterpoint, 1995), Malachi Martin, *The Jesuits* (New York: Simon & Schuster, 1998), and Alain Woodrow, *The Jesuits: A Story of Power* (London; New York: Geoffrey Chapman 1995).

On eighteenth-century Argentine Jesuit history, I have drawn on many books and articles by Guillermo Furlong, SJ, especially *Los Jesuitas y la Cultura Rioplatense* (Buenos

Aires: Ed. Huarpes, 1946) and *Nacimiento y Desarrollo de la Filosofía en el Río de la Plata* (Buenos Aires: Ed. Kraft, 1952). Also William Bangert, *A History of the Society of Jesus* (St. Louis, MO: Institute of Jesuit Sources, 1986), Philip Caraman, *The Lost Paradise: The Jesuit Republic in South America* (New York: Seabury Press, 1976), and Magnus Mörner (ed.), *The Expulsion of the Jesuits from Latin America* (New York: Knopf, 1965).

Jeffrey Klaiber, *The Jesuits in Latin America, 1549–2000: 450 Years of Inculturation, Defense of Human Rights, and Prophetic Witness* (St. Louis, MO: Institute of Jesuit Sources, 2009), presents the anti-Bergoglio case. On the 1974 General Congregation, see Peter Hebblethwaite, *Paul VI: The First Modern Pope* (New York: HarperCollins, 1993). On (Saint) Peter Faber: Mary Purcell, *The Quiet Companion* (Chicago: Loyola Press, 1970).

ARGENTINE HISTORY PRE-1960S

For the early chapters I have drawn on my *Catholicism and Politics in Argentina, 1810–1960* (Basingstoke: Palgrave Macmillan, 1995) as well as my essay on the 1880s Catholic-secularist battle over education in Ivereigh (ed.), *The Politics of Religion in an Age of Revival* (London: ILAS, 2000). The indispensable Argentine church history is Roberto Di Stefano and Loris Zanatta, *Historia de la Iglesia Argentina* (Buenos Aires: Sudamericana, 2009). On Church and state, see M. A. Burdick, *For God and the Fatherland: Religion and Politics in Argentina* (Albany: State University of New York, 1995), G. T. Farrell, *Iglesia y Pueblo en la Argentina: Cien años de pastoral, 1860–1974* (Buenos Aires: Patria Grande, 1976), and Lila Caimari, *Perón y la Iglesia Católica: Religión, Estado y Sociedad en la Argentina, 1943–1955* (Buenos Aires: Ariel, 1995).

Professor John Lynch has many fine books on nineteenth-century Argentina, including *Argentine Dictator: Juan Manuel de Rosas, 1829–1852* (Oxford, UK: Clarendon Press; New York: Oxford University Press, 1981) and *Massacre in the Pampas, 1872: Britain and Argentina in the Age of Migration* (Norman: University of Oklahoma Press, 1998). Among many histories of Argentina in the twentieth century, it is worth mentioning José Luis Romero, *Breve Historia de la Argentina* (Buenos Aires: Editorial Huemel, 1978), Tulio Halperín Donghi, *Argentina en el Callejón* (Montevideo: ARCA, 1964), and Daniel James, *Resistance and Integration: Peronism and the Argentine Working Class, 1946–1976* (Cambridge; New York: Cambridge University Press 1988).

1970S–1980S

Three indispensable books: Donald C. Hodges, *Argentina's "Dirty War": An Intellectual Biography* (Austin: University of Texas Press, 1991), Richard Gillespie, *Soldiers of Perón— Argentina's Montoneros* (Oxford, UK: Clarendon Press; New York: Oxford University Press, 1982), and María José Moyano, *Argentina's Lost Patrol: Armed Struggle, 1969–1979* (New Haven, CT: Yale University Press, 1995).

Gustavo Morello, *Cristianismo y Revolución: Los Orígenes Intelectuales de la Guerrilla Argentina* (Córdoba: EDUCC, 2003), charts the route of young Catholics into violence. See also Carlos Mugica, *Peronismo y Cristianismo* (1973, many editions). The Third World Priests Movement (MSTM) has a copious online archive, and I could access early 1970s copies of the Jesuit theology journal *Stromata* in the Latin-American Centre Library in Oxford.

On the Church and the dirty war of the 1970s: Martín Obregón, *Entre la Cruz y la Espada: La Iglesia Católica durante los Primeros Años del "Proceso"* (Buenos Aires: Universidad Nacional de Quilmes, 2005), is a balanced, document-based analysis of Church-state relations in the first years of the junta. Emilio Mignone's *Iglesia y Dictadura* (Buenos Aires: Ediciones del Pensamiento Nacional, 1986) is published in English as *Witness to the Truth: The Complicity of Church and Dictatorship in Argentina, 1976–1983* (Maryknoll, NY: Orbis Books, 1988). A balanced view of Mignone and the book is offered by his son-in-law Mario Carril, *La Vida de Emilio Mignone: Justicia, Catolicismo y Derechos Humanos* (Buenos Aires: Emecé, 2011).

Horacio Verbitsky, *El Silencio: de Pablo VI a Bergoglio: Las Relaciones Secretas de la Iglesia con ESMA* (Buenos Aires: Sudamericana, 2005) is an attempt to substantiate the Mignone allegations, and his *Doble Juego: La Argentina Católica y Militar* (Buenos Aires: Editorial Sudamericana, 2006) is a Marxist but comprehensively documented attempt to do the same. Olga Wornat, *Nuestra Santa Madre: Historia Pública y Privada de la Iglesia Católica Argentina* (Barcelona: Ediciones B, 2002), is useful for the Yorio/Jalics controversy, and Francisco Jalics recalls their abduction and torture in *El Camino de la Contemplación* (Buenos Aires: Paulinas, 2006). A copy of Yorio's twenty-seven-page letter to the Jesuit curia is in the library of CONICET in Buenos Aires.

Originally published in Italian, Nello Scavo, *La Lista de Bergoglio: Los Salvados por Francisco durante la Dictadura* (Madrid: Ed Claretiana, 2013), collects the stories of the people Bergoglio as provincial rescued from the dictatorship. Bergoglio's own recollections of the dirty war can be found in *El Jesuita* as well as in his 2010 testimony to the ESMA inquiry, on the Internet as "Bergoglio Declara ante el TOF" at the www.abuelas.org.ar site.

A good portrait of Argentina in the 1980s is Jimmy Burns, *The Land That Lost Its Heroes: How Argentina Lost the Falklands War* (London: Bloomsbury, 1987).

1990S–2000S

Luis Alberto Romero, *A History of Argentina in the Twentieth Century* (University Park: Pennsylvania State University Press, 2002), and *La Larga Crisis Argentina: Del Siglo XX al Siglo XXI* (Buenos Aires: Siglo 21, 2013) are useful analyses, as is Jill Hedges, *Argentina: A Modern History* (London: IB Tauris, 2011).

Silvina Premat's book on the shantytown priests and her biography of Padre Pepe Di Paola are full of stories: *Curas Villeros: de Mugica al Padre Pepe* (Buenos Aires: Random House Mondadori, 2012) and *Pepe: El Cura de la Villa* (Buenos Aires: Sudamericana, 2013).

On John Paul II and the 2005 conclave: George Weigel, *Witness to Hope: The Biography of Pope John Paul II* (London: HarperCollins, 2001); John Cornwell, *The Pope in Winter: The Dark Face of John Paul II's Papacy* (London: Viking, 2005); John L. Allen, *The Rise of Benedict XVI: The Inside Story of How the Pope Was Elected* (London: Penguin, 2005). For background on conclaves: Francis A. Burkle-Young, *Passing the Keys: Modern Cardinals, Conclaves and the Election of the Next Pope* (New York: Madison Books 1999).

On Methol Ferré and the future of the Church in Latin America (Chapters 7 and 8): Alberto Methol Ferré and Alver Metalli, *El Papa y el Filósofo* (Buenos Aires: Editorial Biblios, 2013); plus Guzmán Carriquiry Lecour: *Una Apuesta por América Latina* (Buenos Aires: Sudamericana, 2005); *En Camino Hacia La V Conferencia de la Iglesia Latinoamericana: Memoria de los 50 años del CELAM* (Buenos Aires: Claretiana, 2006); (prol. Bergoglio), *El Bicentenario de la Independencia de Los Países Latinoamericanos* (Madrid: Encuentro, 2011).

The archives of *La Nación*, *Clarín*, and *Página 12* have been indispensable for Chapters 7 and 8.

CONCLAVE OF 2013 AND FRANCIS PAPACY

There is good background in Massimo Franco, *La Crisi dell'Impero Vaticano* (Rome: Mondadori, 2013), Various, *Benedict XVI: The Resignation of a Pope* (Rome: La Stampa, 2013); and Andrea Tornielli, *Francis: Pope of a New World* (San Francisco: Ignatius Press, 2013).

The following sources of news and analysis have been invaluable. *Specialist*: Catholic

News Service, Religion News Service, Vatican Radio, La Stampa's *Vatican Insider,* *National Catholic Reporter, National Catholic Register, America* magazine, *Our Sunday Visitor, The Tablet, Catholic Herald, La Croix, Criterio,* Terre d'America, Religión Digital, National Review Online, *First Things,* Aleteia, LifeSite News, Zenit, ABC Religion & Ethics, Salt & Light TV, EWTN, Rome Reports. *Blogs:* John Thavis, Sandro Magister (Chiesa), Catholic Voices Comment. *Newspapers:* (U.S.) *Boston Globe, Washington Post, New York Times, Time* magazine, *USA Today, Atlantic Monthly, Christian Science Monitor, New York Review of Books;* (UK) *Guardian, Times, Financial Times, Economist; Daily Telegraph;* (Argentina) *La Nación, Clarín, Página 12;* (Spain) *La Vanguardia,* La Razón, *ABC;* (Italy) *La Repubblica, La Stampa, Corriere della Sera, Il Messagero. Agencies:* Reuters, Associated Press, Agence France Presse.

BERGOGLIO'S BOOKSHELF: A SELECTION

THEOLOGIANS/SPIRITUAL WRITERS

Congar, Yves. *Vraie et Fausse Réforme dans l'Eglise* (Paris: Éditions du Cerf, 1950), *True and False Reform in the Church,* trans. Paul Philibert OP (Collegeville, MD: Liturgical Press, 2011).

De Lubac, Henri. *Méditation sur l'Eglise* (Paris: Aubier, 2nd ed., 1953), trans. *The Splendor of the Church* (London: Sheed & Ward, 1956).

Gennari, Gianni. Teresa di Lisieux. *Il Fascino della Santità. I Segreti di una "Dottrina" Ritrovata* (Turin: Lindau, 2012).

Guardini, Romano. *Der Gegensatz* (Mainz: Matthias-Grünewald, 1925); *The Lord* (London, New York: Longmans, Green, 1956); and *The End of the Modern World* (New York: Sheed & Ward, 1956).

Kasper, Walter. *Leadership in the Church* (New York: Crossroad, 2003) and *Mercy: The Essence of the Gospel and the Key to Christian Life* (City: Paulist Press, 2014).

Martini, Cardinal Carlo Maria (with Georg Sporschill), *Night Conversations with Cardinal Martini: The Relevance of the Church for Tomorrow* (Mahwah, NJ: Paulist Press, 2013).

Quinn, John R. *The Reform of the Papacy: The Costly Call to Christian Unity* (New York: Crossroad 1999).

Nguyen, Cardinal Van Thuan. *Five Loaves and Two Fish* (City: Publisher, 1969).

Thérèse of the Child Jesus (Saint Thérèse of Lisieux), *Story of a Soul* (City: Publisher, 1925).

LITERATURE

Benson, Robert Hugh. *The Lord of the World* (1907).

Borges, Jorge Luis. *El Martín Fierro* (1953), *El Aleph* (1949), *Ficciones* (1951).

Dostoyevsky, Fyodor. *The Brothers Karamazov* (1880).

Hernández, José. *Martín Fierro* (1879).

Manzoni, Alessandro. *I Promessi Sposi* (1827), trans. *The Betrothed* (many editions).

Marechal, Leopoldo. *Adán Buenosayres* (1948).

POETS

Friedrich Hölderlin, Rainer María Rilke, Gerard Manley Hopkins.

ACKNOWLEDGMENTS

Many on both sides of the Atlantic have nurtured *The Great Reformer*.

In Argentina, where I was lucky to have wise and well-connected friends, I am deeply in debt to Inés San Martín, now the *Boston Globe*'s reporter in Rome, for weeks of work transcribing the interviews and for boundless help and suggestions. Juan Pablo Cannata was an unfailing friend and opener of doors, as were Roberto Bosca and Federico Wals. The *Criterio* board (to which I am proud to belong) offered a home away from home, and its editor, another old friend, José María Poirier, shared his humor, insights, contacts, and stories. Father Carlos Galli in more than one meeting got my head around the *teología del pueblo*, while Fathers Ignacio Pérez del Viso, SJ, Alfonso Gómez, SJ, Fernando Cervera, SJ, Juan Carlos Scannone, SJ, Leonardo Nárdin, SJ, and Rafael Velasco, SJ, helped with materials, interviews, and further clarifications. I am indebted also to the photographer Enrique Cangas for taking me to Villa 21 on my first day, to Marco Gallo of Sant'Egidio for helping me with the interreligious dimension, Daniel Gassman of Caritas for valuable insights into the world of the poor, Evangelina Himitian for being a bridge to evangelicals, and Jorge Milia in Salta and Ana and Walter Albornoz in Santa Fe, for help in a number of ways. For furnishing materials and statistics, thanks to the CONICET library and the Jesuit provincial curia, to Gustavo Vittori of *El Litoral* for excavating an old article, and to Jorge González Mament for letting me use his unpublished memoir, and to Andrés Esteban Bayo for help with photos.

In Rio de Janeiro, my old friend Einardo Bingemer put me up when Francis came to town and opened Jesuit doors in his native Argentina. In Santiago de Chile, Sofia Wulf of Voces Católicas and Father Antonio Delfau, SJ, of *Mensaje* were kind and helpful, as was Juan Valdes, SJ.

To you all, and to those who did not want to be mentioned, a warm creole *abrazo* of thanks.

In Rome, I owe a big *grazie* to a friend, Father Michael Czerny, SJ, for his patient help and invaluable counsel; to María Lia Zerviño for her Bergoglio stories; to Paolo Rodari for clarifying the Curia; to Father Federico Lombardi and the staff of the Vatican press office; to Father Thomas Rosica of Salt & Light, as well as Marco Carroggio and the Santa Croce communications department; and not least to Greg Burke in the secretariat of state. I am in debt, as the text makes clear, to many tireless Vatican news gatherers and analysts who are always helpful when I am in Rome, among them John Allen, Cindy Wooden, Frank Rocca, Philip Pulella, Nicole Winfield, Andrea Tornielli, Robert Mickens, Gerard O'Connell, and Alessandro Speciale.

In New York, my indefatigable agent Bill Barry opened the path to Henry Holt, where Steve Rubin, publisher, and Serena Jones, editor, run a writer's dream team. In Washington, hearty thanks to George Weigel, Kathryn Lopez, and Paul Elie.

And so to England, where warmest thanks go to Father James Hanvey, SJ, Master of Campion Hall, Oxford, for his suggestions, wise guidance, hospitality, and use of the library. Thanks also to the library staff of the Bodleian and the Latin-American Centre in Oxford. And special thanks to my colleagues and the board of Catholic Voices for bearing the extra burden my time away put on them, especially to Jack Valero, Kathleen Griffin, Eileen Cole, Christopher Morgan, and Isabel Errington. But my greatest debt is to my wife, Linda, who lovingly supplied me with everything I could possibly need, got me out of bed at dawn, kept me to deadlines, and once it was over put me on a ferocious diet. Neither she nor the dogs ever once complained about sharing our cottage for so long with an Argentine pope.

Lastly, *merci beaucoup* and *muchísimas gracias* to my desk companions, Saint Thérèse of Lisieux and María Desatanudos, for the extra help only we know about.

Oxfordshire, England
July 2014

INDEX